PENGUIN CLASSICS

PENGUIN ENGLISH POETS
GENERAL EDITOR: CHRISTOPHER RICKS

ISABELLA WHITNEY, MARY SIDNEY and AEMILIA LANYER: *RENAISSANCE WOMEN POETS*

ISABELLA WHITNEY was born in the mid sixteenth century. There is little known about her life, but she appears to have been in service in London. During her life she published two volumes, *The Copy of a Letter* and *A Sweet Nosgay*. Her poems show a concern for women's lack of social and economic power, and evoke the nature of the City of London in the sixteenth century.

MARY SIDNEY (1561–1621) was the daughter of Sir Henry Sidney and younger sister of Philip Sidney. Although she received little formal education, she grew up surrounded by books and intellectual stimulation. She married the Earl of Pembroke in 1577. After the death of her brother in 1586, she oversaw publication of his works, including *Arcadia*, and completed his translation of the *Psalms*. She also translated Garnier's *Antonie*, DuPlessis-Mornay's *Discourse of Life and Death* and Petrarch's *Triumph of Death*, as well as writing some original poetry.

AEMILIA LANYER (1569–1645) was brought up in the home of the Countess of Kent. She was, for a time, the mistress of the Lord Chamberlain, Lord Hunsdon, and had a child by him, but was later married off to Alphonso Lanyer. Her poems advocate and praise female virtue and Christian piety, but reflect a desire for an idealized, classless world.

DANIELLE CLARKE was born in London and educated at St Hugh's College, Oxford. She has published articles on Renaissance women's writing, critical theory and ear~~ ~~ ~~ ~~ and is the co-editor of *'This Double Voice': Gende~~ ~~ ~~ ~~ ~~ ~~~~ ~~ author of *The Politics of Earl~~ ~~ ~~ ~~~~ s currently Lecturer in Englis~~ ~~

D1226007

ISABELLA WHITNEY, MARY SIDNEY
and AEMILIA LANYER:
RENAISSANCE WOMEN POETS

Edited by DANIELLE CLARKE

PENGUIN BOOKS

PENGUIN BOOKS

Published by the Penguin Group
Penguin Books Ltd, 80 Strand, London WC2R 0RL, England
Penguin Putnam Inc., 375 Hudson Street, New York, New York 10014, USA
Penguin Books Australia Ltd, 250 Camberwell Road, Camberwell, Victoria 3124, Australia
Penguin Books Canada Ltd, 10 Alcorn Avenue, Toronto, Ontario, Canada M4V 3B2
Penguin Books India (P) Ltd, 11 Community Centre, Panchsheel Park, New Delhi – 110 017, India
Penguin Books (NZ) Ltd, Cnr Rosedale and Airborne Roads, Albany, Auckland, New Zealand
Penguin Books (South Africa) (Pty) Ltd, 24 Sturdee Avenue, Rosebank 2196, South Africa

Penguin Books Ltd, Registered Offices: 80 Strand, London WC2R 0RL, England

www.penguin.com

First published 2000

15

Set in 10/11.5 pt PostScript Monotype Ehrhardt
Typeset by Rowland Phototypesetting Ltd, Bury St Edmunds, Suffolk
Printed in England by Clays Ltd, St Ives plc

www.greenpenguin.co.uk

CONTENTS

ACKNOWLEDGEMENTS

I am grateful to the following for permission to reproduce the texts in this volume: the British Library for Whitney's *The copy of a letter* and 'The lamentacion of a Gentilwoman', Sidney, 'A Dialogue betweene two shepheards' and Lanyer, 'The Description of Cookeham'; the Bodleian Library for Whitney's *A sweet Nosgay*, Mary Sidney, *Psalmes* and Lanyer, *Salve Deus Rex Judæorum*; the Master and Benchers of the Inner Temple for Mary Sidney's *The Triumph of Death*; Oxford University Press for 'To the Angell spirit', taken from William A. Ringler Jr (ed.), *The Poems of Sir Philip Sidney*; and Penguin Press for 'Even now that Care', taken from David Norbrook and H. R. Woudhuysen (eds), *The Penguin Book of Renaissance Verse*.

Editing texts is a collaborative undertaking which requires the expertise of many minds, and I have been fortunate to have been able to draw upon the burgeoning scholarship on early modern women writers as well as the work of early pioneers. My indebtedness to Margaret Hannay's work on Mary Sidney is clear on virtually every page, and I have learned much from the emerging generation of critics whose work is now beginning to appear: I would like to thank them collectively here. In a more proximate way, I have benefited from discussions of this material and the questions it raises over the course of the last few years. For support, inspiration and criticism I would like to thank Ros Ballaster, Julia Briggs, Elizabeth Clarke, Lorna Hutson, David Norbrook and Diane Purkiss. Many of the ideas presented here have been aired in earlier incarnations, and I would like to thank audiences in Belfast, Dublin, Reading and Oxford for their attention. For specific acts of kindness and pieces of information, I thank Ron Callan, Andrew Carpenter, Janet Clare, Anne-Marie D'Arcy, Màire Doyle, Emily Hamer, Anne Macdona, Susan McNulty, Jim Mays, Clíona Ó'Gallchóir, Catherine Pratt, Philippa Semper, Maria Stuart and Moynagh Sullivan. Elizabeth Macfarlane has facilitated this book in more ways than she knows, providing texts, books, references and, above all, encouragement. I am deeply grateful for her friendship. At Penguin I would like to thank Robert Mighall. Monica Schmoller has been an exemplary copy-editor and I owe her much gratitude. All errors which remain after her careful ministrations are, of course, my own. Finally, I would like to thank Róisín, who has patiently endured these dead poets, and their preoccupied editor, for far too long.

INTRODUCTION

This edition, by bringing together three women poets – Isabella Whitney, Mary Sidney and Aemilia Lanyer – suggests that they are usefully read alongside one another. The assumption is that we can isolate and identify 'women' as a category in the Renaissance, marked by ideological position, and by their 'difference' from male writers. Although feminism led readers and critics to these texts, it has often served to obscure how we read them; anachronistic notions of gender construction, female community and opposition to prevailing ideologies have failed to read these writers and texts on their own terms. This edition aims to re-place women writers *in* the Renaissance by putting them in context, by explaining the poems with reference to the texts and ideas circulating in their contemporary world, and by providing information on the literary, historical and cultural background to each text. This edition does not seek to limit the extent to which these writers' reaction and response to the world and texts around them is determined by their gender, but it does hope to avoid reducing their experience solely to their gender. While it is undoubtedly possible to conclude that women writers' literary choices – generic, linguistic, form of publication – may be to some extent determined by their gendered position, it does not follow that the resulting texts are necessarily about gender. Each of these writers displays some concern with the female subject position, but it cannot be said that this is their primary motivation for writing. Women writers are engaged in the imitation of texts and traditions much as male writers in the period are. It might be argued that women writers are using the written medium to explore a process of 'self-fashioning'[1] and political intervention which was off-limits to them in terms of direct access to the centres of power. These three women poets, who come from differing social, cultural and historical contexts, demonstrate the emergence of the Renaissance female self.

It is important to consider the specific conditions and assumptions about literature more generally in this period; otherwise women writers' engagement with authoritative models can look submissive, slavish and deeply antipathetic to the exercise of textual and personal agency. The expectation, or demand, that literary works should somehow be original is very much a product of the post-Romantic period. For early modern writers, literary quality was measured by the mastery of antecedent models, the ability to imitate them and work variations upon them: while the overall effect of something like Spenser's *Shepheardes Calender* (1579)[2] is a new literary artefact in English, it would be difficult to argue that it was original in the unmediated, inspirational sense suggested by Wordsworth, as it blends Chaucer, Virgil, the French pastoral poet Clément Marot and Mantuan. Rather than value being conferred by the sincerity of a 'spontaneous overflow of powerful feelings',[3] for the Renaissance writer and reader it derives from a process of studied imitation, measured in part by the fitness of language to subject-matter, the skill with which rhetorical tropes and figures are applied, manip-ulated and varied, and the moral effect upon the reader.[4]

Because critics have tended to predicate readings of texts by women upon the oppositional 'separate spheres' model, which assumes that women's lives were limited to the privacy of the household, literary indebtedness has often been seen as submission to male authority, a necessary deference contingent upon the fact of patriarchal power, rather than as the literary currency of the period as a whole.[5] As the poets in this volume illustrate, literary depend-ency should not be viewed negatively: each of them is engaged, more or less closely, with the negotiation and resituating of male models, but none of them is simply capitulating to an all-powerful 'master text', even when that text is as masterly as the Bible itself. Analogous arguments are often advanced in relation to the connec-tion between gender and genre in this period, whereby it is suggested that women writers tend to work in 'permitted areas', that of religion and spirituality in particular.[6] While this is certainly statistically true, it is also true that many works by men in this period address religion and spirituality. Religion was a master-discourse in this period, and we should not let our post-Christian sensibilities occlude the fact that devotion was central to ideology and culture: hence, women's engagement with this area, while it undoubtedly is connect-ed to ideas of virtue, is also mainstream, and often directly political.

None of these writers displays a feminism immediately recognizable to the early twenty-first century, whether political, postmodernist, or even, post-feminist. But none of them seems to have found their sex a particular bar to literary or intellectual ambition: all three demonstrate high aspirations in relation to form, style and subject-matter. The issue of quality has dogged discussion of early modern women writers both among advocates and detractors. This often depends upon assumptions about what a woman writer could achieve, leading either to 'quite good – for a woman' or to 'it must be good because it's by a woman'. These are difficult matters to disentangle without either suspending aesthetic judgement or ignoring the actual conditions underlying the production of women's writing in the Renaissance period. There is unevenness and uncertainty, even technical incompetence, in some of the work included here, but this should be understood within the context not only of the relative inaccessibility of a rhetorical education for most women, but also in relation to the possibility that due to material conditions women's relationship to and usage of language differs from that of men. Mary Sidney, for example, displays not only a desire to innovate verbally, together with an interest in the relationship between style and meaning, but uses a syntactical complexity and compression which often makes her difficult to read. This should not be written off as incompetence but seen as a recurrent feature of sixteenth-century poetry: clarity of meaning is not exactly the prime quality of Donne, Shakespeare or of Philip Sidney. None of the poets included in this volume are Shakespeare or Spenser or Philip Sidney, all acknowledged as extraordinary talents in their own times. But then Turberville, Gascoigne, Googe and Barnes are not Shakespeare, Spenser or Sidney either. Set alongside the so-called 'minor' poets who were their contemporaries, these writers might be seen to suffer a little less by the comparison. Just as literary criticism now seeks to incorporate and interrogate previously undervalued bodies of writing (such as ballads, scurrilous and erotic verse), I suggest that the question of value should not be sidelined, but that it should become a little bit less of a sore point in an effort to reach adequate critical frameworks for the interpretation of women poets.[7]

*

We know little detail about Isabella Whitney's life apart from what she chooses to reveal in her own writings, and what we can infer from biographical information on her brother Geoffrey, famed for his collection of emblems. She was probably born to a gentry family in Cheshire around the middle of the sixteenth century, received some education, and found herself in domestic service in London – movement between households was common for children of all classes. She published two volumes, *The copy of a letter* (1567) and *A sweet Nosgay* (1573). *The copy of a letter* brings together Whitney's own verse epistles on the subject of sexual morality, and 'replies' written by men complaining of female treachery. *A sweet Nosgay* is also a verse miscellany, structured around Whitney's versification of some of Hugh Plat's aphorisms (*The Floures of Philosophie*, 1572), presented to her addressees in requital of past debts and in expectation of future support.

Whitney's work is important for its close connections to the emergent literary culture of the 1570s, and because of the unusual status of its author. Not only is Whitney a woman, rare for venturing into print at this period, but she is also lower-middle class. Her texts can be read as gendered interventions in Tudor poetic culture, interested in reworking classical texts for popular audiences, and the imitation of manuscript cultures in print in the form of the verse miscellany. Unlike print, manuscript circulation was usually accorded higher status, primarily because the writer was able, to a limited extent, to control the readership of the text, and to enter into reciprocal relationships with it.

Whitney uses classical and biblical reference, but many of her sources are popular and vernacular, deriving from earlier English adaptations of classical stories (for example Chaucer and John Gower) as well as more recent translations. Her style is often rough and ready, but she writes within the legacy of the popular ballad form, using the much derided fourteener, and aimed at an emergent urban readership. However, these stylistic choices were common literary currency at this stage in the development of English poetic forms, and as Randall Martin suggests, 'in imitating the customary forms and language of her time, Whitney's poetry is no less historically representative'.[8]

While Whitney is indebted to contemporary models, she is not slavish in her treatment of them; she uses them in the proper spirit of imitation to answer a series of personal and contemporary concerns. Her use of the epistle, for example, is not only based upon Ovid's epistolary heroines in the *Heroides*, but on more popular Tudor adaptations of complaint.[9] Whitney joins a female position of powerlessness with a critique of social and economic forces, and utilizes the epistle form to create a store of personal credit, both by the establishment of good character, and by bestowing the letter upon a recipient whom it is hoped will reciprocate in some way. Notions of mutuality in friendship, the importance of reputation and the condemnation of acquisitiveness run through Whitney's volume. The poems in *The copy of a letter* derive more directly from the Heroidean tradition, but Whitney makes significant modifications: her speakers create authority out of experience, and over-read the classical exempla, making them into sources of instruction, rather than objects to be pitied.

A further point of interest in Whitney's work is her concern with changing social and economic structures, particularly notable in her long poem 'Wyll and Testament', published as part of *A sweet Nosgay*, an innovative and powerful piece of writing which conveys the flavour of sixteenth-century London. It blends irony, testament and topography in an attempt at humorous self-presentation. The 'Wyll' takes a wry look at the relentless mercantilism of 1560s London, and asks searching questions about the effect of such rapid change on social place, service and the nature of personal credit, viewed here as exclusively financial rather than moral. A similar acuity about social relations is apparent in *The copy of a letter*, but from the perspective of relations between the sexes, as Whitney untangles the language of love and sexual desire.

The 'Wyll' is the most innovative of Whitney's poems, as it draws together several traditions, but reapplies them. The poem uses the mock-testament, with its deployment of the figure of the fool and its undermining of an authority which is revealed not to be an authority. Lorna Hutson suggests that mock-testament enables 'the ironic revelation of fraudulent ideas', leaving 'the effigies of impotent, authority-claiming discourses'.[10] Whitney points to London's commercial power, its financial rapaciousness, and its lack of charity, and by seeming to praise its prosperity criticizes the difficulties which accompany its growth, in particular changes in social structure and hierarchy. The city is imaginatively turned into Whitney's 'possession' which is hers to bequeath, pointing to the gap between London's abundant wealth and those who are permitted to possess it. The sense of London as a 'closed shop' is compounded by the fact that the city is recipient, bequest and executor, and the final joke is that Whitney leaves the city nothing that is not there already, thus inverting the trope of generosity structuring the idea of the will. As Hutson writes, 'London . . . is fondly characterized as the heartless friend, whose economy belies the rules of reciprocity and kinship distance, since all here, even neighbours, live amidst an abundance of goods and services that must be openly and immediately transacted for.'[11] Whitney's material dispossession is balanced by an act of poetic possession, whereby she claims London as her property to bequeath, a gesture which simultaneously asserts the acts of writing and publication as economically valuable.[12] Here, as elsewhere in the volume, poetry is seen as a commodity, to be exchanged among friends in order to produce, as Hutson argues, personal credit, a strategy which is reinforced here by Whitney's chosen form.[13] The will is a legal document that substitutes for the processes of exchange engaged in by a living person, a form of writing which organizes the disposal of material goods.

While innovative, the 'Wyll' is not an isolated text; its themes are widely found in writings of the Tudor period, when writers frequently addressed the question of rapid social and economic changes and the disruptions to order and ideology that these brought about. Lawrence Manley argues that writers of Tudor complaint often focused on London as a target for their critique, because of its connection with 'ruthlessly anti-social and amoral commerce', and that the literary techniques involved were the catalogue or list, and 'tropes of inversion'.[14] Both elements are clearly present in Whitney's poem. Her 'list' represents order and disorder, centre and periphery, and thus draws attention to the crumbling of older categories and hierarchies – hence her allusion to the debtors' prison (165ff.) represents the underside of the commercial abundance described elsewhere in the poem. Her listing of places, persons, professions and commodities reinforces a sense of chaos and disorder, and she swings from area to area, and trade to trade, without any apparent sense of connection: in fact, the only connecting thread is Whitney's self-representation in terms of exclusion from the abundance that she describes. The poem is a unique and original contribution, blending the social, satirical and topographical to present a lively portrait of the complexities of London in the 1570s.

Each of the letters reproduced from *A sweet Nosgay* is directed towards a person tied to the author by kinship or friendship. In some, she thanks the recipients for help already received ('To her Sister Misteris. A.B.'), but the letters exploit print to imitate an illusion of closeness to a social context which is clearly absent, in order to create a store of personal credit to offset future insecurity.[15] The letters work a series of variations on the *Heroides*, as each speaker uses the epistolary form to present her 'complaint'. However, unlike the *Heroides*, the lament is not for a lost sexual relationship, but for the lack of social and material connection to the world, i.e. Whitney's own exclusion from the relationships of financial and personal credit which constitute the individual's place in the Tudor social order. Like many miscellanies of the period, *A sweet Nosgay* imitates the dynamics of manuscript culture, but is bound up with the anxieties attendant upon social and literary circulation, particularly for a woman. Hence, the illusion of the letters being exchanged among a closely knit community of known recipients serves to offset the potential opprobrium which might attach to Whitney as a writer circulating without check throughout a wider interpretive community. Furthermore, this potential transgression is contained by the subject-matter treated, and by the power relations implied in the letters. On the one hand, her letters to her sisters ('A modest meane for Maides', 'To her Sister Misteris. A.B.') give household advice without any expectation of return. Whitney upholds gender ideologies, by presenting her writing as filling a hiatus prior to marriage; as Patricia Phillippy argues, in 'To her Sister' Whitney 'depicts the speaker's exile from domesticity as both a lapse and a liberty'.[16] On the other hand, her letters to male recipients suggest a willingness to be subject to their economic power. Whitney's secular, urban poetry is unique for a woman writer of this period, and gives an illuminating insight into the economic and cultural life of a rapidly expanding London. These factors, together with Whitney's use of the popular ballad form and the medium of print, mark her out as quite distinct from the élite piety of Mary Sidney.

Unlike Isabella Whitney, a good deal is known about the life and cultural milieu of Mary Herbert (Sidney), Countess of Pembroke, known as Mary Sidney. She was born in 1561 into an accomplished intellectual family with a wide range of cultural and political connections. She was the recipient of a good education for a girl at this period, and, even if her formal education was scanty, she had access to ideas, books and stimulation, particularly through the influence of her beloved elder brother Philip. Both before and after her marriage to the much older Earl of Pembroke in 1577, she moved in courtly circles, as well as imbibing the brand of militant Protestantism championed by her powerful uncles (see below) and her brother. Her writing began with the completion of the psalm paraphrases begun by her brother (he had finished as far as Psalm 43), in the wake of a series of bereavements – not only the death of Sir Philip (1586), but also of her parents (1586) and her daughter Katherine (1584). Taking on many of Philip's projects, she not only championed poets and writers, but used his work and interests to authorize her own. The paraphrase of the Psalms preoccupied her during much of the decade following his death, but she also undertook other projects: the editing and publication of her Philip's work, translations of Robert Garnier's closet drama *Antonie* (1592) and of Philippe DuPlessis-Mornay's *A Discourse of Life and Death* (1592), the writing of some original poetry, and her translation of Petrarch's *The Triumph of Death* (*c.* 1600–1601).

Mary Sidney's version of the Psalms of David occupies a problematic place within the modes of literary expression: it is neither a close literal translation based upon original sources, nor an entirely original undertaking. However, given the centrality of the imitation of antecedent texts and models to Renaissance literary production, the Sidney Psalter is mainstream in its relationship to its sources – it is only in the post-Romantic period that literary dependence is seen as detrimental to the value of a text. Much feminist criticism has found this apparent capitulation to male authority troubling. But to view the work as a submission to a male authority is to assume that the text being translated is itself stable: 'There is no "real" or pristine Psalter that we can hope to hack our way back to.'[17] The Psalms of David are manifold: written in a variety of genres, over a considerable period of time, and deploying multiple voices. As Donald Davie argues, neither the Psalms *per se*, nor any psalm version of this period, can be understood as 'self-sufficient verbal artefacts'.[18] If there is a submission to authority by Mary Sidney, it is to the divine *status* of the text, not to male power.

Mary Sidney's negotiations of authority are multiple, and need to be taken together: her dependency is textual, familial and devotional. Her paraphrase reveals very few signs of an identifiably *gendered* difference from other metrical versions, except in instances where the sources raise questions of gender or specific problems of voice.[19] Where the Psalms of David overtly use a male voice, Sidney tends to use a gender-neutral formulation rather than a female one, suggesting that she understood the text in the same terms as her contemporaries. Interpretations of voice in the Psalms stress that 'whosoever take this booke in his hande, he reputeth & thinketh all the wordes he readeth . . . to be as his very own wordes spoken in his owne person'.[20] Davie notes that modern readers tend to see 'the "I" of the Psalmist to mean "I" as peculiar unrepeatable individual; not "I" as representative human being'.[21] In other words, the personal application of the meaning of the Psalms is a matter for the individual, rather than something that a versifier should bring to the text. An adequate paraphrase would have to preserve this open-endedness of application, not foreclose it by converting it to individual circumstances. The ambiguities of the psalms are the key to Mary Sidney's undertaking, as she blends and combines a variety of models, texts and precedents to create a body of devotional poetry which simultaneously depends upon authoritative sources and transforms them into something new. While the Sidneian Psalms (Philip and Mary's) can be read as autonomous poems, for a contemporary readership an appreciation of the poetic features of metrical psalms depended upon an ingrained and almost unconscious knowledge of the biblical text from which they derive. The weighing of the poetic and devotional value of versions such as Mary Sidney's requires a recognition of their difference from established versions of this well-known and much-loved text; for most readers this would be either the much maligned Psalter of Thomas Sternhold and John Hopkins and others, *The whole booke of psalmes* (1562), or Miles Coverdale's version (1539), subsequently The Book of Common Prayer. The point here is not only the accurate representation of the divine text according to all available versions and authorities, but the reader's awareness of the variations being worked upon those versions.

The vernacular Psalter rapidly occupied a central place within Protestant theology and worship. It was seen as a repository of analogues for the individual's spiritual state, as well as prefiguring the fate of the Christian (Reformed) Church, suffering from the persecution of Catholic rulers: initially, Protestant thinkers close to Edward VI who went into exile in Geneva at the accession of Mary, and, later, besieged Protestants in France and reformers in the Netherlands under threat from Spain. The Psalms' importance as a source of comfort for the oppressed in private soon merged with political and ideological readings. The universalist claims made by Protestant commentators mean that personal and political applications are intertwined, the comprehensive range of its emotions and descriptions of spiritual states standing in for the scriptures in their entirety. Martin Luther termed the Psalter 'a little Bible; for in it all things that are contained in the whole Bible . . . are condensed into a most beautiful manual'.[22] As Margaret Hannay notes, public psalm singing became 'increasingly partisan', closely associated with the Genevan exiles and French Huguenots.[23] Recourse to key verses in the Psalms became almost axiomatic in the latter half of the sixteenth century; when the Huguenots marched into battle, for example, they sang Psalm 68. A text which contains within its confines a series of clear conflicts between the godly (the Israelites) and their enemies (the Philistines), and where God uplifts the faithful and takes revenge on the ungodly, was easily incorporated into accounts of religious conflict in early modern Europe.

Mary Sidney would have been acutely conscious of these applications – even if her family allegiances had been different, such meanings were inescapable. However, within her own family circle, with its commitment to the military support of Continental Protestants (the three great Protestant earls, Leicester, Huntingdon and Warwick, were her uncles; her brother Philip had extensive contacts with Huguenot radicals and died for the Protestant cause in the Netherlands; a younger brother Robert was the Governor-General of Flushing, at the front line of the Spanish threat), Mary Sidney had plenty of examples of the political uses of the Psalter close at hand. Her Dudley uncles, John, Earl of Warwick, and Robert, Earl of Leicester, had produced psalm versions during their imprisonment in connection with their father's attempt to put the Protestant Lady Jane Grey on the throne.[24] Her father, Henry Sidney, had cited Psalm 114 (In exitu Israel) on his departure from Ireland, hence identifying himself with the position of the godly (as Elizabeth's Lord Deputy) and allying his Irish Catholic charges as the 'Philistines'.[25] Such meanings were a question of content and association, and the product of accreted interpretations, citations and usages: they did not need to be spelled out. The absence of headnotes and aids to interpretation in the Sidney Psalter suggests that its status is that of an élite and subtly coded text, directed to an audience of highly educated Protestants familiar with the kinds of interpretations that Mary Sidney brought to the text, however obliquely. In this, the potential social matrix for the interpretation of the Sidney Psalter has much in common with the poetic versions of the Protestant versifiers Sir Thomas Wyatt, Henry Howard, Earl of Surrey, and Sir John Harington: all manuscript versions designed for circulation among a self-selecting (and selected) audience. Mary Sidney's choice of this form of circulation has as much to do with the anticipation of her readers' ability to decode her text both poetically and politically as it does with a perception that her work should have a limited circulation because of her sex. Audience is one of the key features differentiating the Sidney Psalter from its sources: Calvin's commentaries, translated by Arthur Golding;[26] Bèze's commentaries, translated by Anthony Gilbie;[27] the French Marot and Bèze Psalter;[28] and the Geneva Bible (1560), which appealed to a broad readership in order to urge resistance to what its translators saw as apostate rule. Other vernacular versions demonstrate an evangelizing impulse which extends to a popular audience. Coverdale, for example, begged that

Yee wolde God that oure mynstrels had none other thynge to playe upon, nether oure carters & plowmen other thynge to whistle upon, save Psalmes, hymnes, and soch godly songes as David is occupied withall. And yf women syttinge at theyr rockes, or spynnynge at the wheles, had none other songes to passe theyr tyme withall . . . they shulde be better occupied, then with hey nony noy, hey troly loly, & soch lyke fantasies.[29]

Mary Sidney's version, envisaging an audience defined by Queen Elizabeth, and the presiding presence of her intellectual Protestant brother, has no such motivation: rather, it addresses itself to the spiritual and political responsibilities of those who rule, and the aesthetic question of how to make these highly resonant texts 'speak' poetically in English.

Hannay has suggested that 'the countess did not need to add a political cast to her original',[30] and this is undoubtedly the case: Mary Sidney's psalm versions were directed to a readership connected to her through familial and political allegiances, for whom the Psalter would have been self-explicating in the terms suggested by those 'intensely partisan' sources used by Mary Sidney.[31] Each of these texts was intimately connected with the Dudley–Sidney alliance: the French Psalter was highly influential as a precursor because of its stanzaic and metrical variety, but it was also closely connected with the Protestant cause in France. The Geneva Bible was printed by Rowland Hall, who was the recipient of Leicester's patronage; also, Golding had dedicated his translations of Mornay and Calvin to Leicester.[32] The Earl of Huntingdon had met Théodore de Bèze during the reign of Mary, and both of them knew Gilbie;[33] Bèze's Latin text was dedicated to Huntingdon, and Gilbie's English translation to his wife, Katherine, Mary Sidney's aunt through marriage. These interlocking familial and textual connections suggest a kinship group reinforced by political and religious allegiance, and a knowing readership for the Sidney Psalter.

It is important not to overstate the actual political content of Mary Sidney's work. Its applications are both inherent to the text and supplied by sources and contexts through complex networks of association, but Sidney generally leaves these implications to the discretion of the reader. She frequently softens, or omits, the more extreme political inferences found in her sources, particularly the Geneva Bible's stress upon the right to depose apostate or tyrannical princes (see Psalm 82, for example[34]). A sense of political and dynastic responsibility is only one of Mary Sidney's motivations: although it is true that by the 1590s she was the only remaining spokesperson for the old Dudley–Sidney alliance. A key impetus was the Countess's loyalty to her brother Philip's memory, not only sponsoring literary works that carried on his legacy, but also playing a key role in the publication of his work. Her work on the Psalms needs to be understood in this context, completing what he had begun, as she herself asserts in 'To the Angell spirit'. However, Mary Sidney's allegiance to her brother created an opportunity for her, an opening to write devotional poetry within the complex

matrix of self-assertion and abnegation bequeathed by her circum-
stances and the text that she felt obliged to complete. While Sir
Philip Sidney is the presiding figure hovering over Mary Sidney's
literary output, her concern was that the control of his image
and writing remained within the family: hence while her role has
frequently been presented as one of humility and dependence, it is
equally likely that it is one of appropriation and an assertion of
ownership. This also explains Mary Sidney's fierce adherence to
her Sidney heritage, continuing to use her Sidney arms, and appear-
ing on her entry into London after the period of mourning for her
parents and brother wearing Sidney livery.[35] One of the key points
missed by recent feminist work on Mary Sidney, anxious as it is to
extricate something distinctly 'feminine' – or even 'feminist' – about
her work, and for whom her dependence upon the image of her
brother is faintly troubling, is that in death Philip becomes a manip-
ulable fiction, one which she can adapt to her own ends, just as
subject to her control as she is beholden to his influence and memory.

The Sidney Psalter is a poetic undertaking as well as a political
or theological one. Its principles of composition do not have a
directly public function in mind: Mary Sidney's psalm versions,
although metrical, are not intended for congregational singing,
unlike those of the sources.[36] Her endeavour is indebted to the
sixteenth-century interest in the rhetorical and poetic qualities of
the biblical text. Sir Philip Sidney made perhaps the most famous
statement about the Psalms' poetic status and qualities:

may I not presume a little further . . . and say that the holy David's Psalms
are a divine poem? . . . for what else is the awaking his musical instruments,
the often and free changing of persons, his notable *prosopopoeias*, when he
maketh you, as it were, see God coming in His majesty, his telling of the
beasts' joyfulness and hills leaping, but a heavenly poesy.[37]

This perception came to be widespread, as Israel Baroway argued.[38]
There are two key aspects of the idea of the Psalms as poetry in
relation to the Sidney Psalter. First, devotional fervour and poetic
endeavour were not seen as separate, or even separable, entities, as
Davie has pointed out: 'The Countess's poem is a work of literary
art, but only in the second place; in the first place it is a work of
devotion. To think that its devotional dimension detracts from its

status as art is to devalue everything, including art.'[39] It is difficult for the secular reader to re-create this inseparability: devotion was not a discrete aspect of Renaissance lives, but the very discourse by which they were constructed and articulated. Second, interest in the metrical qualities of the Psalter meant that the creation of metrical versions was a form of fidelity to the text, permitting a respect for the authority of the *form* of the text.

Perceptions like Tyndale's, that 'the scripture useth proverbs, similitudes, riddles or allegories, as all other speeches do . . . As in the English we borrow words and sentences of one thing and apply them unto another and give them new significations',[40] were not entirely new, deriving from a long tradition of patristic theology. What was new was a more specifically aesthetic appreciation of scripture, not only as a useful and convincing allegory, but as something eloquent in itself. The key element is that the poetic qualities of the scriptures imitate and communicate the glories of God. All of Philip Sidney's examples of the highest form of imitation come from the Bible:

The chief . . . were they that did imitate the unconceivable excellencies of God. Such were David in his Psalms; Solomon in his Song of Songs, in his Ecclesiastes, and Proverbs; Moses and Deborah in their Hymns; and the writer of Job.[41]

This line of thinking has an important bearing on the status of Mary Sidney's work.[42] The attempt to re-create David's 'heavenly poesy'[43] in English represented an aspiration to the highest form of literary imitation.[44] That this is not seen as transgressive by her peers (although there were some incredulous voices, such as Sir John Harington, who cast doubt on her ability to undertake the task, not the decorousness of her doing so[45]) is due to the relationship between temporally confined versions, touched by human fallibility, and the universal timeless text from which they derive. The Psalter's authority resides in its absent referent, author and origin: in that sense, the versifier functions as an intermediary between the Word and the power to individualize accorded to the reader by sixteenth-century interpreters. Rather than being a circumscribed attempt to assert the individuality of voice, Mary Sidney's version might be seen in terms of her adherence to the interpretive dynamics of her original, where what Jonathan Goldberg calls the 'unmarking of ownership of voice'[46] is a form of textual and devotional fidelity, rather than a submission to the authority of scripture.

A key aspect of rhetorical interpretations of the Bible in the sixteenth century is the interest in its formal aspects ('art', the poet as maker rather than as prophet). For Sir Philip Sidney, these are conjoined, each informing the other:

And may not I presume a little further, to show the reasonableness of this word *vates*, and say that the holy David's Psalms are a divine poem? If I do, I shall not do it without the testimony of great learned men, both ancient and modern. But even the name of Psalms will speak for me, which being interpreted, is nothing but songs; then that it is fully written in metre, as all learned Hebricians agree, although the rules be not yet fully found.[47]

Baroway cites similar recognitions of the metrical quality of the Psalms from several Elizabethan contemporaries,[48] and while a fog of ignorance prevented any clear comprehension of how Hebraic metre worked, it was dimly understood to be quantitative (i.e. based on syllables, rather than stresses), which may account for both Sidneys' experiments in this area (see Psalms 120–27). More importantly, especially for a modern readership for whom the repeated topoi of the Psalter may carry little emotional force, some of the basic conventions of Hebrew verse were understood, and deployed. One of the most important of these in Mary Sidney's writing is the convention whereby each verse of Hebrew is subdivided into two parts, the second of which recapitulates the thought of the first, using synonymity rather than repetition. Variations upon this structure can be found throughout these psalm versions, and are intensified by her use of rhetorical devices of repetition: chiasmus (inverting the order of repeated words), polyptoton (repetition of words with the same root but different endings), antimetabole (inversion of words), and so on.[49]

Mary Sidney's addition of details and metaphors to her text, for example, the use of classical references, allusions to music and earlier poetic versions of the Psalms, provide evidence of her attitude to her sources.[50] As noted above, the texts upon which she relied were the standard Protestant versions and interpretations in English, French and Latin. However, her approach to these texts appears to have been composite: she does not follow any one authority slavishly, and selects carefully from the interpretations available to her, fusing elements from various sources in order to create a coherent poetic whole. As Hannay et al. note, many of her metaphors are taken from Calvin and Bèze,[51] although Sidney's primary guide to the substance of the Psalms was a combination of the Geneva Bible and The Book of Common Prayer: she consulted both, probably noting differences in phrasing, and where they diverge, generally chose Geneva's interpretation, presumably on the grounds that it was closer to the Hebrew, and she signalled difficulties of translation by placing the ambiguous word or phrase in italics. She also worked with the Marot–Bèze Psalter, and there are some correspondences (noted in the commentary); however, her use of this source seems to be less pervasive than has usually been supposed. It was an authoritative precedent for a Psalter based both on sound interpretive principles and on a commitment to the eloquence of the Psalms in the vernacular. Most commentators are dismissive of the influence of the Sternhold–Hopkins Psalter, but Mary Sidney would have known it well, and there are instances where its phrasing makes its way into her versions, possibly not even consciously.

Mary Sidney's working methods are revealed by the variant psalms, revisions and reworkings. She generally seems to have begun with a paraphrase based upon the Geneva Bible and The Book of Common Prayer; some of the variant psalms from B (Ms. Rawlinson: the transcript of her working copy) fall into this category. At a later stage, having consulted other sources, she reworked, sometimes altering verse form or metre, compressing meanings, and developing imagery and metaphors (see, for example, Psalm 117). Sometimes, there were further revisions, where she altered fine details of phrasing, and rearranged words to create a more powerful verbal patterning – sometimes, after reflection, she reverted to her original wording. Such painstaking attention to detail has prompted the derisory comments of critics like Coburn Freer who argues that 'the Countess herself seems to have been congenitally incapable of leaving a poem alone long enough to produce a definitive copy'.[52] Perhaps Mary Sidney's refusal of a final, definitive version has less to do with indecision than with an understanding of the plural and infinite nature of the text that she was engaged with.

It has been suggested that Mary Sidney began by reworking and revising Psalms 1–43, those undertaken by her brother, and that she used this process as a kind of poetic apprenticeship, before moving on to her own versions.[53] These are certainly indebted in vocabulary and method to Sir Philip Sidney's distinctive lexicon. Many of her coinages owe their technique to Sidney: the use of compound words, zero conversion (noun used as verb, verb used as adjective, etc.), the addition of prefixes and suffixes, and so on. Many usages are found previously only in her brother's work (noted in the commentary), suggesting that she learned much stylistically from preparing his works for the press. Echoes of vocabulary and phrasing from his psalm versions are less surprising: either these derive from her revisions and she is echoing herself, or they are a conscious attempt to make the Psalter into a coherent stylistic whole. Other textual echoes suggest Mary Sidney to be a careful and attentive reader who retained striking words and phrases in her imagination for future use. Tracing the origins and evolution of her diction and phrasing provides a useful insight into her conception of this 'coupled worke',[54] as she creates a composite text, derived from a variety of sources, continental and English, sacred and secular, populist and courtly.

Mary Sidney's version of Petrarch provides a stark contrast to the Psalter; it is a much more literal translation, and it is a secular text. Interpretation of Mary Sidney's translation of *The Triumph of Death* has concentrated on two areas: its literalism and accuracy, and its connection to her mourning for Philip. Her version has been praised particularly for its adherence to the challenging form of *terza rima*. Frances Young described Mary Sidney as 'a translator of great merit', and Robert Coogan says that her version is 'the finest translation of this triumph in the English language'.[55] Others have drawn attention to its syntactic obscurity and clumsy imagery.[56] However, it is not only the literalism, or otherwise, of a translation which makes it carry meaning: 'the specific affiliations of the translator, as well as the time and place in which s/he translates, can affect both the choice of the text to be translated and the method by which it is translated'.[57] A judgement that a translation is literal presupposes that it is read exclusively in relation to its source text, rather than in the context to which it is directed; it also makes an assumption about the stability or presence of the original to be reproduced.[58]

Recent criticism has asserted that Mary Sidney's choice of this particular text from Petrarch's *Trionfi* (the others are Love, Chastity, Fame, Time and Eternity) derives from her mourning, not only for her brother Philip, but also for her parents, Mary and Henry and a younger brother Thomas (d. 1595). There are difficulties with insisting that the text is an encoded elegy for Sir Philip Sidney. First, there is the problem of the identifications in the poem. *The Triumph of Death* reveals a complicated relationship to the voices found in Petrarch's original; shifts between speakers (the poet, Laura, Death) are not always clearly signalled, and it cannot be unequivocally asserted which of the figures in the poem Mary Sidney identifies with.[59] At some level, despite the multiple 'I's in the poem, Sidney projects her voice through that of the poet figure who is chastised and instructed by Laura. If the poem is to be read as an elegy for Philip Sidney's Petrarchan legacy, and the poetic relationship between him and his sister, then some rather eccentric unfixing of gendered positions in the text have to be made: the poet has to be re-gendered as female, and Laura (even more bizarrely) has to be gendered as male. It is difficult to see why Sir Philip Sidney would be celebrated through the figure of Laura, rather than that of the poet. As Goldberg notes, the stance of mourning is 'a site of representation rather than one of identification':[60] the discourse of death cannot be seen as a purely personal issue of individualized grief in this period. A consciousness of mortality is pervasive and its significance is larger than individual loss, connecting with questions of morality, politics, religion and representation.

The other critical objections to a purely biographical reading have to do with textual evidence. If Mary Sidney's text was to be seen as personal in motivation, this would need to be backed by a secure chronology. Sir John Harington's letter accompanying the poem to the Countess of Bedford is dated December 1600, and the poet and recipient of Mary Sidney's patronage, Thomas Moffett, seems to allude to work on Petrarch in his dedication of *The Silkewormes, and their Flies* to the Countess of Pembroke in 1599: 'Let *Petrarke* sleep, give rest to *Sacred Witte*'. However, these dates are not in any sense conclusive. Biographical readings assume that Mary Sidney specifically chose to translate this particular *Triumph*. However, Hannay, using the evidence of the manuscript in which the poem appears, which includes such disparate items as the satirist

Thomas Nashe's 'Choise of Valentines', poems in support of the disgraced soldier and diplomat Robert Devereux, Earl of Essex, and epigrams by Sir John Harington, argues that 'such haphazard preservation certainly leaves open the possibility that the "Triumph of Death" was a fragment of a longer work'.[61] If the translation cannot be seen as exclusively personal in motivation and content, how should it be read? There are two important contexts: the politics of representation, and the relationship of gender and Petrarchanism. The *Trionfi* was a text central to courtly representation in sixteenth-century England, via adaptations of its central motifs and images in numerous media (for example, poetry, courtly entertainments, visual arts). It had a particular connection with the representation of female monarchy, where its depiction of a virtuous, moral, chaste, but powerful female figure triumphing over earthly love and desire could be usefully manipulated. Both Elizabeth I and Mary Queen of Scots were depicted in terms derived from Petrarch's poem.[62] Elizabeth had translated part of *The Triumph of Eternity*, and the 'Siena' portrait, which represents the Queen in terms of her exceptional chastity, uses a quotation from *The Triumph of Chastity*.[63] Court entertainments such as *The Four Foster Children of Desire* (1581) utilize the structure of the *Trionfi*, so that chastity (Elizabeth) is seen to conquer desire.

Whatever message is conveyed by Mary Sidney through the medium of translation, it is carefully balanced: on the one hand, the poem relates the death of a figure repeatedly identified with Elizabeth, ageing by 1600 and notoriously sensitive about the subject of her own mortality; on the other, the text elevates Laura into a powerful moral figure, resisting the control of her image by the poet, who finally secures eternity through her elevation into timelessness. Some of the details found in the poem recall elements of Elizabeth's representation, especially after the demise of the marriage negotiations with Alençon, heir to the French throne, when the cult of virginity took hold.[64] The deliberate recall of earlier representations of Elizabeth (the text consistently stresses Laura's youth and beauty) could be seen as a way of pointing subtly to the gap between the ever more extravagant depictions (pictorial and poetic) of the Queen and the reality of an ageing, declining queen. Such a position can be supported by reference to the problematic relationship of radical Protestants to panegyric and their distrust of iconography. At the very least, *The Triumph of Death* is a poem which sets forth the fundamental elements of Petrarchan poetics (mainly in 'The first chapter'), then undermines them and replaces them with another register of praise dependent upon eternity and mutability. Ultimately, it can be seen to reverse Petrarchan conventions, as the poet is criticized for his concern with earthly things, erotic desire and superficiality, while Laura speaks from a position of authority about the transitory nature of earthly values, and the durability of the divine. The poet is abandoned to a legacy of loss and longing until he can renounce worldly passions. Such a position could be read as a carefully balanced panegyric: on the one hand, viewing the conventional registers of praise for Elizabeth as inappropriate, and on the other, suggesting that the proper form of praise is to stress the divine and eternal in relation to the Queen.

One of the key areas of interest in the poem is its attempt to reverse, or question, the dynamics of Petrarchanism: here, Laura is given a voice for the only time; the poet is subject to her in terms of his disabling desire; and he is excluded from the heavenly vision that she imparts.[65] *The Triumph of Death* does provide some evidence of a gendered intervention on Mary Sidney's part. The validity of female speech is stressed throughout, not only by granting Laura a voice, but also through the stress upon her eloquence (1.9 and 149–50). Laura provides authority for female speech, as her speech is virtuous, is concerned with the spiritual life, and does not call her sexual reputation into question; rather, it serves to assert her virtue and chastity. At times, Mary Sidney avoids using the pronoun 'I' where her Italian source does so, with the result that the identity of the male poet is somewhat undermined, and the relationship between poet and Laura is altered (for example, 1.40–42). Her treatment of the gaze, long acknowledged as a key element in the Petrarchan poet's objectification of the female beloved, is particularly interesting. The structure of male viewer and female object is replicated in the organization of the *Triumphs*, but Mary Sidney intervenes to alter this aspect of the subject–object relationship. The gaze is often negated, or expressed by means of periphrasis, as in 'those sightfull fountaines drye' (1.119), where Petrarch uses a direct reference to 'occhi'. Sometimes the gaze is relocated as female property, as women are the ones who look, rather than being looked *at*. In 1.10–12, Mary Sidney reworks the original – where the narrator looks upon the procession of women – so that it is personified Love which looks upon Laura's exploits, hence erasing the visual power of the narrator. Seeing is often distanced, passive rather than active; Laura is 'presented there to view' (1.110), rather than being directly looked upon. These are small changes, but cumulatively they alter the power dynamics of Petrarchan conventions. Looking, in this poem, is not power for the poet; rather, it is a constant reminder of his exclusion from a privileged community, which has knowledge that he cannot obtain because of his preoccupation with earthly love, an exclusion which derives from his inability to see beyond surfaces: 'Thou sawe'st what was without, not what within' (2.97).

Commentators both contemporary and modern attest to Mary Sidney's exceptional poetic talent and political commitment. Both these were undoubtedly enabled and encouraged by circumstances – fortuitous and tragic. Mary Sidney's familial obligations were intensified in the wake of her brother's death, which turned completing his work into a powerful imperative transcending gender limitations. Such conditions contrast sharply with the situation of Aemilia Lanyer, who used her writing to advance her own social and economic standing by insisting upon an ideal spiritual equality uniting all women.

Much of our information about Aemilia Lanyer's life comes from unreliable sources, but it is possible to piece together some basic facts: she was raised in the household of the Countess of Kent. She had an affair with Lord Hunsdon, the Lord Chamberlain, bore his child and was married off to a musician, Alphonso Lanyer. She clearly spent time with the aristocratic northern Clifford family (mother and daughter) at Cookham (see her poems and commentary), but the circumstances surrounding this are unclear.

Lanyer's sole volume, *Salve Deus Rex Judæorum* (1611), is both heterogeneous and organized around a single agenda: heterogeneous in its deployment of multiple models and modes of address, but single-minded in its advocacy of the virtue of women. Themes and images are echoed across and within the various component parts: dedicatory encomia, the Passion narrative, an apology for Eve and 'The Description of Cooke-ham'. Each represents a different negotiation of the poet's virtue, her sense of female spirituality, and the exemplification of this in the world by her patron Margaret Clifford, Countess of Cumberland, whom she depicts as the living emblem of Christian piety. In presenting her patrons as the living exemplars of Christ (see 'To the Ladie *Lucie*', 1–7), Lanyer immediately signals her interest in questions of representation and textualization, and in the conundrum of how to write the divine. As Diane Purkiss suggests, *Salve Deus* is 'a poem about difficulties of interpretation',[66] particularly where interpretation has been obscured or complicated by assumptions about women's nature. The text's interest in the promotion of female virtue, and the advocacy of a non-hierarchical community of 'good women', has led to the virtual canonization of Lanyer as an early feminist.[67] Critics allude to its 'remarkable feminism' without investigating the terms in which this might be articulated by a woman poet in early modern England.[68] First, a revision of biblical tradition, particularly in relation to the question of Eve's culpability, is not necessarily the subversive gesture that it might appear to be. This issue had been extensively debated by male commentators and theologians as part of the *querelle des femmes*,[69] and the poem participates in the notion that one woman can stand for all women. Lanyer's revision was not unprecedented; she clearly draws upon the theological arguments advanced by Cornelius Agrippa in *A treatise of the Nobilitie and Excellencie of Womankynde* (translated by David Clapam, 1542).[70] Her text does not disrupt prevailing Renaissance models of female virtue, rather it pleads for a proper acceptance of them. Her ideal models are chaste, pious, and dedicated to the reading of spiritually instructive texts (particularly the Psalms, see 'The Authors Dreame to the Ladie *Marie*', 117–20 and 'The Description of Cooke-ham', 87–90). Although the notion of obedience is lacking in Lanyer's poem, there is an overwhelming sense of obligation in the text, particularly in relation to ideas of social hierarchy.[71] Female subjecthood is inextricably linked to notions of female virtue that contemporary commentators would not have found disquieting. The feminism of *Salve Deus* does not address questions such as power, nor does it really analyse patriarchy; rather, it is a poem which is interested in creating a means whereby women can have access to Christ, through identification with a suffering, weakened and largely silent Christ. It is possible that Lanyer's feminism is not primarily concerned with women as a category or group, rather that identification with Christ reverses the social hierarchies from which Lanyer feels herself to be excluded. In other words, her rewriting of biblical tradition is an act of self-fashioning as well as one of gender solidarity and sincere devotion, as the repositioning of women in relation to the Christian heritage is a way for her to negotiate access to her projected patrons in terms which not only flatter them, but provide a rationale for that access.

This is not to deny that Lanyer is a careful and sensitive reader of texts and a consummate manipulator of images. 'Salve Deus' is, effectively, a long meditation on the Bible, to the point where Lanyer 'speaks' through the rearrangement of her sources. She draws attention to revisions of the model of fallen women and virtuous men, by amplifying the gaps and omissions in the biblical text; however, everything that Lanyer advocates can be found in the scriptures. Indeed, this perhaps constitutes her most powerful argument; not that biblical authority has to be undermined, rather that interpretative traditions need to be less selective in relation to their sources, as Lewalski suggests: 'her feminist perceptions can be rendered only in terms of the discourse of scripture, but they force a radical imaginative rewriting of its patriarchal norms to place women at the center'.[72] Hence the central placing of the prophetic dream of Pilate's wife, Procula, the precedent of the queen of Sheba's visit to Solomon (prefiguring the relationship between Christ and the Church), and the stress laid upon Christ's proximity to and sympathy with women counter the Augustinian tradition of seeing women as inherently fallen. Each of these exemplars reveals virtue to be a natural quality of women, and emphasizes that their power to speak derives from their ability to prophesy – in other words, their agency is presented in a way which suggests that their morality and eloquence come directly from God's grace. Lanyer's own authority as a poet derives from the same source, in a deft marshalling of conventional assumptions about women's speech and spirituality in order to allow her to speak. While she utilizes conventional humility topoi, Lanyer merges her identification with 'the voices which have been suppressed'[73] in the New Testament with her strategy of textualization, turning her 'booke' into the mediating figure of Christ, and thereby placing herself as a kind of literary Virgin Mary ushering forth the text, which *is* Christ. Lanyer certainly deploys a 'subversive hermenuetic method',[74] but it is directed to her own authorial presentation and social ambition, rather than to the possibility of a utopian community of women *per se*.

The poem's consistently feminized representation of Christ is a notable feature of *Salve Deus*. The first key aspect of Lanyer's depiction of Christ is her angling of the contexts surrounding his trial and persecution in the Gospels. Throughout the poem, she stresses male guilt and complicity and female innocence, suggesting that women have an innate sympathy with the oppressed, and that they possess a unique understanding that Christ is the Son of God. Thus women are seen to be closer to Christ in terms of status, and in terms of morality, as they bear out Christian principles of mercy, justice and compassion in relation to Christ himself. This essential connection between women and Christian belief is underlined by the structural aspects of *Salve Deus*, particularly the framing of the narrative of the Passion by addresses to the Countess of Cumberland, who is thus seen as the living embodiment of both Christ and the women who surround him. This collapse of historical time reinforces the relevance of the Christian story, and inaugurates Lanyer as the writer of a new feminocentric gospel. The second aspect of Lanyer's depiction of Christ is his multiple representation as a figure immediately appealing to women. Using biblical precedents of Christ as lover and bridegroom (Song of Songs, Revelation), Lanyer reworks the metaphor of marriage to denote a spiritual union between her patrons and Christ. Christ himself is portrayed through frameworks which serve to feminize him, turning him into a spectacle, often eroticized, for women to gaze upon (see 1161–8 and 1305–20), using the model of the Petrarchan *blazon* – the enumeration of the bodily parts of the beloved. As Randall Martin suggests, Lanyer creates an androgynous Christ, whom it is legitimate for women to desire, so that in looking at Christ, Lanyer's female readers look at themselves.[75] This is linked to the poem's conceptualization as a mirror which replaces the self normally reflected in a mirror with a picture of Christ, where the implication is that Christ *is* the self for these women, and reflects their selves back to them. Wendy Wall argues, 'Her work is figured almost obsessively as an interactive mirroring of female virtues, a redemptive textual space in which women might find the image of themselves and other devout women, and in which they, by looking, might purify their sight.'[76] 'Salve Deus' repeatedly displays the physical suffering of

Christ, and stresses his feminine virtues of humility, patience and mercy: Lanyer's Christ is largely a passive Christ subject to aggressive male institutional power.

There has been an increasing consensus that 'Salve Deus' is not purely and simply a religious poem, and that its radical revision of scripture might in fact be a strategy which enables Lanyer to address and negotiate questions of social power and hierarchy. This perception arose from the apparently contradictory social and religious impulses of the poem. As Judith Scherer Herz notes, 'the margins crowded with noble readers, take up almost as much space as the text itself'.[77] However, the division into text and margins cannot be sustained because Lanyer sets up correspondences between the prefatory material and the poem which militate against their separation. The patrons are integral to the poem because they are its interpretive community. Rather than simply flattering her dedicatees, Lanyer seems to be manipulating them in order to create a spiritual equality, contrasting with the intense sense of social hierarchy which emerges from the text. Hence she appeals to a uniting, but hypothetical, category of 'women' – not because of sexual solidarity, but as a way of articulating her self. By placing herself as the guardian of Christ, presenting him to her readers, she hints at a position of social superiority, based on virtue rather than birth; in 'To the Ladie *Anne*' (17–80) she suggests that the hereditary principle is open to abuse, and that social hierarchy is at odds with scriptural precedent: 'Was it not Virtue that distinguisht all?/ All sprang but from one woman and one man' (34–5). Throughout 'Salve Deus', the low birth of Christ is emphasized and worldly riches are rejected; hence, the embracing of Christian virtue functions as a form of social advancement for Lanyer, as she imagines the inversion of social hierarchies through the love of Christ. As Lisa Schnell argues, 'the conventionally humble declaration of unworthiness becomes, paradoxically, a claim to spiritual and epistemological superiority over the woman she would have as her patron'.[78] So, while Lanyer rereads scriptural authority and tradition from a distinctively female point of view, the status of her feminism needs to be carefully considered, as it is shot through with class considerations, and complicated by the attempt of the poet to articulate herself in the context of a social dependence.

'The Description of Cooke-ham' has been hailed as the first

published country-house poem, printed some five years before Ben Jonson's 'To Penshurst' (1616), with which it may be usefully compared. The poem brings together many elements of the country-house poem, drawing upon a series of precedents, particularly those associated with pastoral. As Lewalski has argued, the poem blends the *beatus ille* motif (cf. Horace, *Epode* II; Martial, *Epigram* III.58) with 'the controlling topos of the valediction to a place' (cf. Virgil, *Eclogue* I).[79] Added to this blend are ideas related to the earthly paradise, or *locus amoenus*, topographical description, and the pathetic fallacy (where the natural world reflects human emotion). It should be seen in relation to the rest of the *Salve Deus* volume, as it looks back nostalgically to an ideal exchange between devout and virtuous women in the earthly paradise, which contrasts with the vision of the heavenly paradise adumbrated in the main body of the text. The first part of the poem represents 'a redeemed Eden',[80] an ideal spiritual community of women united in their love of God. The poem is, as Beilin argues, 'a parable of the Fall'[81] as Lanyer sets up parallels between the tree in the Garden of Eden, the tree of the Crucifixion, and the oak tree at Cookham; the worship of the tree is a redemptive gesture, as these women are not tempted, but adoring; the three women might be understood to parallel the three Marys in the Gospel. Not only is this a female paradise, it is also a classless one, unriven by the problematics of social exchange and hierarchy. The second part of the poem, however, provides a stark contrast, as the estate is abandoned and nature mourns the departure of the Clifford women, whose earlier bounty is thereby highlighted. At this point, social concerns come to the fore, as nature's visible copiousness is read retrospectively as a metaphor for patronage, now absent, figured by the sterility and non-production of the natural world.

Although Lanyer, of the three poets represented here, can make the largest claim to feminist ideas, it is important to recognize that this feminism is powerfully shaped by questions of education and social position. In addition, like Whitney and Sidney, Lanyer's shaping of language and ideas into poetic artefacts is in turn moulded by her culture, but is finally turned to new generic and ideological ends.

*

Reading Isabella Whitney, Mary Sidney and Aemilia Lanyer along-
side one another provides a fascinating insight into the range of
female literary experience in the Renaissance. Each poet should be
seen as intervening in contemporary cultural life in quite distinct
ways, ways which are deeply informed by the specific social and
intellectual conditions constructing each writer's position within
the hierarchies of early modern England. At the same time, despite
these differences, some recurrent concerns are apparent. All three
poets display, although through varied discourses and class con-
cerns, an abiding interest in notions of female virtue, and a deep
sense of the potential of their chosen forms. All three recognize the
forms of literary value current in Renaissance culture, and deploy
varied forms of imitation in order to articulate their interests and
anxieties. These three poets are not just women writers, they are
writers who engaged deeply with a range of early modern discourses,
of which gender is but one, but one which underwrites and informs
the terms in which they wrote.

Danielle Clarke
Stoneybatter
Dublin

NOTES

1. The phrase comes from Stephen Greenblatt, *Renaissance Self-Fashioning:
From More to Shakespeare* (Chicago, 1980).
2. See *Edmund Spenser: The Shorter Poems*, ed. Richard A. McCabe, Penguin
Classics (Harmondsworth, 1999).
3. William Wordsworth, Preface to *Lyrical Ballads* (1802), in *The Norton
Anthology of English Literature*, ed. Abrams et al. (6th edition; New York,
1993), vol. 2, p. 143.
4. See George Pigman III, 'Versions of Imitation in the Renaissance',
Renaissance Quarterly 33 (1980), pp. 1–32, and Thomas M. Greene, *The
Light in Troy: Imitation and Discovery in Renaissance Poetry* (New Haven,
1982).
5. This tendency has been particularly marked in relation to women's use
of translation, which has not been as extensively explored as a form of
female literary agency as it should have been, being subsumed into the
search for autonomous voices pioneering new genres. For an argument

asserting a more historically based understanding of translation, see Suzanne Trill, 'Sixteenth-century women's writing: Mary Sidney's *Psalmes* and the "femininity" of translation', in *Writing and the English Renaissance*, ed. William Zunder and Suzanne Trill (London, 1996), pp. 140–58.

6. See the essays collected in Margaret P. Hannay (ed.), *Silent But for the Word: Tudor Women as Patrons, Translators, and Writers of Religious Works* (Kent, Mich., 1985).

7. Moves are starting to be made in this direction; see, for example, Lisa Schnell's powerful argument that we should resist collapsing one woman into '*all women*' (her emphasis), and that we have tended to make early modern women writers speak for 'the feminist energy of our own perceived communities', 'Breaking "the rule of *Cortezia*": Aemilia Lanyer's Dedications to *Salve Deus Rex Judaeorum*', *Journal of Medieval and Early Modern Studies* 27 (1997), p. 95. While I do not agree with all of his conclusions, Jonathan Goldberg's *Desiring Women Writing: English Renaissance Examples* (Stanford, 1997) usefully opens up areas for debate.

8. Randall Martin (ed.), *Women Writers in Renaissance England* (London, 1997), p. 279.

9. See John Kerrigan, *Motives of Woe: Shakespeare and 'Female Complaint', A Critical Anthology* (Oxford, 1991).

10. Lorna Hutson, *Thomas Nashe in Context* (Oxford, 1989), p. 128.

11. Lorna Hutson, *The Usurer's Daughter: Male Friendship and Fictions of Woman in Sixteenth-Century England* (London, 1994), p. 127.

12. See Wendy Wall, *The Imprint of Gender: Authorship and Publication in the English Renaissance* (Ithaca, NY, 1993), p. 301.

13. Hutson, *The Usurer's Daughter*, pp. 122–5.

14. Lawrence Manley, *Literature and Culture in Early Modern London* (Cambridge, 1995), pp. 75–7.

15. See Hutson, *The Usurer's Daughter*, p. 122.

16. Patricia Phillippy, 'The Maid's Lawful Liberty: Service, the Household, and "Mother B" in Isabella Whitney's *A Sweet Nosegay*', *Modern Philology* 95 (1997–8), pp. 439–62.

17. Suzanne Trill, 'Sixteenth-century women's writing', in *Writing and the English Renaissance*, pp. 140–58.

18. See Donald Davie (ed.), *The Psalms in English* (Harmondsworth, 1996), pp. xvi, lii.

19. See Margaret P. Hannay, ' "House-confinéd maids": The Presentation of Woman's Role in the *Psalmes* of the Countess of Pembroke', *English Literary Review* 24 (1994), pp. 44–71.

20. Athanasius, quoted in Margaret P. Hannay, *Philip's Phoenix: Mary Sidney, Countess of Pembroke* (Oxford and New York, 1990), p. 96.

21. Davie, *The Psalms in English*, p. xlv.

22. Quoted in Barbara K. Lewalski, *Protestant Poetics and the Seventeenth-Century Religious Lyric* (Princeton, 1979), p. 42.

23. *The Collected Works of Mary Sidney Herbert, Countess of Pembroke*, ed. Margaret P. Hannay, Noel J. Kinnamon and Michael G. Brennan (eds.), 2 volumes (Oxford, 1998), 2.5. Hereafter referred to as *CW*.

24. Margaret P. Hannay, ' "Princes You As Men Must Dy": Genevan Advice to Monarchs in the *Psalmes* of Mary Sidney', *English Literary Renaissance* 19 (1989), pp. 27–8.

25. Hannay, *Philip's Phoenix*, p. 98.

26. *The Psalmes of David and others.With M. John Calvins Commentaries*, trans. Arthur Golding (1571).

27. Théodore de Bèze, *The Psalmes of David, truly opened and explained by paraphrasis*, trans. Anthony Gilbie (1581).

28. Clément Marot and Théodore de Bèze, *Les Psaumes Vers en Français* (1562).

29. Preface to *Goostly psalmes* (*c.* 1535), Appendix II, in Robin A. Leaver, *'Goostly psalmes and spirituall songes': English and Dutch Metrical Psalms from Coverdale to Utenhove, 1535–1566* (Oxford, 1991), p. 286.

30. Hannay, *Philip's Phoenix*, p. 96.

31. Ibid.

32. Ibid., p. 86.

33. Ibid., p. 88.

34. See also *CW* 2.25–6.

35. Hannay, *Philip's Phoenix*, p. viii.

36. Davie notes that the rhetorical complexity of Mary Sidney's versions makes them unsuitable for performance, *The Psalms in English*, pp. li–lv.

37. *The Defence of Poesy*, in *Sir Philip Sidney*, ed. Katherine Duncan-Jones (Oxford, 1994), p. 104.

38. Israel Baroway, 'The Bible as Poetry in the English Renaissance: An Introduction', *Journal of English and German Philology* 32 (1933), pp. 447–80.

39. Davie, *The Psalms in English*, p. l.

40. William Tyndale, *The Obedience of a Christian Man*, ed. David Daniell, Penguin Classics (Harmondsworth, 2000), pp. 156–7.

41. Sidney, *Defence of Poesy*, p. 107.

42. See Baroway, 'The Bible', pp. 468–70.

43. Sidney, *Defence of Poesy*, p. 104.

44. As Elaine Beilin (among others) suggests, Mary Sidney's 'sex modified what she would do; her woman's training what she could do', *Redeeming Eve: Women Writers of the English Renaissance* (Princeton, 1987), p. 127.

45. John Harington, *Nugae Antiquae* (edition of 1804), 1.173.

46. Jonathan Goldberg, *Desiring Women Writing: English Renaissance Examples* (Stanford, CA, 1997), p. 131.

47. Sidney, *Defence of Poesy*, p. 104.

48. Baroway, 'The Bible', pp. 473–4.

49. See also *CW* 2.19.

50. See *CW* 2.7–11, 2.25, 2.26–9.

51. *CW* 2.21, 2.23–4.

52. Coburn Freer, *Music for a King: George Herbert's Style and the Metrical Psalms* (Baltimore, 1972), p. 74.

53. Beth Wynne Fisken, 'Mary Sidney's *Psalmes*: Education and Wisdom', in Margaret P. Hannay, *Silent But for the Word*, p. 166.

54. 'To the Angell spirit', line 2.

55. Frances Young, *Mary Sidney, Countess of Pembroke* (London, 1912), p. 149; Robert Coogan, 'Petrarch's *Trionfi* and the English Renaissance', *Studies in Philology* 67 (1970), p. 324.

56. Douglas Brooks-Davies (ed.), *Silver Poets of the Sixteenth Century* (London, 1992), p. 442.

57. Trill, 'Sixteenth-century women's writing', p. 143.

58. See Goldberg, *Desiring Women Writing*, pp. 114–16.

59. Ibid., p. 131, on the difficulties created by modern editors adding quotation marks.

60. Ibid., p. 119.

61. Hannay, *Philip's Phoenix*, p. 107.

62. See Danielle Clarke, ' "Lover's Songs Shall Turne to Holy Psalmes": Mary Sidney and the Transformation of Petrarch', *Modern Language Review* 92 (1997), pp. 284–6.

63. See Roy Strong, *Gloriana: The Portraits of Elizabeth I* (New York, 1987), p. 97, and Clarke, ' "Lover's Songs" ', p. 284.

64. See John N. King, 'Queen Elizabeth I: Representations of the Virgin Queen', *Renaissance Quarterly* 43 (1990), p. 58, on this shift. Details of the chastity cult as they relate to *The Triumph of Death* are noted in the commentary to the text.

65. See Hannay, *Philip's Phoenix*, p. 108.

66. Diane Purkiss (ed.), *Renaissance Women: The Plays of Elizabeth Cary, The Poems of Aemilia Lanyer* (London, 1994), p. xxx.

67. See Beilin, *Redeeming Eve*, pp. 177–207, and Barbara K. Lewalski, *Writing Women in Jacobean England* (Cambridge, Mass., 1993), pp. 213–41.

68. Esther Gilman Richey, ' "To Undoe the Booke": Cornelius Agrippa, Aemilia Lanyer and the Subversion of Pauline Authority', *English Literary Renaissance* 27 (1997), p. 108.

69. Ibid., pp. 106–28.

70. Ibid., pp. 109–12.

71. See Tina Krontiris, *Oppositional Voices: Women as Writers and Translators of Literature in the English Renaissance* (London, 1992), p. 106.

72. Lewalski, *Writing Women*, p. 219.

73. Richey, ' "To Undoe the Booke" ', p. 120.

74. Ibid., p. 107.

75. Martin, *Women Writers*, p. 364.

76. Wall, *Imprint of Gender*, p. 322.

77. Judith Scherer Herz, 'Aemilia Lanyer and the Pathos of Literary History', in Claude Summers and Ted-Larry Pebworth (eds.), *Representing Women in Renaissance England* (Columbia, NY, 1997), p. 129.

78. Lisa Schnell, 'Breaking "the rule of *Cortezia*": Aemilia Lanyer's Dedications to *Salve Deus Rex Judaeorum*', *Journal of Medieval and Early Modern Studies* 27 (1997), p. 92.

79. Lewalski, *Writing Women*, p. 235.

80. Beilin, *Redeeming Eve*, p. 202.

81. Ibid.

FURTHER READING

ISABELLA WHITNEY

Editions

The Floures of Philosophie (1572) by Hugh Plat and *A Sweet Nosgay (1573)* and *The Copy of a Letter (1567)* by Isabella Whitney, introduction by Richard J. Panofsky (Delmar, NY, 1982)

Martin, Randall (ed.), *Women Writers in Renaissance England* (London, 1997), selection

Travitsky, Betty S., 'The "Wyll and Testament" of Isabella Whitney', in *English Literary Renaissance* 10 (1980), pp. 76–94

MARY SIDNEY, COUNTESS OF PEMBROKE

Editions

Brooks-Davies, Douglas (ed.), *Silver Poets of the Sixteenth Century* (London, revised edition 1994)

Davie, Donald (ed.), *The Psalms in English*, Penguin Classics (Harmondsworth, 1996), selection

Hannay, Margaret P., Noel J. Kinnamon and Michael G. Brennan (eds.), *The Collected Works of Mary Sidney Herbert, Countess of Pembroke* (Oxford, 1998), 2 volumes

Martin, Randall (ed.), *Women Writers in Renaissance England* (London, 1997), selection

Pritchard, R. E. (ed.), *The Sidney Psalms* (Manchester, 1992), selection

Rathmell, J. C. A. (ed.), *The Psalms of Sir Philip Sidney and the Countess of Pembroke* (New York, 1963)

Ringler, William A., Jr (ed.), *The Poems of Sir Philip Sidney* (Oxford, 1962)
Waller, Gary F. (ed.), *The Triumph of Death and other unpublished poems by Mary Sidney, Countess of Pembroke (1561–1621)* (Salzburg, 1977)

AEMILIA LANYER

Editions

Martin, Randall (ed.), *Women Writers in Renaissance England* (London, 1997), selection
Purkiss, Diane (ed.), *Renaissance Women: The Plays of Elizabeth Cary, The Poems of Aemilia Lanyer* (London, 1994)
Rowse, A. L. (ed.), *The Poems of Shakespeare's Dark Lady: 'Salve Deus Rex Judaeorum' by Emilia Lanyer* (London, 1978)
Woods, Suzanne (ed.), *The Poems of Aemilia Lanyer* (New York and Oxford, 1993)

GENERAL READING

Beilin, Elaine, *Redeeming Eve: Women Writers of the English Renaissance* (Princeton, 1987)
Brant, Clare and Diane Purkiss (eds.), *Women, Texts and Histories, 1575–1760* (London, 1992)
Chedgzoy, Kate, Melanie Hansen and Suzanne Trill (eds.), *Voicing Women: Gender and Sexuality in Early Modern Writing* (Keele, 1996)
Crawford, Patricia, *Women and Religion in England, 1500–1700* (London, 1993)
Erickson, Amy Louise, *Women and Property in Early Modern England* (London, 1993)
Ezell, Margaret, *Writing Women's Literary History* (Baltimore, 1990)
Goldberg, Jonathan, *Desiring Women Writing: English Renaissance Examples* (Stanford, 1997)
Gowing, Laura, *Domestic Dangers: Women, Words and Sex in Early Modern London* (Oxford, 1996)

Grossman, Marshall (ed.), *Aemilia Lanyer: Gender, Genre, and Canon* (Lexington, Ky, 1998)

Hannay, Margaret P., *Philip's Phoenix: Mary Sidney, Countess of Pembroke* (Oxford and New York, 1990)

Hannay, Margaret P. (ed.), *Silent But for the Word: Tudor Women as Patrons, Translators, and Writers of Religious Works* (Kent, Ohio, 1985)

Haselkorn, Anne M. and Betty S. Travitsky (eds.), *The Renaissance Englishwoman in Print: Counterbalancing the Canon* (Amherst, Mass., 1990)

Hull, Suzanne W., *Chaste, Silent, and Obedient: English Books for Women, 1475–1640* (San Marino, Calif., 1982)

Jones, Ann Rosalind, *The Currency of Eros: Women's Love Lyric in Europe, 1540–1620* (Bloomington, Ind., 1990)

Lewalski, Barbara K., *Protestant Poetics and the Seventeenth-Century Religious Lyric* (Princeton, 1979)

Lewalski, Barbara K., *Writing Women in Jacobean England* (Cambridge, Mass., 1993)

Penguin Book of Renaissance Verse 1509–1659, selected and introduced by David Norbrook, ed. H. R. Woudhuysen, Penguin Classics (Harmondsworth, 1992), selection

Wall, Wendy, *The Imprint of Gender: Authorship and Publication in the English Renaissance* (Ithaca, NY, 1993)

Wiesner, Merry E., *Women and Gender in Early Modern Europe* (Cambridge, 1993)

Wilcox, Helen (ed.), *Women and Literature in Britain, 1500–1700* (Cambridge, 1996)

Zim, Rivkah, *English Metrical Psalms: Poetry as Praise and Prayer 1535–1601* (Cambridge, 1987)

TABLE OF DATES

1589   Publication of Puttenham's *The Arte of English Poesie*.

1590   Publication of Spenser's *The Faerie Queene* (Books I–III); birth of Lady Anne Clifford, later Countess of Dorset and Pembroke, one of Lanyer's principal dedicatees.

1592   Publication of Mary Sidney's translation of Garnier's *Antonie* and her translation of Philippe DuPlessis-Mornay's *A Discourse of Life and Death*; marriage of Aemilia Bassano to Alfonso Lanyer.

1595   Death of Mary Sidney's younger brother Thomas.

1599   Proposed visit of Elizabeth I to Wilton (the Pembroke seat); presentation copy of the Sidney Psalter completed; date of composition of Mary Sidney's 'A Dialogue betweene two shepheardes' (published in 1602).

1600   Approximate date of Mary Sidney's translation, *The Triumph of Death*. Earl of Essex's rebellion.

1601   Earl of Essex's trial and execution.

1603   Death of Elizabeth I; James I (James VI of Scotland) ascends the throne.

1611   Publication of Aemilia Lanyer's *Salve Deus Rex Judæorum*.

1616   Publication of Ben Jonson's 'To Penshurst'; death of Aemilia Lanyer's main dedicatee, Margaret, Countess Dowager of Cumberland.

1621   Death of Mary Sidney.

1645   Death of Aemilia Lanyer.

A NOTE ON THE TEXTS

Pressure of space has necessitated the exclusion of the epistles addressed to Isabella Whitney by her friends and relatives, those psalms of Mary Sidney which were lengthy and/or carried little of compelling stylistic or thematic interest, and certain heavily imitative passages of Aemilia Lanyer's *Salve Deus Rex Judæorum*. I have selected those dedicatory epistles likely to be of most interest in the context of the other material included in this edition.

Due to the fact that three poets from different periods are included here, please refer to the Notes and Textual Apparatus for further details of the texts. In general, as little as possible has been altered; *i* and *j* have been standardized, as have *u* and *v*. Contractions have been silently expanded, including 'the' for 'ye', and 'u' has been substituted for 'w' in words such as 'thou' and 'you', but not elsewhere. Where original texts are obscure or illegible, the probable letter, or letters, has been given in square brackets. Emendations are recorded in the Textual Apparatus.

The footnotes to the Sidney Psalter are Mary Sidney's own additions and excisions. The annotations and revisions were recorded by Samuel Woodforde, who transcribed MS's (now lost) working copy of the Psalms, incorporating her changes. Mary Sidney's psalm paraphrases are generally very lightly punctuated and the reader might find it helpful either to read them aloud, or to build up the meaning by looking at the text line by line.

The footnotes to Aemilia Lanyer's *Salve Deus Rex Judæorum* were originally written in the margins.

ISABELLA WHITNEY

from *A SWEET NOSGAY*

To the worshipfull and right vertuous yong Gentylman,
George Mainwaring Esquier: IS. W. wisheth happye
health with good successe in all his godly affayres

When I (good M. MAINWARING) had made this simple
Nosegaye: I was in minde to bestow the same on som dere
frind, of which number I have good occasion to accompt you
chiefe: But waying with my selfe, that although the Flowers
bound in the same were good: yet so little of my labour was
in them that they were not (as I wysht they should) to bee
esteemed as recompence for the least of a great number of
benefits, which I have from time to time (even from our
Childhood hetherto) receaved of you: yet least by me, you
10 m[igh]t be occasioned to say, as ANTIPATER said [b]y
DEMADES of Athens, that he should never [f]ill him with
geveing, I woulde to shew my selfe satisfied, gratifye your
Guifts, and also by the same, make a confession: that by
deedes you have deserved benefits: (which as DIOGENES
saith) is more worth then the geving or unworthy receaving
of many: But ceasing to seeke by benefits (which to do is not
alotted me) to accquit your curtesies, I come to present you
like the pore man which having no goods, came with his
hands full of water to meete the Persian Prince withal, who
20 respecting the good wyll of the man: did not disdayne his
simple Guift: even so, I being willinge to bestow some Present
on you, by the same thinking to make part of amendes for the
much that you have merited, to perfourme the dutie of a
friend, to expresse the good wyll that should rest in Countrie
folke, and not havyng of mine owne to discharg that I go
about (like to that poore Fellow which wente into an others
ground for his water) did step into an others garden for these
Flowers: which I beseech you (as DARIUS did,) to accepte:
and though they be of anothers growing, yet considering they

30   be of my owne gathering and makeing up: respect my labour
and regard my good wil, and not onely receave them, but
vouchsave to be a protector of them from the spightful, which
(perhaps) wil env[y] that I either presented you, or gathered
them, bef[ore] they had done one, or both: and so might
spoyle thi[s] Nosegay, and not to let it come so happily unto
your handes, as I wish it may. And though the Garden of
your godly mind be full fraught with vertuous Flowers, which
I know in your infancie to take roote, and which all may see
now to florish, with an undoubted hope of their yeelding
40   fruite hereafter: yet ordaine to smell to these, and when you
come into a pestilent aire that might infect your sound minde:
yet savour to these SLIPS in which I trust you shal finde
safety: And yf you take pleasure in them, I shal not only be
occasioned to endevour my selfe to make a further viage for a
more dayntier thing (then Flowers are) to present you withall:
but also have good hope that you wil accept this my labour,
for recompence of al that which you are unrecompenced for,
as knoweth god: who I beseeche geve unto you a longe and a
lucky lyfe with increase of all your vertuous studies.

50   From Abchurch Lane, the 20. of October, 1573.
By your welwillyng Countrywoman. IS. W.

The Auctor to the Reader

This Harvest tyme, I Harvestlesse, and serviceless also:
And subject unto sicknesse, that abrode I could not go.
Had leasure good, (though learning lackt) some study to
        apply:
To reade such Bookes, wherby I thought my selfe to edifye.
Somtime the Scriptures I perusd, but wantyng a Devine:
For to resolve mee in such doubts, as past this head of
        mine
To understand: I layd them by, and Histories gan read:
Wherin I found that follyes earst, in people did exceede.

The which I see doth not decrease, in this our present time
10   More pittie it is we folow them, in every wicked crime.
I straight wart wery of those Bookes, and many other mor[e]
As VIRGILL, OVID, MANTUAN, which many
      wonders [bor]e.
And to refresh my mased [mu]se, and cheare my brused
      brayne:
And for to trye if that my limmes had got their strength
      agayne
I walked out: but sodenly a friend of mine mee met:
And sayd, yf you regard your health: out of this Lane you
      get.
And shift you to some better aire, for feare to be infect:
With noysome smell and savours yll, I wysh you that
      respect.
And have regard unto your health, or els perhaps you may:
20   So make a dye, and then adieu, your wofull friends may say.
I thankt him for his carefulnes, and this for answer gave:
I'le neither shun, nor seeke for death, yet oft the same I
      crave.
By reason of my lucklesse lyfe, beleeve mee this is true:
In that (sayd he) you doo a misse, then bad he mee adieu.
For he was hastyng out of Towne, and could no longer
      byde:
And I went home all sole alone, good Fortune was my
      guyde.
And though she ever hath denyde, to hoyce me on her
      Wheele:
Yet now she stood me in some steede, and made mee
      pleasures feele.
For she to *Plat* his Plot mee brought, where fragrant
      Flowers abound:
30   The smell whereof prevents ech harme, if yet your selfe be
      sound.
Amongst those Beds so bravely deckt, with every goodly
      Flower:
And Bankes and Borders finely framde, I mee reposde one
      howre.

And longer wolde, but leasure lackt, and businesse bad mee
    hye:
And come agayne some other time, to stil my gasing eye.
Though loth: yet at the last I went, but ere I parted thence:
A slip I tooke to smell unto, which might be my defence.
In stynking streetes, or lothsome Lanes which els might mee
    infect:
And sence that time, I ech day once have viewd that brave
    prospect.
And though the Master of the same, I yet dyd never see:
40   It seemes he is a Gentylman, and full of courteseye:
For none that with good zeale doth come, doo any one
    resist:
And such as wyll with order get, may gather whilst they
    [lis]t.
Then pyttie were it to destroy, what he with payne did
    plant.
The moderate heere may be suffizde, and he no whit shall
    want.
And for my part, I may be bolde, to come when as I wyll:
Yea, and to chuse of all his Flowers, which may my fancy
    fill.
And now I have a Nosegay got, that would be passing rare:
Yf that to sort the same aright, weare lotted to my share.
But in a bundle as they bee, (good Reader them accept:)
50   It is the gever: not the guift, thou oughtest to respect.
And for thy health, not for thy eye, did I this Posye frame:
Because my selfe dyd safety finde, by smelling to the same.
But as we are not all a lyke, nor of complexion one:
So that which helpeth some we see, to others good doth
    none.
I doo not say, it dyd mee help, I no infection felt:
But sure I think they kept mee free, because to them I smelt.
And for because I lyke them well, and good have found
    therby:
I for good wyll, doo geve them thee, fyrst tast and after trye.
But yf thy mind infected be, then these wyll not prevayle:
60   Sir *Medicus* with stronger Earbes, thy maliadye must quayle.

For these be but to keepe thee sound, which if thou use
    them well:
(Paynes of my lyfe) in healthy state thy mind shall ever
    dwell.
Or if that thy complexion, with them doo not agree:
Refer them to some friend of thine, tyll thou their vertue
    see.
And this I pray thee, whether thou infected wast afore:
Or whether with thy nature strong, they can agree no more.
That thou my Nosegay not misuse, but leave it to the rest:
A number may such pleasure finde, to beare it in their brest.
And if thy selfe wolde gather more, then I have herein
    bound:
70   My counsell is that thou repayre, to Master *Plat* his ground.
And gather there what I dyd not, perhaps thy selfe may
    light:
On those which for thee fitter are, then them which I
    resighte.
Which if thou doo, then render thanks, to him which sowed
    the soyle:
Yf not, thou nedes must him commend, when as thou
    viewst his toyle.
In any wise, be chary that thou lettest in no Swine:
No Dog to scrape, nor beast that doth to ravin styll inclyne.
For though he make no spare of them, to such as have good
    skyll:
To slip, to shere, or get in time, and not his braunches kyll:
Yet barres he out, such greedy guts, as come with spite to
    loote:
80   And without skill, both Earb and Flower pluck rashly by the
    roote.
So wishing thee, to finde such Flowers, as may thee comfort
    bring:
And eke that he which framd the Plot, with vertues styll
    may spring.
I thee commend to mighty JOVE, and thus I thee assure:
My Nosegay wyll increase no payne, though sicknes none it
    cure.

Wherfore, if thou it hap to weare and feele thy selfe much
  worse:
Promote mee for no Sorceresse, nor doo mee ban or curse.
For this I say the Flowers are good, which I on thee bestow:
As those which weare them to the stalkes, shall by the
  sequell know.
One word, and then adieu to thee, yf thou to *Plat* his Plot
90 Repayre: take heede it is a *Maze* to warne thee I forgot.

* FINIS. quod IS. W.

Certain familier Epistles and friendly Letters by the
Auctor: with Replies

To her Brother. G.W.

Good Brother when a vacant time doth cause you hence to
  ryde:
And that the fertyl feelds do make, you from the Cittie
  byde.
Then cannot I once from you heare nor know I how to send:
Or where to harken of your health and al this would be
  kend.
And most of me, for why I least, of Fortunes favour fynd:
No yeldyng yeare she me allowes, nor goodes hath me
  assind.
But styll to friends I must appeale (and next our Parentes
  deare,)
You are, and must be chiefest staffe that I shal stay on heare.
Wherfore mine owne good brother graunt me when that you
  ar here:
10 To se you oft and also hence, I may have knowledge wheare

A messenger to harke unto, that I to you may wryte:
And eke of him your answers have which would my hart
    delight.
Receave of me, and eke accept, a simple token heare:
A smell of such a Nosegay as I do for present beare.
Unto a vertuous Ladye, which tyll death I honour wyll:
The losse I had of service hers, I languish for it styll.

Your lovyng (though lucklesse) Sister, IS. W.

To her Brother. B.W.

Good Brother *Brooke*, I often looke, to heare of your
    returne:
But none can tell, if you be well, nor where you doo sojurne:
Which makes me feare, that I shall heare your health
    appaired is:
And oft I dread, that you are dead, or somthyng goeth amys.
Yet when I thinke, you can not shrinke, but must with
    Maister bee:
I have good hope, when you have scope, you wyll repaire to
    mee.
And so the feare, and deepe dispaire, that I of you then had
I dryve away: and wysh that day wherin we may be glad.
Glad for to see, but els for mee: wyll be no joy at all:
For on my side, no lucke will byde, nor happye chaunce
    befall.
As you shall know, for I wyll show, you more when we doo
    speake,
Then wyll I wryt, or yet resyte, within this Paper weake.
And so I end, and you commend, to him that guides the
    skyes:
Who graunt you health, and send you welth, no lesse then
    shall suffice.
* *Your loving Sister. Is. W.*

A modest meane for Maides In order prescribed, by Is.
W. to two of her yonger Sisters servinge in London

Good Sisters mine, when I shal further from you dwell:
Peruse these lines, observe the rules which in the same I tell.
So shal you wealth posses, and quietnesse of mynde:
And al your friends to se the same, a treble joy shall fynde.

1. In mornings when you ryse, forget not to commende:
Your selves to God, beseching him from dangers to defende.
Your soules and boddies both, your Parents and your
    friends:
Your teachers and your governers so pray you that your
    ends,
May be in such a sort, as God may pleased bee:
10   To live to dye, to dye to live, with him eternally,

2. Then justly do such deedes, as are to you assynde:
All wanton toyes, good sisters now exile out of your minde,
I hope you geve no cause, wherby I should suspect:
But this I know too many live, that would you soone infect.
Yf God do not prevent, or with his grace expell:
I cannot speake, or wryte to much, because I love you well.

3. Your busines soone dispatch, and listen to no lyes:
Nor credit every fayned tale, that many wyll devise.
For words they are but winde, yet words may hurt you so:
20   As you shall never brook the same, yf that you have a foe.
God shyld you from all such, as would by word or Byll.
Procure your shame, or never cease tyll they have wrought
    you yll.

4. See that you secrets seale, tread trifles under ground:
Yf to rehersall oft you come, it wyl your quiet wound.
Of laughter be not much, nor over solemne seeme:
For then be sure th'eyle coumpt you light or proud will you
    esteeme.

Be modest in a meane, be gentyll unto all:
Though cause they geve of contrary yet be to wrath no
    thrall.
Refer you all to hym that sits above the skyes:
30   Vengeance is his, he wil reveng, you need it not devise.

5. And sith that vertue guides, where both of you do dwell:
Give thanks to God, and painful bee to please your rulers
    well,
For fleetyng is a foe, experience hath me taught:
The rolling stone doth get no mosse your selves have hard
    full oft.
Your businesse being done, and this my scroule perusd,
The day wyll end, and that the night by you be not abusde.
I some thing nedes must write, take paynes to read the same:
Hencefoorth my lyfe as wel as Pen shall your examples
    frame.

6. Your Masters gon to Bed, your Mistresses at rest.
40   Their Daughters all which hast about to get themselves
    undrest.
See that their Plate be safe, and that no Spoone do lacke,
See Dores and Windowes bolted fast for feare of any wrack.
Then help yf neede ther bee, to doo some housholde thing:
If not to bed, referring you, unto the heavenly King.
Forgettyng not to pray as I before you taught,
And geveing thanks for al that he, hath ever for you
    wrought.
Good Sisters when you pray, let me remembred be:
So wyll I you, and thus I cease, tyll I your selves do see.

To her Sister Misteris. A.B.

Because I to my Brethern wrote, and to my Sisters two:
Good Sister Anne, you this might wote, yf so I should not
    doo
To you or ere I parted hence,
You vainely had bestowed expence.

Yet is it not for that I write, for nature dyd you bynde:
To doo mee good: and to requight, hath nature mee
    inclynde:
Wherfore good Sister take in gree,
These simple lynes that come from mee.

Wherin I wish you Nestors dayes, in happye health to rest:
With such successe in all assayes, as those which God hath
    blest:
Your Husband with your pretty Boyes,
God keepe them free from all annoyes.

And graunt if that my luck it bee, to linger heere so long:
Til they be men: that I may see, for learning them so strong:
That they may march amongst the best,
Of them which learning have possest.

By that tyme wyl my aged yeares perhaps a staffe require:
And quakyngly as styll in feares, my lims draw to the fire:
Yet joy I shall them so to see,
Yf any joy in age there bee.

Good Sister so I you commend, to him that made us all:
I know you huswifery intend, though I to writing fall:
Wherfore no lenger shal you stay,
From businesse, that profit may.

Had I a Husband, or a house, and all that longes therto
My selfe could frame about to rouse, as other women doo:
But til some houshold cares mee tye,
My bookes and Pen I wyll apply.

Your loving Sister. IS. W.

To her Cosen. F.W.

Good Cosin myne, I hope in helth and safety you abyde.
And sore I long, to here if yet you are to wedlock tyde.
Yf so you be, God graunt that well both you and she it
    spend:
If not when s'ere it haps, I wish that God much joy you
    send.
And when you to the Cuntry come or thither chaunce to
    send:
Let me you see, or have some scroll, that shall of you be
    pend.
And this accompt as nature binds and meryts yours deserve:
I Cosin am, and faithfull Friend, not minding once to
    swerve.
So wishing you as happy health, as ever man possesst:
I end, and you commyt to him that evermore is blest.

Your poore Kinsewoman, Is. W.

A carefull complaynt by the unfortunate Auctor

Good DIDO stint thy teares, and sorrowes all resigne
To mee: that borne was to augment, misfortunes lucklesse
    line.
Or using styll the same, good DIDO doo thy best:
In helpyng to bewayle the hap, that furthereth mine unrest.

For though thy Troyan mate, that Lorde AENEAS hight:
Requityng yll thy stedfast love, for *Carthage* tooke his flight.
And fowly brake his oth, and promise made before:
Whose falshode finisht thy delight, before thy haires were
    hore.
Yet greater cause of griefe compells mee to complayne:
For Fortune fell converted hath, my health to heapes of
    payne.
And that she sweares my death, to playne it is (alas)
Whose end let malyce styll attempt, to bring the same to
    passe.
O DIDO thou hadst liv'de, a happye Woman styll,
If fickle fancie had not thrald thy wits: to retchlesse wyll.
For as the man by whom, thy deadly dolors bred:
Without regard of plighted troth, from CARTHAGE Citie
    fled.
So might thy cares in tyme, be banisht out of thought:
His absence might well salve the sore, that earst his presence
    wrought.
For fyre no lenger burnes, than Faggots feede the flame:
The want of things that breede annoy, may soone redresse
    the same.
But I unhappy moste, and gript with endles griefes:
Dispayre (alas) amid my hope, and hope without reliefe.
And as the sweltyng heate, consumes the Wax away:
So doo the heapes of deadly harmes, styll threaten my
    decay.
O Death delay not long, thy dewtye to declare:
Ye Sisters three dispatch my dayes and finysh all my care.

Is. W.

IS. W. to C.B. in bewaylynge her mishappes

If heavie hartes might serve to be a sacrifice for sinne:
Or els, if sorowes might suffice, for what so ere hath byn:
Then mine Oblacion, it weare made,
Whiche longe have lived in Mourners trade.

The dryrie daye in dole (alas) continuallye I spende:
The noysome nightes, in restlesse Bedde, I bring unto his
       ende:
And when the daye appeares agayne,
Then fresh begyn my plaints amayne.

But this I feare wyll sooner cease: the nomber of my sinne:
Then make amendes, for former misse, that I have lived in:
Because I take not pacientlye
Correction in adversytie.

Wherfore (my God) geve me that gyfte, As he dyd JOB
       untyll:
That I may take with quietnesse, what soever is his wyll:
Then shall my lucklesse lyfe soone ende,
Or frowarde Fortune shall amende.

And for because your sound advice, may ease me in
       distresse:
For that two wittes may compasse more then one, you must
       confesse:
And that, that burthen dothe not deare,
Whiche frende wyll somtyme helpe to beare.

Therfore, in this perplexitie, to you deare frende I write:
You know mine endlesse miserie, you know, how some me
       spite:
with counsell cure, for feare of wracke,
And helpe to beare, that breakes my backe.

So wishing you in health to bide, and troubles not to taste
And geving tendance for your ayde, which I requier in haste
I cease: and humbly me commend,
To the conducting of my Friende,

Your unfortunate Friend. IS. W.

To my Friend Master T.L. whose good nature I see abusde

Dyd not Dame *Seres* tell to you?
    nor fame unto you shew?
What sturdi storms have bin abrod
    and who hath playd the shrew.
I thought the Goddesse in your feelds
    had helped with your crop:
Or els that fame til you had knowne,
    her trump would never stop.
But sith I se their silentnesse,
10   I cease the same to write:
Least I therfore might be condemd
    to do it for a spite.
But this I wish that you my frind
    go chuse some vertues wife:
With whom in feare of God do spend,
    the residue of your lyfe
For whylst you are in single state
    none hath that right regard:
They think all wel that they can win,
20   and compt it their reward.
With sorow I to oft have seene,
    when some wold fleece you much
And oft in writting wolde I say
    good friend beware of such.
But all my wordes they weare as wind
    my labour yll was spent:
And in the end for my good wil,
    most cruelly was shent.

Yf I were boxt and buffeted,
30   good wyll shall never cease:
Nor hand, nor tong, shal so be charmd
    to make me holde my peace.
Wherfore I warne you once againe
    be warie of your selfe:
For some have sworne to lyke you well
    so long as you have pelfe,
Yf warnings styll you do reject,
    to late your selfe shal rew:
Do as you lyst, I wish you well,
40   and so I say adewe.

Your welwiller. Is. W.

IS. W. *beyng wery of writyng, sendeth this for Answere*

No lesse then thankes, I render unto you,
    What? though it be a Beggers bare rewarde
Accept the same: (for Cosyn) this is true,
    Tis all I have: my haps they are so hard:
    None beareth lyfe, is so from Fortune bard,
But this I know, and hope it once to finde
God can, and wyl, exalt the humble minde.

This simple verce: content you for to take
    for answer of your loving letter lardge,
10 For now I wyll my writting cleane forsake
    till of my griefes, my stomack I discharg:
    and tyll I row, in Ladie Fortunes barge.
Good Cosin write not nor any more replye,
But geve mee leave, more quietnes to trye.

Your Cosin IS. W.

The Aucthour (though loth to leave the Citie) upon her
Friendes procurement, is constrained to departe:
wherfore (she fayneth as she would die) and maketh her
WYLL and Testament, as foloweth: With large
Legacies of such Goods and riches which she moste
aboundantly hath left behind her: and therof maketh
London sole executor to se her Legacies performed

A comunication which the Auctor had to London, before
she made her Wyll

The time is come I must departe,
   from thee ah famous Citie:
I never yet to rue my smart,
   did finde that thou hadst pitie.
Wherefore small cause ther is, that I
   should greeve from thee go:
But many Women foolyshly,
   lyke me, and other moe.
Doe such a fyxed fancy set,
10   on those which least desarve,
That long it is ere wit we get,
   away from them to swarve.
But tyme with pittie oft wyl tel
   to those that wil her try:
Whether it best be more to mell,
   or utterly defye.
And now hath time me put in mind,
   of thy great cruelnes:
That never once a help wold finde,
20   to ease me in distres.

Thou never yet, woldst credit geve
    to boord me for a yeare:
Nor with Apparell me releve
    except thou payed weare.
No, no, thou never didst me good,
    nor ever wilt I know:
Yet am I in no angry moode,
    but wyll, or ere I goe
In perfect love and charytie.
30   my Testament here write:
And leave to thee such Treasurye,
    as I in it recyte.
Now stand a side and geve me leave
    to write my latest Wyll:
And see that none you do deceave,
    of that I leave them tyl.

The maner of her Wyll, and what she left to London:

and all those in it: at her departing

I whole in body, and in minde,
    but very weake in Purse:
Doo make, and write my Testament
    for feare it wyll be wurse.
And fyrst I wholy doo commend,
    my Soule and Body eke:
To God the Father and the Son,
    so long as I can speake.
And after speach: my Soule to hym,
10   and Body to the Grave:
Tyll time that all shall rise agayne,
    their Judgement for to have.
And then I hope they both shal meete.
    to dwell for aye in joye:
Whereas I trust to see my Friends
    releast, from all annoy.

Thus have you heard touching my soule,
    and body what I meane:
I trust you all wyll witnes beare,
20   I have a stedfast brayne.
¶And now let mee dispose such things,
    as I shal leave behinde:
That those which shall receave the same,
    may know my wylling minde.
I first of all to London leave
    because I there was bred:
Brave buildyngs rare, of Churches store,
    and Pauls to the head.
Betweene the same: fayre streats there bee,
30   and people goodly store:
Because their keeping craveth cost,
    I yet wil leave him more.
First for their foode, I Butchers lea[v]e,
    that every day shall kyll:
By Thames you shal have Brewers store,
    and Bakers at your wyll.
And such as orders doo observe,
    and eat fish thrice a weeke:
I leave two Streets, full fraught therwith,
40   they neede not farre to seeke.
Watlyng Streete, and Canwyck streete,
    I full of Wollen leave:
And Linnen store in Friday streete,
    if they mee not deceave.
And those which are of callyng such,
    that costlier they require:
I M[e]rcers leave, with silke so rich,
    as any would desyre.
In Cheape of them, they store shal finde
50   and likewise in that streete:
I Goldsmithes leave, with Juels such,
    as are for Ladies meete.

And Plate to furnysh Cubbards with,
    full brave there shall you finde:
With Purle of Silver and of Golde,
    to satisfye your minde.
With Hoods, Bungraces, Hats or Caps,
    such store are in that streete:
As if on ton side you should misse
60   the tother serves you[r] feete.
For Nets of every kynd of sort,
    I leave within the pawne:
French Ruffes, high Purles, Gorgets and Sleeves
    of any kind of Lawne.
For Purse or Knives, for Combe or Glasse,
    or any needeful knacke
I by the Stoks have left a Boy,
    wil aske you what you lack.
I Hose doo leave in Birchin Lane,
70   of any kynd of syse:
For Women stitchte, for men both Trunks
    and those of Gascoyne gise.
Bootes, shoes, or Pantables good store,
    Saint Martins hath for you:
In Cornwall, there I leave you Beds,
    and all that longs thereto.
For Women shall you Taylors have,
    by Bow, the chiefest dwel:
In every Lane you some shall finde,
80   can doo indifferent well.
And for the men, few Streetes or Lanes,
    but Bodymakers bee:
And such as make the sweeping Cloakes,
    with Gardes beneth the knee.
Artyllery at Temple Bar,
    and Dagges at Tower hyll:
Swords and Bucklers of the best,
    are nye the Fleete untyll.

Now when thy folke are fed and clad
90   with such as I have namde:
For daynty mouthes, and stomacks weake
    some junckets must be framde.
Wherfore I Poticaries leave,
    with Banquets in their Shop:
Phisicians also for the sicke,
    Diseases for to stop.
Some Roysters styll, must bide in thee
    and such as cut it out:
That with the guiltlesse quarel wyl,
100   to let their blood about.
For them I cunning Surgions leave,
    some Playsters to apply.
That Ruffians may not styll be hangde,
    nor quiet persons dye.
For Salt, Otemeale, Candles, Sope,
    or what you els doo want:
In many places, Shops are full,
    I left you nothing scant.
Yf they that keepe what I you leave,
110   aske Mony: when they sell it:
At Mint, there is such store, it is
    unpossible to tell it.
At Stiliarde store of Wines there bee,
    your dulled mindes to glad:
And handsome men, that must not wed
    except they leave their trade.
They oft shal seeke for proper Gyrles,
    and some perhaps shall fynde:
(That neede compels, or lucre lures
120   to satisfye their mind.[)]
And neare the same, I houses leave,
    for people to repayre:
To bathe themselves, so to prevent
    infection of the ayre.

On Saturdayes I wish that those,
   which all the weeke doo drug
Shall thyther trudge, to trim them up
   on Sondayes to looke smug.
If any other thing be lackt
130   in thee, I wysh them looke:
For there it is: I little brought
   but nothyng from thee tooke.
Now for the people in thee left,
   I have done as I may:
And that the poore, when I am gone,
   have cause for me to pray.
I wyll to prisons portions leave,
   what though but very small:
Yet that they may remember me,
140   occasion be it shall:
And fyrst the Counter they shal have,
   least they should go to wrack:
Some Coggers, and some honest men,
   that Sergantes draw aback.
And such as Friends wyl not them bayle,
   whose coyne is very thin:
For them I leave a certayne hole,
   and little ease within.
The Newgate once a Monthe shal have
150   a sessions for his share:
Least being heapt, Infection might
   procure a further care.
And at those sessions some shal skape,
   with burning nere the Thumb:
And afterward to beg their fees,
   tyll they have got the some.
And such whose deedes deserveth death,
   and twelve have found the same:
they shall be drawne up Holborne hill,
160   to come to further shame:

Well, yet to such I leave a Nag
    shal soone their sorowes cease:
For he shal either breake their necks
    or gallop from the preace.
The Fleete, not in their circuit is,
    yet if I geve him nought:
It might procure his curse, ere I
    unto the ground be brought.
Wherfore I leave some Papist olde
170   to underprop his roofe:
And to the poore within the same,
    A Boxe for their behoofe.
What makes you standers by to smile,
    and laugh so in your sleeve:
I thinke it is, because that I
    to Ludgate nothing geve.
I am not now in case to lye,
    here is no place of jest:
I dyd reserve, that for my selfe,
180   yf I my health possest.
And ever came in credit so
    a debtor for to bee.
When dayes of paiment did approch,
    I thither ment to flee.
To shroude my selfe amongst the rest,
    that chuse to dye in debt:
Rather then any Creditor,
    should money from them get.
Yet cause I feele my selfe so weake
190   that none mee credit dare:
I heere revoke: and doo it leave,
    some *Banckrupts* to his share.
To all the Bookebinders by Paulles
    because I lyke their Arte:
They e[ver]y weeke shal mony have,
    when they from Bookes departe.

Amongst them all, my Printer must,
    have somwhat to his share:
I wyll my Friends there Bookes to bye
200   of him, with other ware.
So, Maydens poore, and Widdoers ritch
    do leave, that oft shall dote:
And by that meanes shal mary them,
    to set the Girles aflote.
And wealthy Widdowes wil I leave,
    to help yong Gentylmen:
Which when you have in any case
    be courteous to them then:
And see their Plate and Jewells eake
210   may not be mard with rust,
Nor let their Bags too long be full,
    for feare that they doo burst.
To every Gate under the walles,
    that compas thee about:
I Fruitwives leave to entertayne
    such as come in and out.
To Smithfeelde I must something leave
    my Parents there did dwell:
So carelesse for to be of it,
220   none wolde accompt it well.
Wherfore it thrice a weeke shall have,
    of Horse and [m]eat good store,
And in his Spitle, blynd and lame,
    to dwell for evermore.
And Bedlem must not be forgot,
    for that was oft my walke:
I people there too many leave,
    that out of tune doo talke.
At Bridewel there shal Bedelles be,
230   and Matrones that shal styll
See Chalke wel chopt, and spinning plyde,
    and turning of the Mill.

For such as cannot quiet bee,
    but strive for House or Land:
At Th'Inns of Court, I Lawyers leave
    to take their cause in hand.
And also leave I at ech Inne
    of Court, or Chauncerye:
Of Gentylmen, a youthfull roote,
240   full of Activytie:
For whom I store of Bookes have left,
    at each Bookebinders stall:
And parte of all that London hath
    to furnish them withall.
And when they are with study cloyd:
    to recreate theyr minde:
Of Tennis Courts, of dauncing Scooles,
    and fence they store shal finde.
And every Sonday at the least,
250   I leave to make them sport,
In divers places Players, that
    of wonders shall reporte.
Now London have I (for thy sake)
    within thee, and without:
As coms into my memory,
    dispearsed round about
Such needfull thinges, as they should have,
    heere left now unto thee:
When I am gon, with consience
260   let them dispearced bee.
And though I nothing named have,
    to bury mee withall:
Consider that above the ground,
    annoyance bee I shall.
And let me have a shrowding Sheete
    to cover mee from shame:
And in oblivyon bury mee
    and never more mee name.

Ringings nor other Ceremonies,
270   use you not for cost:
Nor at my buriall, make no feast,
     your mony were but lost.
Rejoyce in God that I am gon,
     out of this vale so vile.
And that of ech thing, left such store,
     as may your wants exile.
I make thee sole executor, because
     I lov'de thee best.
And thee I put in trust, to geve
280   the goodes unto the rest.
Because thou shalt a helper neede,
     In this so great a chardge,
I wysh good Fortune, be thy guide, least
     thou shouldst run at lardge.
The happy dayes and quiet times,
     they both her Servants bee
Which well wyll serve to fetch and bring,
     such things as neede to thee.
¶Wherfore (good London) not refuse,
290   for helper her to take:
Thus being weake and wery both
     an end heere wyll I make.
To all that aske what end I made,
     and how I went away:
Thou answer maist like those which heere,
     no longer tary may.
And unto all that wysh mee well,
     or rue that I am gon:
Doo me comend, and bid them cease
300   my absence for to mone.
And tell them further, if they wolde,
     my presence styll have had:
They should have sought to mend my luck;
     which ever was too bad.

So fare thou well a thousand times,
   God sheelde thee from thy foe:
And styll make thee victorious,
   of those that seeke thy woe.
And (though I am perswade) that I
310   shall never more thee see:
Yet to the last, I shal not cease
   to wish much good to thee.
This, xx of October I,
   in ANNO DOMINI:
A Thousand: v. hundred seventy three
   as Alminacks descry
Did write this Wyll with mine owne hand
   and it to London gave:
In witnes of the standers by,
320   whose names yf you wyll have.
Paper, Pen, and Standish were:
   at that same present by:
With Time, who promised to reveale,
   so fast as she could hye
The same: least of my nearer kyn,
   for anything should vary:
So finally I make an end
   no longer can I tary.

FINIS. by IS. W.

*   *   *

THE COPY OF A LETTER, lately written in meeter, by a yonge Gentilwoman: to her unconstant Lover. With an Admonition to al yong Gentilwomen, and to all other Mayds in general to beware of mennes flattery. By Is. W. Newly joined to a Loveletter sent by a Bacheler, (a most faithfull Lover) to an unconstant and faithles Mayden

I.W. To her unconstant Lover

As close as you your weding kept
    yet now the trueth I here:
Which you (yer now) might me have told
    what nede you nay to swere?

You know I alwayes wisht you wel
    so wyll I during lyfe:
But sith you shal a Husband be
    God send you a good wyfe.

And this (where so you shal become)
10   full boldly may you boast:
That once you had as true a Love,
    as dwelt in any Coast.

Whose constantnesse had never quaild
    if you had not begonne:
And yet it is not so far past,
    but might agayne bewonne.

If you so would: yea and not change
  so long as lyfe should last:
But yf that needes you marry must?
20   then farewell, hope is past.

And if you cannot be content
  to lead a single lyfe?
(Although the same right quiet be)
  then take me to your wife.

So shall the promises be kept,
  that you so firmly made:
Now chuse whether ye wyll be true,
  or be of SINONS trade.

Whose trade if that you long shal use,
30   it shal your kindred stayne:
Example take by many a one
  whose falshood now is playne.

As by ENEAS first of all,
  who dyd poore DIDO leave,
Causing the Quene by his untrueth
  with Sword her hart to cleave.

Also I finde that THESEUS did,
  his faithfull love forsake:
Stealyng away within the night,
40   before she dyd awake.

JASON that came of noble race,
  two Ladies did begile:
I muse how he durst shew his face,
  to them that knew his wile.

For when he by MEDEAS arte,
  had got the Fleece of Gold
And also had of her that time,
  al kynd of things he wolde.

He toke his Ship and fled away
50   regarding not the vowes:
That he dyd make so faithfully,
        unto his loving Spowes.

How durst he trust the surging Seas
        knowing himselfe forsworne:
Why dyd he scape safe to the land,
        before the ship was torne?

I think king Aeolus stayd the winds
        and Neptune rulde the Sea:
Then might he boldly passe the waves
60   no perils could him stea.

But if his falsehed had to them,
        bin manifest befor:
They wold have rent the ship as soone
        as he had gon from shore.

Now may you heare how falsenes is
        made manyfest in time:
Although they that comit the same,
        think it a veniall crime.

For they, for their unfaithfulnes,
70   did get perpetuall fame:
Fame? wherfore dyd I terme it so?
        I should have cald it shame.

Let Theseus be, let Jason passe,
        let Paris also scape:
That brought destruction unto Troy
        all through the Grecian Rape.

And unto me a Troylus be,
        if not you may compare:
With any of these parsons that
80   above expressed are.

But if I can not please your minde,
　　for wants that rest in me:
Wed whom you list, I am content,
　　your refuse for to be.

It shall suffise me simple soule,
　　of thee to be forsaken:
And it may chance although not yet
　　you wish you had me taken.

But rather than you shold have cause
90　　to wish this through your wyfe:
I wysh to her, ere you her have,
　　no more but love of lyfe.

For she that shal so happy be,
　　of thee to be elect:
I wish her vertues to be such,
　　she nede not be suspect.

I rather wish her HELENS face,
　　then one of HELENS trade:
With chastnes of PENELOPE
100　　the which did never fade.

A LUCRES for her constancy,
　　and Thisbie for her trueth:
If such thou have, then PETO be
　　not PARIS, that were rueth.

Perchance, ye will think this thing rare,
　　in on woman to fynd:
Save Helens beauty, al the rest
　　the Gods have me assignd.

These words I do not spek, thinking
110　　from thy new Love to turne thee:
Thou knowst by prof what I deserve
　　I nede not to informe thee.

But let that passe: would God I had
  Cassandraes gift me lent:
Then either thy yll chaunce or mine
  my foresight might prevent.

But all in vayne for this I seeke,
  wishes may not attaine it
Therfore may hap to me what shall,
120 and I cannot refraine it.

Wherfore I pray God be my guide
  and also thee defend:
No worser then I wish my selfe,
  untill thy lyfe shal end.

Which life I pray God, may agayne,
  King Nestors lyfe renew:
And after that your soule may rest
  amongst the heavenly crew.

Therto I wish King Xerxis wealth,
130 or els King Cressus Gould:
With as much rest and quietnesse
  as man may have on Mould.

And when you shall this letter have
  let it be kept in store?
For she that sent the same, hath sworn
  as yet to send no more.

And now farewel, for why at large
  my mind is here exprest?
The which you may perceive, if that
140 you do peruse the rest?

¶FINIS. IS. W.

The admonition by the Auctor, to all yong
Gentilwomen: And to al other Maids being in Love

Ye Virgins that from Cupids tentes
   do beare away the soyle
Whose hartes as yet with raginge love
   most paynfully do boyle.

To you I speake: for you be they,
   that good advice do lacke:
Oh if I could good counsell geve
   my tongue should not be slacke?

But such as I can geve, I wyll.
10   here in few wordes expresse:
Which if you do observe, it will
   some of your care redresse.

Beware of fayre and painted talke,
   beware of flattering tonges:
The Mermaides do pretend no good
   for all their pleasant Songs.

Some use the teares of Crocodiles,
   contrary to their hart:
And yf they cannot alwayes weepe,
20   they wet their Cheekes by Art.

Ovid, within his Arte of Love,
   doth teach them this same knacke
To wet their hand and touch their eies:
   so oft as teares they lacke.

Why have ye such deceit in store?
   have you such crafty wile?
Lesse craft then this god knows wold soone
   us simple soules begile.

And wyll ye not leave of? but still
30   delude us in this wise?
Sith it is so, we trust we shall,
        take hede to fained lies.

Trust not a man at the fyrst sight,
        but trye him well before:
I wish al Maids within their brests
        to kepe this thing in store.

For triall shal declare his trueth,
        and show what he doth think:
Whether he be a Lover true,
40   or do intend to shrink.

If SCILLA had not trust to much
        before that she dyd trye:
She could not have ben clene forsake
        when she for help did crye.

Or yf she had had good advice
        Nisus had lived long:
How durst she trust a strainger, and
        do her deare father wrong.

King Nisus had a Haire by fate
50   which Haire while he dyd kepe:
He never should be overcome
        neither on Land nor depe.

The straunger that the Daughter lov'd
        did warre against the King
And alwaies sought how that he might
        them in subjection bring.

This Scylla stole away the Haire,
        for to obtaine her wyll:
And gave it to the Straunger that,
60   dyd straight her father kyll.

Then she, who thought herself most sure
    to have her whole desyre:
Was cleane reject, and left behind
    when he dyd home retyre.

Or if such falshood had ben once,
    unto Oenone knowne:
About the fieldes of Ida wood,
    Paris had walkt alone.

Or if Demophoons deceite,
70   to Phillis had ben tolde:
She had not ben transformed so,
    as Poets tell of olde.

Hero did trie Leanders truth,
    before that she did trust:
Therfore she found him unto her
    both constant, true, and just.

For he alwayes did swim the Sea,
    when starres in Skie did glide:
Till he was drowned by the way
80   nere hand unto the side.

She scrat[ched] her face, she tare her Heir
    (it greveth me to tell)
When she did know the end of him,
    that she did love so well.

But like Leander there be fewe,
    therfore in time take heede:
And alwayes trie before ye trust,
    so shall you better speede.

The little Fish that carelesse is,
90   within the water cleare:
How glad is he, when he doth see,
    a Bayt for to appeare.

He thinks his hap right good to bee,
    that he the same could spie:
And so the simple foole doth trust
    to much before he trie.

O little Fish what hap hadst thou?
    to have such spitefull Fate:
To come into ones cruell hands,
100   out of so happy state?

Thou diddst suspect no harme, when thou
    upon the bait didst looke:
O that thou hadst had Linceus eies
    for to have seene the hooke.

Then hadst thou with thy prety mates
    bin playing in the streames
Wheras Syr Phebus dayly doth
    shew forth his golden beames.

But sith thy Fortune is so yll
110   to end thy lyfe on shore:
Of this thy most unhappy end,
    I minde to speake no more.

But of thy Felowes chance that late
    such prety shift did make:
That he from Fishers hooke did sprint
    before he could him take.

And now he pries on every baite,
    suspecting styll that pricke:
(For to lye hid in every thing)
120   wherewith the Fishers stricke.

And since the Fish that reason lacks
    once warned doth beware:
Why should not we take hede to that
    that turneth us to care.

And I who was deceived late,
    by ones unfaithfull teares:
Trust now for to beware, if that
    I live this hundred yeares.

FINIS, IS. W.

*   *   *

*The lamentacion of a Gentilwoman upon the death of
her late deceased frend William Gruffith Gent.*

A doutfull, dying, dolefull, Dame,
Not fearing death, nor forcing life:
Nor caring ought for flitting fame,
Emongst such sturdy stormes of strife:
Here doth shee mourne and write her will,
Upon her liked Lovers ende:
Graunt (Muses nyne) your sacred skill,
Helpe to assist your mournfull freend:
Embouldned with your Nimphish ayde,
Shee will not cease, but seeke to singe:
And eke employ her willing head,
Her Gruffithes prayse, with ruthe to ringe.

*

With Poets pen, I doo not preace to write,
Minervæs mate, I doo not boast to bee:
Parnassus Mount (I speake it for no spite)
Can cure my cursed cares, I playnly see:
   For why? my hart contaynes as many woes
   As ever *Hector* did amongst his foes.

Eche man doth mone, when faythfull freends bee dead,
And paynt them out, as well as wits doo serve:
But I, a Mayde, am forst to use my head,
To wayle my freend (whose fayth) did prayse deserve:
    Wit wants to will: alas? no skill I have,
    Yet must I needes deplore my *Gruffithes* grave:

For *William*, white: for *Gruffith*, greene: I wore,
And red, longe since did serve to please my minde:
Now, blacke, I weare, of mee, not us'd before:
In liew of love, alas? this losse I finde:
    Now must I leave, both, White, and Greene, and Red,
    And wayle my freend, who is but lately dead.

Yet hurtfull eyes, doo bid mee cast away,
In open show, this carefull blacke attyre:
Because it would, my secret love bewray,
And pay my pate, with hatred for my hyre:
    Though outwardly, I dare not weare the same,
    Yet in my hart, a web of blacke I frame.

You Ladyes all, that passe not for no payne,
But have your lovers lodged in your laps:
I crave your aydes, to helpe mee mourne amayne,
Perhaps your selves, shall feele such carefull claps:
    Which (God forbid) that any Lady taste,
    Who shall by mee but only learne to waste.

My wits be weake an Epitaphe to write,
Because it doth require a graver stile:
My phrase doth serve but rudely to recite,
How Lovers losse doth pinch mee all this while:
    Who was as prest to dye for *Gruffithes* sake,
    As *Damon*, did for *Pithias* undertake.

But *William* had a worldly freend in store,
Who writ his end to small effect (God knowes)
But I. and H. his name did show no more,
40   Rime Ruffe it is, the common sentence goes,
     It hangs at Pawles as every man goes by,
     One ryme too low, an other rampes too hye.

He praysd him out as worldly freends doo use,
And uttered all the skill that God had sent:
But I am shee that never will refuse,
But as I am, so will I still bee bent:
     No blastes shall blow, my lincked love awry,
     Oh! would the Gods, with *Gruffith* I might dye.

Then had it been that I poore silly Dame,
50   Had had no neede to blot this scratched scroule:
Then Virgins fist, had not set forth the same
How God hath gripte, my *Gruffithes* sacred soule:
     But woe is mee, I live in pinching payne,
     No wight doth know, what sorowes I sustayne.

Unhappy may that drowsie day bee nam'd,
Wherin I first possesst my vitall breath:
And eke I wish, that day that I was fram'd,
Instead of life I had received death:
     Then with these woes, I needed not to waste,
60   Which now (alas) in every vayne I taste.

Some *Zoylus* sot, will thinke it lightly doone,
Because I mone, my mate, and lover, so
Some *Momus* match, this scroule will overronne
But love is lawlesse, every wight doth know:
     Sith love doth lend mee such a freendly scope,
     Disdaynfull dogs I may despise (I hope)

Wherfore I doo, attempt so much the more,
By this good hope, to shew my slender arte:
And mourne I must (who) never marckt before,
What fretting force doo holde eche heavy hart:
    But now I see that *Gruffithes* greedy grave,
    Doth make mee feele, the fits which lovers have.

My mournfull Muse, (good Ladyes) take in worth,
And spare to speake the worst, but judge the best:
For this is all, that I dare publish forth,
The rest recorded is, within my brest:
    And there is lodg'd, for ever to remayne,
    Till God doth graunt (by death) to ease my payne.

And when that death is come to pay her due,
With all the paynes, that shee can well invent:
Yet to my *Gruffith*, will I still be true,
Hap death, holde life, my minde is fully bent:
    Before I will our secret love disclose,
    To *Tantals* paynes, my body I dispose.

So live I shall, when death hath spit her spight,
And Lady (*Fame*) will spread my prayse I know:
And *Cupids* Knights, will never cease to write,
And cause my name, through (*Europe*) for to flow:
    And they that know what (*Cupid*) can prevayle,
    Will blesse the ship, that floates with such a sayle.

If I had part of *Pallas* learned skill,
Or if (*Caliope*) would lend her ayde:
By trade of time, great volumes I would fill,
My *Gruffithes* prayse in wayling verse to spread:
    But (I poore I) as I have sayd before,
    Doo wayle, to want, *Minervæs* learned lore.

By helpe (I hope) these ragged rymes shall goe,
Entituled as lovers' ly[n]es should bee:
And scape the chyding chaps of every foe,
100   To prayse that man, who was best likte of mee:
  Though death hath shapte, his most untimely end,
  Yet for his prayse, my tristive tunes I send.

In hope, the Gods who guide the heavens above,
His buryed corps, alive agayne will make:
And have remorce of Ladyes lincked love,
As once they did for good *Admetus* sake:
  Or change him els, into some flower to weare,
  As erst they did, transforme *Narcissus* fayre.

So should I then, possess my former freend,
110   Restor'd to lyfe, as *Alcest* was from Hell,
Or els the Gods, some fragrant flower would send,
Which for his sake, I might both weare and smell:
  Which flower, out of my hand shall never passe,
  But in my harte, shall have a sticking place.

But wo is mee, my wishes are in vayne,
Adue delight, come crooked cursed care:
To bluntish blockes (I see) I doo complayne,
And reape but onely sorrow for my share:
  For wel I know that Gods nor sprites can cure,
120   The paynes that I for *Gruffith* doo endure.

Since wayling, no way can remedy mee,
To make an ende, I therfore judge it best:
And drinke up all, my sorrow secretly,
And as I can, I will abide the rest:
  And sith I dare not mourne, to open showe,
  With secret sighes and teares, my hart shall flow.

Some busie brayne, perhaps will aske my name,
Disposed much, some tidings for to marke:
That dare I not? for feare of flying fame,
130   And eke I feare least byting bugs will barke:
   Therfore farewell, and aske no more of mee,
   For (as I am) a Lover will I dye.

FINIS

MARY SIDNEY,
COUNTESS OF PEMBROKE

THE SIDNEY PSALTER

'Even now that Care'

Even now that Care which on thy Crowne attends
and with thy happy greatnes dayly growes
Tells mee thrise sacred Queene my Muse offends,
and of respect to thee the line out goes,
One instant will, or willing can shee lose
I say not reading, but receiving Rimes,
On whom in chiefe dependeth to dispose
what Europe acts in theise most active times?

Yet dare I so, as humblenes may dare
cherishing some hope they shall acceptance finde;
not waighing less thy state, lighter thy Care,
but knowing more thy grace, abler thy minde.
What heav'nly powrs thee highest throne assign'de,
assign'd thee goodnes suting that Degree:
and by thy strength thy burthen so defin'de,
To others toile, is Exercise to thee.

Cares though still great, cannot bee greatest still,
Busines most ebb, though Leasure never flowe:
Then these the Postes of Dutie and Goodwill
shall presse to offer what their Senders owe;
Which once in two, now in one Subject goe,
the poorer left, the richer reft awaye:
Who better might (O might ah word of woe,)
have giv'n for mee what I for him defraye.

How can I name whom sighing sighs extend,
and not unstopp my teares eternall spring?
but hee did warpe, I weav'd this webb to end;
the stuffe not ours, our worke no curious thing,

Wherein yet well wee thought the Psalmist King
30   Now English denizend, though Hebrue borne,
woold to thy musicke undispleased sing,
Oft having worse, without repining worne;

And I the Cloth in both our names present,
A liverie robe to bee bestowed by thee:
small parcell of that undischarged rent,
from which nor paines, nor paiments can us free.
And yet enough to cause our neighbours see
wee will our best, though scanted in our will:
and those nighe feelds where sow'n thy favors bee
40   unwalthy doo, not elce unworthie till.

For in our worke what bring wee but thine owne?
what English is, by many names is thine.
There humble Lawrells in thy shadowes growne
To garland others, woold themselves repine.
Thy brest the Cabinet, thy seat the shrine,
where Muses hang their vowed memories:
where Wit, where Art, where all that is divine
conceived best, and best defended lies.

Which if men did not (as they doe) confesse,
50   and wronging worlds woold otherwise consent:
Yet here who mynds so meet a Patrones
for Authors state or writings argument?
A King should onely to a Queene bee sent.
Gods loved choise unto his chosen love:
Devotion to Devotions President:
what all applaud, to her whom none reprove.

And who sees ought, but sees how justly square
his haughtie Ditties to thy glorious daies?
How well beseeming thee his Triumphs are?
60   his hope, his zeale, his praier, plaint, and praise,

Needles thy person to their height to raise:
lesse need to bend them downe to thy degree:
Theise holy garments each good soule assaies,
some sorting all, all sort to none but thee.

For ev'n thy Rule is painted in his Raigne:
both cleere in right: both nigh by wrong opprest:
And each at length (man crossing God in vaine)
Possest of place, and each in peace possest.
proud Philistines did interrupt his rest,
The foes of heav'n no lesse have beene thy foes;
Hee with great conquest, thou with greater blest;
Thou sure to winn, and hee secure to lose.

Thus hand in hand with him thy glories walke:
but who can trace them where alone they goe?
Of thee two hemispheres on honor talke,
and Lands and seas thy Trophees jointly showe.
The very windes did on thy partie blowe,
and rocks in armes thy foe men eft defie:
But soft my muse, Thy pitch is earthly lowe;
forbeare this heav'n, where onely Eagles flie.

Kings on a Queene enforst their states to lay;
Main-lands for Empire waiting on an Ile;
Men drawne by worth a woman to obey;
one moving all, herselfe unmov'd the while:
Truthes restitution, vanitie exile,
wealth sprung of want, warr held without annoye,
Let subject bee of some inspired stile,
Till then the object of her subjects joye.

Thy utmost can but offer to hir sight
Her handmaids taske, which most her will endeeres;
and pray unto thy paines life from that light
which lively lightsome, Court, and Kingdome cheeres,

what wish shee may (farre past hir living Peeres
and Rivall still to Judas Faithfull King)
In more then hee and more triumphant yeares,
Sing what God doth, and doo What men may sing.

To the Angell spirit of the most excellent Sir Phillip Sidney

To thee pure sprite, to thee alone's addres't
   this coupled worke, by double int'rest thine:
    First rais'de by thy blest hand, and what is mine
inspird by thee, thy secrett power imprest.
    So dar'd my Muse with thine it selfe combine,
   as mortall stuffe with that which is divine,
Thy lightning beames give lustre to the rest,

That heaven's King may daigne his owne transform'd
   in substance no, but superficiall tire
10   by thee put on; to praise, not to aspire
To, those high Tons, so in themselves adorn'd,
    which Angells sing in their cælestiall Quire,
   and all of tongues with soule and voice admire
Theise sacred Hymnes thy Kinglie Prophet form'd.

Oh, had that soule which honor brought to rest
   too soone not left and reft the world of all
   what man could showe, which wee perfection call
This halfe maim'd peece had sorted with the best.
    Deepe wounds enlarg'd, long festred in their gall
20   fresh bleeding smart; not eie but hart teares fall.
Ah memorie what needs this new arrest?

Yet here behold, (oh wert thou to behold!)
   this finish't now, thy matchlesse Muse begunne,
   the rest but peec't, as left by thee undone.

Pardon (oh blest soule) presumption too too bold:
   if love and zeale such error ill-become
   'tis zealous love, Love which hath never done,
Nor can enough in world of words unfold.

And sithe it hath no further scope to goe,
30   nor other purpose but to honor thee,
   Thee in thy workes where all the Graces bee,
As little streames with all their all doe flowe
   to their great sea, due tribute's gratefull fee:
   so press my thoughts my burthened thoughtes in mee,
To pay the debt of Infinits I owe

To thy great worth; exceeding Nature's store,
   wonder of men, sole borne perfection's kinde,
   Phoenix thou wert, so rare thy fairest minde
Heav'nly adorn'd, Earth justlye might adore,
40   where truthfull praise in highest glorie shin'de:
   For there alone was praise to truth confin'de;
And where but there, to live for evermore?

Oh! when to this Accompt, this cast upp Summe,
   this Reckoning made, this Audit of my woe
   I call my thoughts, whence so strange passions flowe;
Howe workes my hart, my sences striken dumbe?
   that would thee more, then ever hart could showe,
   and all too short who knewe thee best doth knowe
There lives no witt that may thy praise become.

50   Truth I invoke (who scorne else where to move
   or here in ought my blood should partialize)
   Truth, sacred Truth, Thee sole to solemnize
Those precious rights well knowne best mindes approve:
   and who but doth, hath wisdome's open eies,
   not owly blinde the fairest light still flies
Confirme no lesse? At least 'tis seal'd above.

Where thou art fixt among thy fellow lights:
   my day put out, my life in darkenes cast,
   Thy Angell's soule with highest Angells plac't
60 There blessed sings enjoying heav'n-delights
   thy Maker's praise: as farr from earthy tast
   as here thy workes so worthilie embrac't
By all of worth, where never Envie bites.

As goodly buildings to some glorious ende
   cut of by fate, before the Graces hadde
   each wondrous part in all their beauties cladde,
Yet so much done, as Art could not amende;
   So thy rare workes to which no witt can adde,
   in all men's eies, which are not blindely madde,
70 Beyonde compare above all praise, extende.

Immortall Monuments of thy faire fame,
   though not compleat, nor in the reach of thought,
   howe on that passing peece time would have wrought
Had Heav'n so spar'd the life of life to frame
   the rest? But ah! such losse hath this world ought
   can equall it? or which like greevance brought?
Yet there will live thy ever praised name.

To which theise dearest offrings of my hart
   dissolv'd to Inke, while penn's impressions move
80   the bleeding veines of never dying love:
I render here: these wounding lynes of smart
   sadd Characters indeed of simple love
   not Art nor skill which abler wits doe prove,
Of my full soule receive the meanest part.

Receive theise Hymnes, theise obsequies receive;
   if any marke of thy sweet sprite appeare,
   well are they borne, no title else shall beare.
I can no more: Deare Soule I take my leave;

> Sorrowe still strives, would mount thy highest sphere
90   presuming so just cause might meet thee there,
> Oh happie chaunge! could I so take my leave.

By the Sister of that Incomparable Sidney

The Psalmes of Mary Sidney, Countess of Pembroke

Psalm 45, Eructavit cor meum

My heart indites an argument of worth
The prayse of him who doth the scepter sway
My tongue the pen to paint his prayses forth
Shall write as swift, as swiftest writer may
Then to the King these are the Words I say
Fairer art Thou than sons of mortall race
Because high God hath blessed Thee for aye
  My lips as springs do flow with speaking grace.

Thy Honours sword gird to thy mighty side
10   O Thou that dost all mights in might excell
With glory prosper, on with triumph ride
Since justice, Truth, and meekness with Thee dwell
So that right hand of thyne shall teaching tell
Such things to Thee as well may terror bring
And terror such as never erst befell
  To mortall minds at sight of mortall King

Sharp are thy shafts to cleave their hearts in twayn
Whose heads do cast Thy conquests to withstand
Good cause to make the meaner people faine
20   With willing hearts to undergo thy hand

Thy Throne O God doth never falling stand
Thy scepter Ensign of Thy Kingly might
To righteousness is linkt with such a band
    That Righteous hand still holds the scepter right.

Justice in love, in hate thou holdest wrong
This makes that God, who so doth hate and love
Glad–making Oyl, that Oyl on thee hath flung
Which Thee exalts Thy equals farr above
The fragrant riches of Sabean grove
30   Myrrh, Aloes, Cassia all thy robes do smell
When Thou from Ivory Palace dost remove
    Thy breathing Odors all Thy train excell.

Daughters of Kings among thy Courtly band
By honouring Thee, of Thee do honour hold
On Thy right side Thy Dearest Queen doth stand
Richly aray'd in cloth of Ophir gold
O Daughter heare what now to Thee is told
Mark what Thou hear'st, and what Thou mark'st obey
Forget to keep in memory enroll'd
40   The house and folk when first Thou saw'st the day.

So in The King, Thy King a deare delight
Thy beauty shall both breed, and bred maintain
For only hee on thee hath lordly right
Him only Thou with awe must entertaine
Then unto Thee both Tyrus shall be faine
Presents present, and richest Nations moe
With humble suite Thy Royall grace to gain
    To Thee shall do such homage as they owe.

This Queen that can the King her Father call
50   Doth only shee in upper garment shine?
Nay undercloaths, and what she weareth all
Gold is the stuff the Fashion art Divine

Brought to the King in Robe embroydred fine
Her maids of Honour shall on her attend
With such to whom more favour shall assign
    In nearer place their happy days to spend

    Brought shall they be with mirth and mariage joy
And enter so the Palace of the King
Then let no grief Thy mind O Queen annoy
Nor parents left Thy sadd remembrance sting
Instead of Parents Children Thou shalt bring
Of partag'd earth the Kings and Lords to be
My self Thy name in lasting verse will sing
    The World shall make no end of thanks to Thee.

Psalm 47, *Omnes gentes*

All people to Jehovah bring
A glad applause of clapping hands
To God a song of Triumphs sing
Who high of highly feared stands
Of all the earth sole ruling King.

From whose Almighty Grace it growes
That Nations by our power opprest
Our foot on humbled Countrys goes
Who Jacobs honour loved best
An heritage for us hath chose

Here past he by, hark how did ring
Harmonious ayr with trumpets sound
Prayse, prayse Our God, prayse prayse Our King
King of the World you judgments sound
With skilfull song his prayses sing

On sacred throne, not knowing end
For God the King of Kingdoms raigns
The Folk of Abrahams God to friend
He greatest Prince great princes gains
20   Princes the shields that earth defend.

Psalm 48, Magnus Dominus

He that hath Eternall being
Glorious is and glorious showes
In the citty he hath chose
    Where stands his holy hill
Hill, Sion hill of fairest seeing
Citty of the King most great
Seated in a Northly seat
    All Climes with joy doth fill
In each pallace she contayneth
10   God a well known rock remayneth.[1]

One day Kings a day appoynted
There with joyned force to be
See they it? The things they see
    Amaze their mated minds
Flying, trembling, disappoynted
So they feare, and so they fare
As the Wife whose wofull care
    The pangs of childbed finds
Right as shipps from Tarshish going
20   Crusht with blasts of Eurus blowing

Now our sight hath matcht our hearing
In what state Gods Citty stands
How supported by his hands

[1] The two last verses are putt in the margin instead of these expunged: *Ev'ry pallace it enfoldeth/ God for surest refuge holdeth.*

God ever holds the same
In Thy Temples midst appearing
Wee thy favour Lord attend
Righteous Lord both free from end
    Thy fame doth match Thy Name
Thy just hand brings Sion gladness
30   Turns to mirth all Judas sadness.

Compasse Sion in her standing
Tell her Towers mark her forts
Note with care the stately ports
    Her Royall houses beare
For that Ages understanding
Which shall come, when We shall go
Gladd in former time to know
    How many, what they were
For God is Our God for ever
40   Us till death forsaking never.

Psalm 49, Audite haec[1]

World dwellers all give heed[2] to what I say
To all I speake, to rich poore high and low
Knowledg the subject in my heart conceives
Wisdom the Words shall from my mouth proceed
Which I will measure by melodious eare
And ridled speech[3] to tuned harp accord.

---

[1] The very manner of this Psalms being crossd and alterd almost in every line and in many words twice makes me beleive this was an originall book, that is that the book before me was so for none but an author could or would so amend any Copy[.] The Italians call this A Sestine.

[2] *eare*, expunged.

[3] *grave discourse* expunged.

The times of Evill why should they me dismay
When mischeif shall my footstepps overflow.[4]
And first from him[5] whom fickle trust deceaves
Of wealth which his[6] vain confidence doth breed
Since[7] no man can his Brothers life outbeare
Nor yeild[8] for him his ransom to the Lord.

For deare the price that for a soul must pay
And death in bargaining is endlesse slow
Nay tell me whom a longer time he leaves
Rejected from the tomb for treasures meed?
At his sure summons Wise and fools appeare
And others spend the riches they did leave.[9]

A second[10] thinks his house shall not decay[11]
Nor time his glorious[12] buildings overthrow
Nam'd proudly of his name,[13] where folly reaves

10

20

[4] *Why should I fearfull be in the evill day/ When mischeif trading on my heeles shal go*, expungd, but it is further alterd and the first verse is sometime made to run thus *Why should the time of ev'ill my face affray* and then – *work my dismay* but both expungd.

[5] *mischeif from them*, exp.

[6] *their*, expunged.

[7] *for*, expunged.

[8] *pay* expunged.

[9] This third staffe is so blotted and often mended, that it is hardly perceptible what should and what should not stand. At first it stood thus.

> *For deer price they for their soules must pay*
> *That from their treasures can for ever flow*
> *Tho so they live as life them never leaves*
> *With liveles limbs the greedy grave to feed*
> *For wise or foole deaths badg alike doth weare*
> *And strangers spend the riches they did hoord.* Expunged.

The second verse is also thus mended *Deaths service to an end doth never grow*, expunged. The fifth also has *The wise and foole*, expunged. The sixth has *And others*, which is expungd, then *And who then spends*, expunged: Then the word *others* instead of *strangers* is left to stand as the last correction.

[10] *yet who but*, expunged. *Another*, expunged. *yet who thinks not*, expunged.

[11] *Last for aye*, expunged.

[12] *That nor time shall his*, expunged.

[13] *Nor lands nam'd of his name*, expunged.

Such honourd fooles of sense, and they indeed
A brutish life and death as beasts they were
Do live and dy of whom is no record.

These though their race approve their peevish way
Death in the pitt his carrion food doth stow
And lo the first succeding life perceives
The just installed in the great mans stead
Yea farr his prince: for soon that lovely cheare
30   Lovely in house, in tomb becomes abhorrd.[14]

But God my God to interrupt the pray
Of my life from the grave shall not foreslow
For hee it is he only me receaves
Then though one rich do grow and honours seed
Spring with increase yet[15] stand Thou free from feare
Of all his pomp death shall him naught afford.

Please they themselves, which think at happyest stay
To please themselves: yet to their Fathers go
Shall they to endless dark; for Folly reaves[16]

[14] This fifth staff stood thus:

> Yet their fond race admire their foolish way
> While death devours whole flocks of them below
> Where the just man when first his ey perceives
> The morning light shall in their state succeed
> Lording on them when their once lovely cheare
> A lothly tomb for house shall make abhorrd.

Expunged, as also *Lord* in the fifth verse after the correction putt for, *prince*.
[15] *Full harvest bring him*, expunged.
[16] instead of the three first verses of this staffe there stood at first five thus, for which (possibly because therby the staff was too long) the whole Psalm was crossd and mended:

> The living thought his life at happyest stay
> So flatterers in his eares did whispering blow
> But they shall ly where erst their Fathers lay
> In shade of death when life shall never show
> And justly sure, for surely folly reaves etc, expunged.

40   Exalted men of sense; and they indeed
    A brutish life and death as beasts they were
    Do live and dy of whom is no record.

Psalm 50, *Deus Deorum*

    The ever living God the mighty lord
Hath sent abroad his pursevant his Word
To all the Earth, to which in circling race
Rising or falling Sun doth shew his Face
Beauty of Beautys Sion is the place
    Which he will beautify by his appearing
God comes, he comes and will not silent stay
Consuming Flames shall usher him the way
A guard of storms about him shall attend
10   Then by his voice he for the Earth shall send
And make the vaulted heav'n to earthward bend
    That he may judg his people in their hearing.

    Before me here let their appearance make
My Saints saith he who league did undertake
With me to hold my pledg of sacrifice
(This justest doome the Audience of the skys
Shall wondring shew, for no injustice lyes
    When God himself as judg the judgement frameth.)
My people heare to you I speech will use
20   Heare Israel, and I will Thee accuse
For I am God, Thy God, and thus do say
Because Thou dost not dayly offrings pay
Nor Sacrifice to me present alway
    This is not that in Thee my censure blameth.

    Nor bullock I Thy house enstalled holds
Nor goate will take selected from Thy folds
For all the Cattle woody forests shield
For all the flocks a thousand downs do yeeld
All birds all beasts wide wanderers of the field

30   Are mine, all known to mee, and me all knowing
        If I were hungry that I hungry were
        Since earth is mine, and all that earth doth beare
        I would not tell it Thee to begg thy meate
        But do I long the flesh of bulls to eate
        Or do I thirst to quench my thirsty heat
            With blood from throats of bearded cattle flowing

        A Sacrifice to God of Prayses frame
        Perform Thy vowes made in the Highest name
        In troublous times to me for succour send
40   The playning voice, and when I succor lend
        For lending succour to my glory bend
            All that Thou art; these offrings I demand Thee
        This to the Good. Now to the Godles sort
        How fitts it Thee my statutes to report
        And of my Cov'enant in thy talk to prate
        Wheras to live in right reformed state
        Thou dost refuse, nay in Thy heart dost hate
            Casting behind Thy back what I command Thee.

        Seest Thou a thief? a theif with him Thou art
50   Adulterers findst? Thou tak'st Adulterers part
        Thy mouth a denn where Serpent slaunder lyes
        Thy tongue a stamp that coines but fraud and lyes
        Ev'n to disgrace of him; whom to thee tyes
            The sweet strait band of calling one your mother
        Thus while Thou didst, because I silent staid
        This in Thy thought thy wicked fancy said
        God is like me, and like his like doth love
        But my true deeds shall Thy false thoughts reprove
        And to thy face from point to point shall prove
60   Against thee all that thou hast sought to smother.

        Mark this all you, whose crazed holely braine
        Cannot one thought of God in you contain
        Mark this I say, least if with griping hand
        I once lay hold of you, none may withstand
        My matchless might, nor loose the pinching band

So straitly straind, as to be loosed never
In Summe who will that I take in good part
His offring must on Altar of his heart
Offer an earnest love of honouring me
70 And He whose stepps aright be disposed be
That man will I keep still from danger free
    And place with God in safty lasting ever.

Psalm 51, *Miserere mei Deus*

O Lord, whose grace no limits comprehend
Sweet Lord, whose mercys stand from measure free
To me that Grace to me that mercy send
And wipe, O Lord, my sin from sinfull mee
O cleanse, o wash my foul iniquity
    Clense still my spotts still wash away my stainings
    Till stains and spotts leave in me no remaynings.

For I alas, acknowledging do know
My Filthy fault, my faulty filthyness
10 To my soules ey uncessantly doth shew
Which don to Thee, to Thee I do confess
Just judg, true Witness; that for righteousness
    Thy dome may passe against my guilt awarded
    Thy evidence for truth may be reguarded.

My Mother lo, where I began to be
Conceiving me with me did sin conceive
And as with living heat shee cherisht me
Corruption did like cherishing receive
But Lo thy Love to purest good doth cleave
20   And inward truth, which hardly else discerned
    My truant soul in Thy hidd schole hath learned

Then, as Thy self to leapers hast assignd
With hyssop Lord, thy Hyssop purg me so
And that shall cleanse the Leapry of my mind

Make over me Thy mercys streams to flow
So shall my whitness scorn the whitest snow
    To eare and heart send sounds and thoughts of gladness
    That bruised bones may dance away their sadness.

Thy ill-pleasd ey from my misdeeds avert
30 Cancell the registers my Sins contain
Create in me a pure clean spotless heart
Inspire a spirit where Love of right may reign
Ah cast me not from Thee, take not again
    Thy breathing grace; again thy comfort send me
    And let the guard of Thy free sprite attend me.

So I to them a guiding hand will be
Whose faulty feet have wandred from Thy way
And turnd from sin, will make return to thee
Whom turnd from thee, sin erst had led astray
40 O God, God of my health O do away
    My bloody crime, so shall my tongue be raised
    To prayse Thy truth enough can not be praysed.

Unlock my lipps, shutt up with sinfull shame
Then shall my mouth O Lord Thy honour sing
For bleeding fewell of Thy Altars flame
To gain thy grace what boots it me to bring
Burnt offrings are to Thee no pleasant thing
    The sacrifice that God will hold respected
    Is the heart broken soul, the sprite dejected.

50 Lastly, O Lord, howso I stand or fall
Leave not Thy loved Sion to embrace
But with Thy favour build up Salems wall
And still in peace maintain that peacefull place
Then shalt Thou turn a well accepting face
    To Sacred Fires with offerd gifts perfumed
    Till ev'n whole Calves on Altars be consumed.

Psalm 52, *Quid gloriaris*

Tyrant why swel'st Thou thus
    Of mischeif vaunting
Since help from God to us
    Is never wanting
Lewd lys Thy tongue contrives
    Lowd lyes it soundeth
Sharper than sharpest knives
    With lys it woundeth.

Falshood Thy Witt approves
10   All truth rejected
Thy Will all vices loves
    Virtue neglected
Not words from cursed Thee
    But gulfs are powred
Gulfs wherin dayly be
    Good men devoured.

Thinkst Thou to beare it so?
    God shall displace Thee
God shall Thee overthrow
20   Crush Thee deface Thee
The just shall fearing see
    These fearefull chances
And laughing shoot at Thee
    With fearfull glances.

Lo, Lo the wretched wight
    Who God disdaining
His mischeife made his might
    His guard his gaining
I, as an Olive tree
30   Still green shall florish
Gods house the soile shall be
    My roots to nourish.

My trust on his true love
   Truly attending
Shall never thence remove
   Never se ending
Thee will I honour still
   Lord for this justice
There fix my hopes I will
40   Where Thy Saints trust is

Thy Saints trust in Thy name
   Therin they joy them
Protected by the same
   Naught can annoy them.

Psalm 53, *Dixit insipiens*[1]

The foole in foolish Fancy says
There is no God that marks mens wayes
So he and all the Witless train
Such deeds both do, and don maintain
Whose hatefull touch the earth doth stain
   Who good among them? None

Even God that can most nearly pry
Hath cast on them his searching eye
Searching if any God would know
10 What finds he? All astraying go
All so corrupt and cankred so
   Not one doth good, not one.

O Fury! Are Gods people bred
For as they were so are ye fedd
On them, ye Wolvish Canibals

[1] This psalm is crossd in the body of it and with three Crosses at the beginning.

And unto God, which of you calls?
But lo great feare upon you falls
   From what you feared least

For God shall so his people wreake
20 That He whole armys boanes shall breake
Chased by them with shame and scorn
Ah! when shall time away be worne
That Israel Syons Saviour born
   May joy and Jacob rest.

Psalm 54, Deus in nomine tuo

Lord let Thy name my saving succour be
   Defend my wronged cause by Thy just might
Lord let my crying voice be heard of Thee
   Let not my heavy words be counted light
For strangers I against me risen see
   Who hunt me hard, and sore my soul affright
Possest with feare of God in no degree
   But God Thou art my helper in my right
Thou succour send'st to such as succour me
10   Then pay them home, who thus against me fight
And let Thy Truth cutt down their treachery
   So I with offrings shall Thy Altars dight
Praysing Thy name, which thus hast set me free
   Giving me scope to soar with happy flight
Above my Evils, and on my Enemy
   Making me see, what I to see delight.

Psalm 55, Exaudi Deus

My God most glad to look, most prone to heare
An Open eare O let my prayer find
And from my plaint turn not Thy face away

Behold my gestures, hearken what I say
While uttring moanes with most tormented mind
My body I no lesse torment and teare
For lo, their fearfull threatnings wound myne eare
Who greifes on greifes on me still heaping lay
A mark to wrath and hate and wrong assign'd[1]
10   Therfore my heart hath all his force resignd
To trembling pants; Deaths terrors on me prey
I feare, nay shake, nay quivering quake with feare.

Then say I, O, might I but cutt the Wind
Born on the wing the fearfull Dove doth beare
Stay would I not, till I in rest might stay
Farr hence, O farr then would I take my way
Unto the desert and repose me there.
These stormes of Woe, these tempests left behind
But swallow[2] them O Lord in darkness blind
20   Confound their Counsels, lead their tongues astray
That what they meane by words may not appeare
For Mother Wrong within their town each where
And Daughter strife their ensigns so display
As if they only thither were confin'd.

These walk their Citty walls both night and day
Oppressions, tumults, guiles of evry kind
Are Burgesses and dwell the middle neare
About their streets, his masquing robes doth weare
Mischeife cloth'd in deceit with treason lin'd
30   Where only hee, hee only beares the sway.
But not my Foe with me this prank did play
For then I would born with patient chere
An unkind part, from whom I knew unkind
Nor hee whose forehead envys mark had signd
His Trophys on my ruins sought to reare
From whom to fly I might have made assay.

[1] *As if no other tomb were mee assignd*, expunged and the verse in the Staffe enterlin'd in another hand.
[2] *scatter*, but expunged.

But this to Thee, to Thee impute I may
My Fellow, my Companion, held most deare
My soul, my other self, my inward friend
40   Whom unto me, me unto whom did bind
Exchanged secrets, who together were
Gods temple wont to visit; there to pray
O let a suddain Death work their decay
Who speaking faire such cankred malice mind
Let them be buryed breathing from their beere
But purple Morn, black even and mid-day cleare
Shall see my praying voice to God enclin'd
Rousing him up, and naught shall me dismay.

He ransom'd me, he for my safty find
50   In fight where many sought my Soul to slay
He still himself to no succeding heire
Leaving his empire shall no more forbeare.
But att my motion all these Atheists pay
By whom still One, such mischeifes are designd
Who but such Catives would have undermin'd
Nay overthrown, from whom but kindness meere.
They never found? Who would such trust betray?
What butterd words? yet warr their hearts bewray
Their speed more sharp, than sharpest sword or speare
60   Yet softer flowes than balm from wounded rinde.

But my oreloaden soul Thy self upcheare
Cast[3] on Gods shoulders what Thee down doth weigh
Long born by Thee, with bearing paind and pin'd
To care for Thee He shall be ever kind
By him the just in safety held[4] alway
Changeless[5] shall enter, love, and leave the yeare

[3] *Lay*, expunged.
[4] *kept*, expunged.
[5] *fearelesse*, expunged.

But Lord how long shall these men tarry here?
Fling them in pitt of Death where never shin'd
The light of Life, and while I make my stay
On Thee, let who their thirst with blood allay
Have their life holding thred so weakely twin'd
That it half spun, Death may in sunder sheare.[6]

70

Psalm 56, Miserere mei

Fountain of pitty, now with pitty flow
These Monsters on me dayly gaping go
   Daily me devoure these spyes
   Swarms of Foes against me rise
O God that art more high than I am low.

Still when I feare yet will I trust in Thee
Thy Word O God my boast shall ever bee
   God shall be my hopefull stay
   Feare shall not that hope dismay
For what can feeble flesh do unto me?

10

I, as I can, think, speake, and do the best
They to the worst my thoughts, words, doings wrest
   All their hearts with one consent
   Are to work my ruin bent
From plotting which they give their heads no rest

[6] The last 4 verses stood thus before the Correction:–

There let them ly for aye
Let such as would their thirst etc.
Have their l.h.t. no longer twin'd
But e're half spun let Death the same off sheare.

The first of these foure further again thus corrected –

and while on Thee I stay.

but all expunged as appeares and correted by the Authors own hand.

To that intent they secret meetings make
They presse me neare my soul in snare to take
    Thinking slight shall keep them safe
    But thou Lord in wrathfull chase
20 Their League so surely link'd in sunder shake.

Thou didst O Lord with carefull counting look
On evry journy I poor exile took
    Every teare from my sad eyes
    Saved in thy bottle lyes
These matters all are entred in Thy book

Then whensoever my distressed spright
Crying to thee brings these unto thy sight
    What remaineth for my Foes
    Blames and shames and overthrowes
30 For God himself I know for me will fight.

God's never falsed word my boast shall bee
My boast shall be his word to set me free
    God shall be my hopefull stay
    Feare shall not that hope dismay
For what can mortall man do unto mee?

For this to Thee how deeply stand I bound
Lord that my soul dost save my foes confound?
    Ah, I can no payment make
    But if thou for payment take
40 The vowes I pay, thy prayses I resound.[1]

Thy Prayses who from death hast set me free
Whether my feet did headlong carry me
    Making me of Thy free grace
    There again to take my place
When light of life with living men I see.

---

[1] The last verse of this staffe before the correction stood thus: *That still my song thy prayses do resound*, which not pleasing twas thus changd *That still I vow and still thy prayses resound*, but both expunged.

Psalm 57, *Miserere mei*

Thy mercy Lord, Lord now thy mercy show
    On Thee I ly
    To Thee I fly
Hide me hive me as thyne own
Till these blasts be overblown
    Which now do fiercely blow

To highest God I will erect my cry.
    Who quickly shall
    Dispatch this all
10 He shall down from heaven send
From disgrace me to defend
    His love and verity

My soul enraged lyes with lions brood
    Villains whose hands
    Are fiery brands
Teeth more sharp than shaft or speare
Tongues farr[1] better edg do beare
    Than swords to shed thy blood

As high as highest Heav'n can give thee place
20   O Lord ascend
    And thence extend
With most bright most glorious show
Over all the earth below
    The Sunbeames of Thy face!

Me to entangle ev'ry way I go
    Their trap and nett
    Is ready set
Holes they digg, but their own holes
Pitfalls make for their own soules
30   So Lord, O serve them so

[1] Forte *that*.

My heart prepar'd, prepared is my heart
  To spred Thy prayse
  With tuned laies
Wake my tongue, my lute awake
Thou my harp the Consort make
 My self will beare a part

My self when first the morning shall appeare
  My voice and string
  So will Thee sing
40 That this earthly globe and all
Treading on this earthly ball
 My praysing notes shall heare

For God my only God Thy gracious love
  Is mounted farr
  Above each starr
Thy unchanged verity
Heavnly wings do lift as high
 As clouds have roome to move

As high as highest heav'n can give Thee place
50 O Lord ascend
  And thence extend
With most bright most glorious show
Over all the Earth below
 The Sunbeames of Thy Face!

Psalm 58, Si vere utique[1]

You that in judgment sitt
Is this to speake what is in judgment fitt
Is this aright to sentence wronged case
 O you but earthly Adams race
 Though higher sett in honourd place?

[1] This Psalm is cross'd in the MS for correction or change.

Nay is not this the wrong
Which in your hearts you have revolved long
Now to the World in practice to display?
   To whom where justice you should weigh
10   Oppression you in ballance lay

But never did I look
From you for better, since the shape you took
Of men; since first you fedd on breathing wind
   With lying mouth, and wronging mind
   From truth and right you still declin'd.

Not only Serpents hisse
But Serpents poyson in them lodged is.
Poyson such as the Subtile Aspick beares
   Whose tayle ev'n then doth stop her eares
20   When shee the skilfull'st charmer heares

Their teeth Lord, where they stand
Crack in their mouths: crush with thy bruising hand
These lions jawes; as water in dry ground
   So make them sink: when they would wound
   Breake thou their shafts, their shott confound

O let them so decay
As the dishoused snail doth melt away
Or as the Embryo, which formless yet
   Dyes e're it lives, and cannot get
30   Though born to see sun rise, or sett.

O let their springing thorns
Ere bushes waxt they push with pricking horns
Be by untimely rooting overthrown
   With whirlwinds topside turfway blown
   As fruits which fall ere fully grown

Now when the just shall see
This justice justly done by justest Thee
On the unjust, and their no juster brood
    They shall glad at so great a good
40   Bath righteous feet in wicked blood

And thus in heart shall say
Sure a reward doth for the righteous stay
There is a God whose justice never swerves
    But good or ill to each man carves
    As each mans good or ill deserves.

Psalm 60, *Deus repulisti*[1]

O God, who angry leftst us in the field
    Repuls'd, disorderd, scattred, slain
    Again to us be reconcil'd
      O be our guide again
The very Earth Thou madest with trembling quake
    With chinks and chaps it gaping lay
    O sound again her ruptures make
      Stay her in former stay
What most displeasing any heart could think
10   Displeasd Thou didst Thy people show
    Dull horror drank they as a drink
      That makes men giddy grow
But now again Thou hast an ensign spredd
    To cheere Thy last dismayed band
    Which by Thy truths conduction ledd
      In stout array shall stand
March on O God, set Thy beloved free
    Be deafe no more to what we pray
    Hark, hark, I heare so shall it be
20   God from his Temple say!

[1] This whole Psalm in the MS has a Crosse through the body of it.

March then no further make a merry stand
    Here will I part out Sichems feilds
    By perch and pole I'll meate the land
        That Succoths vally yeilds
Mine Gilead Manasse also mine
    Ephraim yeilds me men for warr
    Judah shall right by law define
        When strife breeds doubtfull Jarr
Moab shall wash my feet in servile place
30   At Edom I my shoe will fling
    Thou Palestine (O alterd case)
        Shall of my triumph sing
But who shall bring us to the walled town
    But who shall cause us Edom take
    Who but the God, that threw us down
        And did our hosts forsake
Long long we thus in servitude have layne
    Come heavnly God O come at length
    And ridd us out for vain most vain
40   Is help of human strength.
Then Victory shall us with glory crowne
    When not in men, in God we trust
    And then our foes by him cast down
        Shall lick the deadly dust.

Psalm 61, Exaudi Deus

    To thee I cry
        My crying heare
To Thee my praying voice doth fly
Lord lend my voice a listning eare
    From Country bannished
    All Comfort vanished
To Thee I run when storms are nigh.

Up to Thy hill
Lord make me clime
10   Which else to scale exceeds my skill
For in my most distressed time
Thy eye attended me
Thy hand defended mee
Against my foe for my fortresse still.

Then where a Tent
For Thee is made
To harbour still is my intent
And to Thy wings protecting shade
My self I carry will
20   And there I tarry will
Safe from all shott against me bent

What first I crave
First granting me
That I the royall rule may have
Of such as feare and honour Thee
Let yeeres as manyfold
As can be any told
My King O God keep from the grave.

Before Thy face
30   Grant ever he
May sit, and let Thy truth and grace
His endless guard appointed be
Then singing pleasantly
Praysing uncessantly
I dayly vowes will pay to thee.[1]

[1] This last staffe before the Correction (by the Author or as I guess and under his
own hand) stood thus in two staves:

> He ever shall
> Sit in Gods sight
> While by set turn of heavnly ball
> Age unto age shall yeild his right
> With favour gracing him
> With truth embracing him
> Support him so he never fall

Psalm 63, Deus Deus meus[1]

O God, thou art both God, and good to me
   Thee to find I therfore will
      Employ my skill
When first my Sight the morning light shall see

Within my Soul a thirst of thee dos dwell
   Nay my body more doth crave
      Thy tast to have
Than in this desert dry a springing Well

This desert whence when I my thoughts do reare
10   I no lesse behold thy might
      And glory bright
Than if I in Thy Sanctuary were

For mercys thyne, so kind Thy mercys are
   All life joyes nay life surmount
      Which to recount
My thankfull lips no time, no paine shall spare

As long as life Thy gift, Thy loving gift
   Leaves me not, my joyfull prayse
      Thy name shall rayse
20 Wherin to Thee I praying hands will lift

My hungry Soul most dainty food doth tast
   When of Thee I dreame in night
      Or think in light
Or have my tongue upon thy prayses plac't.

     Then throned high
     Who now sit low
   With prayse I will Thee magnify
   And dayly pay the vowes I ow.

But expunged because as I think the last staff beginning at the 8th verse was shorter than the rest.

[1] This Psalm is crossed in the MS.

Thy Safeguard me from perill hath preserv'd
   Hiv'd by Thee I dry have lain
     From showres of pain
Thy hand to me this life hath still reserv'd.

But who persue, and would me headlong throw
30   Headlong shall themselves be thrown
      With tempest blown
Into the place in lowest earth most low.

The murthring blade shall first their life devoure
   Carkases of life bereft
    Shall there be left
Where foxes teeth shall have them in their power.

As for the King, The King in God shall joy
   So shall they who evermore
    His name adore
40 Who lying mouths will stop, lyars destroy.

Psalm 64, Exaudi Deus[1]

This voice wherin my grief I show
With gracious eare lord entertaine
And let my life in rest remain
By Thee preserv'd from feared foe
O hide me where they may not know.
   Whose wicked witts in wiles are spent
   And rage to working wrong is bent

For their sharp tongues such edg do beare
As fretted stones give whetted Swords
10 They levell so with bitter words
As if not words but shafts they were

[1] This Psalm is crosst too.

Which they embusht and free from feare
    When none could think, where none could see
    Discharg upon poore harmless me

Nay obstinate to ill they go
Discoursing how they Snares may lay
They say who sees? and well they may
For sure they search each corner so
No guile no fraud can ly so low
20   But these will find in any part
            Ev'n in the depth of deepest heart

But Thou O God a shaft shalt send
Death striking them with suddain blow
And their own tongues to their own Woe
Shall all their wounding sharpness bend
Then all shall quake that see their end
    And all the earth their end shall see
    And seing prayse Gods just decree

Meanwhile on his Almighty Name
30 The just man vext by man unjust
Shall cast the Anchor of his trust
And land his comfort on the same
And such whose Consciences not lame
    Upright can stand, and march aright
    Shall boast in God their Captains might.

Psalm 65, Te decet hymnus

    Sion it is where Thou art praysed
    Sion O God where vowes they pay Thee
    There all mens prayers to Thee raysed
    Return possest of what they pray Thee
There Thou my sin prevailing to my shame
Dost turn to smoake of sacrificing flame

O he of blisse is not deceived
Whom chosen Thou unto Thee takest
And whom into Thy Court received
Thou of Thy checkroll number makest
The dainty Viands of thy Sacred store
Shall feed him so he shall not hunger more

From thence it is Thy threatning thunder
Least we by wrong should be disgraced
Doth strike Our foes with feare and wonder
O Thou on whom their hopes are placed
Whom either earth doth stedfastly sustain
Or cradle rocks of restless wavy plain

Thy virtue stayes the mighty mountains
Guirded with power, with strength abounding
The roaring damm of watry fountains
Thy beck doth make surcease her sounding
When stormy uproares tosse the peoples brain
The Civill sea to calm thou bringst again.

Where earth doth end with endlesse ending
All such as dwell thy Signs affright them
And in Thy prayse their voices spending
Both houses of the sun delight them
Both whence he comes, when early he awakes
And where he goes, when evning rest he takes.

Thy eye from heav'n this land beholdeth
Such fruitfull dewes down on it raining
That store house like her lapp enfoldeth
Assured hope of plough-mans gaining
Thy flowing streames her drouth do temper so
That buryed seed through yeilding grave doth grow.

Drunck is each ridg of Thy cupp drinking
Each clod relenteth at Thy dressing
Thy cloud-born waters inly sinking
Fair spring sprouts forth blest with Thy blessing

The fertile yeare is, with Thy bounty croun'd
And where thou go'est, thy goings fatt the ground.

    Plenty bedewes the desert places
    A hedg of mirth the hills encloseth
    The feilds with flocks have hid their faces
    A robe of corn the vallyes cloatheth
Deserts and hills and fields, and vallys all
Rejoice, shout, sing, and on Thy name do call.

Psalm 67, Deus misereatur

God on us Thy mercy show
Make on us Thy blesssings flow
    Thy faces beams
    From heav'n upon us shower
      In shining streams
      That all may see
      The way of Thee
And know Thy saving power.

God the Nations prayse Thee shall
Thee shall prayse the Nations all
    To mirth and joy
    All such as earth possess
      Shall them employ
      For Thou their guide
      Goest never wide
From truth and righteousness

God the nations prayse Thee shall
Thee shall prayse the Nations all
    Then evry field
    As farr as earth hath end
      Rich fruites shall yield

And God our God
With blisse shall load
Who of his blisse depend

God I say with plenteous blisse
To enrich us shall not misse
    And from the place
    The Father of the yeare
    Begins his race
30   To Zephyrs neast
    His races rest
All lands his force shall feare

Psalm 68, Exurgat Deus[1]

Do Thou O God but rise, and in a moments space
    Thy foes shall scatred be, and cast in disarray
    Who hate to Thee conceale, or hate to thee bewray
Affrighted at Thy fearfull look shall fly before Thy face
    Yea so they all shall fly, as smoke away doth go
    Which going goeth to naught, or like the waxy ball
    At least aspect of Fire doth into water flow
So naughty men at sight of God from naught to nought
        shall fall.

    Meane while who justice love, who set their hearts aright
10   When they behold how God doth wicked men destroy
    In mapp of outward prayse shall paint their inward joy
And in his gracious ey shall find but[2] triumph and delight.
    Delight then triumph then, then joy before him show
    Then prayse his name *Who is*, who on the heaven rides
    Who most right judging judg the Widdows cause doth
        know
Who father of the Fatherless in Sacred Temple bides.

[1] This Psalm is crost in the MS.
[2] Forte for *both*.

Thou God with Childrens store the empty house dost fill
Thou of the fetterd foot dost loose the fretting band
But that Rebellious rout, who stiff against Thee stand
20   Exiled from the fields of blisse the cursed sand do till
When Thou O God didst march before thy faithfull train
When through the wastfull wayes Thou didst Thy journy
take
The heavns at sight of Thee with sweating drops did
raine
The earth did bow her trembling knee, yea Sinay mount did
shake.

Mount Sinay shook O God thou God of Israel
At sight of Thee, a sight exceding sight and thought
Who when to promisd soyle Thou hadst Thy people
brought
Upon Thy weary heritage refreshing showers fell
There Thou Thy flock didst feed, therfore[3] Thy sheep
distrest
30   Thou hadst in store layd up each good and healthfull
thing
A virgin army there, with chastness armed best
While armys fledd, by Thee was taught this triumph Song
to sing.

These Kings, these Sons of Warr, lo, lo they fly they fly
Wee house-confined maids with distaffs share the spoyle
Whose hew though long at home the chimnys glosse did
foyle
Since now as late enlarged doves wee freer skyes do try
As that gold-featherd fowle so shall our beautys shine
With beating wavy aire with oare of silverd winge
So dasleth gazing eyes that eyes cannot define
40   If those sweet lovely glittring streams from Gold or Silver
spring.

[3] Forte pro *there for*.

For when th'Almighty had with utter overthrow
The Kings extirpate hence (that this may not seem
    strange)
The very ground her robes black mourning clouds did
    change
And clad herself in weather cleere, as cleare as Salmon snow
    Mount Basan be Thou proud of thy fatt feeding lands
    Of thy empyreall site, mount Basan boast thy fill
    Whose proudly perking top so many tops commands
Mount Basan tho Thou boast and burst Gods hill is Sion
        hill.

    You other hills, whose topps so many topps command
50   What makes you then to leap, what makes you then to
        swell
    This humble mount is that where God desires to dwell
Here here his house, Who Ever is, shall everlasting stand
    Here He twice thousands ten, yea doubled twice retaines
    Of chariots fitt for warr, which carve with hooked wheele
    In midst of whom the Lord in sacred seat remains
As glorious now, as when his weight mount Sinais back did
        feele.

    Thou art gon up on high, with Thee Thy Captive bands
    Whose spoiles Thou hast receiv'd, and wilt to Thyne
        impart
    O God Eternall God, so reverenc't Thou art
60   That even thy Rebels dwell with Thee, as tenants to Thy
        lands
    The Lord our healthfull help, our blessing prayse shall
        have
    Who on us day by day doth good on good amasse
    He only is our God, the God who doth us save
The Lord Eternall keepes the keyes wherby from death wee
        passe.

God of their hatinge heads the crounes with wounds shall
    crowne
Who are against him bent, and who still onward go
In way of wicked will, the bloody streames that flow
Their growing Perrukes water shall in tresses hanging down
    As I my self, said God did once from Basan bring
70 And then from drowning death in deepest Seas did keep
    I now will do again the same, the self same thing
From Basan I will bring my folk, and keep them from the
    deep.

He said; and out of hand, thou didst Thy foot engrain
In blood: In blood of foes thy doggs their tongues did dye
An[d] all O God, my King, beheld with open ey
Thy marching to Thy holy place, they saw, they saw Thee
    plain
The Vantguard was of them, that did with voyces sing
They in the rereward plac'd, on instruments did play
The middleward was maids, and did with timbrells ring
80 The voices, tymbrells, instruments in sweet consort did say

Praise God, O prayse our Lord, when you your meetings
    make
You blessed Jacobs root, you race of Israel
Of whom young Benjamin with sword his foes doth quell
And bullets shott from Judas sling, make more than armour
    ake
We noble Zabulon and Nepthali could name
Two thunderbolts of warr, but God we turn to Thee
Thou gav'st to us this force, O God confirm the same
And what by Thee hath been begun, by Thee let ended be

God for Thy temple sake, for Salem when it stands
90 Where Kings with offred gifts, Thy Altars heads shall
    croune
These furious bulls rebuke, these wanton calves knock
    down
These [want]on furious bulls and calves, these arrow–arm'd
    bands

I meane defeat these troops that do in warrs delight
Make them with humble grace their silver tributes pay
Let Egypt send to Thee her men of greatest might
Let Ethiope with lifted hands Thy speedy favour pray.

And you, you Kingdoms all, that Earthy Kings do share
The King of Kings extoll, I meane the heavnly King
A Song to God the Lord a Songe of prayses sing
100   Let your melodious Instruments his past-praise worth
        declare
For bravely mounted he on highest Heavens back
The rolling spheres to rule doth coachmanlike persist
And from the hight of hights in thundring cloudy crack
Sends down his voice, a voyce of strength, a strength none
        can resist.

Then give to God all strength, of strength the mine and
        spring
Whose brave magnificence, whose sunlike glory showes
No lesse on Israels line, the line himself hath chose
Than in the thundring cloudy crack, his powerfull might
        doth ring.
Thou fearfull art O God, and fearfull things didst show
110   Down from Thy starry Seat, from out Thy Sacred hill
From Him from Him it is his peoples might doth grow
The mighty God of Israel, to him be prayses still.

Psalm 69, Salvum me[1]

Save me O God, O save my drowning Soul
For fast I stick in depth of muddy hole
        Where I no footing find
Now, now, into the watry gulfs I fall

---

[1] This Psalm is crost in the MS.

And with the streame I go
Hoarse is my throat so long I cry and call
So long look for my God, that dymm nay blind
    Mine eyes with looking grow.

Who hate to me and causeless hate do beare
Are more than that to every one one haire
    I from my head can give
Who with no juster cause seek my decay
    More mighty are than I
So what I never took I must repay
But God my Follys in Thy knowledg live
    Thou dost my faults descry.

O mighty Lord, let not discount'nanct be
By my occasion such as trust in Thee
    Let never blushing shame
O God of Isrell flowing from my fall
    Thy Servants faces staine
For what I beare, for Thee I beare it all
Thy cause it is I this disgracefull blame
    And noted blot susteine.

My Brethren me did for a stranger hold
My mothers children so did me behold
    As one they did not know
Zeale of Thy house my Soule did eate and burn
    What shame on Thee was layd
Transferrd on me to my reproach did turn
I wept, I fasted, yet for doing so
    How did they me upbraid?

Changing my weeds in sackcloth sad I mournd
My Sackcloth these to jeasts and jybings turnd
    And both in public place
Of me did prate, and private in their wyne

On me did ryme and sing
But I when Thou the season dost assigne
    To Thee will pray, Lord let Thy saving grace
40   Not faile me help to bring!

Lift me out of this mire; let me not sink
In pudled poole, from such whose thoughts can think
    But hatred to my Soul
And from this bottomless, and banckless deep
    O save, and set me free
Keep, that these streames o'rewhelm me not, O keep
This gulf engulf me not, this gapeing hole
    Shut not her mouth on me

Answer me Lord in that sweet grace of thyne
50   And in Thy mercys numberless encline
    To me Thy aiding eye
Ne from Thy Servant hide Thy helpfull face
    For ev'ils me streightly close
O haste, O heare, O come, and come apace
Unto my Soul, O free it presently
    Redeeme it from my foes.

My shame, my ignominious disgrace
To Thee is known, and still before Thy face
    Are all that beare me spight
60   Which so did rack so rent my tender heart
    That languishing I pin'd
I lookt from Somebody for some kind part
That some would stirr, but all were frozen quite
    No comfort could I find.

Comfort? Nay more to aggravate my Woe
They gave me gall, when I did hungry grow
    And vinacre for drink
Lord make their tables to themselves a snare

Their happyness a nett
70 Make that their eyes, in only darkness stare
And when they go with weakness make them sink
    Such weights upon them sit.

Thy never ceasing indignations shower
Show'r down on them, and in whole rivers poure
    Let Fury of Thyne Ire
On evry side of them lay griping hold:
    Their house be desert ground
Quite desolate their tents, for they are bold
To plague, whom thou but strik'st, and still aspire
80   Thy wounded more to wound.

Add still more cyphers to their sinfull summ
But to Thy justice let them never come
    And from the blessed book
The book of life, that Godly men contains
    Let them clean rased be
But I poore destitute, whose heart sustains
The heavy weight of wo to Thee will look
    Thou God shalt Succour me

Then shall O God my Song extoll Thy name
90 My thankfull prayses magnify Thy Fame
    When Thou shalt dearer hold
Than any Sacrifice, which horned head
    Or hoofed foot doth beare
The Godly grieved ones, who seeking tread
The Paths of God, when they my change behold
    Their hearts to joy shall reare.

For God doth hearken to the poore mans cryes
And never dos the Prisners plaint despise
    Praise him you circling Spheres
100 Thou steadfast earth, Thou Sea, and what in thee

Doth either swim or saile
For Sion shall his safe protection see
And every towre his loved Juda beares
     To build he shall not faile

He shall not faile to build up evry place
And builded bring in habitable case
     That such as do him serve
Not only may therin themselves reside
     But their succeding seed
110 Heires to their heritage may still abide
And all, whose loves of his name well deserve
     No other seate may need.

Psalm 70, *Deus in adjutorium*

Lord, hye Thee me to save
     To help me haste
     Shame let them have
And of confusion taste
That have my soul in chase
Let them be turned back
And no disgraces lack
That joy in my disgrace

Back turned let them be
10   And for reward
     Their own fall see
Who laugh out hard[1]
Ah ha when most I mone
But mirth and joy renew
On them thy trace ensue
And love Thy help alone

[1] This verse lacks a foot.

Make them for ever sing
   To God be Prayse
   And to me bring
20   My downcast state to raise
Thy speedy aid and stay
From Thee my comfort growes
From Thee my Freedom flowes
Lord make no long delay

Psalm 71, In te Domine[1]

On Thee my trust is grounded.
Lord let me never be
   With shame confounded
   But set me free
And in Thy justice rescue me
Thy gracious eare to meward bend
   And me defend.

Be Thou my rock my Tower
My ever safe resort
10   Whose saving power
   Hath not been short
To work my safety, for my Fort
On Thee alone is built; in Thee
   My strong holds be.

Me, O my God deliver
From wicked, wayward hand
   God my help giver
   On whom I stand
And stood since I could understand
20   Nay since by life I first became
   What now I am.

[1] Cross'd in the ms.

Since prison'd in my mother
By Thee I prison brake
   I trust no other
   No other make
My stay, no other refuge take
Void of Thy praise no time doth find
   My mouth and mind

Men for a monster took me
30 Yet hope of help from Thee
   Never forsook me
   Make then by me
All men with praise extolld may see
Thy glory Thy magnificence
   Thy excellence

When feeble yeares do leave me
No stay of other sort
   Do not bereave me
   Of Thy support
40 And fail not then to be my fort
When weakness in me killing might
   Usurps his right

For now against me banded
My foes have talkt of me
   Now unwithstanded
   Who their spyes be
Of me have made a firm Decree
(Lo!)[2] God to him hath bid a Dieu
   Now then persue.

50 Persue say they and take him
No succour can he win
   No refuge make him
   O God begin

[2] MS but the verse lacks it.

To bring with speed Thy forces in
Help me my God, my God, I say
    Go not away.

    But let them be confounded
    And perish by whose hate
      My soul is wounded
60   And in one rate
Let them all share in shamefull state
Whose counsells, as their farthest end
    My wrong intend

    For I will still persever
    My hopes on Thee to rayse
      Augmenting ever
      Thy praise with praise
My mouth shall utter forth always
Thy Truths, Thy Helps, whose summ surmounts
70   My best accounts.

    Thy force keeps me from fearing
    Nor ever dread I ought
      Thy justice bearing
      In mindfull thought
And glorious Acts which Thou hast taught
Me from my youth, and I have shown
    What I have known

    Now age doth overtake me
    And paint my head with Snow
80   Do not forsake me
      Untill I show
The ages, which succeding grow
And every after living wight
    Thy Pow're and might.

How is Thy Justice raysed
Above the height of thought
    How highly praised
    What Thou hast wrought
Sought let be all that can be sought
None shall be found, nay none shall be
    O God like Thee

What if Thou down didst drive me
Into the Gulf of woes
    Thou wilt revive me
    Again from those
And from the Deep, which deepest goes
Exalting me again wilt make
    Me comfort take.

My greatness shall be greater
By Thee: by comfort Thyne
    My good state better
    O lute of mine
To prayse his truth thy tunes incline
My Harp extoll the Holy One
    In juda known

My voice to my Harp join thee
My Soul Sav'd from decay
    My voice conjoin Thee
    My tongue each day
In all mens viewe his justice lay
Who hath disgrac'd and shamed so
    Who work my woe.

Psalm 74, *Ut quid Deus*

O God why hast Thou thus
Repuls'd and scatterd us
Shall now Thy wrath no limits hold?
But ever smoake and burn
Till it to ashes turn
The chosen flock of Thy deare fold

Ah! Think with milder thought
On them whom Thou hast bought
And purchased from endless dayes
10   Think of Thy Birth right lott
Of Sion, on whose plott
Thy Sacred House supported stayes.

Come Lord, O come with speed
This Sacrilegious Seed
Root quickly out and headlong cast
All that Thy Holy Place
Did late adorn and grace
Their hatefull hands have quite defac't

Their beastly trumpets roare
20   Where heavnly notes before
In prayses of Thy might did flow
Within Thy Temple they
Their Ensigns eft display
Their Ensigns which their conquest show.

As men with ax on arme
To some thick Forrest swarm
To lopp the Trees which stately stand
They to Thy Temple flock
And spoyling cutt and knock
30   The curious works of carving hand.

Thy Most, most Holy Place
The greedy Flames do eate
And have such ruthlesse ruins wrought
    That all Thy house is ras't
    So ras't and so defac't
That of that all remaineth nought

    Nay they resolved are
    We all alike shall fare
All of One Cruel Cupp shall taste
40   For not one house doth stand
    Of God in all the land
But they by Fire have laid it waste

    We see the Signs no more
    We wont to see before
Nor any now with Spirit Divine
    Among us more is found
    Who can to us expound
What term these Dolors shall define

    How long, O God, how long
50   Wilt Thou winck at the wrong
Of Thy reviling railing Foe?
    Shall he that hates Thy Name
    And hated paints with shame
Lo, Lo, and do for ever so?

    Woe us, what is the Cause
    Thy hand his help withdrawes?
That Thy right hand farr from us keeps?
    Ah let it once arise
    To plague Thyne Enemys
60   Which now embosom'd idly sleeps.

Thou art my God I know
My King who long ago
Didst undertake the Charge of me
  And in my hard distresse
  Didst work me such release
That all the earth did wondring see

Thou by Thy might didst make
That Seas in Sunder brake
And dreadfull Dragons which before
70   In Deep, or Swam or crauld
  Such mortall stroakes appal'd
They floted dead to every shoare.

Thou crush'st that monsters head
Whom other Monsters dread
And so his fishy flesh didst frame
  To serve as pleasing food
  To all the ravning brood
Who had the Desert for their Dame

Thou wondrously didst cause
80   Repealing Natures Lawes
From thirsty flint a ffountain flow
  And of the Rivers cleere
  The sandy bedds appeare
So dry Thou madest their channels grow

The day array'd in light
The shaddow clothed night
Were made, and are maintained by Thee
  The sun and sunlike rayes
  The bounds of nights and dayes
90   Thy workmanship no lesse they be.

To Thee the Earth doth Owe
That Earth in Sea doth grow
And Sea doth Earth from drowning spare
The Summers corny crown
The Winters Frosty gown
Naught but Thy badg, Thy Livery are.

Thou then still One The same
Think how Thy glorious Name
These brain-sick mens despights hath born
100   How abject Enemys
The Lord of highest skyes
With cursed taunting tongues have torn.

Ah! Give no hawk the power
Thy Turtle to devoure
Which sighs to Thee with mourning moanes
Nor utterly out rase
From tables of Thy grace
The flock of Thy afflicted ones

But call Thy league to mind
110   For horror all doth blind
No light doth in the Land remain
Rape, murder violence
Each outrage, each offence
Each where doth range, and rage, and reign.

Enough, enough We mourn
Let us no more return
Repuls'd with blame, and shame from Thee
But succour us opprest
And give the troubled rest
120   That of Thy Praise their songs may be

Rise God, plead Thyn own Case
Forget not what disgrace
Those Fooles on Thee each day bestow
Forget not with what cryes
Thy Foes against Thee rise
Which more and more to heaven grow

Psalm 76, Notus in Judea Deus

Onely to Juda God his will doth signify[1]
Only in Israel is his Name notorious
His restfull tent doth only Salem dignify
On Sion only stands his dwelling glorious
   There bow and shaft and shield and sword he
      shivered
   Drave Warr from us and Us from Warr delivered.

Above proud Princes, proudest in their theivery
Thou art exalted high, and highly glorifyd
Their weake attempts, Thy valiand delivery
Their Spoyle Thy conquest meet to be historyfyed
   The mighty handless were as men that slumbered
   For hands were mightless, sense and life
      encombered[2]

Nay God, O God, true Jacobs sole Devotion
Thy check the very Carrs, and horses mortify'd
Cast in dull sleep and quite depriv'd of motion

---

[1] Before the Correction (by the Author under his own hand) the first and third verse stood thus though upon the Correction expungd: 1. *That only land knowes God that jury named is*; 3. *His restfull tent in only Salem framed is.*
[2] The last two verses before correction stood thus, tho by the Author expungd. *As men whose senses had to sleep resignd their right/ Nor mighty they their hands nor lands could find their might.*

Most fearfull God! O how must he be fortify'd
　　Whose fearlesse foot to bide Thy onset tarryeth
　　When once Thy wrath displayed Ensign carryeth.[3]

From out of heav'n Thy justice judgment thundered
20　When good by thee were savd, and badd were punished
　　While Earth at Heav'n with feare and silence wondered
　　Yea the most ragefull in their rage astonished
　　　　Fell to prayse Thee, whom Thou however furious[4]
　　　　Shalt eft restraine, if fury prove injurious.[5]

Then let your vowes bee paid, your offring offerred
Unto the Lord, o you of his Protection
Unto the fearfull let your gifts be proffered
Who loppeth princes thoughts, prunes their affection
　　And so himself most terribly doth verify
30　　In terryfying Kings, who Earth do terrify.

Psalm 77, *Voce mea*

To thee my crying call
To Thee my calling cry
I did O God addresse
　　And Thou didst me attend
To nightly anguish thrall

[3] This staff standeth thus expunged:

> Nay God, O God etc.
> At Thy rebuke the very carrs and horses were
> As cast in slumber quite. deprived of motion
> Most fearful God what arms must he what forces beare
> 　　Whose fearless foot before thy presence stayes itself

or

> 　　When bloody ensign of thy wrath displays itself

[4] and what as it remayning is.
[5] Of rage in them reserv'd of thy restraining is, or shalt force restrain if eft they prove injurious. Expungd.

From Thee I sought redresse
To Thee uncessantly
    Did praying hands extend

All comfort fled my soul
Yet God to mind I call'd
Yet calling God to mind
    My thoughts could not appease
Nought else but bitter dole
Could I in thinking find
My Sp'rite with pain appall'd
    Could intertain no ease

Whole Troopes of buisy Cares
Of Cares that from Thee came
Took up their restless rest
    In sleepy sleepless eyes
So lay I all opprest
My heart in office lame
My tongue as lamely fares
    No part his part Supplyes

At length with turned thought
Anew I fell to think
Upon the ancient times
    Upon the yeares of Old
Yea to my mind was brought
And in my heart did sink
What in my former Rimes
    My self of Thee had told

So then to search the Truth
I sent my thoughts abroad
Mean while my silent heart
    Distracted thus did plain
Will God no more take ruth
No further Love impart
No longer be my God
    Unmoved still remain

Are all the Conduits dry
Of his erst flowing grace
Could rusty teeth of time
   To naught his promise turn
Can mercy no more clime
And come before his face
Must all compassion dy
   Must nought but anger burn?

Then (lo) my wrack I see
50 Say I, and do I know
That change lyes in his hand
   Who changeless sitts aloft
Can I ought understand
And yet unmindfull be
What wonders from him flow
   What works his Will has wrought

Nay still Thy Acts I mind
Still of Thy Deeds I muse
Still se Thy glorys light
60   Within Thy Temple shine
What God can any find
(For term them so they use)
Whose Majesty whose might
   May strive O God with Thyne.

Thou only wonders dost
The Wonders by Thee done
All earth doth wonder make
   As when Thy hand of Old
From servitude unjust
70 Both Jacobs sons did take
And sons of Jacobs sonn
   Whom Jacobs sons had sold

The waves Thee saw, saw Thee
And fearfull fledd the field
The Deep with panting breast

Engulfed quaking lay
The clouds Thy fingers prest
Did rushing Rivers yeild
Thy Shafts did flaming flee
80   Through fiery ayry way.

Thy voices thundring crash
From one to other Pole
Twixt roof of starry Sphere
    And Earth then trembling floore
Whilst light of lightning's flash
Did pitchy clouds encleare
Did round with terror roll
    And ratling horror roare.

Meane while through dusty deep
90   On Seas discoverd bedd
Where none Thy trace could view
    A path by Thee was wrought
A path wheron Thy crue
As shepheards use their sheep
With Aaron Moses ledd[1]
    And to glad pasturs brought

Psalm 79, Deus venerunt

The Land of long by Thee possessed
The heathen Lord have now oppressed
Thy Temple holyly maintained
Till now, is now profanely stained
Jerusalem quite spoild and burned
    Hath suffered sacks
    And utter wracks
To stony heapes her houses turned

[1] *Moses with Aaron led*, but expunged.

The lifeless Carkasses of those
That liv'd Thy Servants serve the crowes
The flock so dearly lov'd of Thee
To ravning beasts deere food they be
Their blood doth streame in evry street
    As water spilled
    Their bodys killed
With sepulture can no where meet

To them that hold the neighbour places
We are but objects of disgraces
On ev'ery coast who dwell about us
In ev'ry kind deride and flout us
Ah Lord when shall Thy wrath be ended
    Shall still Thyne Ire
    As quenchless fire
In deadly ardor be extended.

O kindle there Thy furys flame
Where lives no notice of Thy Name
There let Thy heavy anger fall
Where no devotions on Thee call
For hence they be who Jacob eate
    Who thus have rased
    Have thus defaced
Thus desert layd his antient seate.

Lord ridd us from our sinfull combers
Count not of them the passed numbers
But let Thy pitty soone prevent us
For hard extremes have neerly spent us
Free us O God our freedom giver
    Our misery
    With help supply
And for Thy glory us deliver.

Deliver us and for Thy name
With mercy cloath our sinfull shame
Ah why should this their by-word be
Where is your God where now is hee?
Make them, and us on them behold
    That not despised
    But deerly prized
Thy wreakfull hand our blood doth hold.

Where Grace and Glory Thee enthroneth
50   Admitt the groanes the Prisner groaneth
The poore condemned for Death reserved
Let be by Thee in life preserved
And for our neighbours Lord remember
    Th'opprobrious shame
    They lent Thy Name
With sev'nfold gain to them thou render.

So wee Thy Servants we Thy sheep
Whom Thy looks guide, Thy pastures keep
Till death define our living dayes
60   Will never cease to sound Thy praise
Nay when we leave to see the sun
    The aftergoers
    We will make knowers
From age to age, what Thou hast done.

Psalm 81, Exultate Deo

All gladness gladdest hearts can hold
In merryest notes that mirth can yeild
Let joyfull songs to God unfold
To Jacobs God our sword and shield
    Muster hither Musicks joyes
    Lute and Lyre, and Tabrets noyse
    Let no instrument be wanting
    Chasing grief, and pleasure planting

When evry Month beginning takes
10   When fixed times bring Sacred dayes
When any feast his People makes
Let Trumpets tunes report his Praise
    This to us a Law doth stand
    Pointed thus by Gods own hand
  Of his League a sign ordained
  When his plagues had Egypt pained

There heard I, earst unheard by me
The voyce of God, who thus did say
Thy shoulder I from burden free
20   Free set thy hand from baked clay
    Vexed Thou my aid didst crave
    Thunderhidd I answer gave
  Till the streames, where strife did move thee
  Still I did with tryall prove Thee

I badd Thee then attentive be
And told Thee thus O Israel
This is my cov'nant that with Thee
No false nor forreign God should dwell
    I am God Thy God that wrought
30   That Thou wert from Egypt brought
  Open me Thy mouth to feed Thee
  I will care, nought else shall need Thee.

But (ah!) my people scornd my voice
And Israel rebelled still[1]
So then I left them to the choyse
Of froward way and wayward will[2]
    Why alas! why had not they
    Heard my voice and held my way
  Quickly I their foes had humbled
40   And their haters headlong tumbled.

[1] Before the correction but expunged, *Nor Israël would me obey.*
[2] *Of wayward will and froward way.*

Subdued by me, who them annoy'd
Had serv'd them now in servile state
And of my grant they had enjoyd
A lease of blisse with endless Date
    Flowër of the finest wheat
      Had been now their plenteous meat
    Hony from the rocks distilled
    Filled hath, yea over filled.

Psalm 82, Deus stetit

Where poore men plead at Princes barr
What gods, as Gods vicegerents are
The God of gods hath his tribunall pight
    Adjudging right
    Both to the judg and judged wight

How long will yee just doome neglect
How long saith he badd men protect
You should his own unto the helpless give
    The poore relieve
10   Ease him with right whom wrong doth grieve

You should the Fatherless defend
You should unto the weake extend
Your hand to loose, and quiet his estate
    Through lewd mens hate
    Entangled now in deep[1] debate

This should you do, but what do ye
You nothing know, you nothing see
No light no Law; Fy, Fy, the very ground
    Becomes unsound
20   So right, wrong, all your faults confound.

[1] Interlined *in quarel and*, but expungd because a foot too long.

Indeed to you the stile I gave
Of gods, and sons of God to have
But err not Princes, you as men must dy
    You that sitt high
Must fall and low as Others ly.[2]

Since men are such O God arise
Thy self most strong, most just, most wise
Of all the earth King, Judg, Disposer bee
    Since to decree
30   Of all the Earth belongs to Thee!

Psalm 84, *Quam dilecta*

How Lovely is Thy dwelling
Great God to whom all greatness is belonging
To view Thy Courts, farr, farr from any telling
    My Soul doth long and pine with longing
        Unto the God that liveth
        The God that all life giveth
    My heart and body both aspire
    Above delight, beyond desire.

    Alas, the sparrow knoweth
10   The house where free, and fearless shee resideth
Directly to the Neast the swallow goeth
    Where with her sonns she safe abideth
        O Altars Thyne most Mighty
        In warr, yea most Almighty
    Thy Altars Lord, Ah! Why should I
    From Altars thyne excluded ly.

[2] *As others fall with others low must ly*. So it was at first corrected and the other expungd but this being after expung'd, *stet* is putt to the other.

O happy, who remaineth
Thy household man, and still thy prayse unfoldeth
O happy who himself on Thee susteineth
20   Who to Thy house his journy holdeth[1]
      Meeseems I see them going
      Where Mulberrys are growing
How wells they digg in thirsty Plaine
And cisterns make for falling rain

Me seems I se augmented
Still troop with troop, till all at length discover
Sion, wherto their sight is represented
    The Lord of hosts, the Sion lover
      O Lord, O God most mighty
30   In warr, yea most Allmighty
Heare what I begg, hearken I say
O Jacobs God to what I pray.

Thou art the shield us shieldeth
Then Lord behold the face of Thyne Anoynted
One day spent in Thy Courts more comfort yeeldeth
    Than thousands other wise appoynted
      I count it clearer pleasure
      To spend my Ages treasure
Wayting a Porter at Thy Gates
40   Than dwell A Lord with wicked mates.

Thou art the Sun that shineth
Thou art the buckler Lord that us defendeth
Glory and Grace Jehovas hand assigneth
    And good without refusall sendeth
      To him, who truly treadeth
      The Path to pureness leadeth
O Lord of might, most blessed hee
Whose Confidence is built on Thee.

---

[1] *Whose heart thy wayes engraved holdeth*, expunged.

Psalm 86, *Inclina Domine*[1]

Lord bend to me Thyne eare
And me heare
Most poore, and most oppressed
O save my soul distressed
Who deeply am Thy debtor
Save me and make my badd state better
For Thee my God I serve.
From Thee my hope doth never swerve.

Lord pitty of me take
For I make
To Thee my dayly crying
My heart in sorrow lying
With joy O Lord recomfort
For unto Thee my only comfort
My Soul doth strive to rise
With stretched hands and bended eyes.

For Thou art good and kind
Myld of mind
To all their prayërs sending
To Thee then well attending
Thy servant heare his praying
Gravely his petitions weighing
I cry, but when I need
I therfore of Thy help shall speed

Compar'd with other gods
By great odds
Thou Lord excell'st: none taketh
In hand, what thy hand maketh

[1] This Psalm also is Crossed.

All nations by Thee framed
30   Praising the Name, that Thou art named
                    Shall come and as his right
          Shall fall adoring in Thy sight

                    Thou great in deed dost stand
                            From whose hand
                    O only God still floweth
                    Each work that wonder showeth
                    Thy path to me discover
          And I O Lord with walking hover
                    Still in thy truth: O frame
40   My heart to love and feare Thy name.

                    My heart, Lord, all my heart
                            Shall take part
                    In praysing Thee: Thy glory
                    Shall be my endlesse story
                    Thou art a gracious giver
          Of good to me, Thou dost deliver
                    My Soul from pitt of woe
          Even from the pit that lyes most low

                    Se, God, how proud men arm
50   To my harm
                    See how the mighty number
                    My chased Soul incumber
                    Who Thee from eyes repelling
          Reserve Thee in their sight no dwelling
                    But Thou Lord God, my King
          Most mercyfull, wilt mercy bring

                    Thy Pardon prone Thou art
                            To impart
                    To anger slowly going
60   With truth and mildness flowing

      With pitty then behold me
      With Thy Support, my Lord, uphold me
          For I Thy servant am
      And of Thy handmaids body came

      O set on me some Sign
          To define
      Me one by Thee embraced
      That they with shame amated
      May fall by whom my Soul is hated
70   Seing my Succour brought
      By Thee, by Thee my comfort wrought.

Psalm 88, *Domine Deus*

My God, my Lord, my help, my health,
      to thee my crie
      doth restles flie
    both when of Sunn, the daie
    the treasures doth displaie
And night locks up his goulden wealth.

Admitt to presence what I crave
      O bowe thine eare
      my plaint to heare
10   whose Soule with ills, and woes
    soe flowes, so overflowes,
That now my life drawes neere my grave.

With them that fall into the pitt
      I stand esteem'd
      quite forcles deem'd
    As one whoe free from strife
    and stirr of mortall life
Amonge the dead at rest doth sitt

Right like unto the murdred sorte
20 whoe in the grave
  theire biding have
 whome thou do'st no more
 remember as before
Quite quite cutt of from thy supporte.

Throwne downe into the grave of graves
  in darknes deepe
  thou do'st mee keepe
 where lightning of thy wrath
 upon mee lighted hath
30 All overwhellm'd with all thy waves.

Who did knowe mee, whome I did knowe,
  remov'd by thee
  are gone from mee.
 Are gone? that is the best
 they all mee so detest
That nowe abroade I blush to goe

My wasted eye doth melt awaye
  fleeting amayne
  in Streames of paine
40 while I my prayers send
 while I my hands extend
To thee my God and faile no daie.

Alas my lord, will then be time
  when men are dead
  thy truth to spread?
 shall they whome death hath slaine
 to praise thee live againe,
And from theire lowelie lodgings clime?

Shall buried mouthes thy mercie tell
50 Dust and decaie
  thy truth displaie

And shall thy workes of marke
shine in the dreadfull darke?
Thy justice where oblivions dwell?

Good reason then I crie to thee
and ere the light
salute my sight
My plaint to thee dirrect
Lord why dost thou reject
60 My Soule, and hide thy face from mee?

Aye mee, alas, I fainte I die
so still, so still
thou dost mee fill
And hast from youngest yeares
with terrifieng feares
That I in traunce amaz'd doe lie

All over me thy furies paste
thy feares my mynde
doe fretting bynde
70 flowing about mee soe
as flocking waters flowe
No daie can overunne theire haste.

Whoe earst to mee were neere and deere
farr, nowe, O farr
disjoined are
And when I would them see
whoe my Aquaintance be
As darknes they to mee appeare.

Psalm 89, Miserecordias

The constant promises, the loving graces
that cawse oure debt, Eternall Lord to thee
till ages shall fill up theire endles spaces

my thankfull songes unaltred theme shalbe
for of thy bountie, thus my thoughts decree:
It shalbe fully builte, as fairelie founded
and of thy truth attesting heav'ns shall see
the boundles periods, though theirs be bounded.

Loe I have leagu'd (thou saiest) with my ellected
10   and thus have to my Servant David sworne:
thy offspring kings, thy throne in state erected
by my supporte all threates of time shall scorne.
And Lord, as running skies with wheeles unworne
ceasse not to lend this wonder theire comending
Soe with one mynd, oure praise no lesse adorne
this truth the holie troupes thy court attending.

For who with thee among the clowds compareth?
what Angell there thy Paragon doth raigne?
whose Majestie, whose peereles force declareth
20   the trembling awe of thy immortall trayne:
Lord God, whome hoasts redoubt, whoe can maintaine?
with thee in powerfullnes a Rivalls quarrell?
Strongest art thou, and must to end remaine
whome compleate faith doth Armour-like apparell.

Thy Lordlie checke, the Seas prowde courage quailed
and highly swelling lowlie made reside:
To crushe stowte Pharaoh, thy arme prevailed
what one thy foe, did undisperst abide?
The heaven, the Earth, and all in bosome wide
30   this huge rownd engine clipps, to thee pertaineth
which firmelie based, not to shake, to slide
the unseene hindge of North, and South sustaineth:

For North and South were both by thee created
and those crosse pointes our bounding hills behould
Thabor and Hermon, in whose joye related
thy glorious grace to East, and West is tould:

Thy name all power, all puissance doth enfould
Thy lifted hand a might of wonder sheweth.
Justice and Judgment doe thy throne uphould
40   before thy presence, truth with mercie goeth.

Happie the people, whoe with hastie running
poste to thy Courte when trumpets triumphes blowe:
on pathes enlighted by thy faces sunning,
theire stepps Jehova unoffended goe:
Thy name both makes them gladd, and houlds them soe
high thoughts into theire harts thy justice powreth
The worship of theire strength from thee doth flowe
and in thy love theire springing Empire floweth.

For by Jehova's Shield stand wee protected,
50   and thou gav'st Israell theire sacred kinge:
what time in vision thus thy word dirrected
thy loved Prophet, aide I will you bringe
against that violence your state doth wringe
from one among my folke, by choice appointed:
David my Servant, him to act the thinge,
have I with holie Oile, my self annointed.

My hand shall bide his never failing piller
And from mine Arme shall he derive his might
Not closelie undermyn'd by curssed willer
60   Nor overthrowne by foe in open fight.
For I will quaile his vexers in his sight:
All that him hate by mee shalbe mischaunced
My truth my Clemencie, on him shall light
and in my name his head shalbe advaunced.

Advaunced soe, that twixte the watrie borders
of Seas, and floods, this noble land define
All shall obeye Subjected to the orders
which his imperious hand for lawes shall signe.

he unto mee shall saie: Thou father myne:
70   Thou art my God, the forte of my salvation
And I will him my first borne roome assigne
more highly thron'd, then king of greatest nation.

While circling times still ending and begining,
shall runne the race, where stopp nor starte appeares:
My bountie towards him, not ever lynning
I will conserve, nor write my league in yeares.
Naye more: his sonnes, whome fathers love indeeres
shall finde like blisse for legacie bequeathed:
A stedfast throne (I saie) till heavenly spheares,
80   Shall fainte in Course, where yet they never breathed.

Nowe if his children, doe my lawes abandon,
and other pathes then my plaine Judgements choose:
Breake my beheasts, and plainelie walke at randon,
and what I bidd with froward hart refuse
I meane indeede, on theire revolt to use,
Correcting rodd theire Sinne with whipps to chasten
not in theire fault my loves defect excuse
nor loose the promise once my faith did fasten.

My league shall hould my word persist unchaunged:
90   once sworne I have, and sworne in holines:
Never shall I from David be estraunged
his seede shall ever bide, his seate no lesse.
The daies bright guide, the nights pale Governesse
shall claime no longer lease of theire induring
whome I behould as heav'nly wittnesses
in turneles turnes, my termeles truth assuring.

And yet (O nowe) by thee abjected, skorned
scortcht with thy wrath, is thy annointed one:
hated his league, the crowne him late adorned
100   pull'd from his head, by thee, augments his mone

Raz'd are his fortes, his walls to ruyn gone:
not simplest passenger but on him praieth
his neighbours laugh, of all his haters, none
but boasts his wrack, and at his sorrowe plaieth.

Takes he his weapon? Thou the edge rebatest.
Comes to the field to fight? thou mak'st him flie.
Would march with kinglie pompe? thou him unstatest
Ascend his Throne? it overthrowne doth lie
his Ages springe, and tyme of jollitie,
110   winter of woe, before the daie defineth:
For praise, reproch: for honnour infamy,
he overladen beares, and bearing pineth.

Howe long (O Lord) what still in darke displeasure,
wilt thou thee hide? And shall thine angrie thought
still flame? O thinck how shorte oure ages measure:
Thinck if wee all created were for nought:
for whoe is he, whome birth to life hath brought
but life to Death, and Death to grave subjecteth,
from this necessitie, let all be sought:
120   no priviledg exempts, no aide protecteth.

Kynde Lord, where is the kindnes once thou swarest
swarest in truth thy Davids stock should finde:
Shewe lord, yet shewe thou for thy servants carest
houlding those shames in unforgetting mynde:
which wee imbosom'd beare of many a kynde
But all at thee, and at thy Christ dirrected
To endles whome, be endles praise assign'd:
be this againe, I saie be this effected.

Psalm 90, *Domine refugium*

Thou oure refuge, thou oure dwelling
   O Lord hast beene from time to time
longe ere Mountaines prowdelie swelling

above the lowelie Dales did clime:
longe er th'earth embowl'd by thee
    bare the forme it nowe doth beare
yea thou art God, for ever free
    from all touch of age and yeare.

O but man by thee created
    as he at first of Earth arose
when thy word his end hath dated
    in equall state to earth he goes
Thou sai'st (and saieng mak'st it soe:)
    Bee no more (O Adams heyre)
from whence ye came, dispatch to goe
    Dust againe, as Dust ye were.

Graunt a thousand yeares be spared
    to mortall man of life and light
what is that to be compared?
    one daie, one quarter of a night.
when Death upon them stormelike falls
    like unto a Dreame they growe:
which comes and goes, as fancie calls
    nought in Substance, all in showe

As the herbe, that earlie groweth
    which leaved greene, and flowred faire
ev'ning chaunge, with ruyn moweth
    and laies to roste in withering ayre.
Soe in thy wrath wee fade awaie
    with thy furie overthrowne
when thou in sight oure faults do'st laie
    looking on oure sinnes unknowne.

Therefore in thy angrie fuming
    his life of daies his measure spends
All oure yeares in Death consuming
    right like a sownd that sownded ends.

Our daies of life make seventie yeares
    eightie if one stronger be
whose cropp is labor, dollors feares
40   then awaie in poste wee flee.

Yet who notes thy angrie power
    as he should feare, so fearing thee?
Make us count each vitall howre
    make thou us wise, wee wise shalbe.
Turne Lord: shall theis things thus goe still?
    let thy Servants peace obtaine:
us with thy joyfull bountie fill
    endles joys in us shall raigne.

Gladd us nowe, as earst wee grieved
50   send yeares of good, for yeares of ill:
when thy hand hath us relieved,
    shewe us and ours thy glorie still.
Both them, and us, not one exempt
    with thy beawtie beawtifie
supplie with aide what wee attempt
    oure attempts with aide supplie.

Psalm 92, *Bonum est*

O lovelie thing
    to sing and praises frame:
    to thee (O Lord) and thy high name
with early springe
    thy bountie to displaie
    thy truth when night hat[h] vanish't daie
yea soe to singe
    that tenn string'd instrument
    with lute, and harpe and voice consent.

10   For Lord my mynde
     thy workes with wonder fill
     thy dooings are my comfort still
what witt can fynde
     how bravelie thou hast wrought?
     or deepelie sownd thy shallow'st thought?
The foole is blynde
     And blyndlie doth not knowe
     howe like the grasse the wicked growe.

The wicked growe,
20   like fraile, though flowrie grasse
     and fallne to wracke, past helpe doe passe,
But thow not soe.
     But high thow still dost staie:
     and lowe thy haters fall awaie
Thy haters loe
     decaie and perish shall
     all wicked hands to ruyn fall.

Fresh oiled I
     will livelie lift my horne
30   and match the matchless unicorne:
Myne eye shall spie
     my spies in spightfull case
     Myne eare shall heare my foes disgrace:
Like Cedar high
     Or like date-bearing tree
     for greene and growth the just shalbe.

Where God doth dwell
     shalbe his spreading place
     Gods Court shall his faire boughs imbrace
40   Even then shall swell
     his blossoms fatt, and faire
     when aged rynd the stock shall beare.
And I shall tell
     howe God my Rocke is juste
     so just with him is nought unjust.

Psalm 93, *Dominus regnavit*

Cloth'd in state, and girte with might,
    Monarke like, Jehova raignes:
He who Earthes foundacion pight
    pight at first, and yet sustaines.
    He whose stable throne disdaines
Motions shocke, and ages flight:
    He who endles one remaines,
one the same in chaungeles plight.

Rivers, yea, though rivers roare:
10   roaring, though Sea billowes rise:
vexe the deepe, and breake the shore,
    stronger art thou Lord of skies.
    firme, and true thy promise ties,
Nowe and still as heretofore:
    holie worship never dies
In thy house where wee adore.

Psalm 95, *Venite exultemus*

Come, come, let us with joyfull voice
    record and raise
    Jehova's praise:
Come let us in oure safeties rock rejoice.
    Into his presence let us goe
    and there with Psalmes our gladdnes showe
    For he's a God, a God most greate:
    above all Gods, a king in kinglie seate.

What lowest lies in Earthie masse,
10   what highest stands
    stands in his hands
The Sea is his, and he the Sea wright was.

he made the Sea, he made the shore:
come let us fall, let us adore,
come let us kneele with awfull grace,
before the Lord, the Lord oure maker's face.

He is oure God, he doth us keepe
wee by him ledd
and by him fedd
20   his people are, wee are his pasture sheepe
To daie if he some speech will use
Doe not, O doe not you refuse,
with hardned harts his voice to heare:
as Masha nowe, or Meriba it were.

Where mee your Fathers (God doth saie)
did angring move
and tempting prove
Yet ofte had seene my workes before that daie
Twice twentie times my poast the Sunn
30   his yearelie race to end had runn,
while this fond nation bent to ill
did tempt, and trie and vexe and grieve mee still.

Which, when I sawe, thus said I, loe
theis men are madd
and too too badd.
Err in theire hartes, my waies they will not knowe
Thus therefore unto them I sweare
I angrie can no more forbeare
The rest for you I did ordaine
40   I will so work you never shall obtaine.

Psalm 96, Cantate Domino

Singe, and let the songe be newe,
    unto him that never endeth
Sing all Earth, and all in you,
    Singe to God, and blesse his name
of the help, the health he sendeth
    daie by daie newe Ditties frame.

Make each countrie knowe his worth,
    of his acts the wondred storie:
painte unto each people foorth
10   for Jehova greate alone
all the Gods for awe and glorie
    farr above doth hould his throne.

For but Idolls, what are they
    whome besides madd earth adoreth:
he the Skies in frame did laie
    grace and honnor are his guides
Majestie his temple storeth
    might in guard, about him bides.

Kindreds come, Jehova give,
20   give Jehova alltogither:
force and fame where soe you live
    give his name the glorie fitt:
take your offrings, gett you thither
    where he doth enshrined sitt.

Goe adore him in the place,
    where his pompe is most displaied:
Earth O goe with quaking pace,
    goe proclayme Jehova kinge
staieles world shall nowe be staied
30   righteous doome his rule shall bringe.

Starrie roofe, and Earthy floore
   Sea and all thy widenes yeeldeth:
Nowe rejoyce, and leape, and roare;
   Leavie infants of the wood:
fields, and all that on you feedeth,
   Daunce, O daunce at such a good.

For Jehova cometh, loe
   loe to raigne Jehova cometh
under whome yee all shall goe,
40   he the world shall rightlie guide
trulie as a kinge becometh
   for the peoples weale provide.

Psalm 98, Cantate Domino

O singe Jehova, he hath wonders wrought:
   A songe of praise that newenes may comend:
his hand, his holie Arme alone hath brought,
   conquest on all, that durst with him contend.
   he that salvacion his ellect attend,
      longe hidd, at length, hath sett in open viewe:
And nowe the unbeleeving nations taught,
   his heavnlie justice, yeelding each theire due.

His bountie, and his truth, the motives were,
10   promis'd of yore, to Jacob, and his race:
which everie Margine of this heav'nly spheare,
   nowe sees performed, in his saving grace.
   Then Earth, and all possessing Earthly place
      O singe, O shoute, O triumph, and rejoice,
Make lute a parte, with vocall musicke beare
   and entertaine this kinge with trumpets noise.

Roare sea, and all that trace the brynye sands:
    Thou totall Globe and all that thee enjoy:
You Streamye Rivers, claspe your swyming hands
20   you Mountaines echo, each at others joy.
    See on the Lord this service you imploie
        whoe comes of Earth, the crowne, and rule to take:
And shall with upright justice, judge the lands,
    And equall lawes among the dwellers make.

Psalm 100, Jubilate Deo

O all you lands, the treasures of youre joye
    in merrie showte upon the Lord bestowe:
Your service cheerefully on him emploie,
    with triumph songe into his presence goe:
knowe firste that he is God, and after knowe,
    that God did us (not wee our selves) create.
wee are his flocke, for us his feedings growe:
    wee are his folke, and he uphoulds oure state.
With thankfullnes, O enter then his gate:
10   make through each porche of his your praises ring
All good, all grace of his high name relate
    he of all grace, all goodnes is the springe.
        Time in no termes, his mercie comprehends:
        from age to age, his truth itself extends.

Psalm 101, Miserecordiam

When nowe appointed kinge, I king shalbe
    what mercie then what justice use I will:
I heere O Lord, in songe protest to thee:

Till that daie come, thou mee the crowne shalt give
    deepe studie I, on vertue will bestowe
And pure in harte at home retyred live

My lowelie eye shall levell at no ill:
    whoe fall from thee, with mee not one shall stand
theire waies I shall pursue with hatred still

10   Mischevous heads farr of from mee shall goe
       malicious hartes I never will admitt
and whispring biters all will overthrowe.

Ill shall I brooke the prowde ambitious band
    whose eyes looke hie whose puffed harts doe swell
but for truth tellers seeke and searche the land.

Such men with mee my counsulours shall sitt:
    such evermore myne officers shalbe
men speaking right, and dooing what is fitt.

No fraudulent within my howse shall dwell
20   the cunning coyning tongue shall in my sight
be not indur'd much lesse accepted well.

As soone as I in all the land shall see
    a wicked wretch I shall him roote owt right
And of vile men Jehova's cittie free.

Psalm 102, Domine Exaudi

O Lord my cryeng heare:
Lord let my crie come to thine eare
    hide not thy face awaie
      but hast and aunswer mee
    in this most miserable daie
      wherein I praie, and crie to thee.

My daies as smoake are paste,
My bones as flaming fuell waste:
    mowne downe in mee (alas)

10   with sithe of sharpest paine:
  my hart is withred like the wounded grasse
   my stomack doth all foode disdaine.

  So leane my woes mee leave
  that to my bones my flesh doe cleave:
   and so I braie, and howle
    as use to howle, and braie
   the lovelie Pelican, and desart Owle
    like whome I languish longe the daie

  I languish so the daie,
20 the night in watch I wast awaie:
   right as the Sparrowe sitts
    berefte of Spowse or Sonne:
   which irk'd alone with dollors deadlie fitts,
    to companie will not be wonne.

  As daie to daie succeedes:
  so shame on shame to mee proceedes:
   from them that doe mee hate:
    whoe of my wrack so boaste,
   that wishing ill, they wish but my estate,
30   yet thinck of ills the most.

  Therefore my bread is claie
  therefore my teares my wine allaye:
   for how else should it be:
    since thou still angrie arte
   And seem'st for naught to have advanced mee
    but mee advaunced to subvert?

  The Sunn of my life daies:
  enclines to west with falling rayes:
   and I, as haie am dride
    while yet in stedfast seate
40   Eternall thou, eternally dost bide
    thy memorie, no yeares can frett.

O then at length arrise
On Sion cast thy mercies eyes:
   nowe is the time that thou
     to mercie shouldst encline:
   concerning her (O Lord) the time is nowe:
     thy self for mercie didst assigne.

Thy servants waite the daie,
50 when shee, whoe like a carkase laie:
   stretcht foorth in ruyns beere:
     shall so arrise and live,
   that nations all Jehova's name shall feare
     all kings to thee shall glorie give.

Because thou hast a newe
made Sion stand, restor'd to viewe
   thy glorious presence there:
     because thou haste I saie,
   beheld oure woes, and not refus'd to heare
60   what wretched wee did playning praie.

This of record shall bide,
To this, and ev'rie age beside:
   And they comend thee shall:
     whome thou a newe shalt make:
   that from the prospect of thy heav'nly hall
     thy eye of earth survey did take.

Harkning to prisoners grones:
And setting free condemned ones
   that they when nations come,
70   and Realmes to serve the Lord
   In Sion and in Salem might become
     fitt meanes his honnour to record.

But what is this if I,
In the midd waie should fall and die?
   my God to thee I praie

      whoe canst my prayer give:
    Turne not to night, the noonetide of my daie
      since endles thou, do'st ageles live.

  The Earth, the heavens stands
80 Once founded formed by thy hands:
    they perish, thou shalt bide:
      they owld, as clothes shall weare
    till chaunging still, full chaung shall them betide
      uncloth'd of all the clothes they weare.

  But thou art one, still one
  time interest in thee have none:
    then hope, who godlie be
      or come of godlie race
    endles your blisse, as never ending he
90   his presence your unchaunged place.

Psalm 104, *Benedic anima mea*

  Make, O my Soul, the subject of Thy Song
Th'Eternall Lord! O Lord, O God of might
To Thee to Thee all Royall pomps belong
  Cloathed art Thou in state and glory bright
  For what is else this eye-delighting light
But unto Thee a Garment wide and long?
  The Vaulted heaven, but a Curtain right
A Canopy Thou over Thee hast hung?

  The Rafters that his Parlors roof sustain
10   In chev'ron he on chrystall waters binds
He on the winds, he on the clouds doth reign,
    Riding on clouds, and walking on the winds
    Whose winged blasts his Word as ready finds
To post for him as Angels of his traine
    As to effect the purposes he minds
He makes no lesse the flamy fiër faine.

By him the earth a stedfast base doth beare
And stedfast so, as time, nor force can shake
   Which once round waters garment-like did weare
20 And hills in Seas did lowly lodging take
But seas from Hills a swift descent did make
   When swelling high by Thee they chidden were
Thy thunders[1] rore did cause their conduits quake
   Hastning their hast with spurr of hasty feare.

So waters fled, so mountains high did rise
   So humble vallys deeply did descend
All to the place Thou didst for them devise
   When bounding Seas, with unremoved end
   Thou bad'st they should themselves no more extend
30 To hide the Earth, which now unhidden lyes
   Yet from the Mountains rocky sides didst send
Springs whispring murmurs, Rivers roaring cryes.

Of these the beasts, which on the plains do feed
All drink their fill, with these their thirst allay
   The Asses wild, and all that wildly breed
By these in their self-chosen mansions[2] stay
The free-born fowles, which through the empty way
   Of yeilding aire wafted with wingy speed
To Art-like notes of nature-tuned lay
40 Make eareless bushes give attentive heed.

Thou, Thou of heav'n the Windows dost unclose
   Dewing the mountains with Thy Bountys raine
Earth great with young her longing doth not loose
   The hopefull plowman hopeth not in vain
   The vulgar grasse, wherof the beast is faine
The rarer Herb man for himself hath chose
   All things in brief, that life in life maintain
From Earths Old bowells fresh and yongly growes.

---

[1] *Thundry*, expunged.
[2] *Stations*, expunged.

Thence Wine, the Counterpoyson unto Care
50   Thence Oyle, whose juice unplaits the folded brow
      Thence bread, Our best, I say not daintyest Fare
Prop yet of hearts, which else would weakly bow
Thence Lord Thy leaved people budd and blow
      Whose Princes Thou Thy Cedars dost not spare
A fuller Draught of Thy cupp to allow
      That[3] highly raysd above the rest they are.

Yet highly raysd, they do not proudly scorn
      To give small byrds an humble entertain
Whose brickle neasts are on their branches born
60   While in the firrs tyhe storks a lodging gain
      So highest hills rock loving goates sustain
And have their heads with climbing traces[4] worn
      That safe in rocks the Conyes may remain
To yeild them caves, their rocky ribbs are torn.

Thou make'st the Moon the Empresse of the Night
Hold constant Course with most unconstant face
      Thou makest the Sun the Chariotman of light
Well know the start and stopp of dayly race
When he doth sett, and night his beames deface
70   To rome abroad Wood burgesses delight
Lions I meane, who roaring all that space
      Seem then of Thee to crave their food by right.

When he retires, they all from field retire
      And lay them down in Cave their home to rest
They rest, man stirrs to winn a Workman's hire
      And works till sun have wrought his way to West
      Eternall Lord, who Greatest art and Best
How I amaz'd Thy mighty Works admire
      Wisdom in them hath evry part possest
80 Wherto in me no Wisdom can aspire

---

[3] Forte *Though*.
[4] Forte pro *tresses*.

Behold the Earth, How there thy bountys flow
Look on the sea extended hugely wide
   What watry troopes swymm, creep and crawle and go
Of great and small on that, this evry side
There the sayl-winged ships on waves do glyde
   Sea monsters there their plays and pasttimes show
And all at once in seasonable tide
   Their hungry eyes on Thee their feeder throw.

Thou givst, they take, Thy hand itself displayes
90   They filled feel the plentys of Thy hand
All darkned ly deprived of Thy rayes
   Thou takest their breath not one can longer stand
   They dy they turn to former dust and sand
Till Thy life giving spirit do mustering rayse
   New companys to reinforce each band
Which still supplyed, never whole decayes.

So may it, O, So may it ever go
Jehovas Works, his glorious gladnes be
   Who touching mountains, mountains smoking grow
100 Who eyeing Earth, Earth quakes with qivering knee
As for my self, my seely self in me
   While life shall last in song his Worth to show
I framed have a resolute decree
   And thankfull be,[5] till being I forgo.

O that my song might good acceptance find
   How should my heart in Great Jehova joy!
O that some plague this Irreligious kind
   Ingrate to God would from the earth destroy
   Meane while my soul uncessantly employ
110 To high Jehovas prayse my mouth and mind
   Nay all, since all his benefitts enjoy
Prayse him, whom bands of time nor age can binde.

---

[5] *thankfully*, expunged.

Psalm 109, Deus laudem

Since thus, the wicked, thus the fraudulent.
  Since Lyers thus enforce my blame
    O God God of my prayse
    Be not in silence pent
For their malicious words against mee rayse
Engines of hate, and causeless battery frame.

Causeless! Ay me! quite contrary to cause
  My love they do with hate repay
    With treasons lawless spight
10   They answer friendships lawes
And good with Ill, and help with harm requite
What resteth now but that to Thee I pray.

I pray then What? That lorded at command
  Of some vile wretch I may him see
    That fitly still his Foe
    To thwart his good may stand
That judgd from judgment he condemned go
Yea to his plagues his prayër turned be

That speedy death cutt off his wofull life
20   Another take his place and part
     His children Fatherless
     And husbandless his Wife
May wandring begg, and begg in such distresse
Their beggerd homes maybe their best resort

That Usurers may all he hath ensnare
  And strangers reape what he hath sown
    That none him friend at all
    None with compassions care
Embrace his brood, but they to wrack may fall
30 And fal'n may ly in following age unknown

That not his Own alone, but evry crime
   Of Fathers and fore-fathers hand
      May in Gods sight abide
      Yea to Eternall time
Sin of his Mother and his Mothers Side
May in His mind, who is eternall stand

That he and they may be so farr begott
   That neither print of being leave
      What humane nature will
40   For he remembred not
But sought a wretch inhumanely to spill
And would of life an humbled heart bereave

He loved mischeif, mischeif with him go
   He did no good, then do him none
      Be wretchedness his Cloak
      Into him soaking so
As water drunken inwardly dos soake
And oyle through flesh doth search the hidden bone

Be Woe I say his garment large and wide
50   Fast girt with girdle of the same
      So be it, be it aye
      Such misery betyde
Unto all such as thirsting my decay
Against my Soul such deadly falsehood frame

But Thou O God, my Lord, so deale with me
   As dos thy endless honour fitt
      And for Thy glorys sake
      Let me delivrance see
For want and woe my life their Object make
60 And in my breast my heart doth wounded sit

I fade, and fayle,[1] as shade with falling sun
   And as the grassehopper is tost
      Place after place I leese
      While Fast hath nigh undone
The witherd knotts of my disjointed knees
And dryëd flesh all juice and moisture lost

Worse yet, alas, I am their scorn and nodd
   When in their presence I me show
      But Thou, Thou me uphold
70   My Lord my gracious God
O save me in thy mercys manifold
Thy hand Thy work make all men on me know.

They curse me still, but blesse Thou when they curse
   They rise, but shame shall bring them down
      And this my joy shall be
      As badd disgrace, or worse
Shall them attyre, than ever clothed me
Training in train a sinfull shameles gown.

Then, then will I Jehovas works relate
80   Where multitudes their meeting have
      Because still nigh at hand
      To men in hard estate
He in their most extremitys doth stand
And guiltless lives from false condemners save

Psalm 111, Confiteor

A t home abroad most willingly I will
B estow on God my prayses utmost skill
C hanting his Works, works of unmatched might
D eem'd so by them who in their search delight
E ndless the Honour to his power pertains
F rom end as farr his Justice eke remains

---

[1] *fall*, expunged.

G ratious and good and working wonders so
H is wonders never can forgotten go
I n hungry wast he fedd his faithfull crew
10   K eeping his League, and still in promise true
L astly his strength he caused[1] them understand
M aking them Lords of all the heathen land
N ow what could more each promise, doome, decree
O f him confirm[2] sure just unmov'd to be
P reserv'd his folk his league Eternall fram'd
Q uake then with feare, when Holy he is named
R everence of him is perfect Wisdoms well
S tand in his Law, so understand you well
T he prayse of him (though wicked hearts repine)
20   U nbounded bides, no time can it define.

Psalm 113, Laudate pueri

O you that serve[1] the Lord
   To prayse his name accord
Jehova[2] now and ever
   Commending, ending never
Whom[3] all this Earth resounds
From East to Western bound

   He monarch reigns on high
   His glory treads the sky
Like him who can be counted
10   That dwells so highly mounted[4]
   Yet stooping low beholds
   What heav'n and earth enfolds.

[1] *made*, expunged.
[2] *approve*, expunged.

[1] First *feare*, then *praise*, but both expunged.
[2] *His name*, expunged.
[4] *which*, expunged.
   By whom can he be faced/ He who most highly placed, but expungd by the Author
and set as in the text only it was first *His like* etc but *His like* is changd to *like him*.

From dust the Needy Soul
  The Wretch from myry hole
He lifts, yea Kings he makes them
Yea Kings his People takes them
  He gives the barren Wife
  A fruitfull Mothers life[5]

Psalm 114, In exitu Israel

At what time Jacobs race did leave of Egypt take
  And Egypts barbrous folk forsake
Then, then Our God, Our King elected Jacobs race
  His temple there, and throne to place
The sea beheld and fled: Jordan with swift return
  To twynned springs his streams did turn
The mountains bounded so, as fedd in fruitfull ground
  The fleeced Rams do frisking bound
The hillock capre'old so, as wanton by their damms
10   We capre'ol see the lusty lambs
O sea why didst Thou fly? Jordan why swift return?
  To twynned spring what made thee turn
Mountains why bounded ye, as fed in fruitfull ground
  The fleeced Rams do frisking bound?
Hillocks, why capreold ye as wanton with their dams
  We capreoll see the lusty lambs
Nay you and earth with you quake ever at the sight
  O God Jehovas might
Who in the hardest rocks makes standing waters grow
20   And purling springs from flints to flow.

[5] *The barren Wife before/ He stores with children store*, expunged.

Psalm 115, *Non nobis Domine*

Not Us, I say, not Us
But thyn own Name respect Eternall Lord
   And make it glorious
To shew Thy mercy and confirm Thy Word
  Why Lord, why should these Nations say
  Where doth your God now make his stay

You ask where Our God is
In heav'n enthron'd, no mark of mortall eye
   Nor hath nor will he misse
What likes his Will to will effectualy
  What are your Idols we demand
  Gold, Silver, works of workmens hands.

They mouths, but speechless have
Eyes sightless, eares no newes of noise can tell
   Who them their noses gave
Gave not their noses any sense of smell
  Nor hands can feel, nor feet can go
  Nor sign of sound their throates can show

And wherin differ you
Who having made them make of them your trust
   But Israël pursue
Thy Trust in God, the target of the just
  O Aarons house the like do yee
  He is their ayd, their target He.

All that Jehova feare
Trust in Jehova, He our ayd and shield
   He us in mind doth beare
He will to us abundant blessings yeild
  Will ever more with grace and good
  Blesse Jacobs house, blesse Aarons brood.

Blesse all that beare him aw
Both great and small, the Conduits of his store
   He never dry shall draw
But you and yours enrich still more and more
  Blest O thrice blest, whom He hath chose
  Who first with heav'ns did earth enclose

   Where hight of highest skyes
Removed most from floore of lowly ground
   With vaulted Roof doth rise
40 Himself took up[1] his dwelling there to found
  To mortall men he gracious gave
  The lowly ground to Hold and Have

   And why? His prayse to show
Which how can dead men Lord in any wise?
   Who down descending go
Into the place where silence lodged lyes
  But save us We Thy prayse record
  Will now and still O Prayse the Lord

Psalm 116, Dilexi quoniam

The Lord receives my cry
And me good eare doth give
Then love him still will I
And prayse him while I live
  Fast bound in bonds of death
With deadly anguish thralled
  When greife nigh stopt my breath
Upon his name I called

I call'd and thus I said
10 O Lord my bands unbind
I found him prone to ayd
I found him just and kind

---

[1] *hath chose*, expunged.

The simples surest guard
By me of right esteemed
   Whom he distressed heard
From hard distresse redeemed

My soul turmoyld with woes
Now boldly turn to rest
Such changes on Thee shows
20   Who greatest is and best
   My life from death is past
Myne eyes have dry'd their weeping
   My slipping foot stands fast
My self live in his keeping

Beleiving as I spake
Such wo my witts did blind
I said, when I did quake
I all men Lyars find
   Which finding false, To Thee
30   What thanks Lord shall I render
   Who showring blisse on me
Dost me so truly tender

My Cupp with thanks shall flow
In freedome from my thrall
Which I in flames will throw
And on Thy name will call
   To Thee my vowes will pay
Thy People all beholding
   Who deare their Deaths dost weigh
40   That are to Thee beholden

This I thy servant taste
Thy Slave, Thy handmaids son
Whose bands Thou broken hast
And fettring chaines undone
   Who unto Thee for this
A Sacrifice of praising
   To offer will not misse
Thy name with honour raysing

Thou whom no times enfold
50 Shalt have what I did vow
And they shall all behold
Who to Thy Scepter bow
  The place, that Holy place
Before Thy house extended
  The very middle space
In Sion comprehended

Psalm 117, *Laudate Dominum*[1]

P raise, prayse the Lord, All that of lowest sphere
R eside on any side
A ll you I say
I n Countrys scatterd wide
S e in your joyes Jehovas prayse appeare
T hat worthily your songs display
H is worth whose every way
E xceding grace
L ayd upon us doth overlay
10 O ur greatest force; whose promise ever true
R estraind within no space
D ecayeth not, He needs it not renew.

Psalm 119, *Beati Immaculati*

A

An undefiled Course, who leadeth
And in Jehovas Doctrin treadeth
  How blessed He
  How blest they be

[1] This Psalm is crossed.

Who still his Testimonys keeping
Do seek himself with hearty seeking.

For whom in walk Gods way directeth
Sure them no sinfull blott infecteth
    Of deed or word
10   For Thou O Lord
Hast to be done Thy Lawes commanded
Not only to be understanded.

O were my stepps so stay'd from swerving
That I me to Thy hests observing
    Might wholy give
    Then would I live
With constant cheere all chances brooking
To all Thy precepts ever looking.

Then would I worship Thee sincerely
20 When what Thy Justice bidds severely
    Thou shouldst me teach
    I would no breach
Make of Thy Law to me betaken
O leave me not in whole forsaken.

B

    By what correcting line
May a young man make streit his crooked way
    By Levell of Thy Lore Divine
      Sith then with so good cause
    My heart Thee seekes O Lord, I seeking pray
      Let me not wander from Thy lawes.

    Thy speeches have I hidd
Close locked up in Casket of my heart
    Fearing to do what they forbid

10   But this cannot suffice
Thou wisest Lord, who ever blessed art
   Yet make me in Thy statutes wise

      Then shall my lipps declare
Thy Sacred lawes, which from thy mouth proceede
   And teach all nations what they are
      For what Thou dost decree
To my conceit farr more delight doth breed
   Than Worlds of wealth if worlds might be

      Thy precepts therfore I
20 Will my continuall Meditation make
   And to Thy paths will have good eye
      The Orders by Thee set
Shall cause me in them greatest pleasure take
   Nor once will I Thy words forgett.

C

      Conferr O Lord
   This benefitt on me
That I may live and keep thy word
      Open myne eyes
   They may The riches see
Which in Thy law enfolded lyes.

      A Pilgrim right
   On earth I wandring live
O barr me not Thy statutes light
10   I wast and spill
   While still I longing grieve
Grieve longing for Thy judgments still.

      Thou, Proud and high
   Dost low, and lowly make
Curst from Thy Rule, who bend awry

What shame they lay
　　On me, then from me take
For I have kept Thy will alway.

　　Let Princes talk
20　And talk their worst of me
In Thy Decrees my thoughts shall walk
　　　All my Delight
　　Thy witness'd Will shall be
My counsell to advise me right.

D

　　Dead as if I were
　　My Soul to dust doth cleave
Lord keep Thy word, and do not leave
　　　Me here
　　But quicken me anew
　　　When I did confess
　　My sinfull wayes to Thee
As then Thy eare Thou didst to me
　　　Addresse
10　So teach me now Thy statutes true.

　　Make that I may know
　　And throughly understand
What way to walk Thou dost command
　　　Then show
　　Will I Thy wonders all
　　　Very Woe and grief
　　My Soul doth melt and fry
Revive me Lord, and send me Thy
　　　Releife
20　And let on me Thy comfort fall.

　　From the Lyars trace
　　From falshoods writhed way
O save me Lord, and make I may
　　　Embrace

The law Thou dost commend
　For the path ay right
Where Truth unfeigned goes
My tongue to tread hath dayly chose
　　My sight
30　Thy judgment doth as guides attend.

　　Since therfore O Lord
　Still did I still I do
So nearely dearly cleave unto
　　Thy Word
　All shame from me avert
　　Then lo, lo then I
　Will tread yea running tread
The trace which Thy commandments lead
　　When Thy
40　Free grace hath fully freed my heart.

E

Explain O Lord the way to me
That Thy Divine Edicts unfold
And I to end will run it right
O make my blinded eyes to see
And I Thy Law will hold, yea hold
Thy Law with all my hearts delight.

　O be my Guide O guide me so
I Thy commandments path may pace
Wherin to walk my heart is fain
10　O bend it then to things that show
True Witness of Thy might and grace
And not to hungry thirst of gain

Avert my eye it may not viewe
Of vanity the falsed face
And strength my treading in Thy trade

Let doings prove Thy sayings true
To him that holds Thy Servants place
And Thee his aw his feare hath made.

Thou then my feare remove the feare
20   Of Cousning[1] blame from carefull me
For gracious are Thy judgments still
Behold to me Thy precepts deare
Most deare, and most delightfull be
O let Thy Justice ayd me still.

F

Frankly poure O Lord on me
Saving grace to set me free
That supported I may see
Promise truly kept by Thee
    That to them who me defame
    Roundly I may answer frame
    Who because Thy word and name
    Are my trust, thus seek my shame
        Thy true Word O do not make
10   Utterly my mouth forsake
        Since I thus still waiting wake
        When Thou wilt just vengeance take
            Then lo I Thy doctrin pure
            Sure I hold will hold most sure
            Nought from it shall me allure
            All the time my time shall dure
        Then as brought to widest way
        From restraint of streightest stay
        All their thinking night and day
20   On Thy Law my thoughts shall lay
Yea then unto any King
Witness will I any thing
That from Thee can witness bring
In my face no blush shall spring

[1] Forte *comming*, *winning*, expunged.

Then will I set forth to sight
With what pleasure what delight
I embrace Thy precepts right
Whereunto all love I plight
   Then will[1] I with either hand
30   Clasp the rules of Thy command
   There my study still shall stand
   Striving them to understand.

G[1]

Grave deep in Thy remembrance Lord
   Thy promise past
To me whose trust on Thy true word
   Thou builded hast
   For in my Woes
Hence my only comfort growes
   That when I grieve
Still Thy word doth me relieve

Most fowly those that proudly swell
10   Did me deride
Yet I from what thy teachings tell
   Did never slide
   For I did hold
Mindfully Thy wreakes of Old
   And That O Lord
Comfort did to me afford

Yea trembling horror seisd on me
   And I did quake
When I did wicked wretches see
20   Thy lawes forsake

[1] Forte pro *with*.

[1] Crost and in the margin written *Quaere*.

Who though I stand
Farr exild from native land
   Yet still Thy law
Songs of mirth from me doth draw

Each night præsents unto myne eye
   Instead of sleep
Thy awfull name and soundly I
   Thy Doctrin keep
   The spring I know
30   Whence to me all blessings flow
   I firmly stand
In the deeds Thy words command

H^1

Have Others other choyse
I have irrevocably giv'n my voice
   That my lot in Thee O Lord
My wealth shall be in following Thy Word
   Before Thy præsence I
Poure out my heart I pray unfeignedly
   Promise me good hope doth give
Let with good help performance me relieve!
   All all my walks and wayes
10   My thoughts sharp censure carefully survayes
   All my stepps to that I move
Wherto Thy Doctrin testifys Thy love
   Nor walk I slack and slow
Nor day from day do I deferring go
   But with hearty hast do hye
To keep the Words where Thy commandments lye.
   Indeed the wicked pack
To stopp my passage wrought my spoile and wrack
   But to me that was no cause
20   Why once I should the more forget Thy lawes

---

[1] This staff or part (H) is also crost.

    Nay then even then when night
Hides in her darkness most remote from light
    Rising I my bed forsake
To prayse Thy judgments justly Thou dost make
    To all that Thee do feare
I a companion fellowship do beare
    All I say that fear Thee so
That Thy commandments they observing go
    Since all the Earth O Lord
30   Flowes with the goods Thy Goodness dos afford
    This one good thing grant to me
That in Thy lawes I may Thy Scholar be

I

In all kindness Thou O Lord
Hast to me performed Thy Word
This now resteth that I learn
From Thy skill a skillfull tast
Good from evill to discern
On Thy lawes whose trust is plac't

Yet unhumbled I did stray
Now I will Thy words obey
Thou that art so highly good
10   Nothing can Thy goodness reach
Thou where floweth bountys flood
Willing me Thy statutes teach.

What if proud men on me ly
I will on Thy Lawes rely
Wallow they in their delights
Fatt in body, fatt in mind
I the pleasures of my sp'rits
Will unto Thy Doctrin bind

Now I find the good of Woe
20   How Thy hests it makes me know
Of whose mouth the lectures true
Are alone all wealth to me
Millions then, and mines adieu
Gold and Silver drosse you bee

K

Knitt and conformed by Thy hand
   Hath been evry part of me
Then make me well to understand
Conceiving All thou dost command
   That when me Thy fearers see
   They for me may justly joy
   Seing what I lookt from Thee
   On Thy word I now enjoy.

O Lord Thy judgments just I know
10   When Thy Scourges scourged me
Thou in that doing naught didst show
That might Thy promise overthrow
   Let mee then Thy Comfort see
   Kindly sent as Thou hast said
   Bring Thy mercys life from Thee
   On Thy lawes my joyes are layd

Let blame and shame the Proud betide
   Falsly who subverted me
Whose meditations shall not slide
20   But fast on Thy Commandments bide
   So shall I Thy Fearers see
   On my part who know Thy will
   While I purely worship Thee
   Blott nor blush my face shall fill.

L

Looking and longing for deliverance
Upon Thy promise, mightless is My mind
Sightlesse mine eyes, which often I advance
  Unto Thy word
  Thus praying, When O Lord
When will it be I shall Thy comfort find.

I like a smoked bottle am become
And yet the Wine of Thy commandments hold
Ay me! When shall I see the totall summ
10 Of all my woes
  When wilt Thou on my foes
Make wronged me Thy just revenge behold?

Their Pride hath digged pitts me to ensnare
Which with Thy teachings how doth it agree
True, or more truly Truth Thy præcepts are
  By falsehood they
  Would make of me their prey
Let truth O Lord from falsehood rescue me.

Nigh quite consum'd by them on earth I ly
20 Yet from Thy statutes never did I swerve
Lord of Thy goodness quicken me, and I
  Will still persue
  Thy Testimonys true
And all the biddings of Thy lipps observe.

M

 Most plainly Lord the frame of Sky
Doth show Thy word decayeth never
  And constant stay of Earth descry
Thy Word that staid it stayeth ever

For by Thy lawes they hold their standings
   Yea all Things do Thy Service try
But that I joyd in Thy commandings
   I had my self been sure to dye[1]

   Thy Word that hath revived me
10 I will retain forgetting never,
   Let me Thyne own be sav'd by Thee
Whose Statutes are my studys ever
I mark Thy will, the while their standings
   The wicked take my bane to bee
For I no close of Thy commandings
   Of best things else an end I see.

   N

   Nought can enough declare
   How I thy learning love
Wheron all day my meditation lyes
   By whose Edicts I prove
   Farr than my foes more wise
For they a wisdom never failing are

   My teachers all of Old
   May now come learn of me
Whose studyes tend but to Thy witnessd Will
10   Nay who most aged be
   Thought therfore most of skill
In skill I passe for I Thy præcepts hold

   I did reform my feet
   From evry wicked way
That they might firmly in Thy Statutes stand
   Nor ever did I stray
   From what Thy Lawes command
For I of Thee have learned what is meet.

[1] *My self had perisht utterly*, expungd.

How pleasing to my tast
20   How sweet Thy speeches bee
No touch of hony so affects my tongue
    From whose Edicts in me
    Hath such sure wisdom sprung
That all false wayes, quite out of love I cast.

O

O what a Lantern, what a Lamp of light
    Is Thy pure Word to me
To cleere my paths and guide my goings right
    I swear and sweare again
I of Thy statutes will Observer be
    Thou justly dost ordain.

The heavy weights of grief oppresse me sore
    Lord rayse me by Thy word
As Thou to me didst promise heretofore
10   And this unforced prayse
I for an Offring bring, Accept O Lord
    And shew to me Thy wayes.

What if my life ly naked in my hand
    To evry chance exposd
Should I forgett what Thou dost me command
    No, No I will not stray
From Thy Edicts, though round about enclosd
    With snares the wicked lay

Thy Testimonys as my heritage
20   I have retayned still:
And unto them my hearts delight engage
    My heart, which still dos bend
And only bend to do what Thou dost will
    And do it to the end.

P

People that inconstant be
Constant hatred have for me
But Thy Doctrin changeless ever
Holds my love that changeth never
For Thou the closet where I hide
The shield wherby I safe abide
My confidence expects Thy promise just.
Hence away you cursed crew
Gett you gon that ridd from you
I at better ease and leasure
May perform my Gods good pleasure
O Lord as Thou Thy word didst give
Sustain me so that I may live
Nor make me blush as frustrate of my trust.

Be my Pillar, be my stay
Safe then I shall swerve no way
All my Witt and understanding
Shall then work on Thy Commanding
For underfoot Thou treadst them all
Who swerving from Thy Præcepts fall
And vainly in their guile and treason trust
Yea the wicked sort by Thee
All as drosse abjected be
Therfore what Thy Proof approveth
That my love entirely loveth
And such regard of Thee I make
For feare of Thee my flesh doth quake
And of Thy Lawes, Thy Lawes severely just.

Q

Quit and cleare from doing wrong
O let me not betrayed be
Unto them who ever strong
Do wrongly seek to ruin me

Nay my Lord
    Baile Thy servant on Thy word
And let not these that soare so high
By my low stoop yet higher fly

    Eye doth faile while I[1] not faile
10 With eye Thy safety to persue
    Looking when will once prevaile
And take effect Thy promise true
        All I crave
    I at[2] mercys hand would have.
And from Thy Wisdom, which I pray
May cause me know Thy law and way

    Since Thy Servant still I stay
My understanding Lord enlight
    So enlight it that I may
20 Thy Ordinances know aright
        Now, O now
    [3]Time requires O Lord that Thou
Thy Laws defence shouldst undertake
For now Thy Law doth sorely shake

    Hope wherof makes that more deare
I Thy Edicts and Statutes hold
    Than if Gold to me they were
Yea than they were the purest Gold.
        Makes that right
30   Are[4] thy Præcepts in my sight
Makes that I hate each lying way
That from their truth may cause me stray.

---

[1] *I do*, expunged.
[2] *thy*, expunged.
[3] *The*, expunged.
[4] *all*, expunged.

R

Right wonderfull Thy Testimonys be
   My heart to keep them I therfore bend
      Their very threshold gives men light
         And gives men sight
         That light to see
Yea ev'en to Babes doth understanding lend.

Opening my mouth I drank a greedy draught
   And did on them my whole pleasure place
      Look then O Lord and pitty me
10   As erst I see
         Ordaind and taught
By Thee for them whose hearts Thy name embrace

Of all my goings make thy Word the[1] guide
   Nor let injustice upon me reign
      From them that false accusers be
         Lord set me free
         So never slide
Shall I from what Thy statutes do ordeine

Shine on Thy Servants with Thy Faces beames
20   And throughly me Thy commandments teach
      From ffountains of whose watry eyes
         Do welling rise
         Of teares huge streames
Viewing each where Thy Doctrins dayly breach.

S[1]

   Sure Lord Thy Self art just
   And sure Thy lawes be right
   Which justly Thou and rightly dost

[1] *my*, expunged.

[1] This whole part is crossd and in the margin *Quaere* is written.

Command us still to lay
Before our carefull sight
To rule our words, and guide our way.

How neare my heart it goes
And pains me to endure
Thy Words forgotten by Thy foes!
10   Whose pureness doth excell
What is of all most pure
By me Thy Servant loved well

Who though to them most base
And most despisd I grew
Oblivion yet could not deface
Thy Statutes in my breast
For ay Thy Truth most true
And justice still most just doth rest.

Oppression heavy lay
20   And anguish wrung me sore
Yet were Thy præcepts still my joy
Thy præcepts which remaine
Must just for ever more
O teach me, and my life sustaine.

T

To Thee my hearty plaint I send
Lord turn Thyn eare
My plaint to heare
For to Thy law my life I bend
Since I have invoaked Thee
Let me Lord Thy succour see
And what Thy Ordinances will
I will persist observing still.

My cry more early than the day
10   Doth dayly rise
        Because mine eyes
Upon Thy promise wayting stay
    Eyes I say, which still prevent
    Watches best to watchings bent
Esteming it but pleasing paines
To muse on that Thy Word contains.

O in Thy mercy heare my voice
        And as Thy lawes
        Afford the cause
20 So make me Lord reviv'd rejoyce
    Lord Thou seest the graceless crew
    Presse me neare, who me persue
As for the Doctrin of Thy law
They farr from it themselves withdraw.

That Lord Thou seest, and this I see
        Thou evry where
        To me art neare
For true, nay Truth Thy Præcepts be
    Now, though not now first I know
30   For I knew it long agoe
That firmly founded once by Thee
Thy Ordinance no end can see

V

View how I am distressed
And let me be released
For look what me Thy Word hath bidden
Out of mind hath never slidden
    Then bee my Causes Deemer
    Bee then my Souls Redeemer
And as good hope Thy Word doth give me
Let with good help Thy Work redeem me
    Where wickedness is loved
10   There health is farr removed

For since Thy Sole Edicts contain it
Who search not them how can they gain it?
   Thy mercys are so many
   Their number is not any
Then as Thou usest Lord to use me
Revive me now and not refuse me
   Exceding is their number
   That me persue and cumber
Yet what Thy Witness hath defined
20   From that my stepps have not declined.
   I saw and grieved seing
   Their ways who wayward being
With guilfull stubborness withstanded
What by Thy speeches was commanded
   Since therfore plain is proved
   That I Thy laws have loved
Look Lord and heare, Thy bounty showing
Restore my life now feeble growing.
   This in Thy Doctrin reigneth
30   It naught but Truth containeth
This in Thy justice brightly shineth
Thy just Edicts no date defineth.

W[1]

Without all cause the mightyest Peeres
Do me persue but all my Feares
   Herin do end
Least that I should against Thy Word[2] offend
   Thy word wherin I so[3] delight
   As he who after happy fight
     Finds precious spoiles
Sweet recompense of passed painfull toiles[4]

[1] This Part Crost and in the margin *Quaere*.
[2] *law*, expunged.
[3] *do*, expunged.
[4] *foiles*, expunged.

It canot be but I must hate
10 And hate is more than common rate
What fals doth prove
Since on Thy Doctrin true is built my love
The Sun his light doth never bring
But seven times Thy prayse I sing
My Theme I make
The punishments Thou dost in justice take
I know to him that loveth Thee
Shall peace, and peace in plenty be
That no unrest
20 To him shall fall, no trouble him molest
That makes I never make an end
Thy saving succour to attend
Performing still
All that I find præscribed by Thy will.
That makes my carefull heart doth hold
The Words Thy witnesst will enfold
Loving them so
That greater love in heart can hardly grow
That makes my self well keeping stand
30 Both them and that Thy Words command
Knowing to Thee
No deedes of mine unknown can ever be

Y

Yeild me this favour Lord
My plaint may presse into Thy sight
And make me understand aright
According to Thy Word
Admitt to sight I say
The prayër that to Thee I send
And unto me Thy help extend
Who on Thy promise stay
Then from my lipps shall flow
10 An holy hymn of prayse to Thee
When I Thy scholar taught shall be
By Thee Thy lawes to know

Then shall my tongue declare
And teach again what Thou hast taught
All whose Decrees to tryall brought
    Most just nay justice are.
    O then reach out Thy hand
And yeild me ayd I justly crave
Since all things I forsaken have
20   And chosen Thy command.
    I look, I long, O Lord
To see at length Thy saving grace
And only do my gladness place
    In Thy glad–making Word
    I know my soul shall live
And living Thee due honour yeild
I know Thy law shall be my sheild
    And me all succour give
    As sheep from shepheard gon
30 So wander I, O seek Thy sheep
Whoso in mind Thy Præcepts keep
    That I forget not One.

Psalm 120, *Ad dominum*[1]

As to th'Eternall often in anguishes
Earst have I called never unanswered
    Again I call, again I calling
    Doubt not again to receive an answer
Lord ridd my soul from treasonous eloquence
Of filthy forgers craftily fraudulent
    And from the tongue where lodg'd resideth
    Poisned abuse ruin of beleivers
Thou that reposest vainly thy confidence
10 In wyly wronging say by thy forgery

---

[1] This and the seven following Psalms without Rhymes seem to be made in Imitacion of the Greek and Latin lyrics, by quantity of syllables and diversity of foot, a project about Sir Philips age, though our language is not suited so well for it.

What good to thee, what gain redoundeth
What benefit from a tongue deceitfull?
Though like an arrow strongly delivered
It deeply peirce though like to a Juniper
   It coales do cast which quickly fired
   Flame very hott, very hardly quenching.
Ah God, too long here I wander bannished
Too long abiding barbarous injury
   With Kedor and with Mesec harbor'd
20   How? In a tent in a housles harbor
Too long alas, too long, have I dwelled here
With friendly Peaces furious Enemys
   Who when to peace I seek to call them
   Faster I find to the warr they arm them.

Psalm 122, *Lætatus sum*[1]

O what lively delight, O what a jollity
This newes unto me brought newly delivered
That Gods house ruined should be reedifyd
And that shortly we should evry man enter it
   O now Thy galerys lovely Jerusalem
Thy gates shall be my rest, now not unordered
Nor wide scatred as erst, but very citty-like
All commoned in One shall be Jerusalem
   Now there convenient place to the company
10 Gods hand hath gathered shall be alotted out
His passed benefitts jointly to testify
And so prayse him as once praysed him Israël
   Now there shall be the seat, where to be justiced
All shall freely resort weary of injuryes
Seat, whose lofty receit loftily may receive
Davids posterity royaly honored
   Pray then, we I say Peace to Jerusalem
   To you Prosperity friends to Jerusalem

[1] In the margin Quære the Psalm itself crost.

Thy walls thy joïfull fortifications
20 Peace and plenty betide never abandoning
   With good reason I now wish Thee al happyness
Whose blisse is generall unto my Countrymen
With good cause shal I pray dayly Thy bettering
Where Gods Mansion is now to be edifyd.

Psalm 123, *Ad te levavi*

Unto Thee Oppressed Thou great Commander of heavën
   Hev'nly God attending, lift I my earthy seing
Right as a Waiters eye on gracefull Master is holden
   As the look of Waitresse fixt on a lady lyeth
So with erected face untill by thy mercy releived
   O Lord expecting begg wee thy friendly favour
Scorn of proud Scorners, reproach of mighty reproachers
   Our Sprits cleane ruined fills with an inly dolour.
Then friend us, favour us Lord then with mercy releive us
10   Whose scornfull misery greatly Thy mercy needeth.

Psalm 125, *Qui confidunt*

As Sion standeth very firmly stedfast
Never once shaking, so on high Jehova
Who his hope buildeth very firmly stedfast
     Ever abideth.

As Salem braveth with her hilly bulwarks
Roundly enforced, so the Great Jehova
Closeth his Servants as a hilly bulwark
     Ever abiding

Though Tyrants hard yoake with a heavy pressure
10 Wring the just shoulders, but awhile it holdeth
Least the best minded by too hard abusing
       Bend to abuses.

As your well workers[1] so the right beleivers
Lord favour farther, but a vain deceiver
Whose wryed footing not aright directed
       Wandereth in error

Lord him abjected set among the number
Whose doings lawless study bent to mischeife
Mischeif expecteth, but upon Thy chosen
20   Peace be for ever

Psalm 126, In convertendo

   When long absent from lovëly Sion
By the Lords conduct home we returned
We our own senses scarcely beleiving
Thought meere visions moved our fancy
   Then in our merry mouths laughter abounded
Tongues with gladness lowdly resounded
While thus wondring Nations whisperd
God with them most royally dealeth.
   Most true with us Thou royaly dealest
10 Woe is expired sorrow is vanished
Now Lord to finish throughly Thy working
Bring to Jerusalem all that are exiles.
   Bring to Jerusalem all that are exiles
So by Thy comfort lively refreshed
As when southern sunburnt Regions
Be by Cold fountains freshly releived.[1]

[1] *doers*, expunged.

[1] Written as I judg by the Author himself and added.

Oft to the ploughman, so good hap hapneth
What with teares to the ground he bequeatheth
Season of harvest timely returning
20 He before wofull joyfuly reapeth.
    Why to us may not as happily happen
To sow our buisiness wofuly weeping
Yet when buisiness growes to due ripeness
To see our buisiness joyfuly reaped

Psalm 127, Nisi quia

The house Jehova builds not	We vainly strive to build it
The Town Jehova guards not	We vainly watch to guard it.
No use of early rising	As useless is our watching
Not ought at all it helps thee	To eat Thy bread with anguish
As unto weary senses	A sleepy rest unasked
So bounty cometh uncausd	From him to his beloved
No not Thy children hast Thou	By choice by chance by nature
They are they are Jehovas	Rewards from him rewarding
The multitude of infants	A good man holds resembleth
The multitude of arrowes	A mighty archer holdeth.
His[1] happyness triumpheth	Who beare a quiver of them
No countenance of haters	Shall unto him be dreadfull.

10 (line number beside "The multitude of arrowes")

Psalm 128, Beati omnes

All happyness shall Thee betide
    That dost Jehova feare
And walking in the paths abide
    By him first trodden were

[1] *This*, expunged.

The labours of Thy hands
Deserved fruit shall beare
And where Thy dwelling stands
All blisse, all plenty there.

Thy Wife a vine a fruitfull vine
10   Shall in Thy parlour spring
Thy table compasse children thine
    As olive plants in ring
    On Thee I say on Thee
    That fear'st the heav'nly King
    Such happyness shall he
    He shall from Sion bring.

Yea while to Thee Thy breath shall hold
    Though longest running race
Thou Salem ever shalt behold
20   In wealth and wished case
    And childrens children view
    While Jacobs dwelling place
    No plagues of Warr persue
    But gifts of peace shall grace

Psalm 129, Saepe expugnaverunt

Oft and ever from my youth
    So now Israel may say
Israël may say for truth
    Oft and ever my decay
From my youth their force hath sought
Yet effect it never brought.

Unto them my back did yeild
    Place and plain[1] (O hight of Wo)
Where as in a plowed feild

---

[1] *of pain*, expunged.

10   Long and deep did furrows go
But O just Jehova who
Hast their plowropes cutt in two

Tell me you that Sion hate
    What you think shall be your end?
Terror shall your minds amate
    Blush and shame your faces shend,
Mark your wheat on houses top
Such your harvest such your crop

Wither shall you where you stand
20   Gatherd? no, but wanting sap
Filling neither reapers hand
    Nor the binders inbow'd lapp
Nay who you shall reap or bind
Comon kindness shall not find.

Such as travail by the way
    Wheras they their pains employ
Shall not once saluting say
    God speed friends, God give you joy
He in whom all blessing reigns
30   Blesse yourselves, and blesse your pains.

Psalm 130, De profundis

    From depth of greif
    Where droun'd I ly
    Lord for releife
    To Thee I cry
My ernest, vehement crying praying
Grant quick attending hearing weighing.

    O Lord if Thou
    Offences mark
    Who shall not bow

10   To beare the cark
        But with thy justice mercy dwelleth
        Wherby[1] thy worship more excelleth.

            On Thee[2] my soul
            On Thee O Lord
            Dependeth whole
            And on Thy Word
        Though sore with blott of sin defaced
        Yet surest hope hath firmly placed

            Who longest watch
20   Who soonest rise
            Can nothing match
            The early eyes
        The greedy eyes my soule erecteth
        While Gods true promise it expecteth.

            Then Israel
            On God attend
            Attend him well
            Who still Thy friend
        In kindness hath Thee deare esteemëd
30   And often, often erst redeem'd.

            Now as before
            Unchanged hee
            Will Thee restore
            Thy state will free
        All wickedness from Jacob driving
        Forgetting follys faults forgiving.[3]

[1] *and makes*, expunged.
[2] *yea makes*, expunged.
[3] But from this place to the end my Copy is defective, the leaves being torn off. Ita testor Sam[uel] Woodforde who for sir Philip Sidnys sake, and to preserve such a remaine of him undertook this tiresome task of transcribing. 1694/5.

Psalm 132, *Memento Domine*

Lord call to mynde, lord keepe in mynde:
   Thy David, and thy Davids paines
whoe once by oathe, and vowe did bynde
   himself to him, whoe aye remaines
     That mightie one
     The God in Jacob knowne.

My howse shall never harbour mee
   nor bedd allowe my bodie rest:
Nor eyes of sleepe, the lodging be
10   nor eyelidds slenderest slumbers nest
     untill I finde
     a plott to please my mynde.

I finde I saie, my mynde to please:
   a plott, whereon I maie erect
A howse for him to dwell at ease
   whoe is ador'd with due respect
     That mightie one
     The God in Jacob knowne.

The plott thy David then did name
20   wee heard at Ephrata it laie:
Wee heard, but bent to finde the same,
   were faine to seeke another waie
     ev'n to the fields
     that woodie Jear yeelds.

And yet not there, but here, O here,
   wee finde now settled what wee sought
before the Stoole, thy foote doth beare
   nowe entring in, wee as wee ought
     adore thee will
30   and dulie worshipp still.

Then enter lord, thy fixed rest
  with Arke the token of thy strength
And let thy Priests be purelie drest
  In robes of Justice laide at length.
    Let them be gladd
    thy gracefull blisse have hadd.

For David once thy servants sake,
  Doe not oure Kinge his seede reject:
ffor thou to him this oath didst make:
40   This endles oath: I will erect
    and howld thy race
    enthron'd in royall place.

Naie if thy race my league observe
  and keepe the Covenants I sett downe:
Theire race againe I will preserve
  Eternally to weare thy Crowne
    no lesse thy throane
    shall ever be theire owne

For Sion, which I loved best,
50 I chosen have no seate of chaunge:
heere heere shalbe my endles rest,
  heere will I dwell nor hence will raunge
    unto the place
    I beare such love, and grace

Such grace, and love, that evermore
  as blisse from gracious loving mee
shall blesse her victuall, blesse her store,
  that ev'n the poore, whoe in her be
    with store of bread
60   shall fully all be fedd

In her, my priests shall nought annoye
  naie cladd they shall with safetie be:
O howe in her with cawse shall joye,

whoe there as Tennants howld of mee
    whose tenure is
    by grace the fields of blisse.

O howe in her shall sprowte, and springe
    the Scepter Davids hand did beare:
howe I my Christ, my sacred kinge
70   as light in lanthorne placed there
        with beames divine
        will make abrode to shine.

But as for them, whoe spite and hate
    conceave to him, they all shall downe:
Downecast by mee, to shamefull state:
    while on him himself his happie Crowne
        shall up to skies
        with fame and glorie rise.

Psalm 133, Ecce quam

Howe good, and how beseeming well
    it is that wee
    whoe brethren be
as brethren should, in Concord dwell.

Like that deere oile that Aron beares
    which fleeting downe
    to foote, from Crowne
embalmes his bearde and robe he weares:

Or like the teares the morne doth shedd
10   which lie on ground
        empearled round
on Sion, or on Hermons head.

For join'd therewith, the Lord doth give
    such grace, such blisse
    That where it is
men maie for ever blessed live.

Psalm 135, Laudate Nomen

O praise the name, whereby the Lord is knowne
    praise him I saie you that his Servants be:
You whose attendance in his howse is showne,
    and in the Courtes before his howse wee see.
    Praise God, right termed God, for good is he,
      O sweetelie singe,
    unto his name, the sweetest sweetest thinge

For of his goodnes Jacob hath he chose,
    chose Israel his owne Demaine to bee:
10 My tongue shall speake, for well my conscience knowes
    greate is oure God, above all Gods is he.
    each branch of whose inviolable decree
      both Heavens doe keepe
    and Earth, and Sea, and Seas unsounded deepe.

From whose extreames drawne up by his comaund
    In flakie mistes, the reaking vapors rise:
Then high in Clowdes incorporate they stand:
    laste owte of Clowdes raine flowes and lightning flies.
    No lesse a treasure in his storehouse lies
20   Of breathing blasts
    which oft drawne foorth, in winde his pleasure wasts.

He from best man, to most despised beaste
    Egipts firste borne in one night overthrewe:
And yet not so his dreadfull showes he ceaste,
    but did them still in Egipts midst renewe.

not onelie meaner men had cawse to rue,
　　But ev'n the best
　　of Pharaos courte, the king among the rest.

He manie nations mightie kings destroy'd:
30　　Sehon for one, whoe ruld the Amorites,
And huge limbd Oge, whoe Basans crowne enjoy'd,
　　yea all the kingdoms of the Canaanites.
　　whose heritage, he gave the Isralites
　　　His chosen traine
　　　theire heritage for ever to remaine.

Therefore O Lord, thy name is famous still
　　the memorie thy auncient woonders gott:
Time well to world, his message maie fullfill
　　and backe returne to thee, yet never blott
40　　out of oure thoughts, for how can be forgott,
　　　The Lord that soe
　　　forgives his servants, plagues his Servants foe.

What difference, what unproportioned odds,
　　to thee, theis Idolls, gould and silver beare?
which men have made, yet men have made theire Godds:
　　whoe though mouth, eye, and eare, and nose they weare
　　yet neither speake, nor looke, nor smell nor heare.
　　　O Idolls right
　　　whoe Idolls make, or Idolls make your might.

50　But you that are of Israels descent,
　　O praise the Lord, you that of Aron came:
O praise the Lord, you Levies howse assent
　　to praise the Lord you all his fearers frame:
　　your highest praise, to praise Jehovas name.
　　　His praises still
　　　Salem resound, resound O Sion hill.

Psalm 137, Super flumina

Nigh seated where the river flowes
   that watreth Babells thankfull plaine
which then our teares in pearled rowes
   Did help to water with theire rayne
The thought of Sion bredd such woes,
    that though our Harpes we did retaine
      yet useles, and untouched there
      On willowes onelie hang'd they were.

Nowe while our Harpes were hanged soe
10   the men whose captives then wee laie:
Did on oure griefes insulting growe,
   and more to grieve us, thus did saie:
You that of musicke make such showe,
    Come singe us now a Sion laie
      O no, wee have nor voice nor hand
      for such a songe in such a land.

Though farr I lie sweete Sion hill
   in forraigne Soile exilde from thee:
Yet let my hand forgett his skill
20   if ever thou forgotten be
And let my tongue fast glued still
   unto my roofe, lie mute in mee:
      If thy neglect within mee spring
      or ought I doe, but Salem singe.

But thou O Lord, shalt not forgett:
   to quitt the paines of Edoms race:
whoe cawseleslie, yet hottlie sett
   thy holie Cittie to deface.
Did thus the bloodie Victors whett
30   what time they entred first the place:
      Downe, downe with it at anie hand
      make all platt pais, let nothing stand.

And Babilon, that didst us waste,
   thy selfe shall one daie wasted be:
And happie he, whoe what thou haste
   unto us don, shall doe to thee.
Like bitternes shall make thee taste
   like woefull objects cause thee see,
     Yea happie whoe, thy litle ones
40   shall take, and dashe against the stones.

Psalm 139, Domine probasti

O lord in mee, there lieth nought
   but to thy search revealed lies
     for when I sitt
     thou markest it
no lesse thou notest when I rise
yea closest Closett of my thought
   hath open windowes to thine eyes.

Thou walkest with mee, when I walke,
   when to my bedd for rest I goe
10   I finde thee there
     and ev'rie where
not youngest thought in mee doth growe,
No not one word I caste to talke
   but yet unuttred thou dost knowe

If foorth I march, thou goest before
   If back I turne, thou com'st behinde:
     So foorth nor backe,
     thy guard I lacke
Naye on mee to thy hand I finde
20   well I thy wisdome maie adore
   but never reach with Earthie mynde.

To shunne thy notice leave thine eye,
   O whither might I take my waie?
     To Starrie Spheare?
     thy throne is there.
   To dead mens undelightsome staie,
There is thy walke, and there to lie
   unknowne, in vaine I should assaie.

O Sunne, whome light, nor flight can match:
30   Suppose thy lightfull flightfull winges
     Thou lend to mee
     and I could flee
   as farr as thee, the ev'ning brings
Ev'n ledd to west, he would mee Catch
   nor should I lurke with westerne things.

Doe thou thy best O secret night,
   In sable vaile to cover mee:
     Thy sable vaile
     shall vainelie faile
40   with daie unmaskt my night shalbe,
For night is daie, and darknes light
   O father of all lightes to thee.

Each innmoste peece in mee is thyne,
   while yet I in my Mother dwelt:
     All that mee cladd
     from thee I hadd
   thou in my frame, haste straungelie dealt,
Needes in my praise, thy workes must shyne
   so inly them my thoughts have felt.

50   Thou, how my backe was beamewise laide
   and raftering of my ribbs do'st knowe:
     know'st everie pointe
     of bone and jointe
   how to this whole theis partes did growe
In brave imbrodrie faire array'd
   though wrought in shopp both darke, and lowe.

Naie fashionles one forme I tooke,
   thy all, and more, behoulding eye
      My shapeles shape
60   could not escape
   all theis with times appointed by
Ere one had being, in the booke
   of thy foresight enrowld did lie

My God, howe I theis studies prize,
   that doe thy hidden workings showe:
      whose some is such:
      no some so much,
   Naie sum'd as sand they summeles growe
I lie to sleepe, from sleepe I rise
70   yet still in thought with thee I goe.

My God, if thou, but one would'st kill
   then straight would leave my further chase:
      This Curssed broode
      inur'd to blood,
   whose graceles taunts at thy disgrace
have aymed ofte, and hating still
   would with prowde lies thy truth outface.

Hate not I them, whoe thee doe hate?
   thine Lord, I will the censure be:
80   Detest I not,
      the Cankred knott,
   whome I against thee banded see?
O Lord, thou know'st in highest rate,
   I hate them all as foes to mee.

Search mee my God, and prove my hart
   Examyn mee, and trie my thought:
      And marke in mee,
      if ought there be,
   that hath with cawse theire anger wrought.
90 If not (as not) my lives each parte
   Lord safelie guide from daunger brought.

Psalm 140, Eripe me

Protect mee lord, preserve mee, sett mee free,
from men that be, so vile, so violent:
in whose intent, both force, and frawde doth lurke,
my bane to worke, whose tongues are sharper thinges
then Adders stinges, whose rustie lipps enclose,
A poisoned hoord, such in the Aspick growes.

Save I saie lord, protect mee, sett mee free,
from those that be, so vile, so violent:
whose thoughts are spent, in thinking how they maie
10   My stepps betraie, how nett of fowle misshapp
maie mee intrapp, how hidd in traytor grasse
theire Cunning Cord, maie catch mee as I passe.

But this O Lord I hould my God art thou:
thou eare wilt bowe, what time thy aide I praie.
In thee my staie, Jehova, thou do'st arme,
against all harme, and guard my bedd in field.
O then to yeeld theis wicked theire desire
doe not accord, for still they will aspire.

But yeeld O lord, that ev'n the head of those
20   that me enclose, of this theire hott pursuite,
maye taste the fruite: with deadlie venom stronge
of theire owne tongue. Loe, loe, I see they shall
yea Coales shall fall, yea flames shall flinge them low
aye unrestor'd to drowne in deepest woe.

For lyers Lord, shall never firmelie stand,
and from the land whoe violentlie live
mischiefe shall drive. But well I knowe the poore
thou wilt restore: restore th'afflicted wight.
That in thy sight, the just maie howses frame
30   and gladd record, the honnour of thy name.

Psalm 141, Domine clamavi

To thee Jehova thee I lifte my crieng voice
O banish all delaie, and let my plaintfull noise
   by thy quick-hearing eare, be carefully respected:
As sweete perfume to Skies, let what I praie ascend
Let theis up-lifted hands, which praieng I extend
   as ev'ning Sacrifize be unto thee dirrected.

Warde well my wordes (O Lord) for that it is I praie:
A watchfull Sentinell at my Mouthes passage laie,
   at Wicket of my lipps stand aye a faithfull porter:
10 Encline mee not to ill, nor let mee looselie goe
A mate in worke with such, whence no good worke doth
       growe,
   and in theire flattring baites, let mee be no Consorter.

But let the good man wound, most well I shall it take
yea price of his rebukes, as dearest baulme shall make:
   yea more shall for him praie, the more his wordes shall
       grieve mee
And as for theis, when once the leaders of theire crue:
by thee, be brought to stoope, my words most sweetelie
       true,
   shall in the rest so worke, that soone they shall believe
       mee.

Meane while my bones the grave, the grave expects my
       bones,
20 so broken, hewne, disperst, as least respected stones
   by careles Mason drawne, from cave of worthles quarrie:
But thou O Lord (my Lord) since this thy servants eye
repleate with hopefull truste, doth on thy helpe relie
   faile not that trustfull hope, that for thy help doth tarrie.

O soe dirrect my feete, they maie escape the hands
of theire intangling snare, which for me pitched stands:
   and from the wicked netts for mee, with crafte they cover:

Naie for theis fowlers once thyself a fowler be,
and make them fowlie fall, where netts are laid by thee
30   but where for mee they laie, let mee leape freelie over.

Psalm 142, *Voce mea*

My voice to thee it selfe extreamelie straining
    cries praieng lord, againe it crieng praieth
before thy face, the cause of my complaining:
    before thy face, my cases Mapp it laieth
        wherein my Soule is painted
            in doubtfull waies a straunger;
        But lord, thou art acquainted
        and knowest each pathe, where sticke the toiles of
                daunger.
For mee, myne eye to everie coaste dirrected
10   lights not on one that will so much as knowe mee
my life by all neglected
        ev'n hope of helpe is nowe quite perisht from mee.

Then with good cawse, to thee my spirit flieth:
    flieth and saith: O lord my safe abiding
abides in thee, in thee all onelie lieth
    Lott of my life, and plott of my residing.
        Alas, then yeeld me hearing
            for weeryeng woes have spent mee
        And save mee from theire tearing
20   whoe hunte mee hard, and dailie worsse torment
                mee.
O chaunge my state, unthrall my Soule inthralled:
    Of my escape then will I tell the storie:
And with a crowne enwalled
    Of godlie men, will glorie in thy glorye.

Psalm 143, Domine exaudi

Heare my intreatie lord, the suite I send
  with heede attend:
    And as my hope, and trust is
      reposed whole in thee
    soe in thy truth and justice
      yeeld audience to mee.
    And make not least begining
    to judge thy servants sinning
      For Lord what living wight
10   lives sinneles in thy sight.

O rather look with ruth upon my woes,
  whome rutheles foes,
    with longe pursuite have chased,
      and chased nowe hath caught
    and caught in Toombe have placed
      with dead men out of thought.
    Aye mee, what now is lefte mee,
    alas all knowledg refte mee
      All courage faintelie fledd
20   I have nor harte nor head.

The best I can, is this, nay this is all:
  that I can call
    before my thoughts surveyeng
      times evidences ould
    all Deedes with comfort weyeng
      that thy hand writing hould.
    So hand and hart conspiring
    I lifte noe lesse desiring
      Thy grace I maie obtaine
30   then drought desireth raine.

Leave then delaie, and let his crie prevaile
  whome force doth faile.
    or let thy face be hidden
      from one, whoe maie compare
    with them whose Death hath bidden
      adiew to life and care.
    My hopes, let mercies morrowe,
    soone chase my night of sorrowe:
      My help, appoint my waie
40   I maie not wandring straie.

My cave, the closet, where I woonte to hide,
  In troublous tide:
    Nowe from those troubles save mee
      and since my God thou art,
    prescribe howe thou wouldst save mee
      performe my duties parte
    And least awrie I wander,
    in walking this Meander:
      Be thy right Spirite my guide,
50   to guard I goe not wide.

Thy honnour, justice, mercie crave of thee
  O Lord that mee
    reviv'd, thou shouldst deliver
      from pressure of my woes
    and in destructions river
      engulfe, and swallowe those
    whose hate thus makes in anguish
    my Soule afflicted languish
      for meete it is so kinde
60   thy servant should thee finde.

Psalm 144, Benedictus Dominus

Praisd be the lord of might
    my Rocke in all allarmes:
by whome my handes doe fight
    my fingers mannage Armes
My grace, my guard, my Forte,
    on whome my safetie staies
to whome my hopes resorte
    by whome my realme obaies.

Lord what is man that thou,
10   shouldst tender so his fare?
what hath his child to bowe
    thy thoughts unto his care?
whose neerest kynn is nought,
    no image of whose daies
more livelie can be thought
    then shade that never staies.

Lord bend thy arched skies
    with ease to let thee downe:
And make the stormes arrise
20   from mountaines fuming crowne:
Let followe flames from Skie
    to backe their stoutest stand
Let fast thy Arrowes flie
    dispersing thickest band.

Thy heav'nlie helpe extend
    and lifte mee from this flood:
Let mee thy hand defend,
    from hand of forraigne broode
Whose mouth no mouth at all,
30   but forge of false intent
whereto theire hand doth fall
    as aptest instrument.

Then in newe songe to thee,
    will I exaulte my voice:
Then shall O God with mee,
    my tenn string'd lute rejoice.
Rejoice in him I saie,
    whoe Royall right preserves
And saves from swordes decaie
40   his David that him serves.

O Lord thy helpe extend
    and lifte mee from this flood:
let mee thy hand defend,
    from hand of forraigne broode.
Whose mouth no mouth at all
    but forge of false intent
whereto theire hand doth fall
    as aptest instrument.

So then oure sonnes shall growe
50   as plants of timelie springe:
whome soone to fairest showe,
    theire happie growth doth bringe.
As Pillers both doth beare
    and garnish kingelie hall
Oure daughters straight, and faire
    each house embellish shall.

Oure store shall aye be full
    yea shall such fullnes finde:
Though all from thence wee pull
60   yet more shall rest behinde.
The Millions of encreasse,
    shall breake the woonted fowld
yea such the sheepie presse
    the streetes shall scantlie howld.

Oure heardes shall brave the best:
   abrode no foes allarme:
At home to breake our rest,
   no crie the voice of harme.
If blessed terme I maie,
70   on whome such blessings fall
Then blessed, blessed they
   theire God Jehova call.

Psalm 147, *Laudate dominum*

Sing to the lord, for what can better be
   then of our God, that wee the honnor singe?
with seemelie pleasure, what can more agree
   then praisefull voice, and touch of tuned string?
   for loe the lord, againe to forme doth bringe:
      Jerusalems longe ruinated walls,
and Jacobs howse, which all the Earth did see
     dispersed earst, to union now recalls.
        And now by him theire broken hartes made sound:
10   And now by him theire bleeding wounds are bound.

For what could not, whoe can the number tell
   of Starrs, the Torches of his heavnly hall:
And tell so redilie, he knoweth well,
   how everie starr by proper name to call.
   What greate to him? whose greatnes doth not fall
     within precincts? whose power, no lymitts staie?
Whose knowledges, all number so excell
     not numbring number can theire number laie:
        Easie to him, to lifte the lowelie juste:
20   Easie to downe prowde wicked to the Duste.

O then Jehova's cawsefull honnour singe.
   his whome oure God, wee by his goodnes finde:
O make harmonious mixe of voice, and stringe
   to him by whome the Skies, with cloudes are lyn'd.

by whome the rayne from cloudes to dropp assign'd:
supples the Clodds of sommer scorched fields
fresheth the Mountaines, with such needefull spring:
fuell of life to maintaine Cattell yeelds.
From whome younge Ravens, Careles oulde forsake
30   Croaking to him, of allmes, theire foode doe take.

The statelie shape, the force of bravest steede
is farr too weake, to worke in him delight
No more in him can anie pleasure breede,
in flieng footman, foote of nimblest flight.
Naie which is more his fearers in his sight
Can well of nothing but his bountie brave;
which never failing, never let them neede:
whoe fixte theire hopes upon his mercies have.
O then Jerusalem, Jehova praise
40   with honnour due, thy God, O Sion raise.

His strength it is, thy Gates doth surelie barr:
his grace in thee, thy children multiplies:
by him thy borders lie secure from Warr:
and finest flower, thy hunger sattisfies.
Nor meanes he needes, for faste his pleasure flies:
borne by his word, when ought him liste to bidd.
Snows woollie lockes, by him wide scattred are,
and hoarie plagues, with frost as Ashes hidd.
Grosse Icie gobbetts, from his hand he flings:
50   And blowes a could too stronge for strongest things.

He bidds againe, and Ice in water flowes
as water earste, in Ice Congealed laie:
Abrode the Southerne winde, his melter goes,
the streames relenting, take theire woonted waie.
O much is this, but more I come to saie:
The wordes of life he hath to Jacob towld:
Taught Israel, whoe by his teaching knowes,
what lawes in life, what rules he wills to howld.
No nation else, hath found him haulfe so kinde
60   for to his light, what other is not blynde.

Psalm 148, Laudate dominum

Inhabitants of heavenlie land,
   as loving subjects praise your kinge:
You that amongst them highest stand,
   in highest notes Jehova singe.
    Singe Angells all on carefull winge:
      you that his Herauldes flie:
    And you whome he doth Souldiers bringe,
      in field his force to trie.

O praise him Sunn, the Sea of light
10   O praise him Moone the light of sea:
You prettie Starres in robe of night
   as spangells twinckling, doe as they
    Thou Spheare within whose bosome plaie
      the rest that Earth emball
    You waters banke, with starrie baye
      O praise, O praise him all.

All theis I saie advaunce that name,
   that doth eternall being showe:
whoe bidding into forme and frame,
20   not being yet, they all did growe.
    All formed, framed, founded soe,
      till ages uttmost date,
    they place retaine, they order knowe
      they keepe theire first estate.

When Heaven hath praisd, praise Earth a newe:
   You Dragons first, her deepest guests:
Then soundles deepes, and what in you,
   residing lowe, or moves, or rests,
    you flames affrighting mortall brests,
30   you stones, that cloudes doe cast:
    you featherie snowes, from winters nests
      you vapours Sunnes apaste.

You boistrous windes, whose breath fullfills
   what in his word, his will setts downe:
Ambitious Mountaines, curteous hills
   you trees, that hills, and Mountaines crowne
   both you that proude of native ground,
      stand fresh or tall to see:
   And you that have your more renowne,
40   by what you beare then be.

You beastes in woodes, untam'd that raunge,
   you that with men familliar goe:
you that your place by creeping chaunge
   or ayrie streames with feathers rowe.
   you statelie kinges, you subjects lowe,
      you Lordes, and Judges all
   you others, whose distinctions showe
      howe sexe or age maie fall.

All theis, I saie, advaunce that name,
50   more high then skies, more lowe then grownd:
And since advaunced by the same,
   you Jacobs sonnes, stand chieflie bound:
   you Jacobs sonnes, be cheefe to sound,
      your God Jehova's praise,
   so fitt them well, on whome is fownd,
      the blisse on you he laies.

Psalm 150, Laudate Dominum

O lawde the lord, the God of hoasts commend,
   Exaulte his power, advaunce his holines.
   with all your might lifte his Allmightines:
Your greatest praise, upon his greatnes spend.
Make Trumpetts noise in shrillest notes ascend:
   Make, lute, and lire his loved fame expresse;
   him let the Pipe, him let the Tabret blesse:
him Organs breath, that windes or waters lend.

Let ringing Timbrells, so his honnour sownd,
  let sounding Cimballs, so his glorie ringe:
That in theire tunes such melodie be found,
  as fitts the pompe of most triumphant kinge.
    Conclude by all, that ayre or life enfould:
    let high Jehova highlie be extould.

* * *

A Dialogue betweene two shepheards, Thenot, *and* Piers, *in praise of Astrea, made by the excellent Lady, the Lady* Mary *Countesse of* Pembrook, *at the Queenes Majesties being at her house at Anno 15.*

Thenot I sing divine ASTREAS praise,
O Muses! help my wittes to raise,
  And heave my Verses higher.
Piers Thou needst the truth, but plainly tell,
Which much I doubt thou canst not well,
  Thou art so oft a lier.

Thenot If in my Song no more I show,
Than Heav'n, and Earth, and Sea do know,
  Then truely I have spoken.
Piers Sufficeth not no more to name,
But being no lesse, the like, the same,
  Else lawes of truth be broken.

Thenot Then say, she is so good, so faire,
With all the earth she may compare,
  Not *Momus* selfe denying.
Piers Compare may thinke where likenesse holds,
Nought like to her the earth enfoldes,
  I lookt to finde you lying.

Thenot   ASTREA sees with Wisedoms sight,
20   *Astrea* workes by Vertues might,
                   And joyntly both do stay in her.

Piers   Nay take from them, her hand, her minde,
                The one is lame, the other blinde,
                   Shall still your lying staine her?

Thenot   Soone as ASTREA shewes her face
                Strait every ill avoides the place,
                   And every good aboundeth.

Piers   Nay long before her face doth showe,
                The last doth come, the first doth goe,
30   How lowde this lie resoundeth!

Thenot   ASTREA is our chiefest joy,
                Our chiefest guarde against annoy,
                   Our chiefest wealth, our treasure.

Piers   Where chiefest are, three others bee,
                To us none else but only shee;
                   When wilt thou speake in measure?

Thenot   ASTREA may be justly sayd,
                A field in flowry Roabe arrayd,
                   In Season freshly springing.

40 *Piers*   That Spring indures but shortest time,
                This never leaves *Astreas* clime,
                   Thou liest, instead of singing.

Thenot   As heavenly light that guides the day,
                Right so doth thine each lovely Ray,
                   That from *Astrea* flyeth.

Piers   Nay, darknes oft that light enclowdes,
                Astreas beames no darknes shrowdes;
                   How lowdly *Thenot* lyeth!

Thenot   ASTREA rightly terme I may,
50   A manly Palme, a Maiden Bay,
                   Her verdure never dying.

Piers	Palme oft is crooked, Bay is lowe,
	Shee still upright, still high doth growe,
	Good *Thenot* leave thy lying.

Thenot	Then *Piers*, of friendship tell me why,
	My meaning true, my words should ly,
	And strive in vaine to raise her.
Piers	Words from conceit do only rise,
	Above conceit her honour flies;
	But silence, nought can praise her.

60

*   *   *

THE TRIUMPH OF DEATH
TRANSLATED OUT OF ITALIAN BY
THE COUNTESSE OF PEMBROOKE

The first chapter

That gallant Ladie, gloriouslie bright,
The statelie piller once of worthinesse,
And now, a little dust, a naked spright:
Turn'd from hir warres a joyefull Conqueresse:
Hir warres, where she had foyl'd the mightie foe,
whose wylie stratagems the world distresse.
And foyl'd him, not with sword, with speare or bowe,
But with chaste heart, faire visage, upright thought,
wise speache, which did with honor linked goe:
And love's new plight to see strange wonders wrought
with shivered bowe, chaste arrowes, quenched flame,
while-here som slaine, and there laye others caught.
She, and the rest, who in the glorious fame
Of the exploit, hir chosen mates, did share,
All in one squadronet close ranged came.

10

A few, for nature makes true glorie rare,
But eache alone (so each alone did shine)
Claym'd whole Historian's, whole Poete's care.
Borne in greene field, a snowy Ermiline
20 Colored with topaces, sett in fine golde
was this faire companies unfoyled signe.
No earthlie march, but heavenly, did they hould;
Their speaches holie were, and happie those,
who so are borne, to be with them enroll'd.
Cleare starrs they send, which did a Sunne unclose,
who hyding none, yett all did beawtifie
with Coronets deckt with violet and rose;
And as gain'd honor, filled with jollitie
Eache gentle heart, so made they merrie cheere,
30 when loe, an ensigne sad I might descrie,
Black, and in black, a woman did appeere,
Furie with hir, such as I scarcelie knowe
If lyke at Phlegra with the Giants were.
Thou Dame, quoth she, that doeth so proudlie goe,
Standing upon thy youth, and beawties state,
And of thy life, the limits doest not knowe,
Loe, I am shee, so fierce, importunate,
And deafe, and blinde, entytled oft by you,
you, whom with night ere evening I awate.
40 I, to their end, the Greekish nation drewe,
The Trojan first, the Romane afterward,
with edge and point of this my blade I slewe.
And no Barbarian my blowe could warde,
who stealing on with unexpected wound,
Of idle thoughts have manie thousand marr'd.
And now no lesse to you-ward am I bound
while life is dearest, ere to cause you moane.
Fortune som bitter with your sweetes compound
To this, thou right or interrest hast none,
50 Little to me, but onelie to this spoile,
Replide then she, who in the world was one.
This charge of woe on others will recoyle,

I know, whose safetie on my life depends:
For me, I thank who shall me hence assoile.
As one whose eyes som noveltie attend,
And what it mark't not first, it spyde at last,
New wonders with it-self, now comprehends.
So far'd the cruell, deeplie over-gast
with doubt awhile, then spake, I know them now.
60   I now remember when my teethe they past.
Then with lesse frowning, and lesse darkned browe,
But thou that lead'st this goodlie companie,
Didst never yett unto my scepter bowe.
But on my counsell if thou wilt relye,
who maie inforce thee; better is by farre
From age and ages lothsomenesse to flye.
More honored by me, then others are
Thou shalt thee finde; and neither feare nor paine
The passage shall of thy departure barre.
70   As lykes that Lord, who in the heav'n doeth raigne,
And thence, this All, doeth moderatlie guide:
As others doe, I shall thee entretaine:
So answered she, and I with-all descryde
Of dead appeere a never-numbred summe,
Pestring the plaine, from one to th'other side.
From India, Spaine, Gattay, Marocco, Coome,
So manie Ages did together falle.
That worlds were fill'd, and yett they wanted roome.
There sawe I, whom their times did happie calle,
80   Popes, Emperors, and kings, but strangelie growen,
All naked now, all needie, beggars all.
Where is that wealth? where are those honors gonne?
Scepters, and crounes, and roabes, and purple dye?
And costlie myters, sett with pearle and stone?
O wretch, who doest in mortall things affye:
(yett who but doeth) and if in end they dye
Them-selves beguil'd, they find but right, saie I.
What meanes this toyle? Oh blinde, oh more then blinde:
you all returne, to your greate Mother, olde,
90   And hardlie leave your verie names behinde.
Bring me, who doeth your studies well behoulde,

And of your cares not manifestlie vaine,
One lett him tell me, when he all hath tolde.
So manie lands to winne, what bootes the payne?
And on strange lands, tributes to impose,
With hearts still griedie, their oune losse to gaine,
After all theise, wherin you winning loose
Treasures and territories deere bought with blood;
water, and bread hath a farre sweeter close.

100 And golde, and gemme gives place to glasse and wood:
But leaste I should too-long degression make
To turne to my first talke I think it good.
Now that short-glorious life hir leave to take
Did neere unto the uttmost instant goe,
And doubtfull stepp, at which the world doeth quake.
An other number then themselves did shewe
Of Ladies, such as bodies yett did lade,
If death could pitious be, they faine would knowe.
And deepe they did in contemplacion wade

110 Of that colde end, presented there to view,
which must be once, and must but once be made.
All friends and neighbors were this carefull crue
But death with ruthlesse hand on golden haire
Chosen from-out those amber-tresses drewe.
So cropt the flower, of all this world most faire,
To shewe upon the excellentest thing
Hir supreame force, and for no hate she bare.
How manie dropps did flowe from brynie spring
In who there sawe those sightfull fountaines drye,

120 For whom this heart so long did burne and spring.
For hir in midst of moane and miserie,
Now reaping once what vertues life did sowe,
With joye she sate retired silentlie.
In peace cryde they, right mortall Goddesse goe,
And so she was, but that in noe degree
Could death entreate, hir comming to forslowe.
What confidence for others? if that she
Could frye and freese in few nights changing cheere:
Oh humane hopes, how fond and false yow bee.

130 And for this gentle Soule, if manie a teare

By pittie shed, did bathe the ground and grasse,
who sawe, doeth knowe; think thou, that doest but heare.
The sixt of Aprill, one a clock it was
That tyde me once, and did me now untye,
Changing hir copie; Thus doeth fortune passe.
None so his thralle, as I my libertie;
None so his death, as I my life doe rue,
Staying with me, who faine from it would flye.
Due to the world, and to my yeares was due,
That I, as first I came, should first be gonne,
Not hir leafe quail'd, as yett but freshlie newe.
Now for my woe, guesse not by't, what is showne,
For I dare scarce once cast a thought there-too,
So farre I am of, in words to make it knowne.
Vertue is dead; and dead is beawtie too,
And dead is curtesie, in mournefull plight,
The ladies saide; And nowe, what shall we doe?
Never againe such grace shall blesse our sight;
Never lyke witt, shall we from woman heare,
And voice, repleate with Angell-lyke delight.
The Soule now prest to leave that bosome deare
Hir vertues all uniting now in one,
There, where it past did make the heavens cleare.
And of the enemies so hardlie none,
That once before his shew'd his face obscure
with hir assault, till death had thorough gonne.
Past plaint and feare when first they could endure
To hould their eyes on that faire visage bent,
And that dispaire had made them now secure.
Not as greate fyers violently spent,
But in them-selves consuming, so hir flight
Tooke that sweete spright, and past in peace content.
Right lyke unto som lamp of cleerest light,
Little and little wanting nutriture,
Houlding to end a never-changing plight.
Pale? no, but whitelie; and more whitelie pure,
Then snow on wyndless hill, that flaking falles:
As one, whom labor did to rest allure.
And when that heavenlie guest those mortall walles

140

150

160

170 Had leaft: it nought but sweetlie sleeping was
     In hir faire eyes: what follie dying calles
     Death faire did seeme to be in hir faire face.

The second chapter

     That night, which did the dreadfull happ ensue
     That quite eclips't; Naie rather did replace
     The Sunne in skyes, and me bereave of view
     Did sweetlie sprintle through the ayrie space
     The Summer frost which with Tithon's bryde
     Cleereth of dreame the darke-confused face,
     When loe, a Ladie, lyke unto the tyde
     with Orient jewells crown'd, from thousands moe
     Crouned as she; to me, I comming spyde:
10   And first hir hand, somtime desyred so
     Reaching to me; at-once she sygh't and spake:
     whence endlesse joyes yett in my heart doe growe
     And know'st thou hir, who made thee first forsake
     The vulgar path, and ordinarie trade?
     while hir, their marke, thy youthfull thoughts did make?
     Then doune she sate, and me sitt-doune she made,
     Thought, wisedom, Meekenesse in one grace did strive,
     Unpleasing bank in bay, and beeches shade.
     My Goddesse, who me did and doeth revive,
20   Can I but knowe? (I sobbing answered)
     But art thou dead? Ah speake, or yett alive?
     Alive am I: And thou as yett art dead,
     And as thou art shalt so continue still
     Till by thy ending hower, thou hence be led.
     Short is our time to live, and long our will:
     Then lett with heede, thy deedes and speaches goe.
     Ere that approaching terme his course fullfill.
     Quoth I, when this our light to end doeth growe,
     which we calle life (for thou by proofe hast tryde)
30   Is it such payne to dye? That, make me knowe.
     While thou (quoth she) the vulgar make thy guide,

And on their judgements (all obscurlie blynde)
Doest yett relye; no blisse can thee betyde.
Of lothsom prison to eache gentle mynde
Death is the end; And onelie who employe
Their cares on mudd, therin displeasure finde.
Even this my death, which yealds thee such annoye
Would make in thee farre greater gladnesse ryse,
Couldst thou but taste least portion of my joye.

40   So spake she with devoutlie-fixed eyes
Upon the Heavens: then did in silence foulde
Those rosie lips, attending there replyes;
Torments, invented by the Tyrrants olde;
Diseases, which each parte torment and tosse,
Causes, that death we most bitter houlde.
I not denye (quoth she) but that the crosse
Preceeding death, extreemlie martireth,
And more the feare of that eternall losse.
But when the panting soule in God takes breath;

50   And wearie heart affecteth heavenlie rest,
An unrepented syghe, not els, is death.
With bodie, but with spirit readie prest,
Now at the furthest of my living wayes,
There sadlie-uttered sounds my eare possest.
Oh happless he; who counting times and dayes
Thinks eache a thousand yeares, and lives in vayne
No more to meete hir while on earth he stayes.
And on the water now, now on the Maine
Onelie on hir doeth think, doeth speake, doeth write,

60   And in all times one manner still retaine.
Heere-with, I thither cast my failing-sight,
And soone espyde, presented to my view,
who oft did thee restraining, me encyte.
Well, I hir face, and well hir voice I knewe,
Which often did my heart reconsolate;
Now wiselie grave, then beawtifulie true.
And sure, when I, was in my fairest state,
My yeares most greene, my self to thee most deare,
whence manie much did think, and much debate.

70   That life's best joye, was all most bitter cheere,

Compared to that death, most myldlie sweete,
which coms to men, but coms not everie-where.
For I, that journie past with gladder feete,
Then he from hard exile, that homeward goes,
(But onelie ruth of thee) without regreete.
For that faith's sake, time once enough did shewe,
yett now to thee more manifestlie plaine,
In face of him, who all doeth see and knowe,
Saie Ladie, did you ever entretaine
80 Motion or thought more lovinglie to rue
(Not loving honor's-height) my tedious paine?
For those sweete wraths, those sweete disdaines in you,
In those sweete peaces written in your eye,
Diverslie manie yeares my fanzies drewe.
Scarce had I spoken, but in lightning wise
Beaming, I saw that gentle smile appeare,
Somtimes the Sunne of my woe-darkned skyes.
Then sighing, thus she answered: Never were
Our hearts but one, nor never two shall be:
90 Onelie thy flame I tempred with my cheere;
This onelie way could save both thee and me;
Our tender fame did this supporte require,
The mother hath a rodd, yett kinde is she.
How oft this saide my thoughts: In love, naie fire
Is he: now to provide must I beginne,
And ill providers are feare and desire.
Thou sawe'st what was without, not what within.
And as the brake the wanton steede doeth tame,
So this did thee from thy disorders winne.
100 A thousand times wrath in my face did flame,
My heart meane-while with love did inlie burne,
But never will my reason overcame:
For, if woe-vanquisht once, I sawe thee mourne;
Thy life, or honor, joyntlie to preserve,
Myne eyes to thee sweetelie did I turne.
But if thy passion did from reason swarve,
Feare in my words, and sorrowe in my face
Did then to thee for salutation serve.
Theis artes I us'd with thee; thou ran'st this race

110 With kinde acceptance; now sharp disdaine,
Thou know'st, and hast it sung in manie a place.
Somtimes thine eyes pregnant with tearie rayne
I sawe, and at the sight; Behould he dyes;
But if I help, saide I, the signes are plaine.
Vertue for ayde, did then with love advise:
If spurr'd by love, thou took'st som running toye,
So soft a bitt (quoth I) will not suffice.
Thus glad, and sad, in pleasure, and annoye;
whot red, colde pale: thus farre I have thee brought
120 wearie, but safe, to my no little joye.
Then I with teares, and trembling; what it sought
My faith hath found, whose more then equall meede
were this: if this, for truth could passe my thought.
Of little faith (quoth she) should this proceede,
If false it were, or if unknowne from me;
The flames withall seem'd in hir face to breede.
If lyking in myne eyes the world did see
I saie not, now, of this, right faine I am,
Those cheines that tyde my heart well lyked me.
130 And well me lykes (if true it be) my flame,
which farre and neere by thee related goes,
Nor in thy love could ought but measure blame.
That onelie fail'd; and while in acted woes
Thou needes wouldst shewe, what I could not but see,
Thou didst thy heart to all the world disclose.
Hence sprang my zeale, which yett distempreth thee,
Our concord such in everie thing beside,
As when united love and vertue be.
In equale flames our loving hearts were tryde,
140 At leaste when once thy love had notice gott,
But one to shewe, the other sought to hyde.
Thou didst for mercie calle with wearie throte
In feare and shame, I did in silence goe,
So much desire became of little note.
But not the less becoms concealed woe,
Nor greater growes it uttered, then before
Through fiction, Truth will neither ebbe nor flowe.
But clear'd I not the darkest mists of yore?

when I thy words alone did entertaine
150   Singing for thee? my love dares speake no more.
With thee my heart, to me I did restraine
Myne eyes; and thou thy share canst hardlie brooke
Lessing by me the lesse, the more to gayne.
Not thinking if a thousand times I tooke
Myne eyes from thee; I manie thousands cast
Myne eyes on thee; and still with pittying looke.
Whose shine no clowd had ever over-cast:
Had I not fear'd in thee those coles to fyre
I thought would burne too-dangerouslie fast.
160   But to content thee more ere I retyre
For end of this, I somthing will thee tell,
Perchance agreable to thy desire:
In all things fullie blest, and pleased well,
Onelie in this I did my-self displease;
Borne in too-base a towne for me to dwell:
And much I grieved, that for thy greater ease,
At leaste, it stood not neere thy flowrie nest.
Els farre-enough, from whence I did thee please.
So might the heart on which I onelie rest
170   Not knowing me, have fitt it-self elswhere,
And I lesse name, lesse notice have possest.
Oh no (quoth I) for, me, the heavens third spheare
To so high love advanc't by speciall grace,
Changelesse to me, though chang'd thy dwelling were.
Be as it will, yett my greate Honor was,
And is as yett (she saide) but thy delight
Makes thee not mark how fast the howers doe passe.
See from hir golden bed Aurora bright
To mortall eyes returning sunne and daye
180   Breast-high above the Ocean bare to sight.
Shee to my sorrowe, calles me hence awaie,
Therfore thy words in times short limits binde,
And saie in-brief, if more thou have to saie.
Ladie (quoth I) your words most sweetlie kinde
Have easie made, what ever erst I bare,
But what is left of you to live behinde,
Therfore to knowe this, my onlie care,

If sloe or swift shall com our meeting-daye.
She parting saide, As my conjectures are,
190   Thou without me long time on earth shalt staie.

Marie Sydney Countesse of Pembroke

AEMILIA LANYER

SALVE DEUS REX JUDÆORUM

Containing,

1. The Passion of Christ,
2. Eves Apologie in defence of Women.
3. The Teares of the Daughters of Jerusalem.
4. The Salutation and Sorrow of the Virgine Marie
With divers other things not unfit to be read.

Written by Mistris *Æmilia Lanyer*, Wife to Captaine *Alfonso Lanyer*, Servant to the Kings Majestie.

To the Queenes most Excellent Majestie

Renowned Empresse, and great Britaines Queene,
Most gratious Mother of succeeding Kings;
Vouchsafe to view that which is seldome seene,
A Womans writing of divinest things:
　　Reade it faire Queene, though it defective be,
　　Your excellence can grace both It and Mee.

For you have rifled Nature of her store,
And all the Goddesses have dispossest
Of those rich gifts which they enjoy'd before,
But now great Queene, in you they all doe rest.
　　If now they strived for the golden Ball,
　　Paris would give it you before them all.

From *Juno* you have State and Dignities,
From warlike *Pallas*, Wisdome, Fortitude;
And from faire *Venus* all her Excellencies,
With their best parts your Highnesse is indu'd:
　　How much are we to honor those that springs
　　From such rare beauty, in the blood of Kings?

The Muses doe attend upon your Throne,
20   With all the Artists at your becke and call;
The Sylvane Gods, and Satyres every one,
Before your faire triumphant Chariot fall:
    And shining Cynthia with her nymphs attend
    To honour you, whose Honour hath no end.

From your bright spheare of greatnes where you sit,
Reflecting light to all those glorious stars
That wait upon your Throane; To virtue yet
Vouchsafe that splendor which my meannesse bars:
    Be like faire *Phoebe*, who doth love to grace
30   The darkest night with her most beauteous face.

Apollo's beams doe comfort every creature,
And shines upon the meanest things that be;
Since in Estate and Virtue none is greater,
I humbly wish that yours may light on me:
    That so these rude unpollisht lines of mine,
    Graced by you, may seeme the more divine.

Look in this Mirrour of a worthy Mind,
Where some of your faire Virtues will appeare;
Though all it is impossible to find,
40   Unlesse my Glasse were chrystall, or more cleare:
    Which is dym steele, yet full of spotlesse truth,
    And for one looke from your faire eyes it su'th.

Here may your sacred Majestie behold
That mightie Monarch both of heav'n and earth,
He that all Nations of the world controld,
Yet tooke our flesh in base and meanest berth:
    Whose daiés were spent in poverty and sorrow,
    And yet all Kings their wealth of him do borrow.

For he is Crowne and Crowner of all Kings,
50   The hopefull haven of the meaner sort,
Its he that all our joyfull tidings brings

Of happie raigne within his royall Court:
   Its he that in extremity can give
   Comfort to them that have no time to live.

And since my wealth within his Region stands,
And that his Crosse my chiefest comfort is,
Yea in his kingdome onely rests my lands,
Of honour there I hope I shall not misse:
   Though I on earth doe live unfortunate,
60   Yet there I may attaine a better state.

In the meane time, accept most gratious Queene
This holy work, Virtue presents to you,
In poore apparell, shaming to be seene,
Or once t'appeare in your judiciall view:
   But that faire Virtue, though in meane attire,
   All Princes of the world doe most desire.

And sith all royall virtues are in you,
The Naturall, the Morall, and Divine,
I hope how plaine soever, beeing true,
70   You will accept even of the meanest line
   Faire Virtue yeelds; by whose rare gifts you are
   So highly grac'd, t'exceed the fairest faire.

Behold, great Queene, faire *Eves* Apologie,
Which I have writ in honour of your sexe,
And doe referre unto your Majestie,
To judge if it agree not with the Text:
   And if it doe, why are poore Women blam'd,
   Or by more faultie Men so much defam'd?

And this great Lady I have here attired,
80   In all her richest ornaments of Honour,
That you faire Queene, of all the world admired,
May take the more delight to looke upon her:
   For she must entertaine you to this Feast,
   To which your Highnesse is the welcom'st guest.

For here I have prepar'd my Paschal Lambe,
The figure of that living Sacrifice;
Who dying, all th'Infernall powers orecame,
That we with him t'Eternitie might rise:
      This pretious Passeover feed upon, O Queene,
90   Let your faire Virtues in my Glasse be seene.

And she that is the pattern of all Beauty,
The very modell of your Majestie,[1]
Whose rarest parts enforceth Love and Duty,
The perfect patterne of all Pietie:
      O let my Booke by her faire eyes be blest,
      In whose pure thoughts all Innocency rests.

Then shall I thinke my Glasse a glorious Skie,
When two such glittring Suns at once appeare;
The one repleat with Sov'raigne Majestie,
100   Both shining brighter than the clearest cleare:
      And both reflecting comfort to my spirits,
      To find their grace so much above my merits

Whose untun'd voyce the dolefull notes doth sing
Of sad Affliction in an humble straine;
Much like unto a Bird that wants a wing,
And cannot flie, but warbles forth her paine:
      Or he that barred from the Suns bright light,
      Wanting daies comfort, doth comend the night.

So I that live clos'd up in Sorrowes Cell,
110   Since great *Elizaes* favour blest my youth;
And in the confines of all cares doe dwell,
Whose grieved eyes no pleasure ever view'th:
      But in Christs suffrings, such sweet taste they have,
      As makes me praise pale Sorrow and the Grave.

[1] The Lady ELIZABETHS Grace.

And this great Ladie whom I love and honour,
And from my very tender yeeres have knowne,
This holy habite still to take upon her,
Still to remaine *the same*, and still her owne:
    And what our fortunes doe enforce us to,
120   She of Devotion and meere Zeale doth do.

Which makes me thinke our heavy burden light,
When such a one as she will help to beare it:
Treading the paths that make our way go right,
What garment is so faire but she may weare it;
    Especially for her that entertaines
    A Glorious Queene, in whome all woorth remains.

Whose powre may raise my sad dejected Muse,
From this lowe Mansion of a troubled mind;
Whose princely favour may such grace infuse,
130   That I may spread Her Virtues in like kind:
    But in this triall of my slender skill,
    I wanted knowledge to performe my will.

For even as they that doe behold the Starres,
Not with the eie of Learning, but of Sight,
To find their motions, want of knowledge barres
Although they see them in their brightest light:
    So, though I see the glory of her State,
    Its she that must instruct and elevate.

My weake distempred braine and feeble spirits,
140   Which all unlearned have adventur'd, this
To write of Christ, and of his sacred merits,
Desiring that this Booke Her hands may kisse:
    And though I be unworthy of that grace,
    Yet let her blessed thoghts this book imbrace.

And pardon me (faire Queene) though I presume,
To doe that which so many better can;
Not that I Learning to my selfe assume,

Or that I would compare with any man:
  But as they are Scholers, and by Art do write,
150   So Nature yeelds my Soule a sad delight.

And since all Arts at first from Nature came,
That goodly Creature, Mother of Perfection,
Whom *Joves* almighty hand at first did frame,
Taking both her and hers in his protection:
  Why should not She now grace my barren Muse,
  And in a Woman all defects excuse.

So peerelesse Princesse humbly I desire,
That your great wisedome would vouchsafe t'omit
All faults; and pardon if my spirits retire,
160   Leaving to ayme at what they cannot hit:
  To write your worth, which no pen can expresse,
  Were but t'ecclipse your Fame, and make it lesse.

To all vertuous Ladies in generall

Each blessed Lady that in Virtue spends
Your pretious time to beautifie your soules;
Come wait on hir whom winged Fame attends
And in hir hand the Booke where she inroules
Those high deserts that Majestie commends:
  Let this faire Queene not unattended bee,
  When in my Glasse she daines her selfe to see.

Put on your wedding garments every one,
The Bridegroome stayes to entertaine you all;
10   Let Virtue be your guide, for she alone
Can leade you right that you can never fall;
And make no stay for feare he should be gone:
  But fill your Lamps with oyle of burning zeale,
  That to your Faith he may his Truth reveale.

Let all your roabes be purple scarlet white,[1]
Those perfit colours purest Virtue wore,
Come deckt with Lillies that did so delight
To be preferr'd in Beauty, farre before
Wise *Salomon* in all his glory dight:
    20   Whose royall roabes did no such pleasure yield,
    As did the beauteous Lilly of the field.

Adorne your temples with faire *Daphnes* crowne,
The never changing Laurel, alwaies greene;[2]
Let constant hope all worldly pleasures drowne,
In wise *Minervaes* paths be alwaies seene;
Or with bright *Cynthia*, thogh faire *Venus* frown:
    With *Esop* crosse the posts of every doore,
    Where Sinne would riot, making Virtue poore.

And let the Muses your companions be,
    30   Those sacred sisters that on *Pallas* wait;
Whose Virtues with the purest minds agree,
Whose godly labours doe avoyd the baite
Of worldly pleasures, living alwaies free
    From sword, from violence, and from ill report,
    To these nine Worthies all faire mindes resort.

Annoynt your haire with *Aarons* pretious oyle,
And bring your palmes of vict'ry in your hands,
To overcome all thoughts that would defile
The earthly circuit of your soules faire lands;
    40   Let no dimme shadowes your cleare eyes beguile:
    Sweet odours, mirrhe, gum, aloes, frankincense,
    Present that King who di'd for your offence.

Behold, bright *Titans* shining chariot staies,
All deckt with flowers of the freshest hew,
Attended on by Age, Houres, Nights, and Daies,

---

[1] The roabes that Christ wore before his death.
[2] In token of Constancie.

Which alters not your beauty, but gives you
Much more, and crownes you with eternall praise:
   This golden chariot wherein you must ride,
   Let simple Doves, and subtill serpents guide.

50   Come swifter than the motion of the Sunne,
To be transfigur'd with our loving Lord,
Lest Glory end what Grace in you begun,
Of heav'nly riches make your greatest hoord,
In Christ all honour, wealth, and beautie's wonne:
   By whose perfections you appeare more faire
   Than *Phoebus*, if he seav'n times brighter were.

God's holy Angels will direct your Doves,
And bring your Serpents to the fields of rest,
Where he doth stay that purchast all your loves
60   In bloody torments, when he di'd opprest,
There shall you find him in those pleasant groves
   Of sweet *Elizium*, by the Well of Life,
   Whose cristal springs do purge from worldly strife

Thus may you flie from dull and sensuall earth,
Whereof at first your bodies formed were,
That new regen'rate in a second berth,
Your blessed soules may live without all feare,
Beeing immortall, subject to no death:
   But in the eie of heaven so highly placed,
70   That others by your virtues may be graced.

Where worthy Ladies I will leave you all,
Desiring you to grace this little Booke;
Yet some of you me thinkes I heare to call
Me by my name, and bid me better looke,
Lest unawares I in an error fall:
   In generall tearmes, to place you with the rest,
   Whom Fame commends to be the very best.

Tis true, I must confesse (O noble Fame)
There are a number honoured by thee,
80   Of which, some few thou didst recite by name,
And willd my Muse they should remembred bee;
Wishing some would their glorious Trophies frame:
    Which if I should presume to undertake,
    My tired Hand for very feare would quake.

Onely by name I will bid some of those,
That in true Honors seate have long bin placed,
Yea even such as thou hast chiefly chose,
By whom my Muse may be the better graced;
Therefore, unwilling longer time to lose,
90   I will invite some Ladies that I know,
    But chiefly those as thou hast graced so.

The Authors Dreame to the Ladie Marie, *the Countesse* Dowager of Pembrooke

Me thought I pass'd through th'*Edalyan* Groves,
And askt the Graces, if they could direct
Me to a Lady whom *Minerva* chose,
To live with her in height of all respect.

Yet looking backe into my thoughts againe,
The eie of Reason did behold her there
Fast ti'd unto them in a golden Chaine,
They stood, but she was set in Honors chaire.

And nine faire Virgins sate upon the ground,
10   With Harps and Vialls in their lilly hands;
Whose harmony had all my sences drown'd,
But that before mine eyes an object stands,

Whose Beauty shin'd like *Titons* cleerest raies,
She blew a brasen Trumpet, which did sound
Throgh al the world that worthy Ladies praise,
And by Eternall Fame I saw her crown'd.

Yet studying, if I were awake, or no,
God *Morphy*[1] came and tooke me by the hand,
And wil'd me not from Slumbers bowre to go,
20   Till I the summe of all did understand.

When presently the Welkin that before
Look'd bright and cleere, me thought, was overcast,
And duskie clouds, with boyst'rous winds great store,
Foretold of violent stormes which could not last.

And gazing up into the troubled skie,
Me thought a Chariot did from thence descend,
Where one did sit repleat with Majestie,
Drawne by foure fierie Dragons, which did bend

Their course where this most noble Lady sate,
30   Whom all these virgins with due reverence
Did entertaine, according to that state
Which did belong unto her Excellence.

When bright *Bellona*,[2] so they did her call,
Whom these faire Nymphs so humbly did receive,
A manly mayd which was both faire and tall,
Her borrowed Charret by a spring did leave.

With speare, and shield, and currat on her breast,
And on her head a helmet wondrous bright,
With myrtle, bayes, and olive branches drest,
40   Wherein me thought I tooke no small delight.

[1] The God of Dreames.
[2] Goddesse of Warre and Wisdome.

To see how all the Graces sought grace here,
And in what meeke, yet princely sort shee came;
How this most noble Lady did imbrace her,
And all humors unto hers did frame.

Now fair *Dictina*[3] by the breake of Day,
With all her Damsels round about her came,
Ranging the woods to hunt, yet made a stay,
When harkning to the pleasing sound of Fame;

50 Her Ivory bowe and silver shaftes shee gave
Unto the fairest nymphe of all her traine;
And wondring who it was that in so grave,
Yet gallant fashion did her beauty staine:

Shee deckt her selfe with all the borrowed light
That *Phoebus* would afford from his faire face,
And made her Virgins to appeare so bright,
That all the hils and vales received grace.

Then pressing where this beauteous troupe did stand,
They all received her most willingly,
And unto her the Lady gave her hand,
60 That shee should keepe with them continually.

Aurora[4] rising from her rosie bedde,
First blusht, then wept, to see faire *Phoebe* grac'd,
And unto Lady *Maie* these wordes shee sed,
Come, let us goe, we will not be out-fac'd.

I will unto *Apolloes* Waggoner,
A bidde him bring his Master presently,
That his bright beames may all her Beauty marre,
Gracing us with the luster of his eie.

[3] The Moone.
[4] The Morning.

Come, come, sweet *Maie*, and fill their laps with floures,
70   And I will give a greater light than she:
So all these Ladies favours shall be ours,
None shall be more esteem'd than we shall be.

Thus did *Aurora* dimme faire *Phoebus* light,
And was receiv'd in bright *Cynthiaes* place,
While *Flora* all with fragrant floures dight,
Pressed to shew the beauty of her face.

Though these, me thought, were verie pleasing sights,
Yet now these Worthies did agree to go,
Unto a place full of all rare delights,
80   A place that yet *Minerva* did not know.

That sacred Spring where Art and Nature striv'd
Which should remaine as Sov'raigne of the place;
Whose antient quarrell being new reviv'd,
Added fresh Beauty, gave farre greater Grace.

To which as umpiers now these Ladies go,
Judging with pleasure their delightfull case;
Whose ravisht sences made them quickely know,
T'would be offensive either to displace.

And therefore will'd they should for ever dwell,
90   In perfit unity by this matchlesse Spring:
Since 'twas impossible either should excell,
Or her faire fellow in subjection bring.

But here in equall sov'raigntie to live,
Equall in state, equall in dignitie,
That unto others they might comfort give,
Rejoycing all with their sweet unitie.

And now me thought I long to heare her name,
Whom wise *Minerva* honoured so much,
Shee whom I saw was crownd by noble Fame,
100   Whom Envy sought to sting, yet could not tuch.

Me thought the meager elfe did seeke bie waies
To come unto her, but it would not be;
Her venime purifi'd by virtues raies,
Shee pin'd and starv'd like an Anotomie:

While beauteous *Pallas* with this Lady faire,
Attended by these Nymphs of noble fame,
Beheld those woods, those groves, those bowers rare,
By which *Pergusa*, for so hight the name

Of that faire spring, his dwelling place and ground;
110   And throgh those fields with sundry flowers clad,
Of sev'rall colours, to adorne the ground,
And please the sences ev'n of the most sad:

He trayld along the woods in wanton wise,
With sweet delight to entertaine them all;
Inviting them to sit and to devise
On holy hymnes; at last to mind they call

Those rare sweet songs which *Israels* King did frame
Unto the Father of Eternitie;[5]
Before his holy wisedom tooke the name
120   Of great *Messias*, Lord of unitie.

Those holy Sonnets they did all agree,
With this most lovely Lady here to sing;
That by her noble breasts sweet harmony,
Their musicke might in eares of Angels ring.

While saints like Swans about this silver brook
Should *Hallalu-jah* sing continually,
Writing her praises in th'eternall booke
Of endlesse honour, true fames memorie.

[5] The Psalms written newly by the Countesse Dowager of Pembrooke.

Thus I in sleep the heavenli'st musicke hard,
130   That ever earthly eares did entertaine;
And durst not wake, for feare to be debard
Of what my sences sought still to retaine.

Yet sleeping, praied dull Slumber to unfold
Her noble name, who was of all admired;
When presently in drowsie tearmes he told
Not onely that, but more than I desired.

This nymph, quoth he, great *Penbrooke* hight by name,
Sister to valiant *Sidney*, whose cleere light
Gives light to all that tread true paths of Fame,
140   Who in the globe of heav'n doth shine so bright;

That beeing dead, his fame doth him survive,
Still living in the hearts of worthy men;
Pale Death is dead, but he remaines alive,
Whose dying wounds restor'd him life agen.

And this faire earthly goddesse which you see,
Bellona and her virgins doe attend;
In virtuous studies of Divinitie,
Her pretious time continually doth spend.

So that a Sister well shee may be deemd,
150   To him that liv'd and di'd so nobly;
And farre before him is to be esteemd
For virtue, wisdome, learning, dignity.

Whose beauteous soule hath gain'd a double life,
Both here on earth, and in the heav'ns above,
Till dissolution end all worldly strife:
Her blessed spirit remaines, of holy love,

Directing all by her immortall light,
In this huge sea of sorrowes, griefes, and feares;
With contemplation of God's powrefull might,
160   Shee fils the eies, the hearts, the tongues, the eares

Of after-comming ages, which shall reade
Her love, her zeale, her faith, and pietie;
The faire impression of whose worthy deed,
Seales her pure soule unto the Deitie.

That both in Heav'n and Earth it may remaine,
Crownd with her Makers glory and his love;
And this did Father Slumber tell with paine,
Whose dulnesse scarce could suffer him to move.

When I awaking left him and his bowre,
170   Much grieved that I could no longer stay;
Sencelesse was sleepe, not to admit me powre,
As I had spent the night to spend the day:

Then had God *Morphie* shew'd the end of all,
And what my heart desir'd, mine eies had seene;
For as I wak'd me thought I heard one call
For that bright Charet lent by *Joves* faire Queene.

But thou, base cunning thiefe, that robs our sprits
Of halfe that span of life which yeares doth give;[6]
And yet no praise unto thy selfe it merits,
180   To make a seeming death in those that live.

Yea wickedly thou doest consent to death,
Within thy restfull bed to rob our soules;
In Slumbers bowre thou steal'st away our breath,
Yet none there is that thy base stealths controules.

If poore and sickly creatures would imbrace thee,
Or they to whom thou giv'st a taste of pleasure,
Thou fli'st as if *Acteons* hounds did chase thee,
Or that to stay with them thou hadst no leasure.

[6] To Sleepe.

But though thou hast depriv'd me of delight,
190   By stealing from me ere I was aware;
I know I shall enjoy the selfe same sight,
Thou hast no powre my waking sprites to barre.

For to this Lady now I will repaire,
Presenting her the fruits of idle houres;
Thogh many Books she writes that are more rare,
Yet there is hony in the meanest flowres:

Which is both wholesome, and delights the taste:
Though sugar be more finer, higher priz'd,
Yet is the painefull Bee no whit disgrac'd,
200   Nor her faire wax, on hony more despiz'd.

And though that learned damsell and the rest,
Have in a higher style her Trophie fram'd;
Yet these unlearned lines beeing my best,
Of her great wisedom can no whit be blam'd.

And therefore, first I here present my Dreame,
And next, invite her Honour to my feast;
For my cleare reason sees her by that streame,
Where her rare virtues daily are increast.

So craving pardon for this bold attempt,
210   I here present my mirrour to her view,
Whose noble virtues cannot be exempt,
My Glasse beeing steele, declares them to be true.

And Madame, if you will vouchsafe that grace,
To grace those flowres that springs from virtues ground;
Though your faire mind on worthier workes is plac'd,
On workes that are more deepe, and more profound;

Yet is it no disparagement to you,
To see your Saviour in a Shepheards weed,
Unworthily presented in your viewe,
220 Whose worthinesse will grace each line you reade.

Receive him here by my unworthy hand,
And reade his paths of faire humility;
Who though our sinnes in number passe the sand,
They all are purg'd by his Divinity.

To the Ladie Lucie, *Countesse of Bedford*

Me thinkes I see faire Virtue readie stand,
T'unlocke the closet of your lovely breast,
Holding the key of Knowledge in her hand,
Key of that Cabbine where your selfe doth rest
To let him in, by whom her youth was blest:
  The true-love of your soule, your hearts delight,
  Fairer than all the world in your cleare sight.

He that descended from celestiall glory,
To taste of our infirmities and sorrowes,
10 Whose heavenly wisdom read the earthly storie
Of fraile Humanity, which his godhead borrows;
Loe here he comes all stucke with pale deaths arrows:
  In whose most pretious wounds your soule may reade
  Salvation, while he (dying Lord) doth bleed.

You whose cleare Judgement farre exceeds my skil,
Vouchsafe to entertaine this dying lover,
The Ocean of true grace, whose streames doe fill
All those with Joy, that can his love recover;
About this blessed Arke bright Angels hover:
20   Where your faire soule may sure and safely rest,
  When he is sweetly seated in your brest.

There may your thoughts as servants to your heart,
Give true attendance on this lovely guest,
While he doth to that blessed bowre impart
Flowres of fresh comforts, decke that bed of rest,
With such rich beauties as may make it blest.
  And you in whom all raritie is found,
  May be with his eternall glory crownd.

To the Ladie Margaret, *Countesse Dowager of Cumberland*

Right Honourable and Excellent Lady, I may say with Saint *Peter, Silver nor gold have I none, but such as I have, that give I you*: for having neither rich pearles of India, nor fine gold of Arabia, nor diamonds of inestimable value; neither those rich treasures, Arramaticall Gums, incense, and sweet odours, which were presented by those Kingly Philosophers to the babe Jesus, I present unto you even our Lord Jesus himselfe, whose infinit value is not to be comprehended within the weake imagination or wit of man: and as Saint *Peter* gave

10 health to the body, so I deliver you the health of the soule; which is this most pretious pearle of all perfection, this rich diamond of devotion, this perfect gold growing in the veines of that excellent earth of the most blessed Paradice, wherein our second *Adam* had his restlesse habitation. The sweet incense, balsums, odours, and gummes that flowes from that beautifull tree of Life, sprung from the roote of *Jesse*, which is so super-excellent, that it giveth grace to the meanest and most unworthy hand that will undertake to write thereof; neither can it receive any blemish thereby: for as a right

20 diamond can loose no whit of his beautie by the blacke foyle underneath it, neither by beeing placed in the darke, but retaines his naturall beauty and brightnesse shining in greater perfection than before; so this most pretious diamond, for beauty and riches exceeding all the most pretious diamonds and rich jewels of the world, can receive no blemish, nor

impeachment, by my unworthy hand writing; but wil with
the Sunne retaine his own brightnesse and most glorious
lustre, though never so many blind eyes looke upon him.
Therefore good Madame, to the most perfect eyes of your
30   understanding, I deliver the inestimable treasure of all elected
soules, to bee perused at convenient times; as also, the mirrour
of your most worthy minde, which may remaine in the world
many yeares longer than your Honour, or my selfe can live,
to be a light unto those that come after, desiring to tread in
the narrow path of virtue, that leads the way to heaven. In
which way, I pray God send your Honour long to continue,
that your light may so shine before men, that they may glorifie
your father which is in Heaven: and that I and many others
may follow you in the same tracke. So wishing you in this
40   world all increase of health and honour, and in the world to
come life everlasting, I rest.

To the Ladie Anne, Countesse of Dorcet

To you I dedicate this worke of Grace,
This frame of Glory which I have erected,
For your faire mind I hold the fittest place,
Where virtue should be setled and protected;
If highest thoughts true honor do imbrace,
And holy Wisdom is of them respected:
    Then in this Mirrour let your faire eyes looke,
    To view your virtues in this blessed Booke.

Blest by our Saviours merits, not my skil,
10   Which I acknowledge to be very small;
Yet if the least part of his blessed Will
I have perform'd, I count I have done all:
One sparke of grace sufficient is to fill
Our Lampes with oyle, ready when he doth call
    To enter with the Bridegroome to the feast,
    Where he that is the greatest may be least.

Greatnesse is no sure frame to build upon,
No worldly treasure can assure that place;
God makes both even, the Cottage with the Throne,
20 All worldly honours there are counted base;
Those he holds deare, and reckneth as his owne,
Whose virtuous deeds by his especiall grace
    Have gain'd his love, his kingdome, and his crowne,
    Whom in the booke of Life he hath set downe.

Titles of honour which the world bestowes,
To none but to the virtuous doth belong;
As beauteous bowres where true worth should repose,
And where his dwellings should be built most strong:
But when they are bestow'd upon her foes,
30 Poore virtues friends indure the greatest wrong:
    For they must suffer all indignity,
    Untill in heav'n they better graced be.

What difference was there when the world began,
Was it not Virtue that distinguisht all?
All sprang but from one woman and one man,
Then how doth Gentry come to rise and fall?
Or who is he that very rightly can
Distinguish of his birth, or tell at all,
    In what meane state his Ancestors have bin,
40   Before some one of worth did honour win?

Whose successors, although they beare his name,
Possessing not the riches of his minde,
How doe we know they spring out of the same
True stocke of honour, beeing not of that kind?
It is faire virtue gets immortall fame,
Tis that doth all love and duty bind:
    If he that much enjoyes, doth little good,
    We may suppose he comes not of that blood.

Nor is he fit for honour, or command,
50   If base affections over-rules his mind;
Or that selfe-will doth carry such a hand,
As worldly pleasures have the powre to blind
So as he cannot see, nor understand
How to discharge that place to him assign'd:
        Gods Stewards must for all the poore provide,
        If in Gods house they purpose to abide.

To you, as to Gods Steward I doe write,
In whom the seeds of virtue have bin sowne,
By your most worthy mother, in whose right,
60   All her faire parts you challenge as your owne;
If you, sweet Lady, will appeare as bright
As ever creature did that time hath knowne,
        Then weare this Diadem I present to thee,
        Which I have fram'd for her Eternitie.

Your are the Heire apparant of this Crowne
Of goodnesse, bountie, grace, love, pietie,
By birth its yours, then keepe it as your owne,
Defend it from all base indignitie;
The right your Mother hath to it, is knowne
70   Best unto you, who reapt such fruit thereby:
        This Monument of her faire worth retaine
        In your pure mind, and keepe it from al staine.

And as your Ancestors at first possest
Their honours, for their honourable deeds,
Let their faire virtues never be transgrest,
Bind up the broken, stop the wounds that bleeds,
Succour the poore, comfort the comfortlesse,
Cherish faire plants, suppresse unwholsom weeds;
        Althogh base pelfe do chance to come in place,
80   Yet let true worth receive your greatest grace.

So shal you shew from whence you are descended,
And leave to all posterities your fame,
So will your virtues alwaies be commended,
And every one will reverence your name;
So this poore worke of mine shalbe defended
From any scandall that the world can frame:
   And you a glorious Actor will appeare
   Lovely to all, but unto God most deare.

I know right well these are but needlesse lines,
90 To you, that are so perfect in your part,
Whose birth and education both combines;
Nay more than both, a pure and godly heart,
So well instructed to such faire designes,
By your deere Mother, that there needs no art:
   Your ripe discretion in your tender yeares,
   By all your actions to the world appeares.

I doe but set a candle in the sunne,
And adde one drop of water to the sea,
Virtue and Beautie both together run,
100 When you were borne, within your breast to stay;
Their quarrell ceast, which long before begun,
They live in peace, and all doe them obey:
   In you faire Madame, are they richly plac'd,
   Where all their worth by Eternity is grac'd.

You goddesse-like unto the world appeare,
Inricht with more than fortune can bestowe,
Goodnesse and Grace, which you doe hold more deere
Than worldly wealth, which melts away like snowe;
Your pleasure is the word of God to heare,
110 That his most holy precepts you may know:
   Your greatest honour, faire and virtuous deeds,
   Which from the love and feare of God proceeds.

Therefore to you (good Madame) I present
His lovely love, more worth than purest gold,
Who for your sake his pretious blood hath spent,
His death and passion you may here behold,
And view this Lambe, that to the world was sent,
Whom your faire soule may in her armes infold:
    Loving his love, that did endure such paine,
120   That you in heaven a worthy place might gaine.

For well you knowe, this world is but a Stage
Where all doe play their parts, and must be gone;
Here's no respect of persons, youth, nor age,
Death seizeth all, he never spareth one,
None can prevent or stay that tyrants rage,
But Jesus Christ the Just: By him alone
    He was orecome, He open set the dore
    To Eternall life, ne're seene, nor knowne before.

He is the stone the builders did refuse,
130   Which you, sweet Lady, are to build upon;
He is the rocke that holy Church did chuse,
Among which number, you must needs be one;
Faire Shepheardesse, tis you that he will use
To feed his flocke, that trust in him alone:
    All wordly blessings he vouchsafes to you,
    That to the poore you may returne his due.

And if deserts a Ladies love may gaine,
Then tell me, who hath more deserv'd than he?
Therefore in recompence of all his paine,
140   Bestowe your paines to reade, and pardon me,
If out of wants, or weakenesse of my braine,
I have not done this worke sufficiently;
    Yet lodge him in the closet of your heart,
    Whose worth is more than can be shew'd by Art.

To the Vertuous Reader

Often have I heard, that it is the property of some women, not only to emulate the virtues and perfections of the rest, but also by all their powers of ill speaking, to ecclipse the brightnes of their deserved fame: now contrary to this custome, which men I hope unjustly lay to their charge, I have written this small volume, or little booke, for the generall use of all virtuous Ladies and Gentlewomen of this kingdome; and in commendation of some particular persons of our owne sexe, such as for the most part, are so well knowne to my selfe, and others, that I dare undertake Fame dares not to call any better. And this I have done, to make knowne to the world, that all women deserve not to be blamed though some forgetting they are women themselves, and in danger to be condemned by the words of their owne mouthes, fall into so great an errour, as to speake unadvisedly against the rest of their sexe; which if it be true, I am perswaded they can shew their owne imperfection in nothing more: and therefore could wish (for their owne ease, modesties, and credit) they would referre such points of folly, to be practised by evill disposed men, who forgetting they were borne of women, nourished of women, and that if it were not by the means of women, they would be quite extinguished out of the world, and a finall ende of them all, doe like Vipers deface the wombes wherein they were bred, onely to give way and utterance to their want of discretion and goodnesse. Such as these, were they that dishonoured Christ his Apostles and Prophets, putting them to shamefull deaths. Therefore we are not to regard any imputations, that they undeservedly lay upon us, no otherwise than to make use of them to our owne benefits, as spurres to vertue, making us flie all occasions that may colour their unjust speeches to passe currant. Especially considering that they have tempted even the patience of God himselfe, who gave power to wise and virtuous women, to bring downe their pride and arrogancie. As was cruell *Cesarus* by the discreet counsell of noble *Deborah*, Judge and Prophetesse of Israel: and resolution of *Jael* wife of *Heber* the Kenite: wicked

Haman, by the divine prayers and prudent proceedings of beautifull *Hester*: blasphemous *Holofernes*, by the invincible courage, rare wisdome, and confident carriage of *Judeth*: and

40 the unjust Judges, by the innocency of chast *Susanna*: with infinite others, which for brevitie sake I will omit. As also in respect it pleased our Lord and Saviour Jesus Christ, without the assistance of man, beeing free from originall and all other sinnes, from the time of his conception, till the houre of his death, to be begotten of a woman, borne of a woman, nourished of a woman, obedient to a woman; and that he healed woman, pardoned women, comforted women: yea, even when he was in his greatest agonie and bloodie sweat, going to be crucified, and also in the last houre of his death, tooke care to

50 dispose of a woman: after his resurrection, appeared first to a woman, sent a woman to declare his most glorious resurrection to the rest of his Disciples. Many other examples I could alleadge of divers faithfull and virtuous women, who have in all ages, not onely beene Confessors, but also indured most cruel martyrdome for their faith in Jesus Christ. All which is sufficient to inforce all good Christians and honourable minded men to speake reverently of our sexe, and especially of all virtuous and good women. To the modest sensures of both which, I refer these my imperfect indeavours, knowing

60 that according to their owne excellent dispositions, they will rather, cherish, nourish, and increase the least sparke of virtue where they find it, by their favourable and best interpretations, than quench it by wrong constructions. To whom I wish all increase of virtue, and desire their best opinions.

Salve Deus Rex Judæorum

Sith *Cynthia* is ascended to that rest
Of endlesse joy and true Eternitie,
That glorious place that cannot be exprest
By any wight clad in mortalitie,

In her almightie love so highly blest,
And crown'd with everlasting Sov'raigntie;
   Where Saints and Angells do attend her Throne,
   And she gives glorie unto God alone.

To thee great Countesse now I will applie
My Pen, to write thy never dying fame;[1]
That when to Heav'n thy blessed Soule shall flie,
These lines on earth record thy reverend name:
And to this taske I mean my Muse to tie,
Though wanting skill I shall but purchase blame:
   Pardon (deere Lady) want of womans wit
   To pen thy praise, when few can equall it.

And pardon (Madame) though I do not write
Those praisefull lines of that delightfull place,
As you commaunded me in that faire night,
When shining *Phœbe* gave so great a grace,
Presenting *Paradice* to your sweet sight,
Unfolding all the beauty of her face
   With pleasant groves, hills, walks and stately trees,
   Which pleasures with retired minds agrees.

Whose Eagles eyes behold the glorious Sunne
Of th'all-creating Providence, reflecting
His blessed beames on all by him, begunne;
Increasing, strengthning, guiding and directing
All worldly creatures their due course to runne,
Unto His powrefull pleasure all subjecting:
   And thou (deere Lady) by his speciall grace,
   In these his creatures dost behold his face.

Whose all-reviving beautie, yeelds such joyes
To thy sad Soule, plunged in waves of woe,
That worldly pleasures seemes to thee as toyes,
Onely thou seek'st Eternitie to know,

---

[1] The Ladie Margaret Countesse Dowager of Cumberland.

Respecting not the infinite annoyes
That Satan to thy well-staid mind can show;
    Ne can he quench in thee, the Spirit of Grace,
40   Nor draw thee from beholding Heavens bright face.

Thy Mind so perfect by thy Maker fram'd,
No vaine delights can harbour in thy heart,
With his sweet love, thou art so much inflam'd,
As of the world thou seem'st to have no part;
So, love him still, thou need'st not be asham'd,
Tis He that made thee, what thou wert, and art:
    Tis He that dries all teares from Orphans eies,
    And heares from heav'n the wofull widdows cries.

Tis He that doth behold thy inward cares,
50   And will regard the sorrowes of thy Soule;
Tis He that guides thy feet from Sathans snares,
And in his Wisedome, doth thy waies controule:
He through afflictions, still thy Minde prepares,
And all thy glorious Trialls will enroule:
    That when darke daies of terror shall appeare,
    Thou as the Sunne shalt shine; or much more cleare.

[Lines 57–144 consist of a meditation on God's glory and the
Creation, drawn from the Psalms.]

Pardon (good Madam)[2] though I have digrest
From what I doe intend to write of thee,
To set his glorie forth whom thou lov'st best,
Whose wondrous works no mortall eie can see;
His speciall care on those whom he hath blest
150   From wicked worldlings, how he sets them free:
    And how such people he doth overthrow
    In all their waies, that they his powre may know.

[2] To the Countesse of Cumberland.

The meditation of this Monarchs love,
Drawes thee from caring what this world can yield;
Of joyes and griefes both equall thou dost prove,
They have no force, to force thee from the field:
Thy constant faith like to the Turtle Dove
Continues combat, and will never yield
    To base affliction; or prowd pomps desire,
160   That sets the weakest mindes so much on fire.

Thou from the Court to the Countrie art retir'd,
Leaving the world, before the world leaves thee:
That great Enchantresse of weake mindes admir'd,
Whose all-bewitching charmes so pleasing be
To worldly wantons; and too much desir'd
Of those that care not for Eternitie:
    But yeeld themselves as preys to Lust and Sinne,
    Loosing their hope of Heav'n Hell paines to winne.

But thou, the wonder of our wanton age
170   Leav'st all delights to serve a heav'nly King:
Who is more wise? or who can be more sage,
Than she that doth Affection subject bring;
Not forcing for the world, or Satans rage,
But shrowding under the Almighties wing;
    Spending her yeares, moneths, daies, minutes, howres,
    In doing service to the heav'nly powres.

Thou faire example, live without compare,
With Honours triumphs seated in thy breast;
Pale Envy never can thy name empaire,
180   When in thy heart thou harbour'st such a guest:
Malice must live for ever in dispaire;
There's no revenge where Virtue still doth rest:
    All hearts must needs do homage unto thee,
    In whom all eies such rare perfection see.

That outward Beautie which the world commends,
Is not the subject I will write upon,
Whose date expir'd, that tyrant Time soone ends,

Those gawdie colours soone are spent and gone:
But those faire Virtues which on thee attends
190   Are alwaies fresh, they never are but one:
　　They make thy Beauty fairer to behold,
　　Than was that Queenes for whom prowd *Troy* was sold.[3]

As for those matchlesse colours Red and White,
Or perfit features in a fading face
Or due proportion pleasing to the sight;
All these doe draw but dangers and disgrace
A mind enrich'd with Virtue, shines more bright,
Addes everlasting Beauty, gives true grace,
　　Frames an immortall Goddesse on the earth,
200   Who though she dies, yet Fame gives her new berth.

That pride of Nature which adornes the faire,
Like blasing Comets to allure all eies,
Is but the thred, that weaves their web of Care,
Who glories most, where most their danger lies;
For greatest perills do attend the faire,
When men do seeke, attempt, plot and devise,
　　How they may overthrow the chastest Dame,
　　Whose Beautie is the White whereat they aime.

Twas Beautie bred in *Troy* the ten yeares strife,
210   And carried *Hellen* from her lawfull Lord;
Twas Beautie made chaste *Lucrece* loose her life,
For which prowd *Tarquins* fact was so abhorr'd:
Beautie the cause *Antonius* wrong'd his wife,
Which could not be decided but by sword:
　　Great *Cleopatraes* Beautie and defects
　　Did worke *Octavias* wrongs, and his neglects.

What fruit did yeeld that faire forbidden tree,
But blood, dishonour, infamie, and shame?
Poore blinded Queene, could'st thou no better see,
220   But entertaine disgrace, in stead of fame?

[3] *An Invective against outward beuty unaccompanied with virtue.*

Doe these designes with Majestie agree?
To staine thy blood, and blot thy royall name.
   That heart that gave consent unto this ill,
   Did give consent that thou thy selfe should'st kill.

Fair *Rosamund*,[4] the wonder of her time,
Had bin much fairer had shee bin not faire;
Beautie betraid her thoughts, aloft to clime,
To build strong castles in uncertaine aire,
Where th'infection of a wanton crime
230 Did worke her fall; first poyson, then despaire,
   With double death did kill her perjur'd soule,
   When heavenly Justice did her sinne controule.

Holy *Matilda*[5] in a haplesse houre
Was borne to sorow and to discontent,
Beauty the cause that turn'd her Sweet to Sowre,
While Chastity sought Folly to prevent.
Lustfull King *John* refus'd, did use his powre,
By Fire and Sword, to compasse his content:
   But Friends disgrace, nor Fathers banishment,
240   Nor Death it selfe, could purchase her consent.

Here Beauty in the height of all perfection,
Crown'd this faire Creatures everlasting fame,
Whose noble minde did scorne the base subjection
Of Feares, or Favours, to impaire her Name:
By heavenly grace, she had such true direction,
To die with Honour, not to live in Shame;
   And drinke that poyson with a cheerefull heart,
   That could all Heavenly grace to her impart.

This Grace great Lady,[6] doth possesse thy Soule,
250 And makes thee pleasing in thy Makers sight;
   This Grace doth all imperfect Thoughts controule,

[4] *Of Rosamund.*
[5] *Of Matilda.*
[6] To the Ladie of Cumberland the Introduction to the passion of Christ.

Directing thee to serve thy God aright;
Still reckoning him, the Husband of thy Soule,
Which is most pretious in his glorious sight:
   Because the Worlds delights shee doth denie
   For him, who for her sake vouchsaf'd to die.

And dying made her Dowager of all;
Nay more, Co-heire of that eternall blisse
That Angels lost, and We by *Adams* fall;
260 Meere Cast-awaies, rais'd by a *Judas* kisse,
Christs bloody sweat, the Vineger, and Gall,
The Speare, Sponge, Nailes, his buffeting with Fists,
   His bitter Passion, Agony, and Death,
   Did gaine us Heaven when He did loose his breath.

[In lines 265–97, Lanyer calls upon God to aid her in her
task.]

Therefore I humbly for his Grace will pray,
That he will give me Power and Strength to Write,
That what I have begun, so end I may,
300 As his great Glory may appeare more bright;
Yea in these Lines I may no further stray,
Than his most holy Spirit shall give me Light:
   That blindest Weaknesse be not over-bold,
   The manner of his Passion to unfold.

In other Phrases than may well agree
With his pure Doctrine, and most holy Writ,
That Heavens cleare eye, and all the World may see,
I seeke his Glory, rather than to get
The Vulgars breath, the seed of Vanitie,
310 Nor Fames lowd Trumpet care I to admit;
   But rather strive in plainest Words to showe,
   The Matter which I seeke to undergoe.

A Matter farre beyond my barren skill,
To shew with any Life this map of Death,
This Storie; that whole Worlds with Bookes would fill,
In these few Lines, will put me out of breath,
To run so swiftly up this mightie Hill,
I may behold it with the eye of Faith;
   But to present this pure unspotted Lambe,
320   I must confesse, I farre unworthy am.

Yet if he please t'illuminate my Spirit,
And give me Wisdom from his holy Hill,
That I may Write part of his glorious Merit,
If he vouchsafe to guide my Hand and Quill,
To shew his Death, by which we doe inherit
Those endlesse Joyes that all our hearts doe fill;
   Then will I tell of that sad blacke fac'd Night,
   Whose mourning Mantle covered Heavenly Light.

That very Night our Saviour was betrayd,[7]
330   Oh night! exceeding all the nights of sorrow,
When our most blessed Lord, although dismayd,
Yet would not he one Minutes respite borrow,
But to *Mount Olives* went, though sore afraid,
To welcome Night, and entertaine the Morrow;
   And as he oft unto that place did goe,
   So did he now, to meete his long nurst woe.

He told his deere Disciples, that they all
Should be offended by him that selfe night;
His Griefe was great, and theirs could not be small,
340   To part from him who was their sole Delight;
Saint *Peter* thought his Faith could never fall,
No mote could happen in so cleare a sight:
   Which made him say, Though all men were offended,
   Yet would he never, though his life were ended.

[7] Here begins the Passion of Christ.

But his deare Lord made answere, That before
The Cocke did crowe, he should deny him thrice;
This could not choose but grieve him very sore,
That his hot Love should proove more cold than Ice,
Denying him he did so much adore;
350   No imperfection in himselfe he spies,
    But saith againe, with him hee'l surely die,
    Rather than his deare Master once denie.

And all the rest (did likewise say the same)
Of his Disciples, at that instant time;
But yet poore *Peter*, he was most too blame,
That thought above them all, by Faith to clime;
His forward speech inflicted sinne and shame,
When Wisdoms eyes did looke and checke his crime:
    Who did foresee, and told it him before,
360   Yet would he needs averre it more and more.

Now went our Lord unto that holy place,
Sweet *Gethsemaine* hallowed by his presence,
That blessed Garden, which did now embrace
His holy corps, yet could make no defence
Against those Vipers, objects of disgrace,
Which sought that pure eternall Love to quench:
    Here his Disciples willed he to stay,
    Whilst he went further, where he meant to pray.

None were admitted with their Lord to goe,
370   But *Peter*, and the sonnes of *Zebed'us*,
To them good *Jesus* opened all his woe,
He gave them leave his sorows to discusse,
His deepest griefes, he did not scorne to showe
These three deere friends, so much he did intrust:
    Beeing sorowfull, and overcharg'd with griefe,
    He told it them, yet look'd for no reliefe.

Sweet Lord, how couldst thou thus to flesh and blood
Communicate thy griefe? tell of thy woes?
Thou knew'st they had no powre to doe thee good,
380   But were the cause thou must endure these blowes,
Beeing the Scorpions bred in *Adams* mud,
Whose poys'ned sinnes did worke among thy foes,
　　To re-ore-charge thy over-burd'ned soule,
　　Although the sorowes now they doe condole.

Yet didst thou tell them of thy troubled state,
Of thy Soules heavinesse unto the death,
So full of Love, so free wert thou from hate,
To bid them stay, whose sinnes did stop thy breath,
When thou wert entring at so straite a gate,
390   Yea entring even into the doore of Death,
　　Thou bidst them tarry there, and watch with thee,
　　Who from thy pretious blood-shed were not free.

Bidding them tarry, thou didst further goe,
To meet affliction in such gracefull sort,
As might moove pitie both in friend and foe,
Thy sorowes such, as none could them comport,
Such great Indurements who did ever know,
When to th'Almighty thou didst make resort?
　　And falling on thy face didst humbly pray,
400   If 'twere his Will that Cup might passe away.

Saying, Not my will, but thy will Lord be done.
When as thou prayedst an Angel did appeare
From Heaven, to comfort thee Gods onely Sonne,
That thou thy Suffrings might'st the better beare,
Beeing in an agony, thy glasse neere run,
Thou prayedst more earnestly, in so great feare,
　　That pretious sweat came trickling to the ground,
　　Like drops of blood thy sences to confound.

Lo here his Will, not thy Will, Lord, was done,
410   And thou content to undergoe all paines;
Sweet Lambe of God, his deare beloved Sonne,
By this great purchase, what to thee remaines?
Of Heaven and Earth thou hast a Kingdom wonne,
Thy Glory beeing equall with thy Gaines,
    In ratifying Gods promise on th'earth,
    Made many hundred yeares before thy berth.

But now returning to thy sleeping Friends,
That could not watch one houre for love of thee,
Even those three Friends, which on thy Grace depends,
420   Yet shut those Eies that should their Maker see;
What colour, what excuse, or what amends
From thy Displeasure now can set them free?
    Yet thy pure Pietie bids them Watch and Pray,
    Lest in Temptation they be led away.

Although the Spirit was willing to obay,
Yet what great weaknesse in the Flesh was found!
They slept in Ease, whilst thou in Paine didst pray;
Loe, they in Sleepe, and thou in Sorrow drown'd:
Yet Gods right Hand was unto thee a stay,
430   When horror, griefe, and sorow did abound:
    His Angel did appeare from Heaven to thee,
    To yeeld thee comfort in Extremitie.

But what could comfort then thy troubled Minde,
When Heaven and Earth were both against thee bent?
And thou no hope, no ease, no rest could'st find,
But must restore that Life, which was but lent;
Was ever Creature in the World so kinde,
But he that from Eternitie was sent?
    To satisfie for many Worlds of Sinne,
440   Whose matchlesse Torments did but then begin.

If one Mans sinne doth challenge Death and Hell,
With all the Torments that belong thereto:
If for one sinne such Plagues on *David* fell,
As grieved him, and did his Seed undoe;
If *Salomon*, for that he did not well,
Falling from Grace, did loose his Kingdome too:
    Ten Tribes beeing taken from his wilfull Sonne,
    And Sinne the Cause that they were all undone.

What could thy Innocency now expect,
450 When all the Sinnes that ever were committed,
Were laid to thee, whom no man could detect?
Yet farre thou wert of Man from beeing pittied,
The Judge so just could yeeld thee no respect,
Nor would one jot of penance be remitted;
    But greater horror to thy Soule must rise,
    Than Heart can thinke, or any Wit devise.

Now drawes the houre of thy affliction neere,
And ugly Death presents himselfe before thee;
Thou now must leave those Friends thou held'st so deere,
460 Yea those Disciples, who did most adore thee;
Yet in thy countenance doth no Wrath appeare,
Although betrayd to those that did abhorre thee:
    Thou did'st vouchsafe to visit them againe,
    Who had no apprehension of thy paine.

Their eyes were heavie, and their hearts asleepe,
Nor knew they well what answere then to make thee;
Yet thou as Watchman, had'st a care to keepe
Those few from sinne, that shortly would forsake thee;
But now thou bidst them henceforth Rest and Sleepe,
470 Thy houre is come, and they at hand to take thee:
    The Sonne of God to Sinners made a pray,
    Oh hatefull houre! oh blest! oh cursed day!

Loe here thy great Humility was found,
Beeing King of Heaven, and Monarch of the Earth,
Yet well content to have thy Glory drownd,
By beeing counted of so meane a berth;
Grace, Love, and Mercy did so much abound,
Thou entertaindst the Crosse, even to the death:
   And nam'dst thy selfe, the sonne of Man to be,
480   To purge our pride by thy Humilitie.

But now thy friends whom thou didst call to goe,
Heavy Spectators of thy haplesse case,
See thy Betrayer, whom too well they knowe,
One of the twelve, now object of disgrace,
A trothlesse traytor, and a mortall foe,
With fained kindnesse seekes thee to imbrace;
   And gives a kisse, whereby he may deceive thee,
   That in the hands of Sinners he might leave thee.

Now muster forth with Swords, with Staves, with Bils,
490   High Priests and Scribes, and Elders of the Land,
Seeking by force to have their wicked Wils,
Which thou didst never purpose to withstand;
Now thou mak'st haste unto the worst of Ils,
And who they seeke, thou gently doest demand;
   This didst thou Lord, t'amaze these Fooles the more,
   T'inquire of that, thou knew'st so well before.

When loe these Monsters did not shame to tell,
His name they sought, and found, yet could not know
Jesus of Nazareth, at whose feet they fell,
500   When Heavenly Wisdome did descend so lowe
To speake to them: they knew they did not well,
Their great amazement made them backeward goe:
   Nay, though he said unto them, I am he,
   They could not know him, whom their eyes did see.

How blinde were they could not discerne the Light!
How dull! if not to understand the truth,
How weake! if meekenesse overcame their might;
How stony hearted, if not mov'd to ruth:
How void of Pitie, and how full of Spight,
510   Gainst him that was the Lord of Light and Truth:
    Here insolent Boldnesse checkt by Love and Grace,
    Retires, and falls before our Makers face.

For when he spake to this accursed crew,
And mildely made them know that it was he:
Presents himselfe, that they might take a view;
And what they doubted they might cleerely see;
Nay more, to re-assure that it was true,
He said: I say unto you, I am hee.
    If him they sought, he's willing to obay,
520   Onely desires the rest might goe their way.

Thus with a heart prepared to endure
The greatest wrongs Impietie could devise,
He was content to stoope unto their Lure,
Although his Greatnesse might doe otherwise:
Here Grace was seised on with hands impure,
And Virtue now must be supprest by Vice,
    Pure Innocencie made a prey to Sinne,
    Thus did his Torments and our Joyes beginne.

Here faire Obedience shined in his breast,
530   And did suppresse all feare of future paine;
Love was his Leader unto this unrest,
Whil'st Righteousnesse doth carry up his Traine;
Mercy made way to make us highly blest,
When Patience beat downe Sorrow, Feare and Paine:
    Justice sate looking with an angry brow,
    On blessed misery appeering now.

More glorious than all the Conquerors
That ever liv'd within this Earthly round,
More powrefull than all Kings, or Governours
540   That ever yet within this World were found;
More valiant than the greatest Souldiers
That ever fought, to have their glory crown'd:
　　For which of them, that ever yet tooke breath,
　　Sought t'indure the doome of Heaven and Earth?

But our sweet Saviour whom these Jewes did name;
Yet could their learned Ignorance apprehend
No light of grace, to free themselves from blame:
Zeale, Lawes, Religion, now they doe pretend
Against the truth, untruths they seeke to frame:
550   Now al their powres, their wits, their strengths they bend
　　Against one siely, weake, unarmed man,
　　Who no resistance makes, though much he can,

To free himselfe from these unlearned men,
Who call'd him Saviour in his blessed name;
Yet farre from knowing him their Saviour then,
That came to save both them and theirs from blame;
Though they retire and fall, they come agen
To make a surer purchase of their shame:
　　With lights and torches now they find the way,
560   　　To take the Shepheard whilst the sheep doe stray.

Why should unlawfull actions use the Light?
Iniquitie in Darknesse seekes to dwell;
Sinne rides his circuit in the dead of Night,
Teaching all soules the ready waies to hell;
Sathan coms arm'd with all the powres of Spight,
Heartens his Champions, makes them rude and fell;
　　Like rav'ning wolves, to shed his guiltlesse blood,
　　Who thought no harme, but di'd to doe them good.

Here Falshood bears the shew of formall Right,
570 Base Treacherie hath gote a guard of men;
Tyranny attends, with all his strength and might,
To leade this siely Lamb to Lyons denne;
Yet he unmoov'd in this most wretched plight,
Goes on to meete them, knowes the houre, and when:
    The powre of darkenesse must expresse Gods ire,
    Therefore to save these few was his desire.

These few that wait on Poverty and Shame,
And offer to be sharers in his Ils;
These few that will be spreaders of his Fame,
580 He will not leave to Tyrants wicked wils;
But still desires to free them from all blame,
Yet Feare goes forward, Anger Patience kils:
    A Saint is mooved to revenge a wrong,
    And Mildnesse doth what doth to Wrath belong.

For *Peter* griev'd at what might then befall,
Yet knew not what to doe, nor what to thinke,
Thought something must be done; now, if at all,
To free his Master, that he might not drinke
This poys'ned draught, farre bitterer than gall,
590 For now he sees him at the very brinke
    Of griesly Death, who gins to shew his face,
    Clad in all colours of a deepe disgrace.

And now those hands, that never us'd to fight,
Or drawe a weapon in his owne defence,
Too forward is, to doe his Master right,
Since of his wrongs, hee feeles so true a sence:
But ah poore *Peter*! now thou wantest might,
And hee's resolv'd, with them he will goe hence:
    To draw thy sword in such a helpelesse cause,
600   Offends thy Lord, and is against the Lawes.

So much he hates Revenge, so farre from Hate,
That he vouchsafes to heale, whom thou dost wound;
His paths are Peace, with none he holdes Debate,
His Patience stands upon so sure a ground,
To counsell thee, although it comes too late:
Nay, to his foes, his mercies so abound,
    That he in pitty doth thy will restraine,
    And heales the hurt, and takes away the paine.

For willingly he will endure this wrong,
610 Although his pray'rs might have obtain'd such grace,
As to dissolve their plots though ne'r so strong,
And bring these wicked Actors in worse case
Than *Ægypts* King on whom Gods plagues did throng,
But that foregoing Scriptures must take place:
    If God by prayers had an army sent
    Of powrefull Angels, who could them prevent?

Yet mightie JESUS meekely ask'd, Why they
With Swords and Staves doe come as to a Thiefe?
Hee teaching in the Temple day by day
620 None did offend, or give him cause of griefe.
Now all are forward, glad is he that may
Give most offence, and yeeld him least reliefe:
    His hatefull foes are ready now to take him,
    And all his deere Disciples do forsake him.

Those deare Disciples that he most did love,
And were attendant at his becke and call,
When triall of affliction came to prove,
They first left him, who now must leave them all:
For they were earth, and he came from above,
630 Which made them apt to flie, and fit to fall:
    Though they protest they never will forsake him,
    They do like men, when dangers overtake them.

And he alone is bound to loose us all,
Whom with unhallowed hands they led along,
To wicked *Caiphas* in the Judgement Hall,
Who studies onely how to doe him wrong;
High Priests and Elders, People great and small,
With all reprochfull words about him throng:
    False Witnesses are now call'd in apace,
640   Whose trothlesse tongues must make pale death imbrace

The beauty of the World, Heavens chiefest Glory;
The mirrour of Martyrs, Crowne of holy Saints;
Love of th'Almighty, blessed Angels story;
Water of Life, which none that drinks it, faints;
Guide of the Just, where all our Light we borrow;
Mercy of Mercies; Hearer of Complaints;
    Triumpher over Death; Ransomer of Sinne;
    Falsely accused: now his paines begin.

Their tongues doe serve him as a Passing bell,
650   For what they say is certainly beleeved;
So sound a tale unto the Judge they tell,
That he of Life must shortly be bereaved;
Their share of Heaven, they doe not care to sell,
So his afflicted Heart be throughly grieved:
    They tell his Words, though farre from his intent,
    And what his Speeches were, not what he meant.

That he Gods holy Temple could destroy,
And in three daies could build it up againe;
This seem'd to them a vaine and idle toy,
660   It would not sinke into their sinful braine:
Christs blessed body, al true Christians joy,
Should die, and in three dayes revive againe:
    This did the Lord of Heaven and earth endure,
    Unjustly to be charg'd by tongues impure.

And now they all doe give attentive eare,
To heare the answere, which he will not make;
The people wonder how he can forbeare,
And these great wrongs so patiently can take;
But yet he answers not, nor doth he care,
670   Much more he will endure for our sake:
    Nor can their wisdoms any way discover,
    Who he should be that proov'd so true a Lover.

To entertaine the sharpest pangs of death,
And fight a combate in the depth of hell,
For wretched Worldlings made of dust and earth,
Whose hard'ned hearts, with pride and mallice swell;
In midst of bloody sweat, and dying breath,
He had compassion on these tyrants fell:
    And purchast them a place in Heav'n for ever,
680   When they his Soule and Body sought to sever.

Sinnes ugly mists, so blinded had their eyes,
That at Noone dayes they could discerne no Light;
These were those fooles, that thought themselves so wise,
The Jewish wolves, that did our Saviour bite;
For now they use all meanes they can devise,
To beate downe truth, and goe against all right:
    Yea now they take Gods holy name in vaine,
    To know the truth, which truth they doe prophane.

The chiefest Hel-hounds of this hatefull crew,
690   Rose up to aske what answere he could make,
Against those false accusers in his view;
That by his speech, they might advantage take:
He held his peace, yet knew they said not true,
No answere would his holy wisdome make,
    Till he was charged in his glorious name,
    Whose pleasure 'twas he should endure this shame.

Then with so mild a Majestie he spake,
As they might easly know from whence he came,
His harmlesse tongue doth no exceptions take,
700   Nor Priests, nor People, meanes he now to blame;
But answers Folly, for true Wisdomes sake,
Beeing charged deeply by his powrefull name,
    To tell if Christ the Sonne of God he be,
    Who for our sinnes must die, to set us free.

To thee O *Caiphas* doth he answere give,
That thou hast said, what thou desir'st to know,
And yet thy malice will not let him live,
So much thou art unto thy selfe a foe;
He speaketh truth, but thou wilt not beleeve,
710   Nor canst thou apprehend it to be so:
    Though he expresse his Glory unto thee,
    Thy Owly eies are blind, and cannot see.

Thou rend'st thy cloathes, in stead of thy false heart,
And on the guiltlesse lai'st thy guilty crime;
For thou blasphem'st, and he must feele the smart:
To sentence death, thou think'st it now high time;
No witnesse now thou need'st, for this fowle part,
Thou to the height of wickednesse canst clime:
    And give occasion to the ruder sort,
720   To make afflictions, sorrows, follies sport.

Now when the dawne of day gins to appeare,
And all your wicked counsels have an end,
To end his Life, that holds you all so deere,
For to that purpose did your studies bend;
Proud *Pontius Pilate* must the matter heare,
To your untroths his eares he now must lend:
    Sweet *Jesus* bound, to him you led away,
    Of his most pretious blood to make you[r] pray.

Which, when that wicked Caytife did perceive,
730   By whose lewd meanes he came to this distresse;
He brought the price of blood he did receive,
Thinking thereby to make his fault seeme lesse,
And with these Priests and Elders did it leave,
Confest his fault, wherein he did transgresse:
    But when he saw Repentance unrespected,
    He hang'd himselfe; of God and Man rejected.

By this Example, what can be expected
From wicked Man, which on the Earth doth live?
But faithlesse dealing, feare of God neglected;
740   Who for their private gaine cares not to sell
The Innocent Blood of Gods most deere elected,
As did that caytife wretch, now damn'd in Hell:
    If in Christs Schoole, he tooke so great a fall,
    What will they doe, that come not there at all.

Now *Pontius Pilate* is to judge the Cause
Of faultlesse *Jesus*, who before him stands;
Who hath neither offended Prince, nor Lawes,
Although he now be brought in woefull bands:
O noble Governour, make thou yet a pause,
750   Doe not in innocent blood imbrue thy hands;
    But heare the words of thy most worthy wife,
    Who sends to thee, to beg her Saviours life.

Let barb'rous crueltie farre depart from thee,
And in true Justice take afflictions part;
Open thine eies, that thou the truth mai'st see,
Doe not the thing that goes against thy heart,
Condemne not him that must thy Saviour be;
But view his holy Life, his good desert.
    Let not us Women glory in Mens fall,
760   Who had power given to over-rule us all.

Till now your indiscretion sets us free,[8]
And makes our former fault much lesse appeare;
Our Mother *Eve*, who tasted of the Tree,
Giving to *Adam* what shee held most deare,
Was simply good, and had no powre to see,
The after-comming harme did not appeare:
 The subtile Serpent that our Sex betraide,
 Before our fall so sure a plot had laide.

That undiscerning Ignorance perceav'd
770 No guile, or craft that was by him intended;
For had she knowne, of what we were bereav'd,
To his request she had not condiscended.
But she (poore soule) by cunning was deceav'd,
No hurt therein her harmelesse Heart intended:
 For she alleadg'd Gods word, which he denies,
 That they should die, but even as Gods, be wise.

But surely *Adam* can not be excusde,
Her fault though great, yet hee was most too blame;
What Weaknesse offerd, Strength might have refusde,
780 Being Lord of all, the greater was his shame:
Although the Serpents craft had her abusde,
Gods holy word ough[t] all his actions frame,
 For he was Lord and King of all the earth,
 Before poore *Eve* had either life or breath.

Who being fram'd by Gods eternall hand,
The perfect'st man that ever breath'd on earth;
And from Gods mouth receiv'd that strait command,
The breach whereof he knew was present death:
Yea having powre to rule both Sea and Land,
790 Yet with one Apple wonne to loose that breath
 Which God had breathed in his beauteous face,
 Bringing us all in danger and disgrace.

[8] Eves Apologie.

And then to lay the fault on Patience backe,
That we (poore women) must endure it all;
We know right well he did discretion lacke,
Beeing not perswaded thereunto at all;
If *Eve* did erre, it was for knowledge sake,
The fruit beeing faire perswaded him to fall:
   No subtill Serpents falshood did betray him,
800   If he would eate it, who had powre to stay him?

Not *Eve*, whose fault was onely too much love,
Which made her give this present to her Deare,
That what shee tasted, he likewise might prove,
Whereby his knowledge might become more cleare;
He never sought her weakenesse to reprove,
With those sharpe words, which he of God did heare:
   Yet Men will boast of Knowledge, which he tooke
   From *Eves* fair hand, as from a learned Booke.

If any Evill did in her remaine,
810   Beeing made of him, he was the ground of all;
If one of many Worlds could lay a staine
Upon our Sexe, and worke so great a fall
To wretched man, by Satans subtill traine;
What will so fowle a fault amongst you all?
   Her weakenesse did the Serpents words obey,
   But you in malice Gods deare Sonne betray.

Whom, if unjustly you condemne to die,
Her sinne was small, to what you doe commit;
All mortall sinnes that doe for vengeance crie,
820   Are not to be compared unto it:
If many worlds would altogether trie,
By all their sinnes the wrath of God to get;
   This sinne of yours, surmounts them all as farre
   As doth the Sunne, another little starre.

Then let us have our Libertie againe,
And challendge to your selves no Sov'raigntie;
You came not in the world without our paine,
Make that a barre against your crueltie;
Your fault beeing greater, why should you disdaine
830 Our beeing your equals, free from tyranny?
  If one weake woman simply did offend,
  This sinne of yours, hath no excuse, nor end.

To which (poore soules) we never gave consent,
Witnesse thy wife (O *Pilate*) speakes for all;
Who did but dreame, and yet a message sent,
That thou should'st have nothing to doe at all
With that just man; which, if thy heart relent,
Why wilt thou be a reprobate with *Saul*?
  To seeke the death of him that is so good,
840 For thy soules health to shed his dearest blood.

Yea, so thou mai'st these sinful people please,
Thou art content against all truth and right,
To seale this act, that may procure thine ease
With blood, and wrong, with tyrannie, and might;
The multitude thou seekest to appease,
By base dejection of this heavenly Light:
  Demanding which of these that thou should'st loose,
  Whether the Thiefe, or Christ King of the Jewes.

Base *Barrabas* the Thiefe, they all desire,
850 And thou more base than he, perform'st their will;
Yet when thy thoughts backe to themselves retire,
Thou art unwilling to commit this ill:
Oh that thou couldst unto such grace aspire,
That thy polluted lips might never kill
  That Honour, which right Judgement ever graceth,
  To purchase shame, which all true worth defaceth.

Art thou a Judge, and asketh what to do
With one, in whom no fault there can be found?
The death of Christ wilt thou consent unto,
860   Finding no cause, no reason, nor no ground?
Shall he be scourg'd, and crucified too?
And must his miseries by thy meanes abound?
 Yet not asham'd to aske what he hath done,
 When thine owne conscience seeks this sinne to shunne.

Three times thou ask'st, What evill hath he done?
And saist, thou find'st in him no cause of death,
Yet wilt thou chasten Gods beloved Sonne,
Although to thee no word of ill he saith:
For Wrath must end, what Malice hath begunne,
870   And thou must yield to stop his guiltlesse breath.
 This rude tumultuous rowt doth presse so sore,
 That thou condemnest him thou shouldst adore.

Yet *Pilate*, this can yeeld thee no content,
To exercise thine owne authoritie,
But unto *Herod* he must needes be sent,
To reconcile thy selfe by tyrannie:
Was this the greatest good in Justice meant,
When thou perceiv'st no fault in him to be?
 If thou must make thy peace by Virtues fall,
880   Much better 'twere not to be friends at all.

Yet neither can thy sterne browe, nor his great place,
Can draw an answer from the Holy One:
His false accusers, nor his great disgrace,
Nor *Herods* scoffes; to him they are all one:
He neither cares, nor feares his owne ill case,
Though being despis'd and mockt of every one:
 King *Herods* gladnesse gives him little ease,
 Neither his anger seekes he to appease.

Yet this is strange, that base Impietie
890   Should yeeld those robes of honour, which were due;
Pure white, to shew his great Integritie,
His innocency, that all the world might view;
Perfections height in lowest penury,
Such glorious poverty as they never knew:
   Purple and Scarlet well might him beseeme,
   Whose precious blood must all the world redeeme.

And that Imperiall Crowne of Thornes he wore,
Was much more pretious than the Diadem
Of any King that ever liv'd before,
900   Or since his time, their honour's but a dreame
To his eternall glory, beeing so poore,
To make a purchasse of that heavenly Realme;
   Where God with all his Angels lives in peace,
   No griefes, nor sorrowes, but all joyes increase.

Those royall robes, which they in scorne did give,
To make him odious to the common sort,
Yeeld light of Grace to those whose soules shall live
Within the harbour of this heavenly port;
Much doe they joy, and much more doe they grieve,
910   His death, their life, should make his foes such sport:
   With sharpest thornes to pricke his blessed face,
   Our joyfull sorrow, and his greater grace.

Three feares at once possessed *Pilates* heart;
The first, Christs innocencie, which so plaine appeares;
The next, That he which now must feele this smart,
Is Gods deare Sonne, for any thing he heares:
But that which proov'd the deepest wounding dart,
Is Peoples threat'nings, which he so much feares,
   That he to *Caesar* could not be a friend,
920   Unlesse he sent sweet JESUS to his end.

Now *Pilate* thou art proov'd a painted wall,
A golden Sepulcher with rotten bones;
From right to wrong, from equitie to fall:
If none upbraid thee, yet the very stones
Will rise against thee, and in question call
His blood, his teares, his sighes, his bitter groanes:
    All these will witnesse at the latter day,
    When water cannot wash thy sinne away.

Canst thou be innocent, that gainst all right,
930 Wilt yeeld to what thy conscience doth withstand?
Beeing a man of knowledge, powre, and might,
To let the wicked carrie such a hand,
Before thy face to blindfold Heav'ns bright light,
And thou to yeeld to what they did demand?
    Washing thy hands, thy conscience cannot cleare,
    But to all worlds this staine must needs appeare.

For loe, the Guiltie doth accuse the Just,
And faultie Judge condemnes the Innocent;
And wilfull Jewes to exercise their lust,
940 With whips and taunts against their Lord are bent;
He basely us'd, blasphemed, scorn'd, and curst,
Our heavenly King to death for us they sent:
    Reproches, slanders, spittings in his face,
    Spight doing all her worst in his disgrace.

And now this long expected houre drawes neere,[9]
When blessed Saints with Angels doe condole;
His holy march, soft pace, and heavy cheere,
In humble sort to yeeld his glorious soule,
By his deserts the fowlest sinnes to cleare;
950 And in th'eternall booke of heaven to enroule
    A satisfaction till the generall doome,
    Of all sinnes past, and all that are to come,

[9] Christ going to death.

They that had seene this pitifull Procession,
From *Pilates* Palace to Mount Calvarie,
Might thinke he answer'd for some great transgression,
Beeing in such odious sort condemn'd to die;
He plainely shewed that his owne profession
Was virtue, patience, grace, love, piety;
    And how by suffering he could conquer more
960   Than all the Kings that ever liv'd before.

First went the Crier with open mouth proclayming
The heavy sentence of Iniquitie,
The Hangman next, by his base office clayming
His right in Hell, where sinners never die,
Carrying the nayles, the people still blaspheming
Their maker, using all impiety;
    The Thieves attending him on either side,
    The Serjeants watching, while the women cri'd.[10]

Thrice happy women that obtaind such grace
970   From him whose worth the world could not containe;
Immediately to turne about his face,
As not remembring his great griefe and paine,
To comfort you, whose teares powr'd forth apace
On *Flora's* bankes, like shewers of Aprils raine:
    Your cries inforced mercie, grace, and love
    From him, whom greatest Princes could not moove

To speake on[e] word, nor once to lift his eyes
Unto proud *Pilate*, no nor *Herod*, king,
By all the Questions that they could devise,
980   Could make him answere to no manner of thing;
Yet these poore women, by their pitious cries
Did moove their Lord, their Lover, and their King,
    To take compassion, turne about, and speake
    To them whose hearts were ready now to breake.

[10] The teares of the daughters of Jerusalem.

Most blessed daughters of Jerusalem,
Who found such favour in your Saviors sight,
To turne his face when you did pitie him;
Your tearefull eyes, beheld his eies more bright;
Your Faith and Love unto such grace did clime,
990   To have reflection from this Heav'nly Light:
    Your Eagles eyes did gaze against this Sunne,
    Your hearts did thinke, he dead, the world were done.

When spightfull men with torments did oppresse
Th'afflicted body of this innocent Dove,
Poore women seeing how much they did transgresse,
By teares, by sighes, by cries intreat, nay prove,
What may be done among the thickest presse,
They labour still these tyrants hearts to move;
    In pitie and compassion to forbeare
1000   Their whipping, spurning, tearing of his haire.

But all in vaine, their malice hath no end,
Their hearts more hard than flint, or marble stone;
Now to his griefe, his greatnesse they attend,
When he (God knowes) had rather be alone;
They are his guard, yet seeke all meanes to offend:
Well may he grieve, well may he sigh and groane,
    Under the burthen of a heavy crosse,
    He faintly goes to make their gaine his losse.

His woefull Mother wayting on her Sonne,[11]
1010   All comfortlesse in depth of sorow drowned;
Her griefes extreame, although but new begun,
To see his bleeding body oft shee swouned;
How could shee choose but thinke her selfe undone,
He dying, with whose glory shee was crowned?
    None ever lost so great a losse as shee,
    Beeing Sonne, and Father of Eternitie.

[11] The sorrow of the virgin Marie.

Her teares did wash away his pretious blood,
That sinners might not tread it under feet
To worship him, and that it did her good
1020 Upon her knees, although in open street,
Knowing he was the Jessie floure and bud,
That must be gath'red when it smell'd most sweet:
 Her Sonne, her Husband, Father, Saviour, King,
  Whose death killd Death, and tooke away his sting.

Most blessed Virgin, in whose faultlesse fruit,
All Nations of the earth must needes rejoice,
No Creature having sence though ne'r so brute,
But joyes and trembles when they heare his voyce;
His wisedome strikes the wisest persons mute,
1030 Faire chosen vessell, happy in his choyce:
 Deere Mother of our Lord, whose reverend name,
  All people Blessed call, and spread thy fame.

For the Almightie magnified thee,
And looked downe upon thy meane estate;
Thy lowly mind, and unstain'd Chastitie,
Did pleade for Love at great *Jehovaes* gate,
Who sending swift-wing'd *Gabriel* unto thee,
his holy will and pleasure to relate;
 To thee most beauteous Queene of Woman-kind,
1040   The Angell did unfold his Makers mind.

He thus beganne, Haile *Mary* full of grace,[12]
Thou freely art beloved of the Lord,
He is with thee, behold thy happy case;
What endlesse comfort did these words afford
To thee that saw'st an Angell in the place
Proclaime thy Virtues worth, and to record
 Thee blessed among women: that thy praise
  Should last so many worlds beyond thy daies.

[12] The salutation of the virgin Marie.

Loe, this high message to thy troubled spirit,
1050 He doth deliver in the plainest sence;
Sayes, Thou shouldst beare a Sonne that shal inherit
His Father *Davids* throne, free from offence,
Call's him that Holy thing, by whose pure merit
We must be sav'd, tels what he is, of whence;
 His worth, his greatnesse, what his name must be,
 Who should be call'd the Sonne of the most High.

He cheeres thy troubled soule, bids thee not feare;
When thy pure thoughts could hardly apprehend
This salutation, when he did appeare;
1060 Nor couldst thou judge, whereto those words did tend;
His pure aspect did moove thy modest cheere
To muse, yet joy that God vouchsaf'd to send
 His glorious Angel; who did thee assure
 To beare a child, although a Virgin pure.

Nay more, thy Sonne should Rule and Raigne for ever;
Yea, of his Kingdom there should be no end;
Over the house of *Jacob*, Heavens great Giver
Would give him powre, and to that end did send
His faithfull servant *Gabriel* to deliver
1070 To thy chast eares, no word that might offend:
 But that this blessed Infant borne of thee,
 Thy Sonne, The onely Sonne of God should be.

When on the knees of thy submissive heart
Thou humbly didst demand, How that should be?
Thy virgin thoughts did thinke, none could impart
This great good hap, and blessing unto thee;
Farre from desire of any man thou art,
Knowing not one, thou art from all men free:
 When he, to answere this thy chaste desire,
1080 Gives thee more cause to wonder and admire.

That thou a blessed Virgin shouldst remaine,
Yea that the holy Ghost should come on thee
A maiden Mother, subject to no paine,
For highest powre should overshadow thee:
Could thy faire eyes from teares of joy refraine,
When God look'd downe upon thy poore degree?
    Making thee Servant, Mother, Wife, and Nurse
    To Heavens bright King, that freed us from the curse.

Thus beeing crown'd with glory from above,
1090 Grace and Perfection resting in thy breast,
Thy humble answer doth approve thy Love,
And all these sayings in thy heart doe rest:
Thy Child and Lambe, and thou a Turtle dove,
Above all other women highly blest;
    To find such favour in his glorious sight,
    In whom thy heart and soule doe most delight.

What wonder in the world more strange could seeme,
Than that a Virgin could conceive and beare
Within her wombe a Sonne, That should redeeme
1100 All Nations on the earth, and should repaire
Our old decaies: who in such high esteeme,
Should prize all mortals, living in his feare;
    As not to shun Death, Povertie, and Shame,
    To save their soules, and spread his glorious Name.

And partly to fulfil his Fathers pleasure,
Whose powrefull hand allowes it not for strange,
If he vouchsafe the riches of his treasure,
Pure Righteousnesse to take such il exchange;
On all Iniquitie to make a seisure,
1110 Giving his snow-white Weed for ours in change;
    Our mortall garment in a skarlet Die,
    Too base a roabe for Immortalitie.

Most happy news, that ever yet was brought,
When Poverty and Riches met together,
The wealth of Heaven, in our fraile clothing wrought
Salvation by his happy comming hither:
Mighty Messias, who so deerely bought
Us Slaves to sinne, farre lighter than a feather:
   Toss'd to and fro with every wicked wind,
1120   The world, the flesh, or Devill gives to blind.

Who on his shoulders our blacke sinnes doth beare
To that most blessed, yet accursed Crosse;
Where fastning them, he rids us of our feare,
Yea for our gaine he is content with losse,
Our ragged clothing scornes he not to weare,
Though foule, rent, torne, disgracefull, rough and grosse,
   Spunne by that monster Sinne, and weav'd by Shame,
   Which grace it selfe, disgrac'd with impure blame.

How canst thou choose (faire Virgin) then but mourne,
1130 When this sweet of-spring of thy body dies,
When thy faire eies beholds his bodie torne,
The peoples fury, heares the womens cries;
His holy name prophan'd, He made a scorne,
Abusde with all their hatefull slaunderous lies:
   Bleeding and fainting in such wondrous sort,
   As scarce his feeble limbes can him support.

Now *Simon* of *Cyrene* passeth them by,
Whom they compell sweet JESUS Crosse to beare
To *Golgatha*, there doe they meane to trie
1140 All cruell means to worke in him dispaire:
That odious place, where dead mens skulls did lie,
There must our Lord for present death prepare:
   His sacred blood must grace that loathsome field,
   To purge more filth, than that foule place could yield.

For now arriv'd unto this hatefull place,[13]
In which his Crosse erected needes must bee,
False hearts, and willing hands come on apace,
All prest to ill, and all desire to see:
Gracelesse themselves, still seeking to disgrace;
1150   Bidding him, If the Sonne of God he bee,
    To save himselfe, if he could others save,
    With all th'opprobious words that might deprave.

His harmlesse hands unto the Crosse they nailde,
And feet that never trode in sinners trace,
Betweene two theeves, unpitied, unbewailde,
Save of some few possessors of his grace,
With sharpest pangs and terrors thus appailde,
Sterne Death makes way, that Life might give him place:
    His eyes with teares, his body full of wounds,
1160   Death last of paines his sorrows all confounds.

His joynts dis-joynted, and his legges hang downe,
His alabaster breast, his bloody side,
His members torne, and on his head a Crowne
Of sharpest Thorns, to satisfie for pride:
Anguish and Paine doe all his Sences drowne,
While they his holy garments do divide:
    His bowells drie, his heart full fraught with griefe,
    Crying to him that yeelds him no reliefe.

[Lines 1169–1288 are addressed to the Countess of Cumberland, and describe the suffering of all creation at Christ's death, concentrating on the paradox that his death brings eternal life.]

[13] Christs death.

For he is rize from Death t'Eternall Life,[14]
1290 And now those pretious oyntments he desires
Are brought unto him, by his faithfull Wife
The holy Church; who in those rich attires,
Of Patience, Love, Long suffring, Voide of strife,
Humbly presents those oyntments he requires:
    The oyles of Mercie, Charitie, and Faith,
    Shee onely gives that which no other hath.

These pretious balmes doe heale his grievous wounds,[15]
And water of Compunction washeth cleane
The soares of sinnes, which in our Soules abounds;
1300 So faire it heales, no skarre is ever seene;
Yet all the glory unto Christ redounds,
His pretious blood is that which must redeeme;
    Those well may make us lovely in his sight,
    But cannot save without his powrefull might.

This is that Bridegroome that appeares so faire,
So sweet, so lovely in his Spouses sight,
That unto Snowe we may his face compare,
His cheekes like skarlet, and his eyes so bright
As purest Doves that in the rivers are,
1310 Washed with milke, to give the more delight;
    His head is likened to the finest gold,
    His curled lockes so beauteous to behold;

Blacke as a Raven in her blackest hew;
His lips like skarlet threeds, yet much more sweet
Than is the sweetest hony dropping dew,
Or hony combes, where all the Bees doe meet;
Yea, he is constant, and his words are true,
His cheekes are beds of spices, flowers sweet;
    His lips like Lillies, dropping downe pure mirrhe,
1320   Whose love, before all worlds we doe preferre.

[14] Christs resurrection.
[15] A briefe description of his beautie upon the Canticles.

Ah! give me leave (good Lady) now to leave[16]
This taske of Beauty which I tooke in hand,
I cannot wade so deepe, I may deceave
My selfe, before I can attaine the land;
Therefore (good Madame) in your heart I leave
His perfect picture, where it still shall stand,
 Deepely engraved in that holy shrine,
 Environed with Love and Thoughts divine.

There may you see him as a God in glory,
1330 And as a man in miserable case;
There you may reade his true and perfect storie,
His bleeding body there you may embrace,
And kisse his dying cheekes with teares of sorrow,
With joyfull griefe, you may intreat for grace;
 And all your prayers, and your almes-deeds
 May bring to stop his cruell wounds that bleeds.

Oft times hath he made triall of your love,
And in your Faith hath tooke no small delight,
By Crosses and Afflictions he doth prove,
1340 Yet still your heart remaineth firme and right;
Your love so strong, as nothing can remove,
Your thoughts beeing placed on him both day and night,
 Your constant soule doth lodge betweene her brests,
 This Sweet of sweets, in which all glory rests.

Sometime h'appeares to thee in Shepheards weed,
And so presents himselfe before thine eyes,
A good old man; that goes his flocke to feed;
Thy colour changes, and thy heart doth rise;
Thou call'st, he comes, thou find'st tis he indeed,
1350 Thy Soule conceaves that he is truely wise:
 Nay more, desires that he may be the Booke,
 Whereon thine eyes continually may looke.

[16] To my Ladie of Cumberland.

Sometime imprison'd, naked, poore, and bare,
Full of diseases, impotent, and lame,
Blind, deafe, and dumbe, he comes unto his faire,
To see if yet shee will remain the same;
Nay sicke and wounded, now thou do'st prepare
To cherish him in thy deare Lovers name:
   Yea thou bestow'st all paines, all cost, all care,
1360   That may relieve him, and his health repaire.

These workes of mercy are so sweete, so deare
To him that is the Lord of Life and Love,
That all thy prayers he vouchsafes to heare,
And sends his holy Spirit from above;
Thy eyes are op'ned, and thou seest so cleare,
No worldly thing can thy faire mind remove;
   Thy faith, thy prayers, and his speciall grace
   Doth open Heav'n, where thou behold'st his face.

These are those Keyes Saint *Peter* did possesse,
1370   Which with a spirituall powre are giv'n to thee,
To heale the soules of those that doe transgresse,
By thy faire virtues; which, if once they see,
Unto the like they doe their minds addresse,
Such as thou art, such they desire to be:
   If they be blind, thou giv'st to them their sight;
   If deafe or lame, they heare, and goe upright.

Yea, if possest with any evill spirits,
Such powre thy faire examples have obtain'd
To cast them out, applying Christs pure merits,
1380   By which they are bound, and of all hurt restrain'd:
If strangely taken, wanting sence or wits,
Thy faith appli'd unto their soules so pain'd,
   Healeth all griefes, and makes them grow so strong,
   As no defects can hang upon them long.

Thou beeing thus rich, no riches do'st respect,
Nor do'st thou care for any outward showe;
The proud that doe faire Virtues rules neglect,
Desiring place, thou sittest them belowe:
All wealth and honour thou do'st quite reject,
1390   If thou perceiv'st that once it prooves a foe
         To virtue, learning, and the powres divine,
         Thou mai'st convert, but never wilt incline

To fowle disorder, or licentiousnesse,
But in thy modest vaile do'st sweetly cover
The staines of other sinnes, to make themselves,
That by this meanes thou mai'st in time recover
Those weake lost sheepe that did so long transgresse,
Presenting them unto thy deerest Lover;
         That when he brings them backe into his fold,
1400   In their conversion then he may behold

Thy beauty shining brighter than the Sunne,
Thine honour more than ever Monarke gaind,
Thy wealth exceeding his that Kingdomes wonne,
Thy Love unto his Spouse, thy Faith unfaind,
Thy Constancy in what thou hast begun,
Till thou his heavenly Kingdom have obtaind;
         Respecting worldly wealth to be but drosse,
         Which, if abuz'd, doth proove the owners losse.

[Lines 1409–1464 compare Cleopatra's earthly lustful love
unfavourably with the Countess of Cumberland's selfless love
of Christ.]

Though famous women elder times have knowne
Whose glorious actions did appeare so bright,
That powrefull men by them were overthrowne,
And all their armies overcome in fight;
The Scythian women by their powre alone,
1470   Put king *Darius* into shamefull flight:
         All Asia yeelded to their conq'ring hand,
         Great *Alexander* could not their powre withstand.

Whose worth, though writ in lines of blood and fire,
Is not to be compared unto thine;
Their powre was small to overcome Desire,
Or to direct their wayes by Virtues line:
Were they alive, they would thy Life admire,
And unto thee their honours would resigne:
  For thou a greater conquest do'st obtaine,
1480   Than they who have so many thousands slaine.

Wise *Deborah* that judged Israel,
Nor valiant *Judeth* cannot equall thee,
Unto the first, God did his will reveale,
And gave her powre to set his people free;
Yea *Judeth* had the powre likewise to queale
Proud *Holifernes*, that the just might see
  What small defence vaine pride, and greatnesse hath
  Against the weapons of Gods word and faith.

But thou farre greater warre do'st still maintaine,
1490   Against that many headed monster Sinne,
Whose mortall sting hath many thousand slaine,
And every day fresh combates doe begin;
Yet cannot all his venome lay one staine
Upon thy Soule, thou do'st the conquest winne,
  Though all the world he daily doth devoure,
  Yet over thee he never could get powre.

For that one worthy deed by *Deb'rah* done,
Thou hast performed many in thy time;
For that one Conquest that faire *Judeth* wonne,
1500   By which shee did the steps of honour clime;
Thou hast the Conquest of all Conquests wonne,
When to thy Conscience Hell can lay no crime:
  For that one head that *Judeth* bare away,
  Thou tak'st from Sinne a hundred heads a day.

Though virtuous *Hester* fasted three dayes space,
And spent her time in prayers all that while,
That by Gods powre shee might obtaine such grace,
That shee and hers might not become a spoyle
To wicked *Hamon*, in whose crabbed face
1510   Was seene the map of malice, envie, guile;
  Her glorious garments though shee put apart,
  So to present a pure and single heart

To God, in sack-cloth, ashes, and with teares;
Yet must faire *Hester* needs give place to thee,
Who hath continu'd dayes, weekes, months, and yeares,
In Gods true service, yet thy heart beeing free
From doubt of death, or any other feares:
Fasting from sinne, thou pray'st thine eyes may see
  Him that hath full possession of thine heart,
1520   From whose sweet love thy Soule can never part.

His Love, not Feare, makes thee to fast and pray,
No kinsmans counsell needs thee to advise;
The sack-cloth thou do'st weare both night and day,
Is worldly troubles, which thy rest denies;
The ashes are the Vanities that play
Over thy head, and steale before thine eyes;
  Which thou shak'st off when mourning time is past,
  That royall roabes thou may'st put on at last.

Joachims wife, that faire and constant Dame,
1530   Who rather chose a cruel death to die,
Than yeeld to those two Elders voide of shame,
When both at once her chastitie did trie,
Whose Innocencie bare away the blame,
Untill th'Almighty Lord had heard her crie;
  And rais'd the spirit of a Child to speake,
  Making the powrefull judged of the weake.

Although her virtue doe deserve to be
Writ by that hand that never purchas'd blame;
In holy Writ, where all the world may see
1540 Her perfit life, and ever honoured name:
Yet was she not to be compar'd to thee,
Whose many virtues doe increase thy fame:
    For shee oppos'd against old doting Lust,
    Who with lifes danger she did feare to trust.

But your chaste breast, guarded with strength of mind,
Hates the imbracements of unchaste desires;
You loving God, live in your selfe confind
From unpure Love, your purest thoughts retires,
Your perfit sight could never be so blind,
1550 To entertaine the old or yong desires
    Of idle Lovers; which the world presents,
    Whose base abuses worthy minds prevents.

Even as the constant Lawrell, alwayes greene,
No parching heate of Summer can deface,
Nor pinching Winter ever yet was seene,
Whose nipping frosts could wither, or disgrace:
So you (deere Lady) still remaine as Queene,
Subduing all affections that are base,
    Unalterable by the change of times,
1560   Not following, but lamenting others crimes.

No feare of Death, or dread of open shame,
Hinders your perfect heart to give consent;
Nor loathsome age, whom Time could never tame
From ill designes, whereto their youth was bent;
But love of God, care to preserve your fame,
And spend that pretious time that God hath sent,
    In all good exercises of the minde,
    Whereto your noble nature is inclin'd.

That Ethyopian Queene did gaine great fame,
1570   Who from the Southerne world, did come to see
Great *Salomon*; the glory of whose name
Had spread it selfe ore all the earth, to be
So great, that all the Princes hither came,
To be spectators of his royaltie:
    And this faire Queene of Sheba came from farre,
    To reverence this new appearing starre.

From th'utmost part of all the Earth shee came,
To heare the Wisdom of this worthy King;
To trie if Wonder did agree with Fame,
1580   And many faire rich presents did she bring:
Yea many strange hard questions did shee frame,
All which were answer'd by this famous King:
    Nothing was hid that in her heart did rest,
    And all to proove this King so highly blest.

Her Majestie with Majestie did meete,
Wisdome to Wisdome yeelded true content,
One Beauty did another Beauty greet,
Bounty to Bountie never could repent;
Here all distaste is troden under feet,
1590   No losse of time, where time was so well spent
    In virtuous exercises of the minde,
    In which this Queene did much contentment finde.

Spirits affect where they doe sympathize,
Wisdom desires Wisdome to embrace,
Virtue covets her like, and doth devize
How she her friends may entertaine with grace;
Beauty sometime is pleas'd to feed her eyes,
With viewing Beautie in anothers face:
    Both good and bad in this point doe agree,
1600   That each desireth with his like to be.

And this Desire did worke a strange effect,
To drawe a Queene forth of her native Land,
Not yeelding to the nicenesse and respect
Of woman-kind; shee past both sea and land,
All feare of dangers shee did quite neglect,
Onely to see, to heare, and understand
    That beauty, wisedome, majestie, and glorie,
    That in her heart imprest his perfect storie.

Yet this faire map of majestie and might,
1610   Was but a figure of thy deerest Love,
Borne t'expresse that true and heavenly light,
That doth all other joyes imperfect prove;
If this faire Earthly starre did shine so bright,
What doth that glorious Sonne that is above?
    Who weares th'imperiall crowne of heaven and earth,
    And made all Christians blessed in his berth.

If that small sparke could yeeld so great a fire,
As to inflame the hearts of many Kings
To come to see, to heare, and to admire
1620   His wisdome, tending but to worldly things;
Then much more reason have we to desire
That heav'nly wisedome, which salvation brings;
    The Sonne of righteousnesse, that gives true joyes,
    When all they sought for, were but Earthly toyes.

No travels ought th'affected soule to shunne,
That this faire heavenly Light desires to see:
This King of kings to whom we all should runne,
To view his Glory and his Majestie;
He without whom we all had beene undone,
1630   He that from Sinne and Death hath set us free,
    And overcome Satan, the world, and sinne,
    That by his merits we those joyes might winne.

[Lines 1633–1672 assert the uniqueness of Christ, and the
extent of his powers.]

Pure thoughted Lady, blessed be thy choyce[17]
Of this Almightie, everlasting King;
In thee his Saints and Angels doe rejoice,
And to their Heav'nly Lord doe daily sing
Thy perfect praises in their lowdest voyce;
And all their harpes and golden vials bring
    Full of sweet odours, even thy holy prayers
1680   Unto that spotlesse Lambe, that all repaires.

Of whom that Heathen Queene obtain'd such grace,
By honouring but the shadow of his Love,
That great Judiciall day to have a place,
Condemning those that doe unfaithfull prove;
Among the haplesse, happie is her case,
That her deere Saviour spake for her behove;
    And that her memorable Act should be
    Writ by the hand of true Eternitie.

Yet this rare Phoenix of that worne-out age,
1690   This great majesticke Queene comes short of thee,
Who to an earthly Prince did then ingage
Her hearts desires, her love, her libertie,
Acting her glorious part upon a Stage
Of weaknesse, frailtie, and infirmity:
    Giving all honour to a Creature, due
    To her Creator, whom shee never knew.

But loe, a greater thou hast sought and found
Than *Salomon* in all his royaltie;
And unto him thy faith most firmely bound
1700   To serve and honour him continually;
That glorious God, whose terror doth confound
All sinfull workers of iniquitie:
    Him hast thou truely served all thy life,
    And for his love, liv'd with the world at strife.

[17] To the Lady dowager of Cumberland.

To this great Lord, thou onely art affected,
Yet came he not in pompe or royaltie,
But in an humble habit, base, dejected;
A King, a God, clad in mortalitie,
He hath thy love, thou art by him directed,
His perfect path was faire humilitie:
    Who being Monarke of heav'n, earth, and seas,
    Indur'd all wrongs, yet no man did displease.

Then how much more art thou to be commended,
That seek'st thy love in lowly shepheards weed?
A seeming Trades-mans sonne, of none attended,
Save of a few in povertie and need;
Poore Fishermen that on his love attended,
His love that makes so many thousands bleed:
    Thus did he come, to trie our faiths the more,
    Possessing worlds, yet seeming extreame poore.

The Pilgrimes travels, and the Shepheards cares,
He tooke upon him to enlarge our soules,
What pride hath lost, humilitie repaires,
For by his glorious death he us inroules
In deepe Characters, writ with blood and teares,
Upon those blessed Everlasting scroules;
    His hands, his feete, his body, and his face,
    Whence freely flow'd the rivers of his grace.

Sweet holy rivers, pure celestiall springs,
Proceeding from the fountaine of our life;
Swift sugred currents that salvation brings,
Cleare christall streames, purging all sinne and strife,
Faire floods, where souls do bathe their snow-white wings,
Before they flie to true eternall life:
    Sweet Nectar and Ambrosia, food of Saints,
    Which, whoso tasteth, never after faints.

1710

1720

1730

This hony dropping dew of holy love,
Sweet milke, wherewith we weaklings are restored,
Who drinkes thereof, a world can never move,
1740   All earthly pleasures are of them abhorred;
This love made Martyrs many deaths to prove,
To taste his sweetnesse, whom they so adored:
    Sweetnesse that makes our flesh a burthen to us,
    Knowing it serves but onely to undoe us.

[Lines 1745–1824 are devoted to an account of the martyrdom
of St Stephen, based upon Acts 6–7.]

Loe Madame, heere you take a view of those,
Whose worthy steps you doe desire to tread,
Deckt in those colours which our Saviour chose;
The purest colours both of White and Red,[18]
Their freshest beauties would I faine disclose,
1830   By which our Saviour most was honoured:
    But my weake Muse desireth now to rest,
    Folding up all their Beauties in your breast.

Whose excellence hath rais'd my sprites to write,
Of what my thoughts could hardly apprehend;
Your rarest Virtues did my soule delight,
Great Ladie of my heart: I must commend
You that appeare so faire in all mens sight:
On your Deserts my Muses doe attend:
    You are the Articke Starre that guides my hand,
1840   All what I am, I rest at your command.

The Description of Cooke-ham

Farewell (sweet *Cooke-ham*) where I first obtain'd
Grace from that Grace where perfit Grace remain'd;
And where the Muses gave their full consent,
I should have powre the virtuous to content:

[18] Colours of Confessors & Martirs.

Where princely Palace will'd me to indite,
The sacred Storie of the Soules delight.
Farewell (sweet Place) where Virtue then did rest,
And all delights did harbour in her breast:
Never shall my sad eies againe behold
Those pleasures which my thoughts did then unfold:
Yet you (great Lady) Mistris of that Place,
From whose desires did spring this worke of Grace;
Vouchsafe to thinke upon those pleasures past,
As fleeting worldly Joyes that could not last:
Or, as dimme shadowes of celestiall pleasures,
Which are desir'd above all earthly treasures.
Oh how (me thought) against you thither came,
Each part did seeme some new delight to frame!
The House receiv'd all ornaments to grace it,
And would indure no foulenesse to deface it.
The Walkes put on their summer Liveries,
And all things else did hold like similies:
The Trees with leaves, with fruits, with flowers clad,
Embrac'd each other, seeming to be glad,
Turning themselves to beauteous Canopies,
To shade the bright Sunne from your brighter eies:
The cristall Streames with silver spangles graced,
While by the glorious Sunne they were embraced:
The little Birds in chirping notes did sing,
To entertaine both You and that sweet Spring.
And *Philomela* with her sundry leyes,
Both You and that delightfull Place did praise.
Oh how me thought each plant, each floure, each tree
Set forth their beauties then to welcome thee:
The very Hills right humbly did descend,
When you to tread upon them did intend.
And as you set your feete, they still did rise,
Glad that they could receive so rich a prise.
The gentle Windes did take delight to bee
Among those woods that were so grac'd by thee.
And in sad murmure utterd pleasing sound,
That Pleasure in that place might more abound:

The swelling Bankes deliver'd all their pride,
When such a *Phoenix* once they had espide.
Each Arbor, Banke, each Seate, each stately Tree,
Thought themselves honor'd in supporting thee.
The pretty Birds would oft come to attend thee,
Yet flie away for feare they should offend thee:
The little creatures in the Burrough by
50   Would come abroad to sport them in your eye;
Yet fearefull of the Bowe in your faire Hand,
Would runne away when you did make a stand.
Now let me come unto that stately Tree,
Wherein such goodly Prospects you did see;
That Oake that did in height his fellowes passe,
As much as lofty trees, low growing grasse:
Much like a comely Cedar streight and tall,
Whose beauteous stature farre exceeded all:
How often did you visit this faire tree,
60   Which seeming joyfull in receiving thee,
Would like a Palme tree spread his armes abroad,
Desirous that you should there make abode:
Whose faire greene leaves much like a comely vaile,
Defended *Phebus* when he would assaile:
Whose pleasing boughes did yeeld a coole fresh ayre,
Joying his happinesse when you were there.
Where beeing seated, you might plainely see,
Hills, vales, and woods, as if on bended knee
They had appeard, your honour to salute,
70   Or to preferre some strange unlook'd for sute:
All interlac'd with brookes and christall springs,
A Prospect fit to please the eyes of Kings:
And thirteene shires appear'd in all your sight,
Europe could not affoard much more delight.
What was there then but gave you all content,
While you the time in meditation spent,
Of their Creators powre, which there you saw,
In all his Creatures held a perfit Law;
And in their beauties did you plaine descrie,
80   His beauty, wisdome, grace, love, majestie.

In these sweet woods how often did you walke,
With Christ and his Apostles there to talke;
Placing his holy Writ in some faire tree,
To meditate what you therein did see:
With *Moyses* you did mount his holy Hill,
To know his pleasure, and performe his Will.
With lovely *David* did you often sing,
His holy Hymnes to Heavens Eternall King.
And in sweet musicke did your soule delight,
90   To sound his prayses, morning, noone, and night.
With blessed *Joseph* you did often feed
Your pined brethren, when they stood in need.
And that sweet Lady spring from *Cliffords* race,
Of noble *Bedfords* blood, faire streame of Grace;
To honourable *Dorset* now espows'd,
In whose faire breast true virtue then was hous'd:
Oh what delight did my weake spirits find
In those pure parts of her well framed mind:
And yet it grieves me that I cannot be
100   Neere unto her, whose virtues did agree
With those faire ornaments of outward beauty,
Which did enforce from all both love and dutie.
Unconstant Fortune, thou art most too blame,
Who casts us downe into so lowe a frame:
Where our great friends we cannot dayly see,
So great a diffrence is there in degree.
Many are placed in those Orbes of state,
Parters in honour, so ordain'd by Fate;
Neerer in show, yet farther off in love,
110   In which, the lowest alwayes are above.
But whither am I carried in conceit?
My Wit too weake to conster of the great.
Why not? although we are but borne of earth,
We may behold the Heavens, despising death;
And loving heaven that is so farre above,
May in the end vouchsafe us entire love.
Therefore sweet Memorie doe thou retaine
Those pleasures past, which will not turne againe:

Remember beauteous *Dorsets* former sports,
120 So farre from beeing toucht by ill reports;
Wherein my selfe did alwaies beare a part,
While reverend Love presented my true heart:
Those recreations let me beare in mind,
Which her sweet youth and noble thoughts did finde:
Whereof depriv'd, I evermore must grieve,
Hating blind Fortune, carelesse to relieve.
And you sweet Cooke-ham, whom these Ladies leave,
I now must tell the griefe you did conceave
At their departure; when they went away,
130 How every thing retaind a sad dismay:
Nay long before, when once an inkeling came,
Me thought each thing did unto sorrowe frame:
The trees that were so glorious in our view,
Forsooke both flowres and fruit, when once they knew
Of your depart, their very leaves did wither,
Changing their colours as they grewe together.
But when they saw this had no powre to stay you,
They often wept, though speechlesse, could not pray you;
Letting their teares in your faire bosoms fall,
140 As if they said, Why will ye leave us all?
This being vaine, they cast their leaves away,
Hoping that pitie would have made you stay;
Their frozen tops like Ages hoarie haires,
Showes their disasters, languishing in feares:
A swarthy riveld ryne all over spread,
Their dying bodies halfe alive, halfe dead.
But your occasions call'd you so away,
That nothing there had power to make you stay:
Yet did I see a noble gratefull minde,
150 Requiting each according to their kind,
Forgetting not to turne and take your leave
Of these sad creatures, powrelesse to receive
Your favour when with griefe you did depart,
Placing their former pleasures in your heart;
Giving great charge to noble Memory,
There to preserve their love continually:

But specially the love of that faire tree,
That first and last you did vouchsafe to see:
In which it pleas'd you oft to take the ayre,
160   With noble *Dorset*, then a virgin faire:
Where many a learned Booke was read and skand
To this faire tree, taking me by the hand,
You did repeat the pleasures which had past,
Seeming to grieve they could no longer last.
And with a chaste, yet loving kisse tooke leave,
Of which sweet kisse I did it soone bereave:
Scorning a sencelesse creature should possesse
So rare a favour, so great happinesse.
No other kisse it could receive from me,
170   For feare to give backe what it tooke of thee:
So I ingratefull Creature did deceive it,
Of that which you vouchsaft in love to leave it.
And though it oft had giv'n me much content,
Yet this great wrong I never could repent:
But of the happiest made it most forlorne,
To shew that nothing's free from Fortunes scorne,
While all the rest with this most beauteous tree,
Made their sad consort Sorrowes harmony.
The floures that on the banks and walkes did grow,
180   Crept in the ground, the Grasse did weepe for woe.
The Windes and Waters seem'd to chide together,
Because you went away they know not whither:
And those sweet Brookes that ranne so faire and cleare,
With griefe and trouble wrinckled did appeare.
Those pretty Birds that wonted there to sing,
Now neither sing, nor chirp, nor use their wing;
But with their tender feet on some bare spray,
Warble forth sorrow, and their owne dismay.
Faire *Philomela* leaves her mournefull Ditty,
190   Drownd in dead sleepe, yet can procure no pittie:
Each arbour, banke, each seate, each stately tree,
Lookes bare and desolate now for want of thee;
Turning greene tresses into frostie gray,
While in cold griefe they wither all away.

The Sunne grew weake, his beames no comfort gave,
While all greene things did make the earth their grave:
Each brier, each bramble, when you went away,
Caught fast your clothes, thinking to make you stay:
Delightfull Eccho wonted to reply
200   To our last words, did now for sorrowe die:
The house cast off each garment that might grace it,
Putting on Dust and Cobwebs to deface it.
All desolation then there did appeare,
When you were going whom they held so deare.
This last farewell to *Cooke-ham* here I give,
When I am dead thy name in this may live,
Wherein I have perform'd her noble hest,
Whose virtues lodge in my unworthy breast,
And ever shall, so long as life remaines,
210   Tying my heart to her by those rich chaines.

ABBREVIATIONS AND SHORT TITLES USED IN THE NOTES AND TEXTUAL APPARATUS

A&S	Sir Philip Sidney, *Astrophil and Stella*, in *Sir Philip Sidney*, ed. Katherine Duncan-Jones (Oxford, 1994)
AL	Aemilia Lanyer
Ars	Ovid, *Ars Amatoria*, in *The Erotic Poems*, trans. Peter Green, Penguin Classics (Harmondsworth, 1996)
BCP	The Book of Common Prayer, from the Psalms in the Great Bible, *The byble in Englysche* (1539)
BL	British Library
CW	*Collected Works of Mary Sidney Herbert, Countess of Pembroke*, ed. Margaret P. Hannay, Noel J. Kinnamon and Michael G. Brennan, 2 volumes (Oxford, 1998)
Defence	*Defence of Poesy*, in *Sir Philip Sidney*, ed. Katherine Duncan-Jones
DNB	*Dictionary of National Biography*
ELR	*English Literary Renaissance*
FQ	Spenser, *The Faerie Queene*, ed. Thomas P. Roche, Jr, Penguin Classics (Harmondsworth, 1987)
GN	Geneva Bible (Geneva, 1560)
Handlist	Richard A. Lanham, *A Handlist of Rhetorical Terms* (2nd edition; Berkeley, 1991)
Heroides	Ovid, *Heroides*, trans. Harold Isbell, Penguin Classics (Harmondsworth, 1995)
HF	Chaucer, *The House of Fame*, in *The Riverside Chaucer*, ed. Larry D. Benson (Oxford, 1988)
IW	Isabella Whitney
LGW	Chaucer, *The Legend of Good Women*, in *The Riverside Chaucer*
M–B	Clément Marot and Théodore de Bèze, *Les Psaumes en Vers Français*, facsimile of 1562 edition (Droz, 1986)
Met.	Ovid, *Metamorphoses*, trans. Mary Innes, Penguin Classics (Harmondsworth, 1955)
MS	Mary Sidney, Countess of Pembroke
Ms.	manuscript
NT	New Testament
OED	*Oxford English Dictionary* (2nd edition)
OT	Old Testament

Poesie   George Puttenham, *The Arte of English Poesie*, ed. G. D. Willcock
             and Alice Walker (Cambridge, 1936)
ps., pss.   psalm, psalms
Rathmell   *Psalms of Sir Philip Sidney and the Countess of Pembroke*, ed.
             J. C. A. Rathmell (New York, 1963)
SC   Spenser, *The Shepheardes Calender*, in *Edmund Spenser: The
             Shorter Poems*, ed. Richard A. McCabe, Penguin Classics
             (Harmondsworth, 1999)
S–H   Thomas Sternhold and John Hopkins and others, *The whole booke
             of psalmes* (Geneva, 1569)
Spenser   *Edmund Spenser: The Shorter Poems*, Richard A. McCabe (ed.)
TD   *Triumph of Death*
Tilley   M. P. Tilley, *A Dictionary of Proverbs in England in the Sixteenth
             and Seventeenth Centuries* (Ann Arbor, 1950)

An asterisk (*) before a headword in the Notes indicates that the poet's
usage predates that of *OED*, or that the particular sense in which the word
is used is unrecorded.

NOTES

ISABELLA WHITNEY

Additional abbreviations and short titles used

London: John Stow, *A survey of London, written in the year 1598* (Dover, NH, 1994)

Manley: Lawrence Manley, *Literature and Culture in Early Modern London* (Cambridge, 1995)

Martin 1996: Randall Martin, 'Isabella Whitney's "Lamentation upon the Death of William Gruffith"', *Early Modern Literary Studies*

Martin 1997: Randall Martin (ed.), *Women Writers in Renaissance England* (London)

from *A SWEET NOSGAY*

To the worshipfull and right vertuous yong Gentylman, George Mainwaring Esquier ...

ADDRESSEE *George Mainwaring*: little is known of Mainwaring; IW's brother Geoffrey dedicated Emblem 139 (sig. S2^r) of his *Choice of Emblems* (1586) to him, and another (sig. R2^r) to an Arthur Mainwaring.

2. *Nosegaye*: a posy of flowers. Frequently used figuratively. IW here plays on two secondary senses: (i) the protective properties of bouquets against infection – for IW illness is literal and metaphorical, referring to moral and social dis-ease and disorder; (ii) the idea, derived from the word *anthology* (a gathering of flowers), of the placing together of literary texts deemed of value.

3. *accompt*: consider.

4. *Flowers*: reference both to the title of IW's text, and to Plat's *The Floures of Philosophie* (1572). A metaphor for poetry.

8. *benefits*: perhaps financial, but more likely to be friendship.

10. *ANTIPATER*: (?397–319 BC), lieutenant of Philip II, governor of Macedon.

11. *DEMADES of Athens*: (*c.* 380–319 BC). The saying ('never [f]ill him with geveing') is taken from Plutarch's *Life of Phocion* (Loeb vol. VIII), XXX.213.

14. *DIOGENES*: Greek philosopher (*c.* 412/403–*c.* 324/321 BC), a Cynic, who believed in the rejection of conventions, and lived as a mendicant.

18–19. *like the pore man . . . the Persian Prince*: IW seems to connect this figure with Darius, mentioned again below, but it seems more likely to be Xerxes. See Erasmus's *Adages* (II.vii.5), also recorded in Richard Taverner (trans.), *The Garden of Wysdom conteyning pleasant flowres* (London, n.d.), f. 13ᵛ.

28. *DARIUS*: Persian ruler and empire builder.

42. *SLIPS*: small shoots from a plant for grafting or planting; used figuratively here.

44. *viage*: form of voyage (obsolete).

50–51. A variation on a conventional closing to a letter; see Erasmus, *De conscribendis* ('On the Writing of Letters'), in (trans.), C. Fantazzi, *Collected Works XXV: Literary and Educational Writings 3* (Toronto, 1974–), pp. 1–254.

50. *Abchurch Lane*: a street running past St Mary Abchurch, between Lumbardstreet (now Lombard Street) and Canwick Street.

The Auctor to the Reader

1. *Harvestlesse: lacking sustenance, support; *serviceless*: without reward or pay.

3. *though learning lackt*: the lack of education contingent upon IW's social position and her gender position.

4. *my selfe to edifye*: IW asserts authority *and* modesty; her reading is for private edification, not public display.

5. *wantyng a Devine*: the scriptures were seen as suitable reading material for women, but women were to submit to the authority of a clergyman in interpretation.

7. *Histories*: in the sixteenth century a much broader generic category, including mythology, travel narrative, prose fiction and factual history, but generally understood to impart a moral message, hence IW's insight here (8–9).

8. *earst*: formerly; *exceede*: grow, increase.

10. *them*: histories.

11. *wart*: became.

12. *VIRGILL*: (70–19 BC) Latin poet, prized in the Renaissance for his pastoral poetry and for his epic, *The Aeneid*; *OVID*: (43 BC–AD 17) Latin poet who had a central place within the grammar-school curriculum and

whose *Metamorphoses* was one of the most influential Latin texts in the Renaissance. Arthur Golding's translation was published in 1565 (Books I–IV) and completed in 1567; *MANTUAN*: (1448–1516), Italian writer of Latin eclogues; George Turberville's translation *The Eglogs of the Poet B. Mantuan* was printed in 1567.

13. *mased*: bewildered.

17. *shift*: change, replace by another of the same kind; *infect*: infected.

18. *noysome*: harmful, ill-smelling. The metaphor of pestilence is used for misfortune in general and social displacement in particular, but IW may also be responding to the plague year of 1563.

20. *make a dye*: die (colloquial).

23. *lucklesse lyfe*: IW introduces the major theme of *A sweet Nosgay*, namely her lack of fortune and her dependence upon her friends.

26. *sole alone*: the repetition is for emphasis, but *sole* also means single, unmarried.

26–7. *Fortune . . . to hoyce me on her Wheele*: The Wheel of Fortune was a commonplace for the vicissitudes of life.

28. *some steede*: stead, good fortune.

29. *Plat his Plot*: Hugh Plat (?1552–1608), poet and author of texts on gardening, science and household economy. His *Floures of Philosophie* (1572) was printed by Robert Jones, the printer of IW's poems.

33. *hye*: hurry, hasten.

35. *loth*: unwilling.

36. *slip*: a cutting, here an excerpt.

44. *whit*: least amount, nothing. Possibly punning on IW's name, underlining her self-representation as abandoned and without status.

48. *lotted*: allotted.

50. *It is the gever . . . respect*: proverbial, Tilley G97.

53. *complexion*: character, appearance. Plat's text (see note 29 above) is a miscellany from which the reader may choose what suits or pleases; cf. IW's metaphor of gathering flowers as a metaphor for poetic arrangement (46).

58. *trye*: put to the test.

60. *Sir Medicus*: an allegorical figure for a physician.

64. IW refers to the text to be circulated.

70. *Master Plat*: Hugh Plat. See note 29 above.

71. *light*: come upon.

72. *resighte*: recite, narrate; also, possibly, 'to put in new places', cf. IW's reference to the process of arrangement (48–9).

73. *sowed the soyle*: laid the groundwork, i.e. Plat's text.

75. *chary*: careful, cautious; *Swine*: Matthew 7:6, 'Give not that which is holy unto the dogs, neither cast ye your pearls before swine, lest they trample them under their feet, and turn again and rend you'.

76. *ravin*: act of seizing prey.

77. *no spare*: not lacking generosity.

78. *slip*: cut.

82. *eke*: also.

83. *mighty JOVE*: poetic name for Jupiter, chief of the Roman gods.

86. *Promote mee for no Sorceresse*: IW is dissociating herself from female healers, who were often accused of witchcraft.

88. *weare them to the stalkes*: i.e. carry through the moral precepts contained in *A sweet Nosgay*.

90. *a Maze*: apparently referring to the vagaries of Plat's arrangement and indexing, but also asserting *The Floures of Philosophie* as a kind of game which will impart moral value; see *The Floures of Philosophie (1572) by Hugh Plat and A Sweet Nosgay (1573) and The Copy of a Letter (1567) by Isabella Whitney*, introduction by Richard J. Panofsky (Delmar, NY, 1982), p. xi.

Certain familier Epistles and friendly Letters by the Auctor

To her Brother. G.W.

ADDRESSEE Geoffrey Whitney (1548–1601), author of *A Choice of Emblemes* (1586), dedicated to the Earl of Leicester.

1. *hence*: from here, i.e. London.

2. *the Cittie*: the part of London within the city walls, administered by the Corporation of London.

4. *harken*: hear; *kend*: known.

6. *yeldyng yeare*: productive time.

8. *staffe*: (literally) stick, here meaning mainstay; *stay*: rely upon.

11. *harke unto*: call upon, have recourse to.

13–14. IW presents her work as labour, and as a requital for debts past, present and future.

15–16. Alluding to IW's loss of position as a household servant; *languish*: long for.

To her Brother. B.W.

ADDRESSEE Brooke Whitney, the brother to whom Geoffrey Whitney dedicated an emblem (sig. L4ᵛ).

2. *sojurne*: stay.

3. *appaired*: injured, damaged.

5. *Maister*: possibly an allusion to Brooke being apprenticed in some trade.

6. *scope*: possibility; *repaire*: visit.

8. *wysh*: wish for.

10. IW repeats her constant refrain in these epistles, i.e. her luckless state; *byde*: happen.

A modest meane for Maides . . . to two of her yonger Sisters servinge in London

Addressed to her two younger sisters, this poem contains advice about running a household. There are several contemporary manuals on which IW could have drawn, e.g. *Xenophon's Treatise of Householde*, translated by Gentian Hervet (1532). Her letter contrasts with those to male recipients in that it tends to give advice without expectation of return.

14. *infect*: corrupt.

19. *words they are but winde*: proverbial, but from Job 6:26.

20. *brook*: deal with, cope.

21. *word, or Byll*: insult, or legal accusation.

24. *rehersall*: recounting, repetition.

27. *modest in a meane*: moderate in modesty.

28. *no thrall*: not enslaved or subject to.

30. *Vengeance is his*: 'Vengeance is mine; I will repay, saith the Lord', Romans 12:19.

32. *painful bee*: careful, take pains.

34. *The rolling stone doth get no mosse*: proverbial, cf. Tilley S885, recorded by Erasmus in *Adagia* (1500); *hard*: heard.

35. *scroule*: roll of paper usually covered with writing.

41. *Plate*: utensils, often made of silver or pewter.

42. *wrack*: damage, injury.

To her Sister Misteris. A.B.

Given lines 1–2, presumably this is IW's married sister, Anne Baron (see Martin 1997, p. 286). The poem gives an occasion for a comparison of the married and single state, and the contrasting of (public) writing with the tasks of housewifery and motherhood. The good wishes directed towards the recipient of the poem act as a kind of requital for an unpaid debt, suggested in line 4.

2. *wote*: know, variant of wit (verb), to have cognizance of.

4. *You vainely had bestowed expence*: implying that IW had received a financial favour, for which thanks are due.

5. *nature dyd you bynde*: i.e. bonds of kinship obliged you to generosity.

7. *in gree*: with goodwill, favour (archaic).

9. *Nestors dayes*: mythological archetype for longevity and wisdom, and a common formula in the sixteenth century.

10. *assayes*: attempts.

12. *annoyes*: harms.

14–16. Reflecting the humanist respect for learning, and its connection with worldly success and social status.

17. *staffe*: stick, means of support.

22. *huswifery*: the management of a household in all its aspects; *though I to writing fall*: (literally) come upon, encounter, but there is a slight moral edge to the word 'fall', especially given its opposition to 'huswifery'.

25–8. Suggesting that writing is a temporary substitution for the 'proper' womanly task of running a household; *frame about to rouse*: be helpful, profitable, to be of service.

To her Cosen. F.W.

This poem is an expansion of an epistolary commonplace, where the sender wishes the recipient good health and happiness (cf. Erasmus, *De conscribendis*). F.W. is unidentified.

2. *sore*: desperately, keenly.

6. *scroll*: letter (archaic).

7. *this accompt*: consider this.

A carefull complaynt by the unfortunate Auctor

The labelling of this poem as a 'complaynt' indicates its indebtedness to Ovid's *Heroides*, translated by George Turberville in 1567: IW's knowledge of the *Heroides* is clear in *The copy of a letter*. The conventions employed here recall Ovid's 7th epistle, but IW chooses to deploy her own rather than Dido's voice; the third person narration of Dido's plight owes more to Book IV of Virgil's *Aeneid*, which IW may have encountered in Surrey's translation (1557).

1. *DIDO*: queen of Carthage, lover of Aeneas in Virgil's epic, abandoned by him when he is reminded by the gods to found Rome. Cursing the Trojans, she sacrificed herself on a funeral pyre; *stint*: stop.

2. IW places herself in a long line of suffering women, picking up the theme of her own misfortune.

4. *hap*: occasion, cause.

5. *Troyan mate . . . AENEAS*: the Trojan leader in the *Iliad*, whose journey to Italy to found Rome is recounted in Virgil's *Aeneid*; *hight*: named.

6. *Carthage*: city on the north coast of Tunisia, reputedly founded by Dido.

8. *hore*: grey, white with age.

10. *fell*: bitter, vengeful.

11. *that she sweares my death*: Venus, the goddess of love, who was locked into a battle with Juno over Aeneas.

14. *thrald*: enslaved, captured; *retchlesse*: variant of reckless.

15. *dolors*: sorrows.

16. *plighted troth*: pledge one's faith, engage oneself to marry.

18. *salve the sore*: ease the pain.

19. *Faggots*: bunches of sticks, used for kindling; in some accounts Dido is thought to have committed suicide by throwing herself on to a funeral pyre that she had built.

20. *want*: lack.

23. *sweltyng*: sweltering heat, variant of sweltering.

26. *Ye Sisters three*: the Fates, or Parcae. Clotho spins out the thread of life with her distaff, presiding over the moment of birth; Lachesis spins out the events and actions of life, and is sometimes equated with Fortune; Atropos cuts the thread of life with her scissors.

IS.W. to C.B. in bewaylynge her mishappes

1. *heavie hartes*: cf. 'As he that taketh away a garment in cold weather . . . so is he that singeth songs to an heavy heart', Proverbs 25:20; *sacrifice for sinne*: Hebrews 5:1 refers to the function of priests 'that he might offer both gifts and sacrifices for sins'.

3. *Oblacion*: prayer, offering.

5. *dryrie*: dreary, miserable; *in dole*: in misery.

6. *noysome*: offensive, unpleasant.

8. *plaints*: complaints, sufferings; *amayne*: with full force, vehemently.

9. Unclear, but would appear to mean that 'my suffering [this] will cease sooner than my many sins'.

10. *misse*: error, mistake.

13. *JOB*: OT prophet, famed for his patience.

16. *frowarde*: perverse, opposed.

18. *two wittes*: proverbial, cf. Tilley H281.

21. *perplexitie*: difficulty, trouble.

23. *wracke*: ruin, destruction.

26. *tendance*: care, attention, with the implication of ministering to the sick.

To my Friend Master T.L. whose good nature I see abusde

IW distinguishes carefully between the bonds of friendship and those of kin. The identity of the recipient is unknown.

1. *Dame Seres*: Ceres, the goddess of growth and fertility, often identified with Demeter.

2. *fame*: commonly personified and closely connected with fortune.

4. *playd the shrew*: a shrew was a disobedient and ill-tempered wife; here it is used to bring together the idea of the vicissitudes of nature and those of fortune, meaning ill-disposed, intransigent.

5. *the Goddesse*: Ceres, as in line 1.

7–8. *fame . . . her trump*: Fame was commonly pictured blowing a trumpet, cf. *HF* 1243 and 1250.

9. *sith*: since.

16. *residue*: remainder.

20. *compt*: count.

25. *my wordes they weare as wind*: proverbial, cf. Tilley W833, but from Job 6:26.

28. *shent*: form of 'shend', to put to shame, reproach (archaic).

36. *pelfe*: stolen money or riches (usually derogatory).

38. *rew*: regret.

IS. W. beyng wery of writyng, sendeth this for Answere

4. *haps*: troubles.

7. *God . . . wyl, exalt the humble minde*: 'he that shall humble himself shall be exalted', Matthew 23:12.

11. *my stomack*: discontent, irritation (figurative).

The Aucthour (though loth to leave the Citie) upon her Friendes procurement, is constrained to departe . . . and maketh her WYLL and Testament . . .

TITLE *procurement*: bidding, request; *executor*: person charged with the responsibility of discharging goods according to the wishes of the deceased – ironic, clearly, as the chosen executor here is a place, not a person.

A comunication which the Auctor had to London, before she made her Wyll

3. *rue*: regret; *smart*: bitterness, ill fortune.

7–10. As Wendy Wall notes in *The Imprint of Gender* (p. 302), IW figures London as a treacherous lover.

12. *swarve*: turn away, reject.

15. *mell*: mix.

19–24. This allies IW with the genre of Tudor complaint, which demonizes the city as mercantilist, in opposition to an older feudal social order. See Manley, pp. 71–6.

29. *charytie*: closer to 'love' than to its modern meaning of goodwill, generosity.

31. *Treasurye*: storehouse, wealth, playing on its meaning as public or government control of expenditure.

The maner of her Wyll, and what she left to London: and all those in it: at her departing

1. The standard formula found both in actual wills, and in mock-testaments, cf. Robert Copland, *Jyl of braintfords Testament. Newly Compiled* (London, *c.* 1560), sig. Aiiiᵛ, where the 'whole of minde' formula occurs, together with the bequest of the soul to God and sins to the devil, reminiscent of lines 5–12 below.

11–12. The resurrection of the dead on the Day of Judgement.

19. *you all wyll witnes beare*: a will was deemed to be invalid unless it was witnessed.

20. *stedfast brayne*: i.e. that IW is not insane – a circumstance which would invalidate the will.

26. *I there was bred*: the limited biographical evidence we have indicates, together with what we know of Geoffrey Whitney, her brother, that IW was brought up in the country, near Nantwich in Cheshire (*DNB*).

27. *store*: plenty.

28. *Pauls to the head*: St Paul's (the pre-Great Fire of London church) as the chief.

31. *craveth*: requires, demands.

37–8. IW refers to the requirement that fish be eaten in penance, and on fast days.

39. *fraught*: filled with, loaded.

41. *Watlyng Streete*: leading east from St Paul's, following the Roman road; *Canwyck streete*: extension of Watling Street, leading to Eastcheap. Also known as Candlewick Street, and famed for its drapers and fishmongers (Manley, p. 111). Now part of Cannon Street.

42. *Wollen*: woollen (variant).

43. *Friday streete*: lane off Cheapside, running into the West Fish Market; so named because fishmongers were to be found there, and fish was eaten on Fridays. See *London*, p. 328.

47. *M[e]rcers*: dealers in silks, velvets and luxurious cloths. The Mercers Hall was on Cheapside.

49. *In Cheape*: Cheapside ran east–west, parallel with the River Thames to the west of London Bridge, and was famed for its clothiers.

51. *Goldsmithes*: workers of precious metals. Goldsmiths Hall was north of Cheapside, close to the city walls; see *London*, p. 292.

52. *meete*: fitting, suitable.

53. *Plate*: beaten silver or gold; utensils made of these.

55. *Purle of Silver . . . Golde*: a purl is a cord of gold or silver wire used to make a border; it is sometimes used to describe the ornamental edges of lace.

57. **Bungraces*: (?) some kind of adornment for the hair.

61. *Nets*: fine mesh work, used for the hair or for veils.

62. *within the pawne*: where goods were pledged for cash, to be redeemed at a later date. See *London*, p. 202; the most famous 'pawn' in London was at the Royal Exchange, built in 1566.

63. *Gorgets*: originally a piece of armour for the throat, hence a covering for the neck and breast, or a collar or necklace.

64. *Lawne*: fine linen.

66. *knacke*: thing, device (cf. knick-knack).

67. *Stoks*: form of punishment, where the miscreant was chained into a wooden device (stocks) to be ridiculed by the crowd. London also had a Stocks Market; see *London*, pp. 107, 131, 228.

69. *Hose*: leg-coverings; *Birchin Lane*: lane running north–south between Cornhill (or Cornhull) and Lombard Street. Stow calls it Birchoveries Lane (*London*, pp. 107–8).

71. *Trunks*: for trunk-hose, short breeches worn over the hose.

72. *Gascoyne gise*: in the fashion of Gascony, (figurative) a braggart.

73. *Pantables*: common variant of pantofles, slippers for indoor or outdoor wear.

74. *Saint Martins*: St Martins Lane, which ran from Aldersgate in the north to Newgate in the south.

75. *Cornwall*: Cornhill, which ran from west to east, from the Grocers Hall into Aldgate.

78. *by Bow*: St Mary-le-Bow. Its churchyards had stalls selling clothing (see *London*, p. 107).

82. *Bodymakers*: a body was the part of a dress which covered the body.

84. *Gardes*: ornamental edging or trimming found on a garment.

85. *Temple Bar*: the gate at the end of Fleet Street on the west boundary of the city, marking where the jurisdiction of the Corporation of the City of London ended.

86. *Tower hyll*: an open space within the city wall, north of the Tower of London.

87. *Bucklers*: small round shields.

88. *the Fleete*: a prison, previously a royal prison, at the west edge of the city, by the Fleet river, whence its name (see *London*, p. 359).

92. *junckets*: sweetmeats, delicacies, confections.

93. *Poticaries*: those who prepared drugs or herbs for medicinal purposes.

94. *Banquets*: (?) benches, counters.

97. *Roysters*: ruffians, rowdies.

102. *Playsters*: curative applications, often made of cloth.

108. *scant*: lacking, in short supply.

111. *At Mint*: the Royal Mint, in the Tower of London (see *London*, pp. 80–85).

113. *Stiliarde*: the Steelyard was an area of wharves west of London Bridge.

115–16. IW refers here to apprentices.

117. *proper Gyrles*: given the context which follows (119), IW seems to allude here to prostitutes.

119. *lucre*: derogatory term for money.

122. *repayre*: visit, go to.

126. *drug*: drudge.

128. *smug*: smart, well turned out.

131–2. IW asserts her exclusion from trading activity and exchange of goods.

137. *portions*: amounts. Dowries were known as 'portions'; IW may be alluding to her single state (see 'To her Sister Misteris', 25).

141. *the Counter*: an imitation coin, or a token used to represent a real coin.

142. *wrack*: ruin, disaster.

143. *Coggers*: cheats, deceivers.

144. *Sergantes*: enforcers of the law; *draw aback*: punish, prevent from trading.

145. *bayle*: provide security, usually financial, for the temporary release of a prisoner.

146. *coyne is very thin*: (i) lacking money; (ii) referring to the practice whereby coins were debased, hence making them less valuable as currency.

149. *Newgate*: city gate and jail, west of the city walls, adjacent to Holborn Cross and Bridge.

150. *sessions*: court hearing where defendants were sentenced or acquitted.

151–2. I.e., the sessions would clear the prison and prevent overcrowding.

154. *burning nere the Thumb*: the branding of criminals.

157–8. The process of trial leading to the death penalty, which required the verdict of a jury of twelve men.

159. *Holborne hill*: on the north-west edge of the city; the place of execution.

161. *Nag*: horse of poor quality.

164. *preace*: crowd, mob.

165. *not in their circuit*: does not concern them; the Fleet was primarily for debtors, and debt was not a capital offence.

169. *Papist*: a Catholic.

170. *underprop*: prop up.

172. *Boxe*: alms box for charitable donations; *behoofe*: use, benefit.

174. *laugh so in your sleeve*: laugh secretly, to conceal amusement.

176. *Ludgate*: the city gate, also a jail, on the west side of St Paul's.

177. *in case*: in a position to.

181–2. I.e., if I had ever managed to gain credit, and therefore had the opportunity to be in debt.

185. *shroude*: hide, conceal.

193. *Bookebinders by Paulles*: the churchyards surrounding St Paul's were the main location for booksellers and the print trade.

197. *my Printer*: Richard Jones (1564–1613), printer and bookseller. At one point he was located in St Paul's churchyard.

199. *wyll*: urge, desire.

211. *Bags*: presumably bags of money.

213. *Gate under the walles*: the gates located in the walls at various points of entry to the city.

214. *thee*: London.

215. *Fruitwives*: sellers of fruit.

217. *Smithfeelde*: a horse and cattle market to the north-west of the city, on open ground beyond the city walls (see *London*, p. 106).

218. *my Parents there did dwell*: no biographical evidence confirms this; this is presumably part of IW's creation of a fictive persona with strong familial attachments to London.

223. *Spitle*: hospital; usually a charitable foundation which provided shelter and care for the old, poor and sick.

225. *Bedlem*: Stow explains that 'St. Mary Bethlehem, without Bishopsgate, was an hospital . . . to have been a priory, and remaineth for lunatic people, being suppressed and given to Christ's Hospital' (*London*, p. 435).

228. *out of tune*: strangely, madly.

229. *Bridewel*: a palace built by Henry VIII, completed in 1523, just beyond the west extent of the city walls; *Bedelles*: beadles, parish officers who dealt with petty offences.

231. *Chalke wel chopt*: presumably a punishment.

232. *turning of the Mill*: Bridewell was on the River Fleet and had a water-mill (see *London*, p. 339).

234. *strive for House or Land*: IW refers to the numerous land deals consequent upon the dissolution of the monasteries.

235. *Inns of Court*: the four legal societies which had the right to admit barristers to practise.

238. *Court, or Chauncerye*: or the Rolls, where Rolls of Chancery were deposited; also the Lord Chancellor's Court.

247. *Tennis Courts*: enclosed indoor courts, where tennis was played (the game now known as 'real tennis').

248. *fence*: fencing schools.

265. *shrowding Sheete*: a cloth in which a corpse was wrapped prior to burial.

267–8. IW describes a pauper's burial, without a headstone.

269. *Ringings*: tolling of bells to mark a death.

279–80. Ironic, as IW is giving a critique of London's lack of generosity and social conscience, subordinated to the needs of rapacious commerce.

316. *Alminacks*: annual tables containing a calendar of days and months and, usually, astronomical information.

321. *Standish*: ink-pot.

* * *

THE COPY OF A LETTER, *lately written in meeter, by a yonge Gentilwoman: to her unconstant Lover . . .*

This volume was IW's first foray into print (1567), and it conforms quite closely to the vogue for complaints and epistles loosely based upon Ovid's *Heroides*, translated into English by George Turberville in the same year. While drawing upon the potential outlined for the expression of the female voice in Ovid's text (as well as in earlier English usages, such as Chaucer's *LGW*), IW also undertakes a significant revision of these authoritative models. She recasts the sexual treachery of men as a warning to be heeded, rather than as an occasion for lament, thereby providing herself with the authoritative role of advice-giver.

I.W. To her unconstant Lover

ADDRESSEE *Lover*: generally used to refer to a male, but not necessarily in the context of a sexual relationship.

1. *close*: secret.

13. *quaild*: faded, weakened.

25–6. The failure to keep promises is a theme of IW's writing, and here is a particularly masculine failing.

28. *SINONS trade*: Sinon, a Greek character in *The Aeneid*, who allowed himself to be taken prisoner by the Trojans and then persuaded them to bring the Wooden Horse into Troy, whereupon the Greeks hidden inside the horse sacked the city. A byword for deception and treachery.

30. *your kindred stayne*: the belief that wrong-doing would be visited upon one's ancestors through the shame attached to the family name, cf. Shakespeare, *The Rape of Lucrece*, lines 519–25 and 653–5.

31–2. Most of the examples of male treachery that IW cites here are taken from the *Heroides*. Many of them are also treated in *LGW*.

33–4. *ENEAS . . . DIDO*: the subjects of *Heroides* VII and Chaucer's 'The Legend of Dido' in *LGW*.

36. *cleave*: cut in two.

37–40. *THESEUS*: the lover of Ariadne, who helped him escape from the Minotaur's labyrinth only to be abandoned by him. See *Heroides* X. 9–16 and *LGW*, 1796–2227.

41. *JASON*: the leader of the Argonauts in the quest for the Golden Fleece.

42. *two Ladies*: *Heroides* contains two epistles to Jason, from Hypsipyle (VI) and from Medea (XII).

44. *wile*: cunning.

45. *MEDEA*: the archetype of a scheming woman, who used her skill with potions to protect Jason from the tasks he is set in the pursuit of the Golden Fleece, and charmed the dragon who guarded the fleece so that Jason could steal it.

48. *al kynd of things he wolde*: wanted. These include the rejuvenation of Jason's aged father.

49. *his Ship*: the *Argo*, in which his quest for the Golden Fleece was undertaken.

54. *forsworne*: committed to another by oath. The implication is that Jason should be scared that the gods will take revenge for his treachery.

55. *scape*: contraction of 'escape'.

56. *torne*: broken, wrecked.

57. *Aeolus*: in Homer, the ruler of the winds, and Jason's grandfather.

58. *Neptune*: Roman god of the sea.

60. *stea*: stay, hold back.

63. *rent*: broken.

68. *veniall crime*: relatively minor sin.

69–72. IW's use of the device *correctio* ('Correction of a word or phrase used previously', *Handlist*, p. 42) draws attention to her rewriting of received literary models as she stresses the moral foibles of classical heroes.

74–6. *Paris*: originally betrothed to the nymph Oenone (see note to 65–8 of 'The admonition by the Auctor' below) after being taken to Mount Ida as a baby to evade death. He was the son of Priam, King of Troy, and Hecuba, and the younger brother of Hector. Paris stole Helen from the Greeks and took her to Troy, precipitating the Trojan War.

76. *Rape*: theft, violation, carrying off.

77. *Troylus*: the younger brother of Paris, mentioned only in passing in the *Iliad*. In the medieval period Troilus was linked with Criseyde (or Cressida), with whom he fell in love. An exchange of prisoners takes place between the Greeks and the Trojans, and Criseyde is sent to the Greek camp, where she betrays Troilus for the love of Diomede. Troilus thus became a watch-word for fidelity in love.

82. *wants*: things lacking; *rest*: remain.

83. *list*: want, desire.

84. *refuse*: rejected one.

94. *elect*: chosen.

98. *HELENS trade*: Helen, renowned for her beauty, was often associated with loose morality. See Turberville's translation of *Heroides* V, where the Latin word *paelice* (mistress, concubine) is translated as 'harlot', p. 28.

99. *PENELOPE*: the wife of Ulysses, who remained constant during his long absences, fending off suitors by weaving and unweaving a shroud, because it was said that she would remarry when it was completed; synonymous with chastity and constancy. See *Heroides* I.

101. *LUCRES*: Lucrece, the wife of Collatine who boasted to his friends that only his wife would be found chaste and constant in his absence. Unable to resist this challenge, Tarquin stole into her bedchamber and raped her. Deeply ashamed, Lucrece then committed suicide, and her death resulted in the expulsion of the Tarquin dynasty from Rome, and the establishment of republican rule. The story is found in Livy, in William Painter's *The Pallace of Pleasure* (1566) and in *LGW*, 1680–1885.

102. *Thisbie*: the lover of Pyramus. The two lovers were prevented from marrying by their parents, and spoke to one another through a crack in the wall between their houses. They agreed to meet at Ninus' tomb, where Thisbie was frightened by a lion, who bit her cloak as she fled. Pyramus, finding the blood-stained cloak, thought Thisbie was dead and killed himself. On discovering the dead body of Pyramus, Thisbie did likewise. The story is told in *Met.* IV, available to IW in Golding's translation (Book IV.55ff.), as well as in *LGW*, 706–923.

103. *PETO*: alluding to Cardinal William Peto (d. 1558). Chaplain to Henry VIII, he denounced the king's plans to divorce Catherine of Aragon in a sermon. He subsequently devoted himself to arguing against the king's divorce, and hence here is used as an emblem of constancy in a double sense: (i) he stands for the indissolubility of marriage, and (ii) he is known for his adherence to his moral position (see *DNB*).

104. *rueth*: pitied, regretted.

114. *Cassandraes gift*: Cassandra, daughter of Priam and Hecuba, sister of Paris. In later traditions, she was famous for her prophetic powers, mentioned by Ovid in *Heroides* V.

119. *hap*: occur, happen.

120. *refraine*: prevent.

126. *King Nestor*: famed for his longevity.

129. *King Xerxis*: Persian king, reigned 486–465 BC.

130. *King Cressus*: king of Lydia, reigned *c.* 560–546 BC, who claimed to be the richest of men.

132. *on Mould*: earth (archaic).

134. *in store*: in mind.

The admonition by the Auctor, to all yong Gentilwomen: And to al other Maids being in Love

In addition to the rereading of classical texts, this poem provides a meditation on the proverb 'Try before you trust', from Ecclesiasticus 6:7, 'If thou wouldest get a friend, prove him first, and be not hasty to credit him', but here it is relocated to the sphere of relations between the sexes. The poem gives advice on decoding the language of love, as detailed in Ovid's *Art of Love*, for example, and concludes with a commonplace parable (the fish and the hook) which is also, as Paul Marquis argues, a farewell to love, or *commiatio* ('Oppositional Ideologies of Gender in Isabella Whitney's *Copy of a Letter*', *Modern Language Review* 90 (1995), p 320).

1. *Ye Virgins*: referring to women who fall in love; Cupid is the god of love.

6. *advice do lacke*: on the basis of the experience recounted in *The copy of a letter*, IW presents herself as having the authority to give advice to young women on love.

8. *slacke*: lax, idle.

13. *painted*: false, deceptive.

15–16. *Mermaides*: famed for their power to lure mariners to their deaths through deceit and their alluring singing.

17. *Some use the teares of Crocodiles*: proverbial, cf. Erasmus, *Adagia*, 'Crocodili lachrymae'.

19–20. Cf. Chaucer's *Troilus*, who is advised by Pandarus to splash his letter to Criseyde with tears to convince her of the depth of his love, *Troilus and Criseyde* II.1026–7.

21–4. *Ovid . . . Arte of Love*: *Ars* I.659–62.

25ff. IW has in mind here the arts of deception in love described by Ovid in *Ars*.

33. *Trust not a man*: a gendered use of Tilley T595, 'Try before you trust', used extensively here (e.g. lines 37, 41–2, 73–4).

36. *in store*: in mind.

40. *shrink*: shirk responsibility.

41–64. *SCILLA*: not the mythological monster, but the daughter of Nisus, king of Megara. His fate depended upon his lock of purple hair, which was cut off by Scylla in order to betray the city of Minos, according to Ovid, for love. Minos, however, refused to accept her gift, and denied her the love that she had hoped to gain. She swam after Minos' ship and was punished for her crime by being turned into the sea-bird Ciris (or shearer), pursued by the sea-eagle (Nisus). See *Met*. VIII, pp. 178–83.

43–4. Scylla was abandoned by Minos, and punished by her father.

49–52. *Haire by fate*: cf. 'the hair on which his whole destiny depended' (*Met*. VIII, p. 181).

59–60. In Ovid's version Minos does not kill Nisus, but leaves Megara.

65–8. The story of Oenone and Paris is found in *Heroides* V. Oenone was a nymph on Mount Ida, loved by Paris before he discovered his descent from Priam. He abandoned her for Helen of Troy.

69–72. Demophoon and Phyllis fell in love when his ship was washed ashore in a storm. Phyllis gave him her virginity as a sign of her fidelity, but Demophoon left Thrace never to return. Phyllis hanged herself. The primary account is found in *Heroides* II.

71. *transformed so*: an almond tree grew on Phyllis' grave.

73–88. Hero was the priestess of Aphrodite. Leander saw her at a religious festival and fell in love with her. He would swim the Hellespont at night to see her, and was drowned when a storm extinguished the light she used to guide him. The mutual nature of their love distinguishes them from the other figures IW discusses.

81. *She scrat[ched] her face, she tare her Heir*: standard behaviour for grieving women in the *Heroides*.

87. *alwayes trie before ye trust*: the proverb (see Tilley T595) which recurs throughout this poem (e.g. lines 95–6).

89–92. A standard image for deceit and entrapment, found in *Ars* I.47–8.

93. *hap*: luck, situation.

103. *Linceus eies*: Lynceus, one of the Argonauts, famed for his keen sight.

107. *Syr Phebus*: the sun.

114. *prety shift*: a smart move.

117. *pries*: inspects closely.

120. *stricke*: strike.

*   *   *

The lamentacion of a Gentilwoman upon the death of her late deceased frend William Gruffith Gent.

Claims that this poem is IW's are found, without substantive evidence, in Martin 1996; Martin 1997, p. 281; Louise Schleiner, *Tudor and Stuart Women Writers* (Bloomington, 1994), p. 7; and R. J. Fehrenbach, 'Isabella Whitney (fl. 1565–75) and the popular miscellanies of Richard Jones', *Cahiers Élisabéthains* 19 (1981), pp. 86–7. The only connection with her is through the 'W.G.' text included in *The copy of a letter*, and the fact that both collections were printed by Richard Jones, whom IW calls 'my Printer' (see 'The Maner of her Wyll', 197). However, it resembles her style, which is distinctive if fundamentally conventional. Equally, there is no evidence for discounting her authorship. It is included here in a speculative, but sceptical, spirit.

TITLE *William Gruffith*: unidentified, but could correspond to the W.G. found in *The copy of a letter*.

3. *flitting fame*: passing recognition.

5. *write her will*: the primary meaning of her 'will' here is 'wish'.

7. *Muses nyne*: goddesses, who dwelt on Mount Helicon, and presided over the arts, including poetry.

12. *ruthe*: sorrow, regret; *ringe*: express, recalls the ringing of bells for the dead, cf. 'The maner of her Wyll', 269–70.

[ ]

1. *preace*: form of press (obsolete).

2. *Minerva*: Roman goddess of wisdom and the liberal arts, connected to writers and actors.

3. *Parnassus Mount*: the home of the Muses.

6. *Hector*: son of Priam and Hecuba, the hero of the *Iliad*.

8. *paynt them out*: depict, represent fully.

9. *I, a Mayde*: a woman, particularly a single woman. IW identifies herself as unmarried in 'To her Sister Misteris' (25), but given the frequency of male poets' adoption of the female voice, this statement cannot be taken as conclusive evidence of the sex of the speaker.

10. *wayle*: contraction of bewail.

11. *no skill I have*: a version of the conventional modesty topos, associated with the elegy tradition.

13–14. The wearing of colours was often used as a sign of having given a pledge; here they are part of a code of secrecy (see line 21). Each of them carries specific meanings: white denotes chastity; green, love and joy; red, passion and courage.

15. *blacke*: the colour of mourning. Martin 1997 (p. 304n) suggests it also represents constancy.

20. *carefull*: full of care, misery.

21. *bewray*: give away, reveal.

22. *pay my pate*: bring social opprobrium on my head; *for my hyre*: for my service, love. In both cases, the anticipated reaction is a consequence of the fact that the relationship described is an extra-marital one – hence the speaker's moral authority to mourn her 'friend' is uncertain.

25. *passe not*: circulate in the social realm; *for no payne*: in order to avoid the pain of social ostracism.

27. *amayne*: powerfully, strongly.

28. *claps*: setbacks, disasters connected with love.

30. *waste*: pine, lose in love.

31–2. George Puttenham says that epitaphs should be 'pithie, quicke and sententious' (*Poesie*, p. 56).

35. *prest*: eager, keen.

36. *Damon . . . Pithias*: famed for their friendship. Damon was condemned to death by Dionysius, and Pithias stood bail for him, while Damon left to sort out his affairs. Damon returned and Dionysius freed him, moved by

their mutual trust. This popular story was recounted in Thomas Elyot's *Boke Named the Governour* (1531).

39. *I. and H.*: Martin 1997 (p. 305n) suggests Jasper Heywood.

40. *Rime Ruffe*: inferior verse; *common sentence*: general opinion.

41. *at Pawles*: in St Paul's churchyards, the location of booksellers and printers, and where ballads and broadsheets were hung for the public's perusal.

42. *rampes*: climbs.

43. *doo use*: do regularly; the implication is that the tribute is mechanical, lacking in feeling.

45. *refuse*: give up, either the task of memorialization, or the love for her friend.

46. *bent*: inclined, determined, set on a course.

47. *blastes*: misfortunes; *lincked love*: the image is of a chain, or of the entwined lovers' knot, or simply of a couple arm-in-arm; *awry*: off-course.

50. *blot this scratched scroule*: IW repeatedly refers to her texts as 'scroules', cf. 'A modest meane for Maides' (35); 'To her Cosen' (6).

51. *Virgins fist*: the speaker's own act of writing.

52. *gripte*: snatched in his jaws.

54. *wight*: person.

57. *fram'd*: created, made.

59. *waste*: fade, pine away.

61. *Zoylus*: Cynic philosopher of the 4th century BC, here representing the idea of a biting, scathing attack; *sot*: fool, idiot.

63. *Momus*: a god, the personification of fault-finding; *overronne*: read rapidly.

69. *marckt*: understood, noticed.

70. *fretting*: chafing.

73. *good Ladyes*: this may refer to the Muses, or to IW's audience, posited as other women who have lost their lovers.

84. *Tantals paynes*: Tantalus offended Zeus by violating his rules for human conduct; he was punished by being given a huge thirst and placed in a pool of water which drained away whenever he tried to drink – hence 'tantalize'.

86. *Lady (Fame)*: Fame was commonly personified as a woman, cf. *HF*.

91. *Pallas*: Greek goddess of wisdom and the arts (Roman Minerva).

92. *Caliope*: the Muse of epic poetry.

93. *trade of time*: passage of time, continued effort.

96. *want*: lack; *Minervæ*: see note 91 above.

99. *chyding chaps*: scornful voices.

102. *tristive*: sorrowful.

106–10. *Admetus . . . Alcest*: Alcestis and Admetus were married, and he, when dying, was promised longer life if he could find someone to die instead of him. Alcestis offers to die for him, but is returned to life by Heracles who wrestles with Death for her. Hence a prototype of wifely loyalty.

108. *Narcissus*: the youth who fell in love with his own image, and was punished by being turned into a flower. See *Met.* III, pp. 83–7.

117. *bluntish blockes*: idiots, unfeeling fools.

119. *sprites*: spirits.

127. *busie*: inquisitive, nosy.

129. *That*: i.e. the disclosure of her name; *flying*: transitory.

MARY SIDNEY (HERBERT), COUNTESS OF PEMBROKE

Additional abbreviations and short titles used

Antonie: Mary Sidney's translation of Robert Garnier, *The Tragedie of Antonie* (1592), in Diane Purkiss (ed.), *Three Tragedies by Renaissance Women*, Penguin Classics (Harmondsworth, 1998)

Brooks-Davies: Douglas Brooks-Davies (ed.), *Silver Poets of the Sixteenth Century* (London, 1994)

Fisken 1985: Beth Wynne Fisken, 'Mary Sidney's *Psalmes*: Education and Wisdom', in Margaret P. Hannay (ed.), *Silent But for the Word: Tudor Women as Patrons, Translators, and Writers of Religious Works* (Kent, Ohio, 1985), pp. 166–83

Fisken 1989: ' "The Art of Sacred Parody", in Mary Sidney's *Psalmes*', *Tulsa Studies in Women's Literature* 8 (1989), pp. 223–39

Hannay 1985: Margaret P. Hannay, ' "Doo What Men May Sing": Mary Sidney and the Tradition of Admonitory Dedication', in Hannay, *Silent But for the Word*, pp. 149–65

Hannay 1989: ' "Princes You As Men Must Dy": Genevan Advice to Monarchs in the *Psalmes* of Mary Sidney', *ELR* 19 (1989), pp. 22–41

Hannay 1994a: ' "O daughter heare": Reconstructing the Lives of Aristocratic Englishwomen', in *Attending to Women in Early Modern English*, ed. Betty S. Travitsky and Adele F. Seeff (Associated University Press, Newark, NJ, 1994), pp. 34–63

Hannay 1994b: ' "House-confinéd Maids": The Presentation of Woman's Role in the *Psalmes* of the Countess of Pembroke', *ELR* 24 (1994), pp. 44–71

Hannay *Phoenix*: Margaret P. Hannay, *Philip's Phoenix: Mary Sidney, Countess of Pembroke* (New York, 1990)

Kinnamon: Noel J. Kinnamon, 'God's "Scholer": The Countess of Pembroke's *Psalmes* and Beza's *Psalmorum Davidis . . . Libri Quinque*', *Review of English Studies* NS 44 (1997), pp. 85–8

Lewalski: Barbara K. Lewalski, *Protestant Poetics and the Seventeenth-Century Religious Lyric* (Princeton, 1979)

Martin 1997: Randall Martin (ed.), *Women Writers in Renaissance England* (London)

Mornay: Philippe DuPlessis-Mornay, *A Discourse of Life and Death*, translated by the Countess of Pembroke (London, 1592)

Pritchard: R. E. Pritchard (ed.), *The Sidney Psalms* (Manchester, 1992)

Ringler: William A. Ringler Jr (ed.), *The Poems of Sir Philip Sidney* (Oxford, 1962), pp. 267–9

Schleiner: Louise Schleiner, *Tudor and Stuart Women Writers* (Bloomington, 1994)

Steinberg: Theodore L. Steinberg, 'The Sidneys and the Psalms', *Studies in Philology* 92 (1995)

Trill: Suzanne Trill, 'Sixteenth-century women's writing: Mary Sidney's *Psalmes* and the "femininity" of translation', in William Zunder and Suzanne Trill (eds.), *Writing and the English Renaissance* (London, 1996), pp. 140–58

THE SIDNEY PSALTER

'Even now that Care'

This poem appears exclusively in the presentation copy of the Sidney Psalter, prepared for Queen Elizabeth I on her planned visit to Wilton in 1599. There is no surviving evidence of this visit. This dedicatory (untitled) poem, addressed to the monarch, falls into the tradition of admonitory dedication, as MS uses the ideological associations of the Psalter with the Protestant cause, together with evocation of her brother's memory, as a lever to remind the Queen of her duty. It combines encomium with a meditation upon the Countess's role as author, presenting the text as a sign of service, not only to the monarch but also, more pointedly, to God.

3. *my Muse offends*: by taking up precious time, distracting the Queen from affairs of state, but also possibly by overreaching what is 'proper' for a woman.

4. *the line out goes*: the metre exceeds the line.

6. 'Rimes' is self-deprecating, drawing attention away from the central status of this book of the OT; the implication that the Queen does not have time to read the key text of Protestant meditation implies a paradoxical gap between Elizabeth's duty and her actions.

7–8. These lines are a reminder of Elizabeth's responsibility to uphold the faith, by force if necessary, *acts* and *active* being keywords for the Protestant cause.

11–12. Antithesis elevates Elizabeth, and the importance of MS's undertaking.

13–14. The reference to divine authority in relation to Elizabeth's monarchy offsets her sex and reminds her of her responsibilities in religion.

19. *these*: referring to the lines in the dedicatory poems; *Postes*: announcers, heralds.

20. *owe*: presumably duty and loyalty.

21–2. The paraphrase was begun by Sir Philip Sidney and finished by Mary. Poets represented her as the living image of her brother, the position that she adopts in both dedicatory poems. Cf. Spenser's dedicatory sonnet to the Countess of Pembroke: 'His goodly image living evermore,/ In the divine resemblaunce of your face', *FQ*, p. 32.

24. *defraye*: undertake.

26. *unstopp*: let loose.

27. *hee did warpe, I weav'd this webb*: this image has several senses. (i) It picks up on the connection between 'textile' and 'text', referring to the collocation of texts, translations and intertexts for the Psalter; (ii) it is an appropriation of an accepted female activity to the end of presenting MS's authorship; (iii) it provides a powerful metaphor for collaborative authorship, which implies, to some extent correctly, that MS's role was that of the 'finisher'.

28. *stuffe*: substance; the origin of the text in the Psalms of David, and its status as the Word of God.

30. *denizend*: admit an alien to residence and citizenship.

31. *thy musicke*: the language of the Queen, hence English.

32. MS refers to previous metrical versions of the Psalms in English, probably the stilted metres of the Sternhold–Hopkins Psalter. The clothing metaphor is developed from line 27; it presupposes a clear separation between words and meanings, where the language is the 'dress', or the external covering of the ideas; *repining*: complaining.

34. *liverie robe*: the distinctive set of clothes worn by the servants (or soldiers) attached to a noble household.

35. *parcell*: portion; *undischarged rent*: the gratitude, praise and faith owed to God.

37. *our neighbours*: Protestant allies on the Continent.

38. *scanted in our will*: the implication is that 'will', namely support for Continental Protestantism, is not matched by action.

42. *by many names*: through a variety of claims.

43. *There humble Lawrells*: referring to 'our worke' (41), i.e. the text, produced under Elizabeth's influence, to be returned to her.

44. *repine*: refuse, shrink from.

45. *Cabinet*: a small chest where private papers were kept. The implication is that the proper place for the Psalms is in the heart of the believer. Cf. 119B:8, 119P:5, 139:6–7; BCP 143:41.

46. *hang their vowed memories*: Elizabeth is presented as the fitting recipient for the fruits of the Muses.

49–52. The sense is a continuation of the previous stanza: if men did not admit Elizabeth to be the proper owner of the arts, she is nevertheless an appropriate patron for the Psalms of David.

52. *Authors state*: the author's estate, i.e. David's regal status.

53–4. The king is David, and Elizabeth as a queen is a fitting recipient; the chiasmus in line 54 – 'loved choise', 'chosen love' – pinpoints Elizabeth's typological role as England's David, the champion of the Protestant faith against the predations of Catholicism.

55. *Devotions President*: alluding to Elizabeth's role as Supreme Governor of the Church of England.

57. *ought*: anything; *justly square*: absolutely appropriate.

58. *haughtie*: elevated.

59. *beseeming*: fitting, appropriate; *Triumphs*: songs of jubilation or victory, following the defeat of an enemy. Used frequently by MS; see Pss. 68, 89, 98 etc. Bèze had added the type of victories or triumphs to the five basic classifications of type of Psalms set forth by Luther (see Lewalski, p. 43).

60. This line suggests the internal generic variety of the Psalms (see Lewalski, pp. 45–9); *zeale*: another keyword in the Protestant lexicon, meaning ardent devotion; *plaint*: complaint, lament.

63. The line refers to the centrality of the Psalter in Protestant devotion, the notion that this text is open to all believers; *assaies*: attempts to reach.

64. *sorting . . . sort*: some are fitting for all, but the Queen is the only one for whom all the Psalms are appropriate, underlined by the use of chiasmus.

65. MS is following a tradition of drawing parallels between the narrative of the rule of David and the reign of Elizabeth, to reinforce her identification with the godly Protestants rather than the Catholic philistines.

69–70. Drawing a parallel between David's conflict with the Philistines, who tried to undermine his godly rule, and attacks on Elizabeth from Catholic powers ('foes of heav'n').

76. *thy Trophees*: i.e. land and sea are the visible signs of conquest.

77–8. MS refers to the storm which wrecked the ships of the Armada in 1588.

81. I.e., Kings were required to entrust their states to Elizabeth's authority; the presiding figure here is the reversal of hierarchies.

82. The dependence of mainland countries on the power of an island; echoing the idea of reversed hierarchies.

83. I.e., In the face of established order. This idea was a common notion, and the argument that Elizabeth's 'worth' was exceptional and therefore justified female regiment was often deployed.

84. MS invokes the notion of Elizabeth as *primum mobile*, but possibly alluding to her chastity as well.

87. MS's deferral of praise for martial exploits, economic success and so on is consonant with the notion that women should not aspire to higher poetic genres, such as epic (cf. 79–80).

96. MS refers to the ideal connection between the Word of God, and contingent acts which will elicit the praise of men. Its political implications are analysed in Hannay 1989.

To the Angell spirit of the most excellent Sir Phillip Sidney

Like the preceding poem, this text is uniquely preserved in the presentation copy of 1599. It continues many of the themes of 'Even now that Care', but with more concentration on the politically resonant figure of Sir Philip Sidney, who, Elizabeth scarcely needed reminding, had presumptuously opposed her marriage to the Duke of Alençon because of his Catholicism, and had died defending the Protestant cause on her behalf. The poem is more personal in tone, adapting the traditional pattern of elegy, where the general lament (threnos) is followed by an individualized one; this classical structure enables MS both to adhere to convention and to adopt the stance of grief as authorization for her writing. The complex variations played upon the humility topos, together with the stance of submission to the authority of God, and Sir Philip Sidney, should be balanced by considering the fulsome praise for the Psalter to be found among her contemporaries, most notably in John Donne's poem 'Upon the translation of the Psalmes by Sir Philip Sydney, and the Countesse of Pembroke his Sister', in *The Divine Poems*, ed. Helen Gardner (Oxford, 1952), pp. 34–5. It is interesting also for its regendering of the Muse as male (in the shape of God/Sir Philip Sidney).

1. *to thee alone's addres't*: this contradicts the more general audience envisaged in 'Even now that Care', but implies that Sir Philip Sidney embodies the ideals that MS is trying to convey in her work.

2. *double int'rest*: literally, that Sidney began the work, and its completion is due to his inspiration, but extends the financial metaphors of 'Even now that Care' (35–6).

4. *imprest*: imprinted, stamped upon; but also to advance or lend money; to raise money or manpower for battle.

15. *honor brought to rest*: referring to Philip Sidney's death at Zutphen in defence of the Protestant cause in September 1586.

16. *reft*: deprived.

18. *halfe maim'd peece*: 'halfe maim'd' because of MS's own contribution.

24. *but peec't*: patched; continuing the text as textile images from 'Even now that Care' (27–8).

26–7. *zeale ... zealous*: keywords for commitment within the radical Protestant spiritual lexicon.

30. *honor thee*: this has a double referent – Philip Sidney and God.

31. *Graces*: three goddesses signifying charm, grace and beauty.

35. *debt of Infinits*: i.e. the infinite things that I owe.

38. *Phoenix*: the mythical bird who was reborn from its own ashes. The image alludes to Philip Sidney's varied interests, from the reinvigoration of English poetry to the rebirth of true religion.

43–4. MS builds upon the financial metaphors of 'Even now that Care', and alludes in passing to the biblical idea of the Book of Deeds determining entry to heaven, found frequently in the Psalter, e.g. 51:30; 56:25; 69:81–5; 139:62–3.

47. *would*: form of *will*, meaning 'wishes'.

48. *who knewe thee best*: MS stakes her claim here as the most proximate, and therefore the most authoritative mourner, commented upon by contemporaries also keen to appropriate his image for their own ends. See, for example, Spenser (p. 176) in *The Ruines of Time* (316–19):

> Then will I sing, but who can better sing,
> Than thine owne sister, peerles Ladie bright,
> Which to thee sings with deep harts sorrowing,
> Sorrowing tempered with deare delight.

49. *become*: in the sense of *befit*. A reclamation of MS's authority in the light of numerous attempts on the part of Elizabethan poets to assert themselves as Sidney's heirs; e.g. Spenser's appropriation of MS's voice (or text) and incorporation of it into the structure and lexicon of his *Astrophel* volume of elegies (1595), see Spenser, pp. 372–9.

55. *owly blinde*: a typical coinage, found earlier only in Sidney's *Arcadia* (*OED*).

57–63. MS's choice of vocabulary is highly reminiscent of many other elegies on her brother, but echoes strongly the poem attributed to her by Spenser (p. 382) in his *Astrophel*:

> But that immortall spirit, which was deckt
> With all the dowries of celestiall grace:
> By soveraine choyce from th'hevenly quires select,
> And lineally deriv'd from Angels race ('Dolefull Lay of Clorinda', 61–4).

75. *ought*: anything.

77. The idea that poetry would bring perpetual fame was a Renaissance commonplace, derived from Horace.

85. *theise Hymnes, theise obsequies*: not only are the poems a living memorial, they are also a form of praise; MS here suggests the generic diversity of the Psalms.

The Psalmes of Mary Sidney, Countess of Pembroke

The notes to each psalm are accompanied by a headnote outlining its significance (where relevant) within Protestant thinking; words or phrases suggested by MS's many intertexts are not routinely recorded but are noted where they illuminate the final text. The Latin titles have been retained. Details of the metrical features of each psalm can be found in *CW* 2.470–83. The complex textual history of the Sidney Psalter is given in the Textual Apparatus; an explanation of Ringler A, B and C is to be found there and textual variants noted.

Psalm 45

MS stresses the importance of the 'daughters' of God, and their mediatory role. The phrasing emphasizes the handmaid as a participant in praise and worship. See Hannay 1994a, p. 34; Hannay 1994b, pp. 52–7; and Fisken 1985, pp. 172–5. An epithalamion for Solomon's marriage, but interpreted as an allegory of the relationship between Christ and the Church, figured through Solomon's taking of a heathen wife, who has given 'her selfe wholy to her husband' (S–H, p. 26).

2. *him who doth the scepter sway*: a periphrasis for the use of 'King' in other versions, e.g. GN's 'I wil intreat in my workes of the King' (45:1).

5. The sources have no such preparatory statement, and the signalling of shifts between speakers is a recurrent feature of MS's rendition. She is particularly careful to differentiate between the objective narrative of the body of the Psalms, and the presentation of individualized utterances, especially those of God.

29. *Sabean grove*: Arabian. Not in any source.

33. *CW* (2.363) notes that MS avoids the source's reference to polygamy.

45. *faine*: eager, joyful.

49. BCP's and GN's 'kings daughter' is here a 'Queen', and S–H has her 'within her closet'.

52. MS means that the material is gold, but the craftsmanship is divine; *Fashion*: making.

54. MS's 'maids of Honour' would be the correct Elizabethan term; 'maides of honor' is the *OED*'s first citation of this term; cf. GN 'the virgins' (45:14).

62. **partag'd*: divided into parts. Usually connected with discussions of inheritance – hence MS is more astute about the importance of women to land distribution than the sources.

Psalm 47

S–H suggests this as a song of worship and thanks for the descendants of Jacob, prefiguring the time of Christ. A similar reading is suggested by GN's gloss (47:1a).

3. The psalm as a triumph is introduced by MS, but it is suggested by later lines of the psalm (6–8, 11–12).

6. The reference to grace is added, and builds up in the following two lines to a suggestion of the importance of foreign intervention, sanctioned by God's grace.

18–20. MS suggests the connection between God and earthly princes, as in BCP and GN, but also that they have a duty to uphold God's law ('Princes the shields that earth defend').

Psalm 48

A song of thanks for the deliverance of Jerusalem from its enemies, which underlines God's help. M–B suggests that Jerusalem represents the Church, delivered from its opponents (p. 154).

5. *Sion*: MS's usual spelling for 'Zion'.

8. MS places the detail of Sion's situation before its effect on its surroundings.

13. The rhetorical question conveys the kings' astonishment at what they see; *it*: the city of Jerusalem.

14. *mated*: equalled, matched.

20. *Eurus*: the East wind. Added by MS.

31. *Compasse*: survey.

32. *Tell her Towers*: count.

Psalm 49

S–H presents this as a psalm about providence: God will punish earthly riches and vanity, and will reward the righteous. Hence its central theme is that of mutability (*CW* 2.365). GN concurs, adding that all will get their just deserts 'in the day of the resurrection' (headnote, f. 245r).

TITLE fn. *A Sestine*: a sestina; technically a poem of six stanzas each of six lines and a final triplet, with the same six words at the line-ends in six different sequences. MS's poem bears only a superficial resemblance to the sestina proper.

5. *measure*: one of MS's favourite usages, here it literally means 'to listen', but alludes wittily to her own task of putting the Psalter into metre. Other versions do not have this stress on the ear, nor the musical pun on 'accord' (6).

6. *ridled speech*: referring to the 'parable' and 'darke speach' of the biblical version (BCP 49:4), i.e. the process of turning the hidden meanings of the biblical text into poetic speech. *CW* 2.365 supplies Calvin's 'and I will open my riddle upon the harp' (verse 5).

11. *outbeare*: bear forth, sustain.

15. *he*: death.

16. *meed*: reward.

19–24. MS follows the biblical sources quite closely, but works them into an effective patterning, condensing some details and expanding others. Line 20 incorporates an *ubi sunt* motif, similar to *TD* 1.79–100 (*CW* 2.366).

21. *reaves*: deprives.

29. *farr his prince*: i.e. far above his lord; *cheare*: face, countenance.

32. *foreslow*: delay, neglect.

34. *seed*: propagate, increase.

37. *stay*: circumstance, situation.

38. Clarified by GN: 'He shal enter into the generacion of his fathers' (49:19).

Psalm 50

S–H argues that this is a psalm prophetic of how 'God will call all nations by the Gospell' (p. 29) and of how he will require thanksgiving and praise, frowning on those who prefer ceremony to the love of God. It is thus a key psalm for reformers, and MS seems to have paraphrased it with care.

2. *pursevant*: herald, messenger, usually in a courtly context.

11. *vaulted heav'n*: arched, rounded. Added by MS.

14. *league did undertake*: made a covenant. The word also means an alliance, and this is an example of MS importing the language of politics into her translation; once again here, MS indicates the distance between herself and the speaker (God) by using 'saith he', which is not in her sources.

16. *Audience of the skys*: the heavens shall act as witness.

21. *thus do say*: added by MS.

25–6. Clarified by GN's 'I wil take no bullocke out of thine house, *nor* goates out of thy foldes' (50:9); **enstalled*: placed within a stall.

28. *downs*: pelts, skins.

40. *playning*: lamentation, complaint.

44. MS imports technical vocabulary, using 'statutes' for 'lawes' (BCP) and 'ordinances' (GN 50:16).

45. *prate*: chatter, blab, with the implication of untruth.

46–7. MS's choice of 'right reformed state/ Thou dost refuse' for GN's 'thou hatest to bee reformed' (50:17) is an interesting equation of the idea of reformed religion with righteousness.

51–2. The image of the serpent is added, but is frequently found in this connection elsewhere in the Psalter (cf. 58 and 140).

52. The equation between coining money (with a stamp which put an image on metal: a fairly recent usage, dating from 1572–3; *OED* records no figurative usage until 1607, in *Coriolanus*) and the coining of words is a commonplace in this period, due to their analogous functioning, both circulate as tokens of value.

53–4. A circumlocution for 'brother'; the two figures are united by the 'sweet strait band' of their mother.

58. MS creates an opposition here between 'true deeds' and 'false thoughts' not found in the source.

66. *straitly*: narrowly, tightly.

Psalm 51

This is David's prayer for God's pardon, and protection from his enemies, after his adultery with Bathsheba. It is also a prayer for Jerusalem, which represents the true Church (GN, p. 164). S–H interprets its theme as closer to Original Sin, 'naturall corruption' (p. 31), and therefore a prayer for forgiveness and for the increase of God's graces towards the Church. One of the seven penitential psalms, it was frequently recited by condemned prisoners before execution and its recitation in English rather than Latin was interpreted as demonstrating adherence to the reformed cause. See *CW* 2.6, and Foxe's *Book of Martyrs*, ed. G. A. Williamson (London, 1965), pp. 197, 272, 276 and 329 for examples.

1. *grace*: the idea of grace is not usually found in the text of this psalm, and has been added.

2. *measure*: free from limit or enumeration, cf. Ps. 49:5.

4–7. A considerable expansion of sources, full of characteristic word-play (*sin/sinfull*; *spotts . . . stainings/stains and spotts*). Interpretation later in the psalm, and in MS's sources, makes it clear that this is original sin, to be washed away by the sacrament of baptism, see lines 15–21; *still*: continually.

9. MS has developed an extended image based on chiasmus.

10. *uncessantly*: without ceasing. The notion of the 'soules ey' is added, reflecting Protestant self-scrutiny.

13. *dome*: judgement.

14. **reguarded*: the context seems to dictate the accepted sense, especially as the form 'regarded' is found in Ringler A, but this may predate the *OED* citations, where the word means 'to guard doubly'.

15–18. See commentary in Hannay 1994a, pp. 58–9; Fisken 1985, p. 178.

17. *living heat*: it was believed that the embryo was nourished by the heat of the mother. See Thomas Laqueur, *Making Sex: Body and Gender from the Greeks to Freud* (Cambridge, Mass., 1990), p. 27.

20. *inward truth*: reflecting the Protestant stress on the soul and conscience, and picking up on BCP's 'thou requirest truth in the inward partes' (51:6).

22. The extended allusion to lepers is added, giving inner sin an outward shape, using the metaphor of illness to describe God's mercy and grace. It has been developed from the meanings of 'hyssop', see following note.

23. *hyssop*: a herb, used medicinally and in Jewish purification rites. Its function is explained in Leviticus 14.

24. *Leapry*: leprosy.

26. The image is of the flaking of the purified, healed skin.

30. *Cancell the registers*: the sense is 'erase the records where my sins are contained'.

34. *breathing grace*: for GN's 'holie Spirit' (51:11). MS gives a more Protestant cast to her version.

38. *turnd from sin*: a literal rendering of the meaning of 'converted' (GN 51:13).

43. *shutt up with sinfull shame*: not in the sources, and could be interpreted as reflecting MS's consciousness of the anomaly in 'speaking' God's word as a woman.

52. *Salems*: Jerusalem's. This is MS's usual contraction.

Psalm 52

This psalm describes the tyranny of David's enemy Doeg. David encourages his people to put their faith in God, thanking God for his deliverance. GN and S–H suggest that 'In this Psalme is lively set forthe the kingdome of Antichrist' (headnote, f. 245v). Hannay 1985, pp. 161–2, notes that Bèze draws a parallel with the St Bartholomew Massacre (where the French Catholic king slaughtered his Protestant subjects) in his discussion of this psalm.

2. *vaunting*: boasting, displaying.

25. *wight*: man.

28. *His guard his gaining*: clarified by GN's 'trusted unto the multitude of his riches' (52:7).

Psalm 53

The psalm describes the cruelty of the wicked and their unexpected punishment, and prays for the deliverance of the Godly.

2. *marks*: notes. The second half of the line is added.

3. *Witless train*: stupid followers. This idea is MS's; sources concentrate on corruption and wickedness.

7–8. This idea of God as all-seeing is an addition, which reflects a heightened awareness of God's vigilance.

10. *astraying*: created for the metre, but hinting at 'going astray', which is how this idea is expressed in Ringler A: 'They all have strai'd, are cancred all'.

11. *cankred*: infected with evil, depraved.

13. *O Fury!*: the apostrophe conveys the biblical sources' rhetorical questions.

15. *Wolvish Canibals*: suggesting savagery and self-consumption, namely that sin is destroying them; 'Wolvish' means greedy, savagely.

19. *wreake*: punish, chastise.

Psalm 54

GN suggests that David, in danger, invokes the name of God to destroy his enemies, promising sacrifice if he is delivered.

1. *succour*: help, aid.

2. MS imports legal vocabulary to describe the idea of God taking up the cause of his chosen people.

5. *strangers*: foreigners, aliens.

10. *pay them home*: pay them according to what they deserve.

12. *dight*: adorn, decorate.

Psalm 55

This psalm is concerned with David's suffering at the hand of his enemy Saul, and his petition to God to relieve his misery; he then sets out the grace of God 'as if he had already obtayned his request' (S–H, p. 34). GN has much the same headnote. Hannay *Phoenix* (p. 98) cites MS's uncle, John Dudley, Earl of Warwick's paraphrase of this psalm, when he was imprisoned for his support of Lady Jane Grey, and interprets it as 'a cry for revenge against friends who had betrayed him'.

3. *plaint*: lamentation, complaint.

9. *A mark*: an object at which something is aimed.

9fn. *enterlin'd*: interlined, or written between the lines.

11. *pants*: palpitations.

17. *desert*: all English versions have 'wildernesse', but M–B has 'deser[t]s' which may have suggested this usage (p. 176).

19. *swallow them*: taken from the idea of the tongue in succeeding lines, but used metaphorically, to mean 'envelop'.

20–21. GN's 'Devide' is interpreted here to mean 'place a division between words and meanings'.

22. *Mother Wrong*: added by MS to BCP's general sense of corruption and iniquity in the city (55:9–11); *each where*: everywhere, on every side.

26. *guiles*: designs, deceptions.

27. *Burgesses*: inhabitants, citizens; *dwell the middle neare*: dwell near the centre.

28. *masquing robes*: clothes worn in lavish theatrical entertainments at court; here a byword for deceit and hypocrisy. Added by MS, perhaps to point to the paradox of courtly display and spiritual neglect, and extended by the clothing imagery in line 29 ('cloth'd', 'lin'd'). This might not only apply to Saul, but to Elizabeth too.

30. *hee*: the enemy (Saul).

32. *chere*: countenance.

33. *part*: for 'party'.

36. *made assay*: attempted.

44. MS focuses on the disjunction between words and thought, not in her source; *mind*: harbour, conceal.

45. *beere*: a stand for a coffin.

46. *even*: evening.

48. MS tones down David's arrogance a little; S–H has 'he doth not say me nay' (55:18).

52. *forbeare*: desist (to destroy his enemies).

53–7. The meaning here is obscure, but the general idea is that 'God shall hear my prayer and take what is due from the unbelievers; who but wretches would reject me, from whom they received nothing but kindness, true friendship and trust?'.

55. *Catives*: wretched villains.

58. *butterd words*: cf. GN's 'The wordes of his mouth were softer than butter' (55:21); the sense is derogatory.

61. *upcheare: encourage.

69–70. *make my stay/ On*: rely on, lean on.

71–2. *life holding thred*: a classical reference to the three fates, Atropos, Lachesis and Clotho, introduced by MS. She omits David's final pledge of grace to God. Kinnamon (p. 85, n. 3) suggests a possible source in George Buchanan's Latin paraphrase.

Psalm 56

This psalm recounts David's complaint about his enemies, and his demand for aid. He puts his trust in God, and promises to carry out his vows 'whereof this was the effect to praise God in his Church' (GN, headnote, f. 246v).

2. *gaping*: desiring to obtain, but also 'with mouths wide open', leading into 'devoure' (3), which is supplied by BCP's 'man goeth about to devoure me' (56:1).

5. *I am low*: added to balance the line.

7. *boast*: usually derogatory, but not exclusively; it can just mean 'a loud declaration' (*OED* 1).

12. *wrest*: twist, pervert.

18. *slight*: contempt, indifference, but also craft or guile.

26. *spright*: spirit.

31. *falsed*: proved false (pronounced as two syllables).

33. *stay*: support.

38–40. Cf. 'Even now that Care' and 'To the Angell spirit'.

Psalm 57

David, having been betrayed, is trapped in a cave with his enemy Saul. He calls upon God, certain that he will come to his aid, in anticipation of which he gives praise and thanks.

1. Like many of the other psalms this uses chiasmus as a central rhetorical figure, starting here with the opening line, which also deploys epizeuxis and antimetabole. See Beilin, *Redeeming Eve: Women Writers of the English Renaissance*, pp. 147–8, for further discussion.

4. Using the idea of God as refuge, MS puns; **hive*: give shelter to, developing the meaning of 'hide'.

5. *blasts*: blasts of fortune; *overblown*: blow over (using metaplasm), suggested by GN's 'til *these* afflictions over-passe' (57:1). MS extends the natural imagery; a blast can be a wind or gust (*OED* 1, 2), rage (*OED* 2b) or an infection which destroys life, attributable to a malignant power (*OED* 6). A general term for a curse (*OED* 6c), it carries a series of specific meanings which make the texture of MS's rendering considerably denser. These may be derived from GN's observation that 'he compareth his afflictions . . . to a storme, what commeth & goeth' (57:1b).

17fn. *forte*: probably.

31. *prepar'd*: implying that prayer and meditation are required; the question of the authority of spiritual speech (asserted here by MS) would have been more problematic for a female speaker dealing directly with the Word of God.

33. *laies*: short lyrics or narrative poems intended to be sung. An accurate term for the project of a metrical psalter. Cf. *Defence*: 'But even the name psalms will speak for me, which being interpreted, is nothing but songs' (p. 99, lines 10–11).

34. MS uses GN's injunction to the tongue, 'awake my tongue' (57:8), perhaps because it reflects the dormancy of the female voice within the Psalter. The phrase 'my lute awake' was familiar from Thomas Wyatt's lyrics (see Wyatt, *The Complete Poems*, ed. R. A. Rebholz (Harmondsworth, 1978), p. 144); Wyatt was himself a translator of the penitential psalms (*Poems*, pp. 195–216).

45. From 'heavens' (GN 57:10), compounding the connection between the harmony of music, and the harmony of the spheres.

Psalm 58

David describes those who flatter him, and their intention to destroy him, and his enemy Saul. He appeals to God's justice in order to destroy the ungodly. Unsurprisingly, this psalm, together with the group which surrounds it, had a particular place in Protestant thinking, serving as a justification for their faith, as well as a call to arms. See also Psalm 82.

1–3. MS develops the biblical text, 'judge ye rightly' (GN 58:1), by using legal vocabulary ('sentence', 'case'). S–H's rendering makes it clear that the psalm is addressed to rulers: 'Ye rulers which are put in trust' (58:1), as does M–B's *Entre vous conseillers* (p. 184), which gives MS's version a further nuance if we consider that her dedicatory poem envisaged Elizabeth singing these psalms, and acting out in policy what they narrate; *aright*: rightly, justly.

8–10. A continuation of the legal metaphor laid down in the opening stanza; 'justice' and 'weigh' being ironically countered by 'oppression' and 'ballance'; *practice*: MS's term has a specifically political cast (*OED* 5b and c), but also a distinctly Protestant nuance; it was often used to allude to the schemes of Catholics to overthrow the Reformed faith.

12–13. MS avoids the attribution of sin to the mother, unlike BCP's 'The ungodly are frowarde even from their mothers wombe' (58:3) and S–H (58:3).

18. *Subtile Aspick*: crafty, wily snake (*Aspick* is a by-form of 'asp'). The sense is that they are worse than the serpent, which could at least close its ears to the enchanter.

27. **dishoused*: ousted from a house.

28–30. 'Embryo' is a very unusual word at this period (*OED*), and MS uses it accurately to render 'the untimelie frute of a woman' (GN 58:8, BCP 58:7). Her notion of it as 'formless yet' is indebted to Renaissance gynaecology, which believed that the foetus gained shape in the womb, under the influence of the humours, behaviour and intake of the mother (see n. 17 to Ps. 51 above). The idea of 'dishoused' then might apply by analogy to both snail and embryo, with the concept of maternity reinforcing the results of sin and unrighteousness. MS resists the direct implication of the biblical text, 'and let them not see the Sunne' (BCP 58:7), asserting that 'Though born' it 'cannot get' to see the sun. See Hannay 1994a, p. 44; Hannay 1994b, pp. 61–2; and Fisken 1985, pp. 176–7.

34. *topside turfway*: topsy-turvy.

42. *stay*: await.

Psalm 60

David now rules over Judea, and because of the signs of favour shown to him by God it is clear 'that God elected him king' (S–H, p. 37); the psalm assures the people that they will prosper if they accept David as their king and put their trust in God. David prays to God to help him finish his task. This psalm had important implications not only for the Genevan exiles, but for all those interested in resistance theories, because it implies that monarchs are chosen by God and that it is with his blessing that their regiment will prosper. Analogies with David were frequent in the early years of Elizabeth's rule, in order to create a sure authority for a Protestant reign.

6. *chaps*: fissures or cracks in a surface.

7. *sound*: from the context this must mean 'whole'.

8. Keep her in her former state.

11. The metaphorical undercurrents are brought out; cf. 'thou hast given us a drinke of deadly wine' (BCP 60:3).

15. *conduction*: implementation, management.

22. *part out*: distribute in shares.

23. *perch and pole*: a perch, also called a pole, was a rod of fixed length used for measuring land; *meate*: divide up.

24–30. All these examples are taken directly from the biblical sources.

37. This sentiment is added, although the sense of it is in the biblical source (GN 60:11–12).

Psalm 61

Threatened, David asks to be confirmed in his kingship, offering praises in return.

21. The enemies David alludes to are the Ammonites and Absalom.

26–8. BCP says 'graunt the king a long life: that his yeeres may endure throughout all generations' (61:6). MS omits the second part of this statement, using GN instead: 'his yeres shalbe as manie ages' (61:6), possibly tactless in a volume presented to the ageing and childless Elizabeth in 1599. Given that her recipient was both well-read in the Bible and possessed of an excellent memory, its omission may have been just as tactless.

35fn. *under his own hand*: Woodforde has temporarily forgotten that he is transcribing the writings of a woman; however, it is interesting to note that he automatically associates 'Author' with the male sex.

Psalm 63

After the threat from Saul in the desert of Ziph, David gives thanks for his deliverance, trusting in God's mercy. The psalm prophesies the downfall of God's enemies, and the happiness of his followers.

3. *Employ my skill*: a self-referential comment on the task of the paraphraser of the Psalms, not found in the source.

5. *thirst of thee*: thirst for thee.

9. *reare*: raise up.

23. *in light*: while waking, in contrast to dreaming (22).

26. *Hiv'd*: given shelter; the usual formula used by MS for the biblical phrase 'under the shadow of thy wings wil I rejoice' (BCP and GN 63:8). Cf. Ps. 57:4.

Psalm 64

David prays, condemning 'false reporters and slanderers' (S–H, p. 39), declaring their punishment to be a comfort to the just and for the glory of God.

1. *wherin my grief I show*: MS's addition to the sense of the biblical text.

3. *in rest*: either 'in peace' or 'for the rest of my life'.

6. *wiles*: schemes, plots.

9. *fretted*: worn or ridged.

12. *embusht*: lying in ambush (past participle).

15. *obstinate to ill*: stubbornly adhering to wrongdoing.

17–21. I.e., they look to find deception and sin to such an extent that they find it everywhere.

26. *quake*: quake with laughter.

Psalm 65

This psalm gives praise and thanksgiving to God for his election and government, for his blessings and the earth, 'but specially toward his Church' (GN, headnote, f. 248r).

6. MS's own image for God's mercy and forgiveness.

9–11. MS treats God's 'Court' (GN 65:4) rather like earthly ones, where the servant is fed at the monarch's or householder's expense; *checkroll*: a list containing the names of persons in the sovereign's service and chargeable to the royal exchequer; also a list of the servants of any large household; *Viands*: foodstuffs.

18. *restless wavy plain*: the sea.

22. *beck*: gesture, like a nod, which communicates a command; *surcease*: cessation.

23–4. MS mingles two aspects of the psalm here to use the uproar of the natural world as a metaphor for civil disorder, GN's 'tumultes of the people' (65:7).

26. *affright*: scare, terrify.

31–6. On the cycle of birth and death, see Fisken 1985, p. 179. See also John 12:24.

37. *Drunck is each ridg*: GN clarifies with 'Thou waterest abundantly the forrowes thereof' (65:10).

39. *cloud-born*: either 'carried by the clouds', but more likely 'born of the clouds'.

46. The clothing imagery is MS's addition, derived from GN's 'clad'.

Psalm 67

S–H describes this psalm as 'a sweet prayer' (p. 40) by means of which the faithful may obtain the favour of God, so that his judgements may be universally known. It also gives thanks for the fact that God is the 'governour of all nations' (p. 40). GN views it as a prayer of the Church for God's favour, and as a prophecy of the coming of the kingdom of God 'which shulde be universally erected at the comming of Christ' (headnote, f. 248v).

15. MS means 'never deviating'.

17–18. These lines repeat 9–10, as the biblical verse 67:5 repeats 67:3, a repetition underlined by the use of anadiplosis.

30. *Zephyrs neast*: the West wind's nest, a detail added by MS.

Psalm 68

David praises the mercies of God and the many ways in which he makes these known. God's Church, because of his promises and victories, exceeds all known things, and hence his people are 'moved to praise God for ever' (S–H, p. 41). Hannay 1985 (p. 162) notes that this psalm was used as a battle-hymn by the French Huguenots.

1–8. While expanding and developing, notably the images of smoke and wax in verse 2 of the psalm, MS follows the sense quite closely here; cf. S–H, 'as the fire doth melt the waxe and winde blowes smoke away' (68:2).

3. *bewray*: reveal, expose.

8. *naughty ... naught ... nought*: the word-play suggests the wicked ('naughty') will become insignificant ('naught') before being annihilated ('nought', meaning nothing).

9. *aright*: justly.

11. *In mapp of outward prayse*: hinting at the relationship of outer speech to inner spiritual happiness. Speech, even psalmody, is only an outline, a two-dimensional guide to what lies within; the inadequacy of verbal representation is also suggested by 'paint', which could denote a vivid visual representation, or even (in a transferred sense) a verbal picture, but also frequently had slightly negative implications.

12. *but*: nothing except.

13. *triumph then*: an appropriate term for this psalm, which encloses within it a triumph in the Roman sense – songs of victory together with the display of spoils. Cf. Pss. 89:42, 98:14, 100:4, etc.

18. *Thou of the fetterd foot*: i.e. prisoners; *fretting*: chafing, gnawing.

20. *the cursed sand do till*: the image conveys barrenness – nothing can be grown on sand, 'Continue in scarcenesse' (BCP 68:6).

23. *sweating*: exuding moisture.

24–5. The linkage through reversal (antimetabole) and repetition is MS's.

29. The NT idea of God's people as a flock of sheep is MS's addition.

29fn. *Forte pro*: probably for.

31–2. These lines foreground and introduce the singing of triumphs by women: this is the only precedent of female speech in the Psalter, and MS stresses not only the speakers' virtue ('A virgin army ... with chastness armed', line 31), but also emphasizes their divine authority: 'by Thee was taught this triumph Song to sing'.

34. *house-confined*: the edge, or charge, of this phrase is not in BCP's 'they of the household' (68:12) or in S–H's 'women which remayne at home' (68:12). *CW* 2.450 suggests that 'the passage may have been too bold for her to let it stand', hence its revision to 'we share the spoils that weake in howse did ly' (*CW* 2.79).

35. *hew*: colour; *chimnys glosse*: soot; *foyle*: cover or discolour.

37–40. Cf. GN, 'yet shal ye be as the wings of a doove that is covered with silver, and whose fethers are like yelowe golde' (68:13).

42. *extirpate*: rooted out.

44. *as Salmon snow*: the place referred to is Zalmon, in the land of Canaan, which is the spelling used in GN (68:14).

46. *empyreall*: relating to Empyrean, the sphere of fire or the highest heaven; the abode of God and the angels. Added by MS.

61. *healthfull*: wholesome.

64. *the keyes*: a detail not found in the sources.

68. *growing Perrukes*: wigs, but meaning here 'a head of hair'; the word is

taken directly from M–B (p. 218). The sense is that blood will water their hair.

77. *Vantguard*: advance party.

78. *rereward*: the back of the party.

79. *middleward*: the middle section of the procession; *timbrells*: tambourines.

90–92. BCP says 'so shall kings bring presents unto thee' (68:29), which MS turns into an account of kingly vanity. The 'furious bulls' and 'wanton calves' are the usual sacrificial animals, to be destroyed and subdued just like the rebellious rulers.

102. *coachmanlike*: cf. the image of God as the horseman of heaven (14).

Psalm 69

S–H suggests that Christ and his elect are represented through David's anguish, because his enemies are punished, just as Judas was. MS does not make this interpretation explicit. David exhorts all the world to praise, 'prophecying of the kingdome of Christ and the building of Juda' (S–H, p. 42). GN presses this point home more forcefully, saying that David's misery 'is set forthe as a figure of Christ and all his members' (headnote, f. 249r). Gary Waller discusses the revisions to this psalm (see 'The Text and Manuscript Variants of the Countess of Pembroke's Psalms', *Review of English Studies*, NS 26 (1975), p. 14).

16. *descry*: discern.

17. *discount'nanct*: discouraged.

19. *blushing shame*: MS frequently uses the blush to convey shame. Kinnamon (p. 87) suggests that the image is added from the *interpretatio* in Bèze's Latin text, which was not translated by Gilbie.

29–30. Clarified by GN with 'the rebukes of them that rebuked thee, are fallen upon me' (69:9).

36. *prate*: babble, speak nonsense; *private in their wyne*: 'the drunkards sang *of me*' (GN 69:12). The distinction between public and private is not in the sources.

44. **banckless*: lacking a bordering shelf or slope. See M–B (p. 224): 'ces eaux qui n'ont rive ne fons'.

53. *streightly*: tightly, but with the added sense of 'urgently'.

61. MS's vocabulary is close to contemporary love poetry.

62–3. The image of others 'frozen' from kindness or pity is MS's addition.

66. *gall*: bitterness.

69. This detail is added by MS.

81. *cyphers*: zeros, which when placed after a figure increase its value; hence, multiplying 'their sinfull summ'.

85. *rased*: expunged, wiped out.

Psalm 70

David prays to be delivered quickly, desiring the humiliation of his enemies and the comfort of all those that seek the Lord.

1. *hye*: come, hurry.

Psalm 71

David prays to God that he might be delivered from his son Absalom and his co-conspirators. *CW* comments: 'This is obviously a draft, since stanza 5 does not fit the rhyme scheme' (2.451).

6. **meward*: to me. A common construction, frequently deployed by MS.

22. *prison'd in my mother*: the image of enclosure refers to physical confinement as well as to the idea of being imprisoned by Original Sin.

27–8. This follows 'my prayse shalbe alway of thee' (BCP 71:5), but the implication that 'mouth and mind' are idle without devotion echoes contemporary injunctions about the need to occupy women with godly employment.

40–42. The sense here is that weakness will overcome strength, 'usurp[ing]' it.

45. **unwithstanded*: unopposed. *OED* cites 'unwithstood', used by Samuel Daniel in his *Civil Wars* (1595).

46–9. Those who spy on me have vowed to forsake God, and pursue.

60. *in one rate*: *OED* has 'at a rate', meaning 'equally', which makes sense here.

62. *farthest end*: ultimate intention.

79. *paint my head with Snow*: for GN's 'graie head' (71:18).

81–2. Until I show to succeeding generations.

83. **after living*: that lives after; *wight*: man.

89–91. MS introduces the idea of active searching here.

93. *Gulf of woes*: the idea, and the phrase, is added by MS.

108. *conjoin*: join with.

109–12. Awkward because of the lack of a connecting verb, cf. BCP's 'My tongue also shall talke of thy righteousnesse al the day long: for they are confounded and brought unto shame that seeke to doe me evill' (71:22).

Psalm 74

This psalm is a complaint about the destruction of the Church and true religion by its enemies. However, trust in God's power and might must be affirmed by the glorification of his name, the salvation of the poor and the destruction of his enemies.

10. *Birth right lott*: for 'the tribe of thine inheritance' (BCP 74:3). Both

'lott' and 'plott' (11) are derived from GN's gloss on 'the rod of thy inheritance' (74:2): 'Which inheritance thou hast measured out for thy self as with a line or rod', suggesting inheritance as a piece of land.

19. The idea of replacing songs of praise is MS's, as is the notion of a dissonant music ('beastly trumpets').

23. *eft*: often.

33. *ruthlesse*: without pity.

45. *Spirit Divine*: prophet, as explained by GN, 'there is not one Prophet more' (74:9).

48. *Dolors*: sorrows.

50. *winck at*: turn a blind eye to.

53. *hated paints with shame*: those that hate God's name seek to discredit it (paint it with shame).

60. **embosom'd*: concealed.

63. *the Charge of me*: responsibility for me.

65. *release*: deliverance.

70. *or Swam or crauld*: either swam or crawled.

71. *appal'd*: enfeebled, weakened.

73. *that monsters head*: Leviathan's.

75. *fishy flesh*: BCP and GN have 'meate' (74:15).

77. *ravning*: voracious, greedy.

78. *Dame*: mother, provider; a contraction for 'Dame Nature', leading to the next stanza. Idea added by MS.

80. Added by MS, from the biblical notion that God performs a miracle, underlined by the use of 'wondrously' in the previous line.

81. *thirsty flint*: conveying that the rock is the antithesis of water.

85–6. An example of MS's tendency to embellish.

91–3. Clarified by the sources: 'Thou hast set al the borders of the earth' (BCP 74:18, GN 74:17), which she points up by her use of chiasmus. Due to God, land and sea co-exist in harmony.

96. *Thy badg, Thy Livery*: a sign or emblem and a distinctive suit of clothes indicating service to a lord; 'badg' corresponds to the 'corny crown' of summer, 'Livery' to the 'Frosty gown' of winter.

99. *brain-sick*: addled, frenzied; *despights*: scorn, disdain.

102. *torn*: pulled down, pulled apart.

103. *hawk*: a metaphor for 'Enemys'; the image, added by MS, is of the bird of prey devouring the innocent dove. Kinnamon (p. 86) notes that this detail is taken from Bèze's Latin metrical version.

106. *out rase*: expunge, delete.

107. *grace*: idea added by MS.

111–14. Details added by MS; *Rape*: its primary sense was that of theft. Kinnamon (p. 86) suggests that lines 112–14 are influenced by Bèze's Latin version, 'Regnant undique vis, rapina, cædes'.

114. *Each where*: everywhere. Note the verbal patterning here: *range / rage / reign*.

121. *plead Thyn own Case*: an importation of legal vocabulary (cf. Pss. 58:1– 3, 9–10; 82:1–3; 89:78; 119Q:1–6), suggested by BCP's 'maintaine thine owne cause' (74:23).

Psalm 76

This psalm describes God's power, and his care in defending his people from harm, by destroying the army of Sennacherib. Hence the faithful are to give thanks.

1. MS introduces the idea of God's chosen people.

1fn. *under his own hand*: see Psalm 61, note to 35fn.

6. *Drave*: past tense of 'drive' (archaic).

7–10. MS adds the idea of recording and praising God's power.

10. *meet*: fitting; **historyfyed*: recorded or celebrated in history.

11–12. Note the use of chiasmus: *mighty handless / hands . . . mightless*.

14. *check*: rebuke (BCP and GN 76:6); *Carrs*: chariots; *mortify'd*: for BCP's 'fallen' (76:6) and GN's 'cast a slepe' (76:6), so – killed, put to death.

17–18. The sense is 'even the fearless hesitate or delay to encounter you once your anger has been shown'.

22. *ragefull*: full of fury; rare, but used by Sir Philip Sidney in the *Arcadia* (recorded in *OED*).

Psalm 77

Here David recounts his despair and temptation, but calling God's former favours to mind, he strengthens his faith, and resists. Fisken 1989 (pp. 228– 9) comments on the stylistic features of this psalm.

1–2. The repetition (antimetabole and polyptoton) is suggested by the source: 'I will crie unto God with my voyce: even unto God will I crie with my voyce' (BCP 77:1).

4. *attend*: listen to.

5. *thrall*: in bondage, servitude.

13. *dole*: heaviness, trouble. MS is working freely here.

29–32. MS uses a passive for GN's active, conveying the anguished state of mind, underlined by the use of 'sink' in relation to the heart.

36. *plain*: lament, in a formal sense.

37. *ruth*: pity.

41. *Conduits*: channels.

43. *rusty teeth of time*: MS's own image.

49. *wrack*: ruin.

57. *mind*: remember.

62. This appears to be a *caveat* applied to the previous line.

73–80. MS uses her own images, cf. GN's 'the depths trembled. The cloudes powred out water: the heavens gave a sounde: yea, thine arrowes went abroade' (77:16–17); the chiasmus in line 73 is sanctioned by repetition in the sources: 'The waters sawe thee, O God, the waters sawe thee' (BCP and GN 77:16).

75. *panting*: heaving.

86. *pitchy*: black, like tar; *encleare*: make bright.

91. *trace*: way.

Psalm 79

The Israelites complain to God about the destruction of their temple by Antiochus, requesting help against his tyranny, so that religion will not be destroyed by the heathen.

7. *wracks*: vengeances.

16. *sepulture*: burial.

29. *they be who Jacob eate*: like those who destroyed Jacob.

30. *rased*: destroyed.

32. *desert layd*: laid waste.

33. *combers*: a burden or an affliction.

34. *passed numbers*: for BCP's 'olde sinnes' (79:8) and GN's 'former iniquities' (79:8).

42. The idea of clothing sin with mercy is MS's.

48. *wreakfull*: characterized by vengeance.

59. The source does not refer to death, or the limits to the length of life.

61–4. BCP does not evoke death specifically: 'So we shall give thee thankes for ever: and will alway be shewing foorth thy prayse from generation to generation' (79:14).

Psalm 81

An exhortation to praise God for his gifts, and his condemnation of their ingratitude. GN condemns the use of ceremonies, but MS stresses the place of music in the praise of God.

5. *Muster*: gather, assemble; often with military overtones, as suggested by 'sword and shield' (4).

6. *Tabrets*: small tabor or timbrel.

7–8. These lines are added to the sense of the biblical source.

13. MS clarifies that this is God's voice, not her own or the Psalmist's.

27. *cov'nant*: this word is not used in the sources: BCP has 'I will assure thee' (81:9).

31–2. Clarified by the source: 'open thy mouth wide, and I shall fill it' (BCP 81:11), also GN 81:10.

34. Before the correction this line was 'Nor Israël would me obey', which is closer to the biblical source ('Israel would not obey me', BCP 81:12) than the revised line, suggesting that MS worked through various levels of paraphrase; hence the plethora of revisions.

41. *who them annoy'd*: who is hateful or odious to them.

43. *of my grant*: by my permission.

Psalm 82

This psalm concerns justice, and David asserts that God works through judges and princes. He criticizes their partiality and lack of righteousness, and encourages them to reform. When they fail to do so, David calls upon God to execute justice himself. The psalm could be used as part of a pro-resistance argument as it suggests that apostate or degenerate rulers will be deposed through God's will. GN's gloss asserts this: 'The Prophet sheweth that if princes and judges do not their duetie, God, whose authoritie is above them, wil take vengeance on them' (82:1a). Cf. Martin 1997, p. 312.

1–5. Clarified by BCP's 'God standeth in congregation of princes: he is a judge among gods' (82:1). MS has altered the meaning, so that God as judge stands among the poor men as well as guiding princes. Steinberg (p. 7) argues that in these opening lines MS 'is actually glossing the Hebrew'.

1. The legal terminology is MS's addition and it suggests the responsibility of monarchs to uphold divine law and to dispense justice on God's behalf.

2. *vicegerents*: those who take the place of others in the exercise of official duties.

3. *pight*: past tense of 'pitched' (archaic); *tribunall*: court of justice; an unusual word in this period – Spenser uses it in the *Faerie Queene* (recorded in *OED*).

5. *wight*: man, person.

6. *doome*: judgement.

8. *his own*: property, possessions.

13. *loose*: free, release; *quiet*: ameliorate; *estate*: situation, circumstances.

14. *lewd*: ignorant, unlearned, but also someone not in holy orders, so, figuratively, the ungodly.

18. *No light no Law*: for BCP's 'but walke on still in darknesse' (82:5); the idea of the law is introduced to reinforce the abnegation of the monarch's responsibilities.

23. See Hannay 1989 for a political interpretation. Pritchard (p. 17) suggests that this line provides 'implicit criticism of secular hierarchy, insisting on monarchs' subjection to the supreme law-giver'.

25fn. *stet*: let it stand, remain.

Psalm 84

David wants to return to God's tabernacle in order to be able to praise God. He commends the courage of the people who pass through the wilderness to gather in Zion.

10. *free, and feareless*: these attributes are added to the biblical account by MS.

18. *household man*: MS views 'they that dwell in thy house' as a type of household servant.

20. *holdeth*: maintains, pursues.

21. *Meeseems*: it seems to me.

22–3. A dry place where it is necessary to dig for water. GN's gloss on 'vale of Baca' states: 'That is, of mulberietrees which was a baren place: so that they which passed through, must dig pits for water' (84:6e).

33. *shield . . . shieldeth*: MS was fond of this kind of word-play (polyptoton).

42. *buckler*: (literally) a small round shield, more generally a defender.

Psalm 86

David prays for deliverance, recounting his sufferings and his mercies. He wishes to obtain guidance from God so that he may fear and glorify him.

3–5. MS expands on 'for I am poore and in miserie' (BCP 86:1), adding 'oppressed' from S–H 86:1, implying that it is the soul which is suffering (4), and the notion of being in God's debt (5).

21. MS avoids the mention of humility found in BCP: 'ponder the voyce of my humble desires' (BCP 86:6).

21–4. See the revision in Ringler A:

> then heare o lord with heedfull mynd
> these carefull suites of my commending.
> I only call when much I neede:
> needes of thy help I then must speed (*CW* 2.126, lines 11–14)

24. *speed*: benefit, prosper.

26. To a great extent.

44. *my endlesse story*: endless narrative.

47. *pitt of woe*: cf. S–H, 'the lower hell' (86:13) and GN, 'the lowest grave' (86:13).

54. MS means 'they make no room for you in their souls'. This idea is not in the sources.

63–4. Rendering the source with the sex of the speaker in mind requires some juggling, cf. BCP's 'helpe the sonne of thine handmaide' (86:16).

68. *amated*: disheartened, cast down.

71. The next line is missing; this stanza has only seven lines instead of eight.

Psalm 88

A complaint of the faithful, feeling that they have been abandoned by God. The Psalmist calls on God, fighting despair.

14. *esteem'd*: valued; from S–H 'I am esteemed as one of them' (88:4).

15. MS avoids the gender specificity of the biblical source: 'and am as a man without strength' (GN 88:4, and BCP 88:3).

25. *grave of graves*: BCP has 'pit' (88:5).

36. *abroade I blush to goe*: a slightly different implication, cf. GN's 'I am shut up, and can not get forthe' (88:8) and BCP's 'I am so fast in prison: that I can not get forth' (88:8).

38. *fleeting*: fading away, vanishing; *amayne*: vehemently.

43–60. Fisken 1989 (p. 232) discusses MS's use of interrogatives in her rendition of this passage.

52. *of marke*: of note.

58. *plaint*: lamentation, prayer.

69. *fretting*: chafing, limiting.

Psalm 89

David praises God for the covenant made between him and the elect; he complains of the decline of his kingdom and the sense that the promise has been broken. He prays to be relieved from suffering and death, and reaffirms the validity of God's promises.

1. *constant promises*: CW 2.399 suggests a source in Bèze's 'carmen'.

2. *debt*: introduced by MS, to convey giving thanks for the bounty and mercy of God.

3. MS conveys BCP's simple 'will I ever' (89:1), as well as the idea of praise carrying on 'from one generation to another' (89:1).

5. *decree*: appoint, ordain.

8. *boundles periods*: ages without end.

9. **leagu'd*: made a league.

13–14. Kinnamon (p. 87) suggests that the image of the chariot is added by MS from Bèze's 'carmina'.

16. *the holie troupes*: 'the congregation of the saints' (BCP and GN 89:5).

21. *hoasts*: troops, enemies; *redoubt*: dread, fear; *maintaine*: continue, keep up the fight or rivalry.

22–4. For, loosely, 'to bee had in reverence of all them that are about him' (BCP 89:8). See Ephesians 6:11–17 (*CW* 2.400).

25. *quailed*: weakened.

28. I.e., which one of thy foes remained unscattered? (**undisperst*).

29. *all in bosome wide*: applied to the surface of something, i.e. delineating an area.

30. *clipps*: includes, encompasses; *pertaineth*: belongs.

32. *hindge*: axis. This detail is not found in the sources.

34. **crosse pointes*: one of the points of the compass between two cardinal points.

35. *Thabor and Hermon*: mountains east and west of Jerusalem.

37. *puissance*: power, might.

39–40. Cf. 'Mercy and truth are still with thee, and goe before thy face' (S–H 89:14). MS alters 'face' into 'presence', underlining God's status as monarch.

42. *poste*: travel with haste.

43. **sunning*: radiance.

52. *Prophet*: GN uses 'thine Holie one', identified in the gloss as 'Samuel and others' (89:19q).

53. *violence:* the idea is added here; *wringe*: (literally) to wrest out of position, but here closer to vex or distress.

59. He will not be undermined by the wicked, even those close to him.

61. *quaile*: overpower, destroy.

62. *mischaunced*: have bad luck.

70. *forte*: detail added by MS.

71. Added by MS, possibly from Bèze's paraphrase and/or *interpretatio* which uses the term 'primogenitum' (Kinnamon, p. 87).

75. *lynning*: from the verb 'to lin', meaning 'ceasing' (cf. Rathmell, p. 214).

78. The technical vocabulary of inheritance ('legacie', 'bequeathed') is MS's innovation.

80. *fainte*: falter.

84. *froward*: perverse, ungovernable.

96. *turneles*: having no end or limit.

97. **abjected*: cast down, rejected, from Bèze's paraphrasis, 'abieceris' (Kinnamon, p. 87).

100. *augments his mone*: increases his suffering.

102. *passenger*: one who passes by, cf. S–H's 'commers by' (89:42); *praieth*: rob, steal.

104. *wrack*: destruction, downfall; *plaieth*: rejoice, take pleasure.

105–8. The addition of question and answer conveys the antitheses of the psalm in the sources; *rebatest*: make dull, or blunt (the point of a weapon); *thou mak'st him flie*: suggested only in GN's 'Thou . . . hast not made him to stand in the battel' (89:43); **unstatest*: deprive of state or rank.

110. In other words, his youth is defined by woe before the appointed time.

115–16. MS here alters the first person singular pronoun to the first person plural; *ages measure*: span of life.

117–18. MS means 'where is the man who having been born, will not die?' Note the use of the figure *gradatio*.

119–20. These lines are added to the sense of the biblical text.

125. *imbosom'd*: enclosed within the chest.

126. *at thy Christ*: the biblical sources, obviously, do not mention Christ. Suggested by GN's gloss, although a common interpretation: 'They laugh at us which paciently waite for the comming of thy Christ' (89:51l).

Psalm 90

Moses prays to God to make his people thankful, seeing that they are not moved by the shortness of life, nor by illnesses. He asks God to turn their hearts and to look kindly on their enterprises.

4. *Dales*: valleys.

5. **embowl'd*: moulded into a globe or sphere.

9–16. This stanza renders one verse of the biblical text: 'Thou turnest man to destruction: againe thou saiest, Come againe ye children of men' (BCP 90:3).

11. *dated*: given a timespan to.

12. *equall state*: just as he was born.

15–16. Adapted from BCP, the service for the Burial of the Dead: 'we therfore committe hys bodye to the grounde, earth, to earthe: ashes to ashes, dust, to dust'; recalling Genesis 3:19, 'thou art dust, and to dust shalt thou returne'.

17. *Graunt*: suppose that.

34. MS uses 'measure' to indicate a time-span, and God's control of that timespan, drawing on the sense of the word as 'proportion' or 'limit' (*OED* II. 11 and 12). See also Ps. 89:115.

39. *dollors*: sorrows.

40. *in poste*: at speed, in haste.

49. *Gladd*: cause to rejoice; *earst*: formerly.

52. *us and ours*: us and our children.

53–6. This is MS's addition, drawing on the generalized prayer at the end of Psalm 90.

Psalm 92

This psalm exhorts the people to praise God for his works, in which David rejoices. Evil-doers do not realize that when they are flourishing most they will be destroyed. The final part describes the happiness of the just, who are 'planted in the house of God in praise of the Lord' (S–H, p. 60).

2. *frame*: make, create.

4. *early springe*: first sign of day, dawn.

8–9. MS follows the biblical text, but offers no apology for using music to praise God (*CW* 2.403).

10. *my mynde*: detail is added by MS.

13–14. MS uses an inexpressibility topos to underline the wonder of God's works.

16–18. MS merges her rendition of this verse with the image which comes in the following verse: 'An unwise man doeth not well consider this: and a foole doeth not understande it. When the ungodly are green as the grasse, and when al the workers of wickednesse do florish' (BCP and GN 92:6–7).

20. *fraile, though flowrie*: 'fraile' because God will destroy them; 'flowrie' because they appear to be other than they are. The biblical text refers only to 'grasse'.

21. *wracke*: destruction.

32. **spightfull*: disgraceful, shameful; *case*: situation, state.

Psalm 93

The Psalmist praises the power of God in the creation of the world, provoking him to consider his promises. Schleiner (pp. 74–5) notes that the metre is identical to *A&S*, 10th song, 'O dear life' (pp. 91–3).

3. *pight*: pitched, laid down.

11. *vexe*: disturb, trouble.

Psalm 95

This is 'an earnest exhortation' (S–H, p. 62) to praise God for his government of the world and his Church; and to reject the rebellion of the Israelites' forefathers, who tempted God in the wilderness, and were barred from the Promised Land.

8. *kinglie seate*: detail added by MS.

12. **Sea wright*: 'wright' means 'maker, craftsman', so 'maker of the sea'.

13. *the shore*: the biblical source refers to 'his hand prepared the dry land' (BCP 95:5).

15. *awfull*: respectful (full of awe).

29. I.e., forty years; S–H uses the formulation 'Twise twenty yeares' (95:10).

31. *fond*: foolish.

34. *madd*: in the sense of 'frenzied, violent', rather than 'insane'.

Psalm 96

This psalm encourages both Jews and Gentiles to praise God for his mercy; S–H adds that 'this specially ought to be referred to the kingdome of Christ' (p. 62), an interpretation which MS eschews.

5. *health*: closer in meaning to 'well-being'.

6. *Ditties*: compositions, songs.

8. **wondred*: wonderful, marvellous.

9. *painte*: describe, represent.

14. *madd*: distracted.

15. *in frame did laie*: formed into a structure, developing the source: 'it is the Lorde that made the heavens' (BCP 96:5).

17. *storeth*: contains, protects.

18. *in guard*: as a form of defence or protection.

27. *quaking pace*: trembling with fear.

29. *staieles*: unceasing, ever-changing; cf. *Antonie*, II.250.

30. *doome*: judgement.

34. *Leavie infants*: MS develops the natural images found in the biblical text.

36. *Daunce*: introduced by MS, from the suggestion of the movement of the trees, and the idea of rejoicing. It renders the sentiment of GN's gloss through personification: 'If the insensible creatures shal have cause to rejoice, when God appeareth, much more we, from whome he hath taken malediction and sinne' (96:12i).

41. *becometh*: as is fitting.

42. *weale*: general good, well-being.

Psalm 98

This psalm is an exhortation to all to praise God for his power, mercy and fidelity in his promise to Christ, by whom he has communicated his salvation to all nations (S–H, p. 63).

5. *ellect*: those chosen by God for salvation; MS uses this word where the sources do not.

9. *bountie*: generosity.

11–12. MS takes some licence with natural images: 'all the ends of the earth have seene the salvation of our God' (BCP 98:4, GN 98:3).

11. *Margine*: end, edge.

14. MS adds the idea of the triumph (see Pss. 68:13, 89:42).

15. I.e., make the lute join (bear a part) with the voice; *vocall musicke*: for

GN's 'Sing praise to the Lord upon the harpe, even upon the harpe with a singing voice' (98:5).

18. *totall Globe*: for BCP's 'round world' (98:8).

19. **Streamye*: running, flowing in a stream.

20. The idea of echo is introduced by MS here.

22. An expansion, with the emphasis on earthly regiment: 'he is come to judge the earth' (GN 98:9).

24. *equall lawes*: for BCP and GN's 'equitie' (98:10, 98:9).

Psalm 100

All men are exhorted to serve God, who has admitted the faithful into his courts to praise his name. It is written in the form of a Spenserian sonnet, cf. Psalm 150.

4. *triumph songe*: introduced by MS.

7. *feedings*: pastures.

10–11. MS forges a closer connection between God's court and the singing praises: 'be thankfull unto him, and speake good of his name' (BCP 100:3); *porche*: suggested by M–B's 'portes' (p. 330).

Psalm 101

David describes the government of his house and kingdom; he will punish the wicked and protect the godly.

1. MS clarifies to whom the voice of the speaker belongs: 'Even now that Care' imagines Queen Elizabeth reciting the Sidney Psalter, so that this psalm would take on particular resonance as it becomes a public pledge of responsibility to upholding the law of God.

3. *protest*: affirm.

7. This profession of modesty is not in the sources, but MS renders 'I wil set no wicked thing before mine eies' (GN 101:3).

13. *brooke*: endure, tolerate.

16–18. *counsulours*: this more technical (and contemporary) term is introduced by MS – cf. GN, 'they maie dwell with me' (101:6) – as is 'officers'. The stanza is a piece of advice about the need for monarchs not to be misled by their advisors. This may have been topical in the wake of the death of Burghley (1598), and an increasing sense that Elizabeth's government was drifting. See John Guy (ed.), *The Reign of Elizabeth I: Court and Culture in the Last Decade* (Cambridge, 1995) and Penry Williams, *The Later Tudors: England 1547–1603* (Oxford, 1995), ch. 9.

20. *cunning*: guileful, sly; **coyning*: (literally) the making of coin, often applied to the creation of new words; so, figuratively, invention or fabrication.

Psalm 102

The psalm is a prayer used by those in captivity in Babylon, followed by the praise of God to be passed down through the generations, leading to the conversion of the Gentiles and the establishment of the Church.

10. *sithe*: developing MS's verb to make a comparison between the downcast heart and the cutting of grass.

14. *cleave*: BCP has 'my bones will scarce cleave to my flesh' (102:5), where 'cleave' means 'to adhere, cling to'. MS's reversal owes something to S–H's 'my bones cleave to my skin' (102:5); see also GN 102:5.

15–16. This chiastic formulation for suffering is added.

17. This line contracts GN's 'I am like a pelicane in the wildernes: I am like an owle of the deserts' (102:6). *CW* cites Bèze's paraphrase as the source for the pelican (2.410).

19–24. Some expansion of the biblical text: 'I watche and am as a sparowe alone upon the house toppe' (GN 102:7), notably the more specific interpretation of 'alone' in line 22, and its extension in lines 23–4; *dollors*: sorrows.

28. *wrack*: ruin, revenge.

29–30. Clarified by GN, 'they that rage against me, have sworne against me' (102:8).

32. *allaye*: dilute.

35–6. MS imparts a politically tinged language of service to the sense of the text, cf. 'for thou hast taken me up, and cast me downe' (BCP 102:10).

36. *subvert*: overthrow.

37–8. The fusion of the passing of the speaker's life with the going down of the sun is developed from BCP's 'My dayes are gone like a shadow' (102:11).

39. This precise detail is added, see 'I am withered like grasse' (GN 102:11).

42. *frett*: wear away, erode.

50. *carkase*: added by MS to communicate the idea of Zion as plundered, empty of inhabitants; *CW* suggests that it is from Bèze's Argument, which states that the Church is 'most like a dead carkasse then to a living body' (2.410).

51. *beere*: grave, sepulchre, extending the imagery of death in the preceding line.

55–7. The psalm text (BCP, S–H) makes this into a prophecy, but MS uses the past tense, suggesting, as did some contemporaries, that Protestant England is Zion (i.e. the Church) rebuilt.

58–60. BCP's future tense is rendered as the past tense, so that this passage becomes a rendition of thanks to God for his favour to the Protestants in their struggles against Catholicism; *playning*: lamentation, complaint.

61. The written record will endure.

64. *a newe*: i.e. those yet to be born; cf. 'The people yet uncreated' (S–H 102:18).

65. **prospect*: place giving a commanding view.

66. *survey*: act of looking at something from a commanding position.

77. Developing the idea of being cut down in the midst of life, by splicing it with the progression of the day.

81. *bide*: stay, endure.

82. *weare*: in the sense of 'wear out'.

83–4. The meaning is clearer in BCP: 'And as a vesture shalt thou change them, and they shalbe changed' (102:27).

Psalm 104

This psalm is a thanksgiving for the creation of the world and God's government through providence.

8. The idea of a canopy (like that found over a throne) is MS's.

9–10. Cf. GN for clarification: 'Which laieth the beames of his chambers in the waters' (104:3); *In chev'ron*: in heraldry, a bar bent like two rafters meeting at an angle.

12. BCP and GN mention a chariot (104:3), which is subsumed here into 'Riding on clouds'.

13. The image comes from the source, 'and walketh upon the wings of the winde' (BCP and GN 104:3).

16. He even makes the burning fire eager.

22. **chidden*: reproved, rebuked.

23. *conduits*: channels, suggestive of a structure which ducts water to produce a fountain: this inference is pursued in the next line's 'spurr'.

24. *spurr*: making speed.

28. *unremoved end*: fixed limits.

30. **unhidden*: concealed.

38. *wingy*: soaring.

39. MS expands the Psalmist's image of the birds singing, using compounds to convey her idea: the 'lay', or song, is produced by nature, but resembles art; **Art-like*: having the appearance of art or according to the rules of art.

40. **eareless*: an unusual word meaning without ears, referring to stalks of corn without ears (there is only one citation in *OED* from ?1400); also, lacking ears, and, by extension, the sense of hearing.

41. *unclose*: cause to open, i.e. God sends rain from heaven. Cf. *TD* 1.25.

42. *Dewing*: making wet, as with dew.

45. *vulgar*: common. The 'grasse' is for the beasts, in contrast to the 'rarer Herb' (46) for men; *faine*: desirous.

47–8. This notion is implicit rather than explicit in the biblical text.

49. *Counterpoyson*: antidote.

50. *unplaits*: disentangles, unfurrows. A rare word, used here in the context of the applying of oil for the complexion.

53–6. MS reads the text of the psalm metaphorically, substituting the flourishing of God's people through his bounty for the Bible's continuing description of the power and benevolence of God: 'The trees of the Lorde also are full of sappe: even the Cedars of Libanus, which hee hath planted' (BCP 104:16).

54. *spare*: exempt.

58. *entertain*: lodging, reception (noun).

59. *brickle*: fragile, brittle.

63. *Conyes*: rabbits.

64. **ribbs*: rocky projecting ridges.

67. *the Chariotman of light*: detail is added by MS.

69. *deface*: obliterate, obscure, but with a play on the idea of both sun and moon having a 'face' (cf. line 66); the sun is temporarily deprived of its 'face'.

70. *Wood burgesses*: citizens of the forest.

71. *all that space*: i.e. all the time while the sun is not visible.

72. The point of this allusion is that the lions only find food by God's providence, as GN's gloss makes clear: 'they onely finde meat according to Gods providence, who careth even for the brute beastes' (104:21l).

73. If Ringler B's reading is adopted, then 'he' refers to the moon; if Ringler A's, then it refers to the sun.

75. *Workman's hire*: a workman's wage.

77–80. MS deviates from the strict sense of the psalm, introducing the first person pronoun, and suggesting the impossibility of aspiring to God's wisdom: 'O Lord, how manifold are thy works: in wisdome hast thou made them all' (BCP and GN 104:24).

83. *troopes*: numbers.

85. **sayl-winged*: having sails that serve like wings (*OED* suggests the Latin *velivolus*, 'flying with sails').

87. *in seasonable tide*: in due course, at the right time.

94. *mustering*: gathering, showing forth. The word's military associations are suggested in the following line.

101. *seely*: happy, lucky, blessed by God. This is not found in the source.

108. *Ingrate*: disagreeable, unacceptable.

109–12. MS works in extra details: 'praise thou the Lord, O my soule, praise the Lord' (BCP 104:35).

Psalm 109

David, falsely accused by Saul's flatterers, calls on God to destroy his enemies. By this means the psalm foreshadows Judas's betrayal of Christ.

Hannay notes that Bèze's interpretation of this psalm is virtually a call to commit regicide (*Phoenix*, p. 93).

2. *enforce*: assert, argue forcefully.

4. *pent*: shut up, confined.

6. *Engines*: offensive weapons, i.e. battering-ram; *battery*: series of blows, in a military context. This imagery is added by MS.

13. *lorded*: ruled over tyrannically.

15. *his Foe*: possibly Satan, as identified by BCP with 'let Satan stand at his right hand' (109:5).

20. *part*: position.

22. *husbandless*: rendering 'his wife a widowe' (BCP 109:8, GN 109:9). The word is rare at this period.

24. **beggerd homes*: playing on the uses of 'beg' in the preceding line; 'beggared' means 'made destitute'.

27. *friend*: assist, act as a friend to (verb).

38. *print of being*: image, likeness and/or trace.

39. What human nature should or ought to do, i.e. 'shewe mercie' (GN 109:16).

41. *spill*: slay, kill.

43. The source uses 'cursing' rather than 'mischeif' (GN 109:17).

50. *girt*: encircled.

53. *thirsting*: desiring.

63. *Place*: primarily social, meaning 'position'; *leese*: lose, am deprived of.

66. The fading of the flesh is in the biblical text, but derives from GN's gloss: 'For hungre, that came of sorow, he was leane, and his natural moysture failed him' (109:24n).

76–7. I.e., they shall be seen to be in a greater state of sin than ever David was. Not in the sources.

78. *Training in train*: pulling, or dragging along a train (as in cloth). Added by MS.

82. *in hard estate*: 'the poore' (GN 109:31).

Psalm 111

David gives thanks to God for his mercies and his works in relation to his Church and sets out what constitutes true wisdom and knowledge. The psalm is an acrostic.

9. The idea is of spiritual 'food' given to his Church, suggested by BCP's 'He hath given meate unto them that feare him' (111:5).

17. *well*: origin.

Psalm 113

The psalm is an exhortation to praise God for his providence, especially in relation to his Church.

3–4. Note MS's verbal patterning: *now/ever* echoed in line 4, and the internal rhyme: *commending/ending*.

14. *myry*: muddy, marshy.

Psalm 114

This psalm describes how the Israelites were delivered from Egypt, and the miracles that God performed, which should remind us of God's great mercies, especially towards his Church. MS's father, Henry Sidney, Lord Deputy of Ireland, cited the psalm on his departure (Hannay *Phoenix*, p. 98).

1. *Jacobs race*: the Israelites.

2. *barbrous*: MS uses the etymologically accurate sense of the word, as is clear from GN's gloss on 'barbarous people', 'from them that were of a strange langage' (114:1a).

7. *bounded*: leapt.

9–10. Reworking 'and the hilles as lambs' (GN 114:4); **capre'old*: skipped, capered.

11–16. These lines turn the statements of 5–10 into interrogatives, just as the biblical text does, verses 5 and 6 echoing verses 3–4 almost exactly.

20. *purling*: rippling, undulating. Cf. 'every purling spring/ Which from the ribs of old Parnassus flows' (*A&S* 15.1–2).

Psalm 115

This is a prayer of the faithful against oppression by idolatrous tyrants, asking for God's aid.

1–2. God promised to deliver them not for their sake, but for his Name.

8. *mark of mortall eye*: target of human sight.

11. This line is not in the source.

20. *having made them*: i.e. having made idols.

22–4. *target*: a small shield or buckler.

32–4. The idea of God's grace flowing like a stream is MS's.

Psalm 116

David, under threat from Saul, hides in the desert and perceives God's great love towards him.

4. MS's meaning is close here to BCP's 'therefore will I call upon him as long as I live' (116:2).

6. *thralled*: bound, entrapped.

10. *bands unbind*: continuing the idea of anguish as physical bondage from the previous stanza, meaning 'I beseech thee deliver my soule' (BCP 116:4).

15. *heard*: hard.

17. *turmoyld*: agitated, in distress.

19. The 'changes' are presumably the benefits or mercies described in the biblical text (BCP 116:7).

20. This idea is not found in the sources.

25. The implications are different from the sources' 'I beleved, therefore did I speake' (BCP and GN 116:10).

32. *tender*: regard favourably, have mercy upon.

34. *thrall*: misery, confinement.

35. This detail is not found in the sources, but it is an element of ritual sacrifice. See Exodus 29:40.

38. I.e., In the presence of God's people.

39. *Who deare*: the subject is 'Thee' (37), i.e. God.

40. MS omits the Bible's reference to 'Saints' (GN 116:15).

41. Still referring to the 'cup of salvacion' (GN 116:13) above at line 33.

44. A development of the previous line, found in GN: 'thou hast broken my bonds' (116:16).

Psalm 117

David encourages the Gentiles to praise God because he has promised them, as well as the Jews, life everlasting through Jesus Christ. This psalm is an acrostic, which may account for Ringler B's rather rough and unfinished version. Because of the brevity of the psalm, rather than noting parallels, version A is given in the Textual Apparatus.

Psalm 119

David encourages the children of God to frame their lives according to his word, and shows what true service to God entails. MS's version uses multiples of 8 lines for each section (with the exception of P, which has 28 lines); each section opens with the appropriate letter of the alphabet and uses a different stanzaic form.

A

7–9. Made clearer by GN's 'Surely they worke none iniquitie, that walke in his waies' (119:3).

12. *understanded*: the verb form is dictated by the rhyme.

13. *stay'd from swerving*: prevented from deviating.
14. *hests*: commands.
17. *brooking*: making use of.
23. *betaken*: be assigned.

B

8. MS adds the image of the 'Casket', where documents were kept, to denote inwardness and privacy. Cf. Pss. 119P:5, 139:6–7 and 143:41.
15. *teach all nations*: this phrase comes from Matthew 28:19.

C

10. *spill*: be brought to ruin or misery.
11–12. MS uses antimetabole here: *longing grieve/Grieve longing*.
13–14. Clarified by GN's 'Thou hast destroied the proude' (119:20).
15. *bend awry*: turn away, stray.

D

5. *quicken*: revive.
14–15. 'Show' implies a different function for the speaker than 'I wil meditate in thy wonderous workes' (GN 119:27).
17. *melt and fry*: expanding GN's 'My soule melteth for heavines' (119:28).
21. *trace*: way, path, course of action.
22. *writhed*: convoluted, twisted, hence indicative of deceit.
28. *My tongue*: continuing the idea of renouncing lies, and perhaps insinuating a degree of anxiety about the validity of women's speech.
37–8. *tread/ The trace*: an example of MS's development of this section's imagery into an ongoing metaphor (which also runs through Psalm 119 as a whole: the idea of the spiritual journey).
40. *Free grace*: a characteristically Calvinist interpretation, suggested by GN's gloss (119:32e).

E

4. MS gives a more concrete image for the lack of spiritual understanding; BCP and GN ask: 'Give me understanding' (119:34). *CW* supplies Calvin verse 34: 'blynded with fleshly reason' (2.426).
9. *fain*: desirous, keen.
10–11. *things that show/ True Witness*: for GN's 'testimonies' (119:36).
13. Kinnamon (p. 87) suggests that 'avert' is derived from Bèze's *interpretatio*, which uses 'Averte'.
14. *falsed face*: added by MS, a common formula for vanity.
15. *strength*: make stronger.
16. MS fills out the line by teasing out the meaning of GN's 'thy promes' (119:38).
20. *Cousning*: false, deceiving.

F

6. *Roundly*: plainly, bluntly; *frame*: make.

11–12. A different slant from GN; MS introduces waiting as wakeful vigilance, and interprets 'thy judgement' (119:43) as inevitably punitive.

15. *allure*: tempt, entice.

16. *dure*: last.

17–18. BCP and GN's 'And I wil walke at libertie' (119:45) is conveyed by the contrast between the 'widest way' and the narrowness of 'restraint'. Cf. GN's gloss which refers to those who do not follow God's word as being 'ever in nets and snares' (119:45c).

28. *plight*: pledged.

G

Gfn. *Quaere*: literally, seek, look for, so here meaning 'query, question'.

1. *Grave*: fix indelibly.

14. *wreakes*: retributions.

29–30. MS fleshes out the text of the psalm with the GN gloss: 'That is, all these benefits' (119:56g).

H

1. Let others choose as they will.

2. **irrevocably*: incapable of being undone, but playing on the Latin root (*revocare*) meaning 'to call back' in relation to the use of 'voice' later in the line.

3. *my lot*: fate, destiny, but rendering GN's gloss 'I am persuaded that to kepe thy Law is an heritage and great gaine for me' (119:57a), where heritage is the equivalent of lot, meaning the share or division of an inheritance.

7–8. Approximately, 'Your earlier promise gives me hope; allow your benevolence to carry out what will help me'; cf. version A (*CW* 2.199): 'Pitty me for thy words sake'.

15. *hye*: hurry.

18. *wrought*: brought about, contrived; *spoile*: injury, robbery; *wrack*: ruin, devastation.

21–22. An expansion for GN's 'at midnight' (119:62).

32. *Scholar*: recapitulating the conclusion of 119F, where God's commandments are set forth as the speaker's 'study' (31). *CW* notes that 'the image of the Psalmist as God's scholar . . . runs throughout Calvin's commentary on Ps. 119' (2.456). See also GN's headnote to the Book of Psalms: 'If we wolde seke his incomprehensible wisdome, here is the schole of the same profession' (f. 235r).

I

3. *resteth*: remains.

4. *a skillfull tast*: effective means of testing, judgement.

7. *unhumbled*: MS equates GN's 'afflicted' with pride, i.e. before being touched with the love of God; *stray*: cf. GN's 'I went astraie' (119:67).

9–11. Each line is a dilation on the sense of the biblical text: 'Thou art good and gracious' (GN 119:68).

19. Now I understand your virtues through my misery.

20. *hests*: laws, rules.

21. *lectures*: instructive counsels.

K

4. *Conceiving*: a pun on God's creation of the child within the womb, and on spiritual understanding.

10. When your stick (or rod) punished me.

17. *betide*: happen, befall.

L

2. *mightless*: without power. This affliction is not mentioned in the biblical text, and it is introduced here to produce an internal echo with the next line.

3–4. The idea of turning the eyes to God's (written) Word is not in the sources.

9. *totall summ*: i.e. 'How long wilt thou afflict thy servant?' (GN 119:84c).

13. *ensnare*: capture, not only in the sense of violence, but also of craftiness.

15–16. Kinnamon (p. 87) supplies: 'Delitiis illi corpusque animumque saginent'.

M

1. *frame*: structure, disposition.

3. *stay*: support, something which steadies; *descry*: declares, reveals.

4. *staid*: created; *stayeth*: remains, endures.

5. *standings*: i.e. they remain constant, unchanged.

7. *But*: unless, except.

13. *standings*: (?) positions.

14. *bane*: destroyer, causer of death.

N

5–6. The presence of enemies is a constant source of knowledge and wisdom, via their negative example.

9. MS's vocabulary implies the involvement of the intellect in spiritual meditation. This might be taken as a metacommentary on her own practice.

10–12. MS renders GN's 'I understode more then the ancient, because I kept thy precepts' (119:100), but the mention of 'skill' seems to allude to the act of versification, which is then deftly attributed to the grace of God through adherence to his commandments.

13. Ringler A's reading is close to BCP and GN's 'I have refrained my fete' (119:101), but the pun on poetic feet is a common Sidneian (and early

modern) one, and it would fit in with the project of metrical reform evinced by the experimentation found in the Sidney Psalter, see Coburn Freer, *Music for a King: George Herbert's Style and the Metrical Psalms* (Baltimore, 1972), pp. 72ff.

18. *meet*: fitting, appropriate.

O

10. *unforced*: given freely.

16–18. It is, of course, the speaker who is surrounded by the snares of the wicked.

22. *bend*: incline, be disposed.

P

2. The emendation (and neither reading can ultimately be preferred over the other) reflects GN's gloss, where those who believe in God's word must ignore the false thinking 'bothe of him self and of others' (119:113a).

5. *closet*: (i) a small room, usually used for private purposes; (ii) a secret, hidden place; (iii) somewhere where valuables were kept.

14. *blush*: for the shame attendant upon failing to keep God's law.

15. The detail of the pillar is MS's addition to 'Staie thou me' (GN 119:117).

21. *treason*: suggesting a connection between divine and earthly rule.

23. **abjected*: cast down, rejected. Taken, *CW* suggests, from Bèze's repeated use of 'abjicis' in his paraphrase (2.429).

24–5. Clarified by GN's 'therefore I love thy testimonies' (119:119).

Q

6. *Baile*: freed from imprisonment, dependent upon a pledge to present the person for trial. Kinnamon (p. 87) suggests Bèze's *interpretatio*: 'Sponde pro servo tuo'.

9–10. Characteristic Sidneian punning, which gives an assertive account of the tenacity of the speaker's faith.

13. Echoing S–H's 'thy health so much I crave' (119:123).

14. *would have*: wish, desire.

18. *enlight*: illuminate, shed light upon.

25–32. The grammatical structure here is periodic, where the subject is 'hope' throughout the stanza.

25. *makes that*: i.e. makes it so.

R

4. *sight*: in the sense of 'insight'.

6. *Babes*: supplied for BCP and GN's 'the simple' (119:130), and echoing Psalm 8:2, 'Out of the mouth of babes and suckelings' (GN).

15. *false accusers*: MS's interpretation of 'the oppression of men' (GN 119:134), betraying a recurrent concern with reputation.

S

13. GN's 'I am smale and despised' (119:141) is interpreted as a social category by MS, a possibility raised by S–H: 'as one of base degree' (119:141), and M–B: 'bas de condition' (p. 416).

T

2–4. Following GN closely, but using what is, by this stage of the sequence, MS's own idiolect for the rendition of the Psalms: 'heare me, o Lord, and I wil kepe thy statutes' (119:145).

7. *will*: dictate, ordain.

21. *graceless crew*: for GN's 'They . . . that followe after malice' (119:150), hence godless, without grace.

29. I know now, although I did not at first.

V

5. *Deemer*: one who judges or discriminates.

10. *health*: both spiritual and physical health, rendering 'salvacion' (GN 119:155).

11. *Thy Sole Edicts*: your statutes alone.

15. *usest*: used to do; *use*: behave towards.

32. *no date defineth*: for GN's 'endure for ever' (119:160).

W

6. *happy*: in the sense of 'fortunate, lucky'.

8. This line, and its sentiment, is added by MS.

9–11. For GN's 'I hate falsehode and abhorre it' (119:163). BCP has 'lyes' (119W:3), but MS omits the object of the verb here, restored in A, see *CW* 2.210.

10. *common rate*: common currency, widely found.

21. *makes*: adds up to, means.

22. *saving succour*: for GN's 'salvacion' (119:166); *attend*: pay attention to.

25. *makes*: brings about, causes; *carefull heart*: cf. M–B, 'Mon coeur a mis tes edicts en effet/ Songneusement, me gardant de meffaire' (p. 419).

29. That (my love for God's commands) causes me to remain firm in the proper observance of God's laws.

Y

1. This line is added by MS, although the sentiment is implicit in the biblical source.

2. *presse*: in the sense of 'beseeching', as a courtier might 'press' a suit at court.

8. *stay*: wait, depend.

9. *flow*: MS uses GN's gloss on 'speake', 'The worde signifieth to powre forth continually' (119:171b).

11–12. MS stays close to GN, 'when thou hast taught me thy statutes'

(119:171), but her image of the scholar derives from the gloss earlier in this section: 'As thou hast promised to be the scholemaster unto all them, that depend upon thee' (119:169a).

13–14. MS's rendition draws upon the meaning of 'intreate' (GN 119:172, 'My tongue shal intreate of thy worde') as 'to treat or handle a subject or question' (*OED* v. 2 and 3).

18. *yeild me*: echoing the opening line of this section.

24. **glad-making*: producing gladness.

Psalm 120

David's prayer, made while beset by the falsehoods of Saul's flatterers.

TITLE fn. Referring to the fact that these psalms are quantitative, i.e. based upon the number of syllables, rather than rhymes or stress. (Pss. 121 and 124 are not included in this selection.)

5–6. MS stresses the biblical text's concern with lies and slander, underlining the political aspects of David's complaint, e.g. 'treasonous eloquence' renders GN's 'lying lippes' (120:2), and cf. S–H's 'lyers lips' (120:2).

9. *reposest*: put one's trust in.

11. *redoundeth*: resulting in, bringing some advantage.

13–16. MS blends GN's text and gloss: 'It is as the sharpe arrowes of a mightie man, and as the coles of juniper' (120:4). GN's gloss reads: 'He sheweth that there is nothing so sharpe to perce, nor so hote to set on fyre as a sclanderous tongue' (120:4d). Neither BCP nor S–H include the detail of the juniper. *CW* notes that darts made from burning juniper were 'known to be difficult to extinguish' (2.432).

18. This line is added by MS.

20. GN mentions 'the tentes of Kedar' (120:5), but MS makes it into an image of exile; **housles*: destitute of shelter.

Psalm 122

David gives thanks that God has accomplished his promise, and that his Ark is placed in Zion, and prays for the prosperity of the Church. Steinberg (pp. 14–15) discusses MS's proximity to the meaning of the Hebrew text.

3. *reedifyd*: restored, rebuilt.

5–6. MS omits some details and adds others, e.g. 'galerys', and turns the psalm's first person plural into a singular: 'Our fete shal stand in thy gates, o Jerusalem' (BCP and GN 122:1).

7–8. GN's gloss makes it clear that MS's 'scatred' refers to people: 'By ye artificial joyning and beautie of the houses he meaneth the concord and love that was betwene the citizens' (122:3c).

8. *commoned*: shared, held in common. See M–B's 'Unie avecques tous les tiens' (pp. 425–6).

13. *justiced*: tried in a court of law.

20. *betide*: happen, come about.

Psalm 123

This psalm is a prayer of the faithful, who were persecuted in Babylon and by Antiochus.

1–2. MS provides a more exalted vocabulary for God, and works the interpretation into her version ('Oppressed'); **earthy*: consisting of earth, figuratively here meaning human mortality. See also M–B's 'Nous eslevons nos yeux' (p. 427).

3. *Waiters*: literally, one who waits, but with the additional sense of one who pays court to a superior.

4. **Waitresse*: a handmaid, but with the same implications as 'waiter' (see previous note).

5. *erected*: raised up.

6. What is implicit in the source is made explicit here via the use of indirect speech; cf. GN's 'Have mercie upon us, o Lord, have mercie upon us' (123:3).

8. *inly dolour*: heartfelt sorrow.

Psalm 125

The Psalmist describes the steadfast faith of the believers in the midst of their sufferings, and prays for their safety and the destruction of the evil-doers. Each stanza corresponds to one biblical verse.

5. *Salem*: Jerusalem; *braveth*: (i) challenges; (ii) displays with pride; (iii) puts on a splendid show; *bulwarks*: ramparts, fortifications.

9. *Tyrants hard yoake*: MS adds a political cast, although this meaning is explicit in this psalm as a whole.

11. *minded*: disposed towards, inclined.

15. *wryed*: either concealed, hidden, or swerved from the proper course, hence do wrong, err.

Psalm 126

This psalm was composed after the return of God's people from Babylon, and shows the miracle of their deliverance after seventy years of captivity (cf. Jeremiah 25:12, 29:10).

7. *wondring Nations*: for GN's 'the heathen' (126:2).

8. *royally*: splendidly, liberally.

9. The echo of the previous line reproduces the patterning of the psalm text, where verse 3 recapitulates verse 2. Cf. *A&S* 5.

10. This line, and its sentiment, is added to the text by MS.

16fn. See note to Psalm 61.35fn.

17–20. MS expands upon the image in the biblical text, perhaps because of the history of the ploughman as a figure of social protest and religous authority: 'Thei that sowe in teares, shal reape in joye' (GN 126:5); *hap*: fortune.

Psalm 127

The Psalmist demonstrates that the state of the world, 'bothe domestical and political' (GN f. 263r), is due to God's providence, and that to bring up children is a particular gift from God. GN's glosses make it clear that the psalm is to be read as an allegory for the place of the divine in the running and ordering of the state, but MS evades this parallel.

1–2. The compressed syntax makes the meaning slightly obscure, cf. GN's 'Except the Lord buylde the house, thei labour in vaine that buylde it: except the Lord kepe the citie, the keper watcheth in vaine' (127:1).

7–8. MS rephrases; see GN's 'Beholde, children are the inheritance of the Lord, and the frute of the wombe his rewarde' (127:3). Hannay 1994b (pp. 64–5) cites this as an 'example of male commentaries read with a female eye', leading to 'a significant deletion', as MS edits out Bèze's comment about the effortless production of children, apparently created without 'labor or industrie'.

Psalm 128

The state of blessedness is not universal, but confined to those who fear God and follow his edicts.

1. *betide*: happen to, befall.

11. Your children will be around your table; *compasse*: go around.

23. This detail is added by MS.

Psalm 129

The Psalmist warns the Church to give thanks, even in affliction, because it will be delivered by God, who will also destroy its enemies.

9–10. The image is biblical: 'The plowers plowed upon my backe, and made long forrowes' (BCP and GN 129:3). It seems to refer to the oppressions heaped upon the Church by its enemies and the relief given to the afflicted by God (see *CW* 2.435).

12. *plowropes*: presumably the ropes attaching the plough to whatever was pulling it.

13–14. MS provides her persona with an interrogative rather than a direct statement.

15. *amate*: dismay, dishearten.

16. *shend*: disgrace, spoil, ruin.

22. *inbow'd*: bent inwards, concavely.

Psalm 130

God's people confess their sins and cry to him for mercy, which he grants. This is one of the penitential psalms, and martyrs in England often sang it before going to the stake (see Hannay 1985, p. 162). Its stylistic features, metre and setting are discussed in Fisken 1989 (p. 229) and Schleiner (p. 74).

7–10. God, if you note our sins, who will remain, except by virtue of your mercy?; *cark*: something which burdens the spirit, distress, anxiety.

12. Therefore worshipping you is more excellent.

17–18. Not in the biblical source, but reinforcing the idea of Original Sin found within Calvinist belief.

19–24. MS reworks the comparision found in GN to create a more forceful representation of religious desire: 'My soule waiteth on the Lord more then the morning watche watcheth for the morning' (130:6).

30. *erst*: formerly, previously.

36fn. The text of Ringler B breaks off at this point. The text is therefore supplied from Ringler C; *Ita testor*: Latin, thus testifies.

Psalm 132

The faithful pray to God to fulfil the promise previously made to David, regarding his successors and the building of the Temple, so that they might pray there as foretold in Deuteronomy 12:5.

12. *plott*: (i) piece of land; (ii) strategy. MS's treatment of finding a site for the Ark is more complex than that of the source, but uses the same structure of 'place' upon which to found the 'habitacion' (GN 132:5).

20. *Ephrata*: Ephrathah. The same form as BCP (132:6).

24. *Jear*: *CW* (1.437) suggests that this is a transliteration of a Hebrew word; GN translates it as 'forest', BCP as 'wood' (132:6).

40. The caesura marks the transition into God's word and his reiteration of his promises.

49–54. GN at this point returns to reported speech, rather than retaining the first person pronoun as MS does.

57. *victuall*: provisions, food; *store*: reserves, stocks, usually of food.

59. *store*: plenty.

61. *my priests shall nought annoye*: i.e. my priests will not suffer in any way.

64. *howld of mee*: possess from me. The object is 'fields of blisse' (66).

69. The reference to Christ is MS's addition, although it is found in GN's gloss to an earlier verse, referring to the eternal dominion of David's descendants (132:12h).

74. *downe*: throw or knock down.

Psalm 133

This psalm praises brotherly love among God's servants.

1. *beseeming*: fitting, appropriate.

5. The oil is 'a figure of the graces, which come from Christ the head unto his Church' (GN 133:2b).

6. *fleeting*: flowing, abounding.

11. **empearled*: 'Formed into pearl-like drops' (*CW* 2.438). Suggested by S–H's 'silver drops' (133:4).

Psalm 135

The Psalmist exhorts all the faithful to praise God for his works, but particularly for his grace towards his people, wherein his majesty is displayed to the confounding of all idolaters.

9. *owne Demaine*: for GN's 'Israel for his chief treasure' (135:4); BCP has 'his owne possession' (135:4).

10. The biblical text moves immediately into the direct statement, found in the following line: 'I knowe that the Lord is great, and that our Lord is above all gods' (BCP and GN 135:5). MS thus posits speech as originating with conscience, rather than being an autonomous utterance.

14. *unsounded*: see S–H, 'which he hath framde of nought' (135:6); hence MS would be stressing the idea of creation *ex nihilo* as she does throughout the paraphrase. See also M–B, 'gouffres de la mer' (p. 449).

15. *extreames*: for 'the ends of the earth' (GN 135:7).

16–17. An expansion for 'cloudes' (GN 135:7); **flakie*: consisting of flakes; *reaking*: emitting smoke or vapour; *incorporate*: united in one body.

24. *dreadfull showes*: for 'tokens and wonders' (BCP and GN 135:9).

26. *rue*: sorrow, regret.

28. Cf. 'upon Pharaoh, and upon all his servants' (GN 135:9).

31. *huge limbd Oge*: this detail occurs in Deuteronomy 3:10–11.

37–40. MS's own formulation for 'thy remembrance is from generation to generation' (GN 135:13). It means, roughly, 'Although time will do its work in the world, the memory created by your ancient miracles will never be expunged from our thoughts.'

43. *unproportioned odds*: the general idea is that idols are so unequal to God (disproportionate odds) that they are irrelevant. The idea is MS's.

48–9. I.e., those who make idols are like them ('Idolls right'), as are those who make them into an article of faith.

Psalm 137

This psalm describes the decay of religion when God's people were in exile, which caused them great sorrow and suffering. The Israelites wish God to punish the Edomites (who provoked the Babylonians to attack them). The psalm also prophesies the destruction of Babylon, where they had been so cruelly treated.

1. *Nigh*: close, nearby.

3. *pearled*: formed into drops; *rowes*: a series of something. The stress here is on the profusion of tears.

19. *forgett his skill*: GN does not use a possessive pronoun here, and BCP uses a feminine: 'let my right hand forget her cunning' (137:5), suggesting either absent-mindedness on MS's part, or that she did not regard her psalm versions as necessarily being in *her* voice, or as being gendered in any obvious way.

21. *still*: without moving, but also remain.

26. *quitt*: acquit, avenge.

27. *hottlie*: with passion, intemperance.

29. *whett*: prepare for attack.

32. *platt pais*: a flat place, from the French, but not in M–B.

33. MS just addresses Babylon; GN has 'O daughter of Babel' (137:8).

37–8. Expanding upon the biblical source and the theme of revenge, repaying like with like.

Psalm 139

In order to avoid hypocrisy David demonstrates that there is nothing which is hidden from God. He confirms this by citing the creation of man. David then declares his fear of God, denouncing those who condemn him as enemies. This psalm has been widely praised; see Rivkah Zim, *English Metrical Psalms, Poetry as Praise and Prayer 1535–1601*, pp. 190–92; Martin 1997, p. 313; and Donald Davie, *The Psalms in English*, calls it 'the most splendid Englishing . . . of these verses' (p. xlv).

6–7. Thought is here imaged as an interior and private place. The 'closett' was frequently deployed as a metaphor for interiority, cf. 119B:8, 119P:5, etc.; *closest*: not proximity, but 'most closed', i.e. most private.

12–14. Following, but varying GN's 'For there is not worde in my tongue, but lo, thou knowest it wholly, o Lord' (139:4) – the idea here is that thought precedes language; *youngest*: i.e. most undeveloped.

13. *caste*: plan, devise.

21. *Earthie mynde*: mortal; 'Thy knowledge is to wonderful for me: it is so high that I can not atteine unto it' (GN 139:6).

22. *notice . . . eye*: these terms render GN's 'thy Spirit' and 'thy presence' (139:7).

24. *Starrie Spheare*: for GN's 'heaven' (139:8).

26. **undelightsome*: affording no delight; 'If I lie downe in hel, thou art there' (GN 139:8).

28. *assaie*: attempt, try.

29–35. A variation upon the biblical text, filled with word-play – *light/flight* echoed by *lightfull/flightfull*. It renders GN's 139:9–10: 'Let me take the wings of the morning, and dwell in the uttermost partes of the sea: Yet thether shal thine hand lead me, and thy right hand holde me.' The 'west' is the equivalent of 'uttermost partes', but it enables MS to integrate the image of the sun, moving from east to west, more fully.

30. *flightfull*: adapted for flight. The word would have been familiar to MS in a different sense (transitory, fleeting) from texts that we know she had read: Golding's translation of Calvin's commentary on the Psalms; Golding's translation of Ovid's *Metamorphoses*; and from his completion of Sir Philip Sidney's translation of DuPlessis-Mornay's *Woorke concerning the Trewnesse of Christian religion*. (See *OED*.)

35. *lurke*: remain hidden.

37. *sable*: black.

43. *innmoste peece*: for BCP and GN's 'reines' (139:13), meaning 'the seat of the feelings or affections' (*OED*).

47–9. Clarified by GN's 'I wil praise thee, for I am fearfully and wonderously made: marvelous are thy workes, and my soule knoweth it wel' (139:14).

50–56. An expansion of the biblical text, to which MS brings her own characteristic imagery: 'My bones are not hid from thee, thogh I was made in a secret place, and facioned beneth in the earth' (GN 139:15). MS refers to the development of the foetus in the womb, but presents it as the craftsmanship of God. This is suggested by GN's gloss: 'That is, in my mothers wombe, which he compareth to the inward partes of the earth' (GN 139:15k). The image of embroidery comes from Bèze, as noted by Fisken 1985, pp. 177–8; Pritchard, p. 16; and Hannay 1994b, pp. 62–4.

50. **beamewise*: like or as a beam.

51. **raftering*: framed with rafters.

56. *shopp both darke, and lowe*: the womb.

57–60. Cf. GN: 'Thine eyes did se me, when I was without forme' (139:16);

the idea in MS's version and in the Bible is that of God knowing the soul before it takes corporeal shape, expressed in the oxymoron 'shapeles shape'.
66-8. The word-plays on 'sum' (*some*, *sum'd*, *summeles*) derive from GN's 'how great is the summe of them!' (139:17).
72. *further chase*: continuing pursuit.
75. *at thy disgrace*: in order to effect your disgrace.
77. **outface*: deny, contradict.
81. *knott*: group, band.

Psalm 140

David complains of the wickedness of his enemies and prays to God for help in defeating them.
5. The image is from the biblical text; *rustie lipps*: morally corrupt.
23. *flinge them low*: i.e. 'into the depe pittes, that thei rise not' (GN 140:10).
25. *lyers*: for GN's 'backbiters' (140:11).
26-7. The word order is confusing: 'mischief shall drive [those] who live violently [from] the land'.
29. I.e., 'the just shal dwell in thy presence' (GN 140:13).

Psalm 141

Persecuted by Saul, David cries to God for aid. The psalm counsels patience while waiting for God to avenge one's enemies.
2. *plaintfull*: full of misery.
7. *Warde*: guard, protect.
9. *Wicket*: gate.
10. *Encline*: from M–B's 'N'encline point mon coeur aux vices' (p. 468).
12. *baites*: the use here combines the ideas of something enticing and something damaging.
15. Clarified by GN: 'for within a while I shal even praie in their miseries' (141:5).
24. *tarrie*: delay.
26. *pitched*: set, set up.
28-30. An expansion of GN's 'Let the wicked fall into his nettes together, whiles I escape' (141:10), but also glancing at the gloss: 'Into Gods nettes, wherby he catcheth the wicked [by] their owne malice' (141:10i).

Psalm 142

The Psalmist, in calmness, wishes to kill Saul, but instead directs his prayer to God, who prevents him from doing so.
1-2. Following GN: 'I cryed unto the Lord with my voyce: with my voyce

I praied unto God' (142:1). MS conveys the repetition, and the urgency which this implies; *straining*: deriving from S–H's 'And with my strained voice unto the Lord God prayed I' (142:1).

4. *my cases Mapp*: the outward shape of inner torment, but 'case' really refers to 'a state of affairs', 'condition'.

5. *painted*: continuing the idea of the expression of torment as being represented, with the implication that this is to some extent inadequate, or a falsification.

8. *where sticke the toiles of daunger*: cf. GN, 'thei prively laied a snare for me' (142:3).

10. *lights*: alights, settles, finds.

11. *life*: for GN's 'soule' (142:4).

15–16. See GN: 'Thou art mine hope, and my porcion in the land of the living' (142:5; also BCP 142:6). 'Porcion' is rendered by the play on *Lott* and *plott*, as it means a share of something allotted to someone, something dealt out by destiny (or providence) *and* a part of an estate given through inheritance or marriage; 'porcion' is used for a dowry, which would involve both a transfer of land (for women of MS's class) and the determination of one's fate in life, to an extent.

21. **unthrall*: set free, liberate; *inthralled*: imprisoned, shut up. MS follows the metaphorical sense of the biblical text, 'Bring my soule out of prison' (GN 142:7).

22. MS takes the opportunity to profess God's name and power, building upon GN: 'that I maie praise thy Name' (142:7).

23. *enwalled*: surrounded.

Psalm 143

This psalm is a prayer for the 'remission of sinnes' (GN, headnote) where the speaker acknowledges that he was justly persecuted by his enemies. He desires to be restored to 'grace' (GN) so that he may spend his life in the proper service of God.

1. *suite*: MS adds the language of courtly favour, where the believer supplicates God. See also line 6.

6. Part of the entreaty, derived from the practices of the court, where the monarch gave an 'audience' to petitioners.

9. *wight*: man.

11. Added by MS; *ruth*: pity, punned upon in following line.

17–20. MS's own interpretation for the confusion and suffering outlined in GN (143:4).

23–6. See GN: 'I meditate in all thy workes, *yea*, I do meditate in the workes of thine hands' (143:5). MS develops this, giving a sense of what these 'workes' may be – the evidence of time and history – and then God's deeds which unusually she images as God's 'writing'. She may be thinking directly of the evidence of God's 'hand writing' before her in the shape of the Psalter. This connection may have been suggested by S–H's 'Yea in thy works I meditate, that thy hands have create' (143:5), where 'works' could have signified 'texts'.

29–30. The biblical text does not mention 'grace' here, although GN alludes to it in the headnote.

31–6. MS moves to the third person, where the source uses the first, and to the passive voice from the active; *Leave then delaie*: 'Heare me spedely' (GN 143:7).

41. *My cave, the closet*: i.e. God. Both are images of retreat, meditation and privacy, added by MS; see GN's 'I hid me with thee' (143:9).

47–50. Going astray is suggested in GN's gloss: 'as sone as we decline from Gods wil, we fall into errour' (143:10l); **Meander*: winding course, labyrinthine way.

52–3. *that mee/ reviv'd*: for the more archaic 'quicken' (BCP and GN 143:11).

55–6. The image of the river of destruction is MS's addition.

Psalm 144

The Psalmist gives thanks to God for the restoration of his kingdom and for his victories. He asks for the destruction of his enemies, and vows to give praise to God.

5–8. MS contracts the list found in GN, but follows closely: 'He is my goodnes and my fortres, my tower and my deliverer, my shield, and in him I trust, which subdueth my people under me' (144:2).

10. *tender so his fare*: offer what he needs.

17. *bend*: GN has 'bowe' (144:5), which MS has already used above (11).

21. *flames from Skie*: lightning.

22. *their*: (?) the enemies'.

27. *Let mee thy hand*: let me be defended by thy hand.

28. For 'the hand of strangers' (GN 144:7), perhaps suggested by BCP's 'hand of strange children' (144:7).

29–32. MS fuses text, gloss and her own metaphor. GN has 'Whose mouth talketh vanitie, and their right hand is a right hand of falsehode' (144:8), glossed thus: 'For thogh thei shake hands, yet thei kepe not promes' (144:8g). Added to this is the mouth as a 'forge' where lies are made, perhaps deriving from the frequent imagery in the Psalms of the tongue as a sharpened file (e.g. GN 64:8–9); hence their 'hand doth fall' to the 'forge' as 'aptest instrument' because their handshakes deceive, but also because of the action of forging something by beating down upon metal with an instrument of some kind.

37. This transitional statement is added by MS.

38–40. Note the word-play: *preserves/saves/serves*; *Royall right*: divine authority, for GN's 'It is he that giveth deliverance unto Kings' (144:10), supported by the gloss which stresses that although 'God may use wicked Kings for the working out of His divine plan, those that set forth the glory of God in rule, rather than serving their own ends are properly called God's servants' (144:10i).

41–8. This verse virtually repeats verse 4, as does verse 11 repeat verses 7–8 in the biblical source.

53–6. MS alters the meaning here, stressing the role of daughters in sustaining royal rule, perhaps with a submerged pun on 'beare', and as adornments ('both doth beare/ and garnish'). She also develops the implication of the source that these 'Pillers' are also caryatids: 'the corner stones, graven after the similitude of a palace' (GN 144:12); cf. BCP's 'our daughters may bee as the polished corners of the temple' (144:12). MS expands the terms of the simile so that daughters are to be valued as if they are pillars propping up royal houses: 'each house embellish shall'. See Hannay 1994b, pp. 57–8.

59–60. I.e., even if we take everything from our stores, there will still be plenty left.

63. *sheepie presse*: (to) crowd like sheep, resembling sheep.

64. *scantlie*: barely; contrasting with the preceding images of abundance and plenty.

65–8. There is a metaphorical undertow here, when set against the biblical text: 'That our oxen may be strong to labour: that there be none invasion, nor going out, nor no crying in our stretes' (GN 144:14).

Psalm 147

This is a psalm of praise for God's bounty, providence and justice towards his creation, but particularly to his Church which he reunites after the exile.

1–4. MS adds details regarding the manner of praise, asserting its appropriateness, with 'seemelie', for GN's 'comlie' (147:1).

5–6. For BCP and GN's 'The Lord doeth buyld up Jerusalem' (147:2); *to forme*: outward shape; *ruinated*: demolished.

8. *dispersed earst, to union*: for 'gather together the dispersed of Israel' (GN 147:2).

9–10. Note the use of anaphora ('repetition of the same word or phrase at the beginning of successive lines or clauses', *Handlist*) for emphasis; *bleeding wounds*: a Petrarchan image for GN's 'bindeth up their sores' (147:3).

12. *Torches*: an added detail, giving a courtly flavour to the description.

16. *precincts*: (literally) limits, boundaries; it also refers to the area of consecrated ground surrounding a church.

19–20. These lines draw a series of careful contrasts (as well as deploying anaphora): *to lifte/to downe, lowelie juste/prowde wicked*.

21. *cawsefull*: deserved.

26–7. MS improvises, adding the earlier detail of the rain watering the mountains: 'and maketh the grasse to growe upon the mountaines' (GN 147:8); *supples*: makes soft; *clodds*: lumps of turf.

28. *fuell of life*: periphrasis for 'fode' (GN 147:9).

29–30. The idea comes from M–B: 'Aux corbillats leur nourriture' (p. 485); MS adds the detail that the ravens have been abandoned by their elders ('careles oulde'), and their distinctive 'croaking' (M–B's 'Cracquetans'); *allmes*: used to emphasize God's providence and mercy, as outlined in GN's gloss (147:9g).

46. *ought*: anything; *liste*: desires, wishes.

47–8. Developing the metaphors found in BCP and GN: 'He giveth snow like wool, and scattereth the hoare frost like asshes' (147:16); *hoarie*: greyish white.

49. *gobbetts*: lumps, chunks.

51. *Ice in water*: ice into water.

53. *melter*: something which causes melting. A rare usage, found in a different sense in Coverdale (Jeremiah 6:29).

59–60. MS renders 'He hathe not dealt so with everie nacion, nether have they knowen his judgements' (GN 147:20), but adds the notion of blindness to God's laws and wisdom.

Psalm 148

A psalm of praise, wherein all God's creatures are exhorted to praise him.

1. Interpreting 'from the heaven' (GN 148:1).

2. The idea of the relationship with God being akin to that between ruler and subject is added by MS.

5. *all on carefull winge*: cf. GN's gloss stating that the angels 'are members of the same bodie' (148:2a).

6. *Herauldes*: those who announce the advent of a monarch, those who lead the way.

9. *Sea of light*: MS's expansion, designed to act via chiasmus with the next line, so that sun and moon are seen to mirror each other.

10. *light of sea*: presumably because of the moon's mutability and its power over tides.

11–12. MS's expansion of the literal sense of the biblical text: 'praise ye him all bright starres' (GN 148:3); *spangells*: (figurative) stars; spangles were small thin pieces of metal with a hole in the centre so that they could be attached by a thread to a garment.

13–14. I.e., the sphere (God's dominion) within which all the other planets turn.

14. *emball*: encompass with a sphere.

19. *forme and frame*: substance and shape. Note the reuse of these words via polyptoton at line 21.

23–4. MS's idea of order is expressed through terms relating to social place.

25. *When Heaven hath praisd*: transitional phrase added by MS.

31. The image of snow as a flock of birds is MS's own.

32. **apaste*: food, bait.

35. MS adds the epithets.

36–40. Considerably expanded. MS uses periphrasis for the contrast made by GN's 'fruteful trees and all cedres' (148:9). See M–B: 'Arbres fruictiers, Cedres tres-hauts' (p. 488).

37. *proude*: (i) protruding; (ii) highly valued.

42. Denoting tame beasts in contrast to the 'untam'd' of the previous line.

45–6. For GN's 'Kings of the earth and all people, princes and all judges of the worlde' (148:11). MS makes explicit the contrast between high and low, princes and subjects.

47–8. MS's interpretation is added to GN's 'Yong men and maidens, also olde men and children' (148:12), i.e. that in duty to praise God, hierarchies are of no importance. This was a key argument in relation to access to the Psalter; see Golding, *The Psalmes of David and Others* (1571), sig. *iir.

Psalm 150

This psalm is an exhortation to praise God for all his wonderful works. As with Psalm 100, MS uses the sonnet form. Trill (p. 153) notes that this psalm 'represents the culmination of earthly praise, a point which is encapsulated in both the form and the content of Sidney's translation'.

1–4. MS does not work particularly closely with the biblical source, although she does adhere loosely to its meaning.

6. *lute, and lire*: alliterative equivalents for 'the viole and the harpe' (GN 150:3).

11–12. Added by MS.

*   *   *

A Dialogue betweene two shepheards, Thenot, *and* Piers, *in praise of Astrea . . .*

This poem is a pastoral dialogue, and may be compared with the 'Dolefull Lay of Clorinda' (Spenser, pp. 380–84, 662), a pastoral elegy attributed (by Spenser at least) to MS. It is appropriate to the pastoral mode in that it consists of a poetic competition between shepherds, each questioning and testing forms of praise for the Queen. Such singing competitions, which raise questions about poetic style and decorum, would have been familiar to MS through her brother's pastorals in the *Arcadia* (which she had prepared for the press; see Hannay *Phoenix*, pp. 70–78), but also through such powerful precedents as Spenser's *Shepheardes Calender* (1579). Pastoral was well known for its potential for coded political criticism, as Sidney had noted in his *Defence* (p. 119), and like the carefully framed critique of Elizabeth found in MS's dedicatory poems, this poem's panegyric carries a critical edge. As Helen Hackett suggests, 'Piers represents a dogmatic Protestant point of view, from which panegyric is problematic in its potential for idolatrousness' ('Courtly writing by women', in *Women and Literature in Britain 1500–1700*, pp. 176–7). 'A Dialogue' makes its point covertly; it is possible that MS is pointing to the gap between the extravagance of the forms of representation used for the Queen towards the end of her reign, and the reality of her fading powers. Hannay *Phoenix* (p. 166) speculates that the poem 'could imply that Queen Elizabeth herself may not equal the reality of Astraea, the goddess of justice'. Having noted this, however, it is important to recognize the rhetorical technique deployed, which enables the eloquent delivery of compliment at the same time as it is undermined: MS uses *occultatio*, the method of argument whereby something is emphasized by pointedly passing over it (see *Handlist*, p. 104).

1. *Thenot*: stock pastoral character, found in Spenser's *SC*, 'Februarie', 'Aprill' and 'November'; in 'November' he professes his modesty, and advocates Colin's transition to singing 'of sorrowe and deathes dreeriment' (36); here the argument produces an encomium by exhibiting the insufficiency of human wit and poetic language; *ASTREA*: a frequently used name for Elizabeth I.

2. *Muses*: the nine deities who presided over the arts and provided inspiration.

4. *Piers*: stock pastoral character, found in *SC*, 'May', where he represents a Protestant minister, standing for plain speech and Protestant values, and also in 'October'.

6. *a lier*: the identification of poetry with falsehood is one of the propositions in Stephen Gosson's *Schoole of Abuse* (1579), refuted by Sidney in his *Defence*.

10–11. Piers mocks Thenot's claim of poetic adequacy, prompting him to alter his terms from those of the natural world (8–9) to those of morality (13).

15. *Momus*: the god of satire; hence, ignoring those who demur.

21. *stay*: remain, persist.

22–3. The sense is that without Astrea wisdom and virtue are ineffective, but Piers asserts the inseparability of Astrea and what she embodies, as well as the vacuousness of words which carry little or no meaning.

26. *Strait*: immediately, instantly.

28–9. I.e., her divine powers exceed her actual physical presence.

32. *annoy*: trouble, difficulty.

34–5. Piers rejects Thenot's attempt to praise Astrea via comparison, suggesting that this diminishes her singularity.

36. *in measure*: with moderation, temperately.

38. *arrayd*: adorned, decorated.

40–41. Piers rejects Thenot's natural metaphor, arguing that the seasons are mutable, whereas Astrea is constant.

42. The distinction works to undermine both Thenot's conception of poetry, but also his skill.

46. *enclowdes*: overshadows.

50. This points to Elizabeth's own careful negotiation of her femininity and her monarchy, particularly through the idea of the body politic (male) and the body natural (female); a deliberate inversion, as the palm was linked with the feminine graces and the bay with male virtue and poetry (see Martin 1997, p. 336).

51. *verdure*: greenness, but with the implication of profusion.

56. Thenot finally manages to distinguish ideas ('meaning') and language ('words').

58. *conceit*: in Philip Sidney's sense of 'invention', but with the implication of human vanity.

* * *

THE TRIUMPH OF DEATH TRANSLATED OUT OF ITALIAN BY THE COUNTESSE OF PEMBROOKE

For an interpretation, see Introduction, pp. xxvi–xxx.

The first chapter

1. *gallant Ladie*: Petrarch's Laura, renowned for her beauty and virtue, and for her power to inspire his verse.

2. *statelie piller*: exemplar; the pillar signifies constancy (*Poesie*, p. 97).

3. *naked spright*: pure spirit. Cf. Sidney, 3rd eclogue (Ringler, p. 101, line 78).

4. *warres*: referring to the preceding *Trionfi*, where Laura has triumphed over Love and Chastity.

5. *mightie foe*: Love, often figured in *I Trionfi* as Cupid.

6. *wylie stratagems*: the devious methods used by Cupid to entrap his victims; cf. *A&S* 36.11.

11. *shivered bowe*: cf. Psalm 76:5.

15. *squadronet*: small squadron.

16. Cf. Piers's argument in 'A Dialogue betweene two shepheards', lines 34–5.

19. *a snowy Ermiline*: a small ermine, and an emblem of chastity, used by Sidney (Ringler, p. 89, line 116), but more famous from the 'Ermine' portrait of Elizabeth I, in Roy Strong, *Gloriana: The Portraits of Queen Elizabeth I* (New York and London, 1987), plate 71.

20. *topaces*: topaz, a golden yellow gemstone, symbolic of chastity.

21. *unfoyled*: (i) not injured, marred or impaired; (ii) not overcome, unbeaten.

25. *unclose*: uncover, disclose.

27. Echoing *SC*, 'Aprill' eclogue, lines 59–63.

30–31. An allegorical representation of death.

33. *Phlegra*: a plain, usually known as Phlegrean, where the earthly giants rebelled against Olympus at the beginning of 'the age of hard iron' (*Met.* I, pp. 32–3).

37–8. Death was commonly depicted as blind, and wearing a black robe in emblem books; she is 'deafe' because she rejects all pleas for mercy.

40–41. Death is asserting her power to bring down nations and empires, hence her universal power.

43. *warde*: stave off, resist.

45. *marr'd*: injured, spoiled.

46. *to you-ward*: towards you.

48. *compound*: join, combine.

49–50. Laura's reply to Death reminds her that she only has a right to her body, not her soul; *spoile*: figuratively, 'body', but also alluding to goods taken by force in war.

52–3. Laura's reply can be read in relation to the Queen's refusal to name a successor; MS provides the plural 'others', where Petrarch uses a singular, hence giving the phrase a wider application; *recoyle*: retreating, rebounding, especially of a firearm when discharged (rare).

54. *assoile*: help, aid, but with a stress on the idea of forgiveness.

60. I.e., passed into the jaws of Death.

63. Submit to my authority.

65–6. Death now advances the argument that dying is an escape from time into eternity, developed in the following *Trionfi* (Fame and Eternity).

69. *barre*: affect, afflict.

72. *entretaine*: receive, communicate with.

73. *descryde*: discerned, saw.

75. *Pestring the plaine*: overloading, but with the added idea of *plague* through *pest* and *pestilence*.

76. *Gattay*: Cathay.

78. *they wanted roome*: i.e. needed yet more space.

83. *purple dye*: the imperial colour.

85. *affye*: trust.

86. *yett who but doeth*: but who is there that doesn't?

88. *blinde*: the ignorance of those being addressed, i.e. Laura and her troop of ladies.

89. *greate Mother*: the earth.

92. *vaine*: dismissive, unfeeling.

93. *One*: the object of 'Bring me' (91).

97. *you winning loose*: i.e. having once won, inevitably you will lose.

99. *farre sweeter close*: happier conclusion.

104. I.e., was drawing close to its final moments.

107. *lade*: burden, oppress. The women are still weighed down by their earthly bodies.

108. *faine*: eager, desirous.

113. *ruthlesse*: pitiless. The allusion to the plucking of a single golden hair comes from the myth that Proserpine (queen of the underworld) bestowed death by taking a lock of hair. See Virgil, *The Aeneid*, Book IV.

118. *brynie: salt water, hence the line is a periphrasis for 'tears'. It is the poet/speaker who weeps, in contrast to the dry eyes of Laura in the following line.

119. *sightfull fountaines drye*: MS evades the scopic economy of Petrarch's poem, substituting this phrase for Petrarch's more direct 'occhi'.

126. *forslowe*: slow, delay; i.e. even the virtue of Laura could not stave off Death.

128. *frye and freese*: standard Petrarchan conceit, but 'freese' is relatively rare, used only by Spenser (*Amoretti* LV.8); *cheere*: appearance.

135. *Changing hir copie*: (i) change style or behaviour; (ii) assume another character.

136. *thralle*: bondage, confinement.

137. *rue*: regret.

138. *faine*: willingly, eagerly.

140. The poet argues that as he was older than Laura, then logically he should have died before her.

141. *quail'd*: destroyed.

150. *Angell-lyke*: cf. 'To the Angell spirit', line 59 and *FQ* V.9.29.

151. *prest*: keen, anxious.

153. *the heavens cleare*: the clouds lift to see and admire Laura; also to admit her to heaven.

154. *enemies*: for Petrarch's 'devils'.

155. I.e., on that occasion, none of the devils dared to show his face; *obscure*: presumably meaning 'dark'.

157. I.e., when 'plaint' and 'feare' had gone.

160–65. The idea seems to be that Laura's demise is not like a fire that burns itself out, but a gradual fading away.

164. *nutriture*: a very rare word, derived from Latin *nutritura*, meaning here 'fuel'.

169. *heavenlie guest*: the soul; *mortall walles*: the body.

171–2. See Mornay (sig. D2ᵛ) for a similar sentiment: 'But bring wee quietnesse of mind, constancie, and full resolution [to dying], wee shall not finde anie daunger or difficultie at all.'

The second chapter

1. *happ ensue*: follow on from the event.

3. *bereave*: deprive, but playing on the idea of mourning.

5. *Tithon's bryde*: the goddess of the dawn, Eos, or Roman Aurora; her reputation is as a predatory lover.

6. *Cleereth*: remove something which troubles or clouds, i.e. night changed to day.

7. *tyde*: season; this must be spring (see *TD* 1.133, 'sixt of Aprill'), traditionally the season for lovers.

14. *trade*: path, also way of life; cf. *CW* 2.62–3: 'save from those,/ who make a trade of cursed wrong'.

15. *marke*: something to be aimed at, a target to shoot at; alluding therefore to Laura's role as muse and inspiration, the object producing the poet's ambition.

17. I.e., she surpasses Venus' three attributes, as they are all united in one.

18. *bay*: replacing Petrarch's pun on *laurel/ Laura*, but a symbol of chastity; *beeches*: an emblem of the lamenting lover.

22–7. Laura offers the poet a *consolatio*, frequently found in medieval dream poetry, which explains that death is the gate to eternal life, and offers consolatory wisdom.

28–9. The poet's question reveals his lack of understanding, as he associates 'light' with life on earth, not with eternal life in God. See Mornay (sig. D4ʳ), 'Death only can restore us both life and light'.

31. *the vulgar*: generally used for the 'common people', but here it also has a wider sense, meaning 'mortals'.

36. *mudd*: the earthly; translating Petrarch's 'fango', which has implications of dross and the mortal body. See Brooks-Davies, p. 445n.

43–51. The poet speaks (43–5) and then Laura sets forth the reasons why death is feared, and explains that there is nothing frightening except the anticipation of death (46–51).

43. MS does not include Petrarch's list of tyrants.

46–7. The idea of the 'crosse' which precedes death allies Laura's death with Christian tradition; *martireth*: the choice of vocabulary compounds the overtly Christian overtones – the word is unusual, found in *FQ* IV.7.2 and in MS's translation of *Antonie*, II.498.

49. *panting soule*: MS's interpolation, which recalls the Psalms, particularly Ps. 42: 'As the hart braieth for the rivers of water, so panteth my soule after thee, O God' (GN 42:1).

51. **unrepented*: not regretted.

54. I.e., she heard the voices of those around her.

55. *happless*: unfortunate.

58. *Maine*: mainland.

63. *encyte*: encourage.

65. **reconsolate*: for Petrarch's 'racconsolato'; bring consolation, comfort.

68. *My yeares most greene*: young, youthful.

70. *cheere*: experience.

75. *ruth*: pity.

80–81. Brooks-Davies (p. 445) glosses: 'did you ever love me for my pains (though that love would have to be compatible with your love of Honour)?'

85. *in lightning wise*: like lightning.

89. *Our hearts but one*: never were our hearts anything except one, i.e. united.

90. *cheere*: countenance. The idea here and in the following lines is the need to temper the poet's ardour.

97. I.e., the poet concentrated on outer beauty not inner virtue (the beauty of the soul).

98. *brake*: bit; the bridled horse symbolizes the control of lust.

102. Petyt Ms. (see headnote to *TD* in Textual Apparatus) has a semi-colon in the middle of this line, which has been omitted here.

106–8. I.e., 'If your passion overcame your reason, then my words and expression served to correct you.'

112. *pregnant with tearie rayne*: full of tears.

116–17. Continuing the horse metaphor from line 98.

118–19. Petrarchan oxymorons.

122. *equall meede*: reward, recompense.

128. *faine*: glad, eager.

132. The only thing that could be criticized in your love was its lack of moderation.

139. *tryed*: tempered, tested.

142–3. The contrast between speech (the poet) and silence (Laura) continues the previous contrast between display and concealment (141).

150. This line is not in Petrarch's text.

152–3. The meaning is obscure; perhaps, 'You can endure your lot with difficulty, parting with less (i.e. Laura and earthly love) in order to gain more.'

158. *coles*: an image for the fire of desire.

178. *Aurora*: goddess of the dawn.

AEMILIA LANYER

Additional abbreviations and short titles used

Curtius: Ernst Curtius, *European Literature and the Latin Middle Ages*, trans. Willard R. Trask (Princeton, 1953)

HH: Katherine Usher Henderson and Barbara F. McManus (eds.), *Half Humankind: Contexts and Texts of the Controversy about Women in England 1540–1640* (Chicago, 1985)

Keeble: N. H. Keeble (compiler and ed.), *The Cultural Identity of Seventeenth-Century Woman: A Reader* (London, 1994)

Schnell: Lisa Schnell, 'Breaking "the rule of *Cortezia*": Aemilia Lanyer's Dedications to *Salve Deus Rex Judaeorum*', *Journal of Medieval and Early Modern Studies* 27 (1997), pp. 77–101

Woods: Suzanne Woods (ed.), *The Poems of Aemilia Lanyer* (New York and Oxford, 1993)

Unless stated otherwise biblical references are to the Authorized or King James Version (1611).

SALVE DEUS REX JUDÆORUM

TITLE *Salve Deus Rex Judæorum*: Hail God, King of the Jews. This is the inscription placed upon the cross (Matthew 27:37).

To the Queenes most Excellent Majestie

1. *Britaines Queene*: Anne of Denmark (1574–1619), wife of James I, and patron of masque writers and musicians.

2. *succeeding Kings*: alluding to her sons, Henry (d. 1612), and Charles and James, both of whom were, in their turn, kings.

3. *Vouchsafe*: be willing.

4. AL stresses that a woman writing of the divine is 'seldome seene' (3); she does not say that it is never *done*.

11–15. Paris was given a golden ball, or apple, and told to award it to the most beautiful of three goddesses, who each promised him a gift in return: Pallas Athena (wisdom), Juno (power) and Venus (the most beautiful woman in the world, Helen of Troy).

16. *indu'd*: endowed.

19. *Muses*: the nine goddesses who presided over the arts. See also note 1 above.

21–2. AL alludes to the dynamics of the masque here, where the savage forces of nature ('Sylvane Gods': the gods of the forest, and 'Satyres': half man half goat, renowned for their untamed sexuality) are contained and overcome by the power of majesty.

23. *Cynthia*: goddess of the moon. AL uses Roman and Greek names for deities interchangeably.

29. *Phoebe*: another name for the goddess of the moon.

31. *Apollo*: god of the sun.

35–6. A humility topos; AL suggests that her lines will be elevated by the Queen's attention.

37. *this Mirrour*: the text, which reflects the Queen's virtues, but also sets forth an image of what those virtues should be through the precedent of Christ. AL uses this metaphor frequently, and it combines several meanings: (i) the idea of the mirror of art being held up to nature, hence functioning as a metaphor for poetic imitation; (ii) the idea of the mirror as reflecting the faults of the world; (iii) the association of the mirror with female vanity, which AL subverts by suggesting that her readers look into the 'Mirrour' of her text to see the image of Christ, which 'reflects' their virtue and spiritual devotion.

41. *dym steele*: a steel glass was thought to give a truthful reflection, but AL alludes to her low style (35).

44. *mightie Monarch*: Jesus Christ.

48. The divine right of kings, whereby kings were seen to be appointed to their role by God.

50. *meaner sort*: lower orders.

55. *his Region*: within Christ's power and jurisdiction.

57–60. AL refers to her lack of means and wealth, but sees it as conferring a degree of spiritual authority.

73. *Eves Apologie*: one of AL's major revisions of biblical interpretation, in the main text of 'Salve Deus' (761–832).

76. *the Text*: i.e. the biblical accounts. AL's reinterpretation of Eve's fault as the lesser sin in comparison with men's murder of Christ is a key element of her engagement with biblical tradition. See 'Salve Deus' (761ff.).

78. *defam'd*: slandered, falsely accused.

79. *great Lady*: Eve. This positive representation of Eve's fault represents a fundamental overturning of tradition, which had repeatedly used Eve to discredit female virtue.

85. *Paschal Lambe*: the Passover lamb, seen as a symbol for the sacrifice of Christ; this follows on from AL's vision of the Queen attending a feast (83–4). The idea of the feast is not only identified with the Eucharist, but also, as Schnell (pp. 84–5) argues, places AL in the position of bestowing a gift (Christ) which cannot be reciprocated, thus placing herself as socially superior to the patrons she seems to be petitioning.

86. *figure*: representation, with the implication that her text is a shadow of the real thing.

89. *Passeover*: the Jewish festival commemorating the liberation of the Israelites from Egyptian oppression, narrated in Exodus 12:22–7.

91–4. Anne of Denmark's daughter, Elizabeth, later married to Frederick, Prince Palatine, and a central figure in Continental Protestantism.

97. *my Glasse*: see note 37(i) above.

99. *repleat*: full of.

103–6. A variation on the humility topos, which signifies lack of skill ('untun'd voyce'; 'humble straine'), but also a virtuous identification with the modesty of Christ.

110. AL had spent part of her youth in the court of Elizabeth I, see Woods, pp. xviii–xix.

113. *But*: except.

116–20. AL refers to Princess Elizabeth, building upon the identification with Elizabeth I, whose motto was *semper eadem* (always the same); the Princess is thus the continuation of the Queen's chastity and devotion.

119–20. I.e., what leads most to devotion is bad fortune, whereas the 'great Ladie' has faith in and of itself.

132. *wanted*: lacked.

153. *Jove*: Jupiter, the sovereign god of the Romans.

157–60. By appealing to Queen Anne's greater piety and virtue, AL also enables the defects of her work to be excused, as what is lacking will be supplied by the knowledge and devotion of her noble and royal readers, in relation to whom AL places herself consistently at a disadvantage.

To all vertuous Ladies in generall

1–2. The unspoken terms of comparison throughout this poem are the relationship between women and virtue, set against the oft-cited propensity of women to spend time beautifying themselves. Hence AL's 'Glasse' (7) is for the soul, not for the face, reflecting images of virtue back to the women who look into it.

3. *hir*: Virtue.

5. *deserts*: merits.

6. *Queene*: Virtue.

7. *daines*: condescends.

9. *Bridegroome*: Christ. A biblical image figuring the relationship between Christ and the Church (the bride).

15–21. *purple scarlet white*: colours symbolizing Christ's Passion, referred to in 'Salve Deus' (1110–12).

22–3. *Daphnes crowne*: Daphne was a virgin huntress pursued by Apollo, who prayed to Zeus to save her from violation, at which point she was transformed into a bay-tree, hence the identification with constancy.

25. *Minerva*: Roman goddess of wisdom.

26. *Cynthia*: goddess of the moon and also of chastity; *Venus frown*: Venus, goddess of love, would frown because women are devoted to Cynthia and hence to chastity.

27. *Esop*: hyssop, a herb used for treating leprosy, also associated with cleansing the soul from sin. Its use is discussed at length in Leviticus 14.

32. *baite*: temptation.

35. *nine Worthies*: the Muses.

36. Aaron was anointed with oil by Moses, as first priest of Israel (Leviticus 8:12). A feature of women's attention to their appearance is here converted into a sign of their membership of a spiritual community.

41. Perfumes and herbs used to anoint the dead, especially those of high status.

43. *Titan*: god of the sun; *staies*: stops, remains.

44. *hew*: shade, appearance.

45–6. The personifications indicate the passing of time, which changes outer beauty into spiritual beauty.

49. Christ's injunction to the disciples (see Matthew 10:16); AL directs her readers to serve as examples of virtue in the world.

52. *Glory*: here meaning that earthly pleasures should not obscure the gift of grace (pejorative).

56. *Phoebus*: god of the sun.

59. *he*: Christ; *stay*: remain.

62. *Elizium*: Elysian Fields, a paradise inhabited by the virtuous after death; *Well of Life*: implying, here and in the following line, the cleansing waters of baptism (cf. Proverbs 10:11).

66. *new regen'rate*: newly created; *second berth*: birth into the life of the spirit.

The Authors Dreame to the Ladie Marie, *the* Countesse Dowager of Pembrooke

ADDRESSEE Mary Sidney, Countess of Pembroke (1561–1621). AL places her centrally as a patron and as a writer, with a specific stress upon her gender. The form of the dream poem was a long established convention for the praise of a patron (e.g. Chaucer's *The Book of the Duchess*), and AL's homage evokes MS's works, including her Psalm paraphrases; the conceptual framework of the poem is not unlike MS's own translation of *TD*.

1. *Edalyan Groves*: probably the city of Idalium, in Cyprus, which had shrines dedicated to Athena (Minerva) and Aphrodite (Venus).

9. *nine faire Virgins*: the Muses.

10. *Vialls*: viols; *lilly*: lily white.

13. *Titon*: god of the sun.

14. *brasen*: made of brass; Fame was frequently depicted as blowing a brass trumpet.

18. *Morphy*: Morpheus, the god of sleep and dreams; a figure directing the dreamer's education is a feature of dream poems.

20. *summe*: totality, but also significance.

21. *Welkin*: sky.

23. *duskie*: dark.

33. *Bellona*: there is little sanction for Bellona as a goddess of wisdom, as indicated by AL's marginal gloss (now a footnote), and what follows suggests a possible confusion with Minerva, the goddess of wisdom.

35. *manly mayd*: presumably because of her combination of virtues, her height and her martial appearance.

36. *Charret*: chariot.

37. *currat*: cuirass (variant), a form of armour consisting of a breastplate and backplate fastened together.

39. Symbols of military victory.

42. *shee*: Bellona.

43. *noble Lady*: Mary Sidney, Countess of Pembroke.

45. *Dictina*: Dictynna, mentioned by Arethusa when recounting her attempt to escape from Alpheus; Arethusa calls upon her aid, and Dictynna covers her in a mist to hide her from her pursuer (*Met*. V, p. 132).

50. *traine*: followers.

52. *staine*: impugn, cast a shadow over.

53. *borrowed light*: by contrast with the true virtue shining from the Countess of Pembroke.

59. *her*: Mary Sidney; *the Lady*: Bellona.

61. *Aurora*: strictly, the dawn, rather than the morning, as the AL's marginal gloss (now a footnote) states.

63. *Lady Maie*: goddess of the spring.

64. *out-fac'd*: outdone, faced down.

65. *Apolloes Waggoner*: Phaeton, the charioteer of the sun-god Apollo.

67. *marre*: spoil.

68. *luster*: outer light, used pejoratively here, as it refers to surface glitter or shine.

75. *Flora*: goddess of the spring and flowers; *dight*: adorned.

81. *sacred Spring*: the spring on Mount Helicon, sacred to the Muses.

85. *umpiers*: judges.

88. *either*: Art, or Nature.

103. *Her*: Envy.

104. *Anotomie*: skeleton, emaciated body.

105. *this Lady*: the Countess of Pembroke.

108. *Pergusa*: a lake in Sicily, described in *Met.* V (p. 126), where Pluto falls in love with Proserpine and from where he carries her off. It may be used here because of its depiction of an ideal place; *hight*: is called.

113. *trayld . . . in wanton wise*: referring to the flowing river from the spring, meandering along the ground.

115. *devise*: improvise, reflect.

117. AL refers to the Psalms of David; *frame*: make.

118. *Father of Eternitie*: God.

120. *great Messias*: the Messiah, i.e. Christ.

121. *holy Sonnets*: the Psalms; 'Sonnets' is used in its technical sense of 'small songs'.

125–6. Given that swans were thought only to sing just before death, the stress here is on the eternal life enjoyed by the saints. 'The music of its swans rivals the songs that Cayster hears on its gliding waters' (*Met.* V, p. 126). See also note 108 above.

133. *unfold*: reveal, declare.

138–44. Recalling the conventional terms of praise for Sidney, cf. MS's 'To the Angell spirit', and Spenser's 'Astrophel' (pp. 372–80); *dying wounds*: AL implicitly parallels Philip Sidney's death from his wounds at Zutphen in 1586 with Christ's wounds, which restored mankind to life.

145. *faire earthly goddesse*: Mary Sidney, Countess of Pembroke.

146. *Bellona*: here, correctly, the goddess of war.

149. *deemd*: considered.

151–2. AL is unusual in suggesting that MS surpasses her brother; most elegists stress her role as Sidney's living image on earth.

161. *reade*: understand, interpret.

176. *Charet*: chariot; *Joves faire Queene*: Juno.

180. *seeming death*: comparisons between sleep and death are conventional.

187. *Acteons hounds*: Actaeon caught a glimpse of the goddess Diana bathing, was punished for his presumption by being turned into a stag, and then was pursued by his own hounds and dismembered. See *Met.* III, pp. 77–80.

195. *more rare*: more elevated, special.

199. *painefull*: diligent, taking great pains; *no whit*: not at all.

202. *her Trophie*: achievement.

206. *to my feast*: to read or, perhaps, hear her poem.

211. *exempt*: ignored, excluded.

212. The steel glass represents truth.

213–16. AL contrasts her low offerings, which have grown from the earth, with MS's higher works, which come from deeper sources; 'workes' refers not only to her poetry, but also to the idea that they have been mined from beneath the earth, and are therefore to be compared with precious metals and minerals.

218. *Shepheards weed*: AL is making a point about the difference in quality between her work and that of MS, allying her own with pastoral, conventionally thought of as the lowest poetic form, although her text owes little to pastoral traditions, despite her identification of Christ with a shepherd (cf. John 10:11–17).

223. *passe the sand*: frequently used in the Bible to signify 'uncounted multitudes, or a weight impossible to measure', see 'sand' entry in *Cruden's complete concordance to the Bible* (revised edition, Cambridge, 1977).

To the Ladie Lucie, Countesse of Bedford

ADDRESSEE Lucy, Countess of Bedford (d. 1627), wife of Edward Russell, Earl of Bedford, a prominent patron of poets and writers (e.g. Donne, Jonson, Florio), and a member of Anne of Denmark's court.

2. *closet*: small interior room, associated with privacy; here, as in MS's Psalms, an image for the heart (cf. 119B:8, 119P:5, 139:6–7 and 143:41). Virtue stands holding the key of knowledge (3) to unlock the Countess of Bedford's heart to let Christ enter.

4. *Cabbine*: closet, or cabinet; here used to denote the seat of the soul.

5. *him*: Christ; *her youth*: Virtue's.

8–9. I.e., Christ came down from heaven to earth, to be incarnated as a mortal human being.

11. AL refers to Christ's incarnation as man.

12. AL recalls the martyrdom of St Sebastian, who was pierced with arrows.

19. *Arke*: Woods (p. 33) suggests that this refers to AL's poem, but it seems equally likely that it describes Christ, as there has been no discernible change of subject and the following verse also concentrates on Christ; the Ark is the place where the Covenant resides, the location of God's word.

24. *blessed bowre*: the Countess's heart.

To the Ladie Margaret, *Countesse Dowager of Cumberland*

ADDRESSEE Margaret Clifford, Dowager Countess of Cumberland (d. 1616) was the daughter of the Earl of Bedford and the wife of the third Earl of Cumberland. She is AL's principal dedicatee (cf. 'The Description of Cooke-ham') and is frequently addressed throughout the text of 'Salve Deus', as well as here. Her only child, Anne (see following poem), was bypassed by her father's will, and both mother and daughter engaged in a protracted legal battle to possess their land.

1–3. From Acts 3:6; the profession of lack of wealth is a dedicatory convention.

5. *Arramaticall*: aromatic.

6. *Kingly Philosophers*: the wise men who presented gifts to the infant Jesus.

9–10. AL alludes to the parable in Acts, where Peter cures the lame man (3:6–7).

11–13. Woods (p. 34) asserts that these descriptions apply to 'Salve Deus' itself. They rework the material possessions mentioned in line 2 into spiritual metaphors.

14. *second Adam*: Christ, as it were the second Son of God; Christ was understood to have been sent by God to atone for Adam's fall and to redeem mankind, much as the Virgin Mary was seen as a second Eve.

16. *tree of Life . . . roote of Jesse*: Christ, who came from the line of David; David's father was Jesse. See Isaiah 11:1, Romans 15:12.

19. *right*: true, authentic.

20. *blacke foyle*: referring to the use of a thin sheet, usually of metal, beneath a jewel to make it shine more brightly; more generally, the setting for a jewel.

26. *impeachment*: harm.

30. *inestinable treasure*: Christ's Passion, and the redemption that it offers.

To the Ladie Anne, *Countesse of* Dorcet

ADDRESSEE Anne Clifford (1590–1676), only daughter of the Duke of Cumberland and Margaret Clifford (see dedication above); she married first, the Earl of Dorset, and subsequently, Philip Herbert, Earl of Pembroke (Mary Sidney's younger son).

2. *frame*: structure.

7–8. AL represents her text as a mirror of the virtues of her dedicatee, but the stress also falls on the close relationship between the Countess of Dorset and Christ, whom she will see in the 'Mirrour' of the text.

13–15. AL alludes to the parable of the virgins (Matthew 25:1–13), interpreted as willingness to serve Christ. Cf. 'To the Vertuous Reader' (228ff.).

16. See Matthew 23:11–12 on the reversal of earthly positions in the Kingdom of Heaven.

17–24. These are standard Christian sentiments regarding the right of the virtuous to inherit the Kingdom of Heaven. Given that AL's own social status is inferior to that of her envisaged patrons, these notions of a kind of democracy of virtue are appropriate here, as she imagines a levelling of social divisions.

24. *booke of Life*: the register where deeds are recorded in order to adjudicate the right to inherit the Kingdom of Heaven.

25. *Titles of honour*: noble titles, usually given for service to the monarch.

36. *Gentry*: the middling land-owning class. AL makes the point that everyone descends from Adam and Eve, and that high social status is an honour, not an essential right, because all families, however noble, have ancestors (perhaps biblical ones) who are not known.

41–56. AL's attack on hereditary titles and ownership seems to be closely connected to the fact of her dedicatee's long legal battle, with her mother's help, to inherit her father's estate.

41–4. AL implies here that while titles are inherited, the virtue that originally gave rise to them is not.

45–8. Earthly honour is contrasted here with heavenly immortality; *that blood*: the stock of honour and virtue.

55. *Stewards*: those charged with the management of an estate.

59. *worthy mother*: Margaret Clifford, Countess Dowager of Cumberland. See the poem to her above, and headnote.

63. *this Diadem*: jewel – Christ, but by association AL's poem.

79. *pelfe*: wealth.

97–8. Images of the futility of AL's poem, in connection to the virtue and devotion of the Clifford women.

100. *stay*: remain.

121–2. Renaissance commonplace, see Curtius, pp. 138–44.

123–4. A commonplace regarding the levelling effect of death.

129. Christ as cornerstone of the Church, cf. Ephesians 2:20, 'Christ himself being the chief corner stone'.

131. Christ as rock, found in I Corinthians 10:4.

133–4. Clifford, by her virtue, beauty and piety, will minister to Christ's people, by example rather than action.

139. *recompence*: requital.

141. *wants*: inadequacies.

To the Vertuous Reader

TITLE The reader that AL has in mind is specifically a *female* reader.

1. *property*: habit, characteristic.

19–25. The fact that men were born from women is a frequent argument in defence of woman in this period, often connected to the fact that it was a woman who gave birth to Christ. See Rachel Speght, *A Mouzell for Melastomus* (1617), ed. Barbara K. Lewalski (Oxford, 1996), pp. 15–16.

27–31. I.e., men's unjust imputations are examples where women should avoid confirming these prejudices.

34ff. AL's citation of virtuous biblical women to support her argument that women have been unjustly vilified by men is paralleled in many contemporary texts on this topic. See *HH* for examples.

34–5. *Cesarus . . . noble Deborah*: Deborah and Barak delivered Israel from the oppression of Sisera (Judges 4:10–17).

36. *Jael*: Sisera fled to Jael's tent; she offered him refuge, and while he was sleeping killed him with a hammer and a tent-peg (Judges 4: 21).

37–8. *Haman . . . Hester*: Esther protected her people and had their enemy Haman hanged (Esther 5–7).

38–9. *Holofernes . . . Judeth*: Judith's decapitation of Holofernes to save her people from Nebuchadnezzar's army is narrated in the Apocryphal Book of Judith 13.

40. *chast Susanna*: Susanna was accused of sexual incontinence by two men; the slander was discovered by Daniel who had them put to death (see Apocryphal Book of Susanna).

50–51. After his resurrection Christ appeared to Mary Magdalene and another woman named Mary (see Matthew 28:1–7).

Salve Deus Rex Judæorum

1. *Cynthia*: Queen Elizabeth I, often eulogized as Cynthia, goddess of the moon.

3–4. The assertion of inexpressibility serves to elevate that which cannot be described.

4. *wight*: person.

9–12. AL is fulfilling one of the traditional functions of poetry: the assurance of immortality after death; *great Countesse*: Margaret Clifford, Countess of Cumberland.

15–16. The apparent profession of modesty is balanced by the assertion that the object of praise is beyond most writers' expression, not just that of a woman.

18–19. This is the subject of the poem appended to 'Salve Deus', 'The Description of Cooke-ham', but also functions here as a kind of *locus amoenus*, or earthly paradise, to contrast with the persecution of Christ and his agony in the Garden of Gethsemane. It asserts a (possibly fictitious) patronage relationship between the Countess and AL, as she was 'commaunded' to write on a given topic.

20. *Phœbe*: the moon.

21. *Paradice*: cf. 'The Description of Cooke-ham' (19ff.) for a depiction of an earthly paradise.

34. *waves of woe*: alluding to her widowed status, loss of estates and absence from Cookham.

35. *toyes*: trivialities, irrelevances.

38. *well-staid*: resilient, temperate.

49–52. This sentiment is common throughout the Psalter, see, for example, 73 and 119A.

51. The image of God guiding the believer and helping him avoid traps is recurrent in the Psalter, e.g. 17:5, 119:110, 142:3.

[. . .]

150. I.e., Christ protects those he loves from evil-doers and harm.

155. *equall*: equally.

156. *the field*: neither joy nor pain distract the Countess of Cumberland from God's love.

157. *Turtle Dove*: an emblem of constancy in love, because of its habit of choosing a mate for life.

159. *prowd pomps desire*: the wish for vain splendour.

161. This refers to the Countess of Cumberland's retreat from court, but it also metaphorically suggests a movement from worldly action to rural contemplation.

163. *great Enchantresse*: the temptations of the world and its fleeting pleasures.

165. *wantons*: those who act wantonly, in a dissipated way.

169–70. AL's vocabulary makes an implicit comparison between the court of an earthly king and service to a heavenly king.

172. *Affection*: the meaning is closer to 'affectation' (pejorative).

173. *forcing*: advocating, arguing.

174. This image derives from the Psalter; see 61:4.

179. *empaire*: harm, damage.

180. *such a guest*: Christ.

185–90. Invectives against women's preoccupation with outward beauty to the detriment of their virtue is an oft-rehearsed trope in the seventeenth century. See excerpts in Keeble (pp. 61, 80, 83).

187. The stress is upon the transitory nature of beauty, in contrast to the eternal happiness brought by faith in God.

188. *gawdie*: brash, false.

192. *that Queene*: Helen of Troy, usually viewed by Renaissance writers as the most beautiful woman in the world.

193. *matchlesse*: without comparison; *Red and White*: colours taken to signify conventional beauty.

196. See Daniel Touteville, where female beauty is 'the divels masking-suite, wherewith impietie and impuritie doe many times disguise them-selves' (*Asylum Veneris, Or a Sanctuary for Ladies* (1616), p. 20).

197–8. AL contrasts transitory physical beauty which leads to immorality with the inner beauty of the virtuous soul.

201. *pride of Nature*: the beauty bestowed by nature.

204. I.e., those who take most pride in what threatens them.

208. *the White*: part of the target used in archery.

210. *lawfull Lord*: Helen was married to Menelaus.

211–12. The story of Lucrece is the most famous treatment of the theme of beauty tempting the overthrow of chastity. Lucrece's husband Collatinus boasts that his wife's chastity exceeds that of any other woman, and argues that beauty and chastity can co-exist, only to inflame Tarquin's lust. Tarquin then assaults her chastity, raping her in the absence of her husband; her shame leads her to kill herself.

213–16. Antony, the Roman general, fell in love with Cleopatra, and abandoned his wife Fulvia. After Fulvia's death, he married Octavia, the sister of his fellow triumvir and rival, Octavius Caesar. This was a marriage of convenience, made for the purposes of political alliance, and despite Octavia's chastity and virtue, Antony ruined his reputation and career by continuing to love Cleopatra. This narrative was well known to Renaissance readers from North's translation of Plutarch and through dramatic versions by MS and Shakespeare.

217. *forbidden tree*: Cleopatra, but by inference, beauty more generally; there is an oblique reference to Eve's temptation of Adam, where her beauty led Adam into temptation, bringing about the Fall of Man, as AL argues later in the poem (761ff.).

225. *Fair Rosamund*: mistress of Henry II, rumoured to have been poisoned by her rival, Eleanor of Aquitaine. See Samuel Daniel's 'Complaint of Rosamund' (1592).

226. The word-play (*fairer/faire*) highlights once more the conflict between moral virtue and physical beauty.

227. *aloft to clime*: to move beyond her proper social position.

228. An adaptation of a proverbial phrase, meaning to entertain a daydream, an unobtainable fantasy.

231. *perjur'd*: guilty of having broken an oath.

233. *Matilda*: chaste virgin who resisted the sexual advances of King John, paying for her virtue with her life. See Michael Drayton's *Matilda* (1594); *haplesse*: unfortunate, ill-fated.

235. *Sweet to Sowre*: proverbial, see Erasmus, *Adagia* (1500).

237. *refus'd*: i.e. 'King John, having been refused'.

238. *compasse*: bring about, achieve.

241. *Here Beauty*: still referring to Matilda, whose beauty is presented as an outward sign of inner virtue.

249. *This Grace*: referring back to 'Heavenly grace' in the previous line.

253. *Husband of thy Soule*: Christ, in contrast to an earthly husband.

256. *vouchsaf'd*: was willing.

257. *Dowager of all*: widow with a title or property gained from her husband, so here the living heir of Christ.

258. *Co-heire*: joint heir.

259. The fall of the rebellious angels from heaven, and man's expulsion from the Garden of Eden.

260. *Judas kisse*: the kiss that Judas gave to Christ in order to betray him to his persecutors.

261–4. These details of Christ's death are taken from the Gospels.

262. *buffeting*: beating.

[. . .]

297–8. AL here invokes God as a muse figure.

301. *stray*: go astray, i.e. that she should not go beyond what is proper, if guided by God's grace.

305–6. A recognition of the difference of AL's poetry from that of scripture; her insistence on 'plainest Words' (311) suggests her modesty, but also truth and sincerity.

309. *Vulgars breath*: the approval of the common people.

310. *Fames lowd Trumpet*: Allegorical treatments of Fame frequently depicted her blowing a trumpet.

312. *undergoe*: treat.

314. *map of Death*: outline, representation. See also MS's usage of this term in Ps. 68:11 (and see note).

316–18. This image of striving comes indirectly from the Psalms; see 61:2 and MS 61:8–10.

319. *pure unspotted Lambe*: Christ, envisaged as a lamb in the Book of Revelation and in I Peter 1:19.

322. *holy Hill*: Mount Zion.

327–8. When Christ was crucified the sky went black; it was an eclipse of the sun.

333. *Mount Olives*: a hill just outside Jerusalem, also known as the Garden of Gethsemane, where Christ went to pray on the eve of his Crucifixion.

338. *offended*: (?) embarrassed, i.e. that his disciples would deny him before morning. This is the word used in AV, Matthew 26:31 and Mark 14:27.

340–46. *Saint Peter*: for Peter, see Matthew 26:33, 35.

342. *mote*: spot, blemish.

348. AL deploys a Petrarchan opposition to signal the paradox of Peter's treachery.

357. *forward*: presumptuous. AL stresses Peter's pride.

360. *averre*: assert, insist upon.

362. *hallowed*: sanctified, made sacred.

364. *corps*: living body.

365. The mention of 'Vipers' (Christ's enemies and executioners) in the context of the garden provides an implicit parallel between this garden and the Garden of Eden, which AL goes on to link later in the poem. The connection between the Fall of Man, and humanity's redemption by Christ, is crucial to the poem.

370. *sonnes of Zebed'us*: James and John.

375. *overcharg'd*: overcome, oppressed.

381. *Adams mud*: mortality. Adam's punishment was death, to return to the dust from which he had been created (Genesis 3:19).

383. *re-ore-charge*: burden or oppress once again.

384. *condole*: sympathize with.

388. *whose sinnes did stop thy breath*: because Christ died for the sins of the world, and to save mankind.

389. *straite*: narrow.

391. *tarry*: wait, delay.

395. *moove pitie*: provoke pity.

396. *comport*: endure, bear.

397. *Indurements*: sufferings, hardships.

399–400. AL refers to Christ's prayer to God to spare him; the 'Cup' is the Crucifixion.

405. *glasse neere run*: hourglass, through which the sand has almost passed, indicating the passage of time.

409. *his Will, not thy Will*: the will of God the Father, rather than that of Christ.

412–13. Echoing the parable of the pearl of great price, told in Matthew 13:45–6.

415–16. AL alludes to the prophecies in the Old Testament, interpreted by Christians to prefigure the coming of Christ, the Book of Isaiah particularly.

419. *three Friends*: Peter, James and John.

421. *colour*: reason, with the implication of an excuse.

423–33. *Watch and Pray*: cf. Matthew 26:41, 'Watch and pray, that ye enter not into temptation'.

429. *stay*: support.

434. *bent*: set, inclined.

437. *so kinde*: so fully human.

439. *Worlds of Sinne*: the notion that Christ was to redeem all the sins of humanity.

440. *matchlesse*: unsurpassed, unprecedented.

441. *challenge*: in this context, invite, bring forth.

445–9. Solomon's son Rehoboam inherited his father's kingdom, but added to the oppressions that Solomon had laid upon his people. He refused to take the advice of wise men, and the ten tribes of Israel rebelled.

451. *laid to*: attributed to.

452. I.e., Christ was far from being pitied by man.

454. *remitted*: cancelled.

455. *rise*: happen, occur.

462. All four Gospels give an account of Christ's betrayal.

463. *visit them againe*: Christ predicts his resurrection.

464. *apprehension*: understanding, perception.

469–70. See Matthew 26:45, 'Sleep on now, and take your rest: behold the hour is at hand'; *they*: the soldiers who took Jesus Christ away to his death.

471. *a pray*: something to be captured, killed.

472. *blest . . . cursed*: because on the one hand humanity was freed from death, but on the other Christ was crucified.

476. *so meane a berth*: alluding to Christ's birth in a stable, Luke 2:7.

478. *entertaindst*: dealt with, endured.

482. *Heavy*: weighed down, depressed; *haplesse*: hopeless, unfortunate.

483–8. *thy Betrayer*: Judas Iscariot, whose betrayal of Jesus with a kiss identified Christ to his captors. He was one of the twelve disciples.

485. *trothlesse*: disloyal.

486. *fained*: false, hypocritical.

489. *Bils*: broadswords, falchions.

492. *purpose*: intend.

494–6. See John 18:4, where Christ's foreknowledge of this event is related.

506. *dull*: stupid.

508. *ruth*: pity.

516. AL refers to the fact that the officers sent to arrest Christ asked his identity several times; see John 18:5–8.

523. *Lure*: a hawking term; the bait designed to bring the hawk in from flight.

524. Christ did not exercise his power to deliver himself from death, but took the sacrifice upon himself to redeem humankind.

529. *Obedience*: to the will of God the Father, as displayed by Christ's submission to God's will in his prayers in the Garden of Gethsemane.

531. Love here is a personification, as are the other abstractions detailed in this stanza.

532. *his Traine*: those that follow behind the 'Leader' (531).

536. *blessed misery*: this oxymoron conveys the fact that through Christ's suffering, humanity was given the chance of eternal life, cf. line 528.

546. *apprehend*: understand, perceive.

547. *No light of grace*: those who persecute Christ are excluded from God's grace, because they have no faith in Christ as redeemer.

551. *siely*: innocent, simple.

553. *unlearned*: ignorant of Christ's redemptive power.

556. *them and theirs*: his persecutors and their families.

558. *purchase*: claim, hold on (noun).

560. The metaphor of Christ as shepherd is found in John 10.

561. Christ was judged at dawn; see John 18:28.

566. *rude*: savage, ignorant; *fell*: fierce.

569. I.e., due legal process is followed, even though its judgement is immoral.

576. *these few*: the disciples accompanying Christ.

577. *wait on*: endure.

579. *spreaders of his Fame*: the Apostles, who will spread Christ's message after his death; see Acts.

583–600. This passage recounts the fact that Simon Peter cut off the ear of the high priest's servant.

595. *forward*: keen.

597. *wantest*: lacks.

601. *he*: Christ.

602. *vouchsafes*: promises, pledges. AL moves here into a description of Christ as suffering victim.

610. I.e., Christ has the power to overthrow his enemies, but chooses not to in order to save mankind.

613. *Ægypts King*: there are frequent allusions in the OT to God's revenge on the king of Egypt for holding the Israelites in slavery; see Exodus 7–13, Psalms 68, 78.

614. *But*: except; *foregoing Scriptures*: the prophecies of Christ's death found in the OT, see Mark 14:49, where Christ says 'the scriptures must be fulfilled'; *take place*: have precedence.

627. *prove*: try, test.

629. I.e., Christ was divine, and the disciples were mortal.

630. *flie*: flee, desert.

633. *bound*: tied, obligated; *loose*: free, punning on 'bound'.

634. *unhallowed*: profane, unsanctified.

635. *Caiphas*: Caiaphas, the high priest of Jerusalem, who tried Christ.

639. *apace*: quickly.

640. *trothlesse*: false.

644. *faints*: expires, dies.

645. *Light*: spiritual sustenance, life.

649. *Their tongues*: those of the men who accused Christ; *Passing bell*: a bell announcing a death.

651. *sound*: convincing.

652. *bereaved*: deprived.

655–6. I.e., the witnesses did not exactly betray Christ, but rather used his own words against him.

657–8. Cf. 'We heard him say, I will destroy this temple that is made with hands, and within three days I will build another made without hands'

(Mark 14:58); it is an allusion to the Crucifixion and Resurrection of Christ, as AL clarifies in lines 661–2 and 665–6. Christ refuses to answer when this claim is put to him.

667. *forbeare*: resist.

672. *Lover*: lover of mankind.

678. *fell*: fierce, ruthless.

681–2. AL uses the darkness accompanying Christ's Crucifixion (Matthew 27:45) to describe the spiritual blindness of Christ's persecutors.

684. *Jewish wolves*: the association of the Jews with the killing of Christ was a central element in anti-Semitism during the medieval and Renaissance periods.

688. *prophane*: treat with irreverence; violate.

689. *chiefest Hel-hounds*: the high priest, who demanded that Jesus answer the accusations of the false witnesses.

694. *his holy wisdome*: periphrasis for 'Jesus Christ'.

695. The line is slightly ambiguous; the Gospels recount the twisting of Christ's words against him: 'Art thou then the Son of God? And he said unto them, Ye say that I am' (Luke 22:70).

697. *so mild a Majestie*: i.e. Christ's refusal to defend himself.

699. *exceptions*: offence, pique.

701. *Folly*: the high priest.

706. Addressing Caiaphas, Christ asserts that the high priest's question (i.e. whether he is the Son of God) is its own answer – because it fulfils the OT prophecy and because the high priest takes Christ's assertion that he is the Son of God as convincing testimony.

712. *Owly eies*: because the owl can only see well in the dark.

714. I.e., placing the blame on Christ rather than upon themselves.

715. *smart*: pain, sting – by extension, the sting of death.

716–18. The death sentence, passed by Caiaphas, on the strength of Christ's own testimony.

719–20. Matthew and Luke report that the crowd hit Christ and spat upon him (27:30; 18:32).

727. *bound*: tied up, in bondage; *to him you led away*: i.e. 'you were led away', where 'you' must be Pilate, given the next line.

728. *pray*: prey.

729. *Caytife*: wretch, i.e. Judas, who betrayed Christ.

730. *lewd*: evil, wicked.

731–6. Judas, when he realized that he too was condemned, hanged himself. The priests took the pieces of silver ('the price of blood', Matthew 27:6, used in line 731), and buried them outside the sanctuary. See Matthew 27:3–7.

735. *unrespected*: not valued, hence making a point about the differences between Judaism and Christianity.

740. *cares not*: is not concerned by.

741. *elected*: chosen.

743. *Christs Schoole*: under Christ's tutelage (Judas was one of the twelve disciples).

745. *Pontius Pilate*: the Roman governor of Jerusalem, who had the final say in capital cases.

749. *noble Governour*: Pilate.

750. *imbrue*: stain.

753–60. AL expands upon the biblical verse, giving Pilate's wife a voice of her own.

758. *desert*: claim for favour.

760. The argument that men were granted power over women, but proved inadequate in their use of it, is a central element in 'Eve's Apologie' which follows. While not overturning the hierarchy of the sexes, AL argues that men should take responsibility for their own actions and not blame women. Critical engagement with the story of Adam and Eve, central to the understanding of sex roles in early modern England, is a recurrent feature of the so-called 'pro-woman' arguments of the early seventeenth century. See Speght and Sowernam in Keeble, pp. 9–11 and 17–19, and the texts in *HH*.

761. *Till now*: this should be understood as a continuation of the previous stanza, despite the use of a full point in line 760. Up to the moment ('Till now') of Christ's Crucifixion, men's power to rule over women was undisputed, but this event, orchestrated by men, and opposed by women, calls that power into question.

762. *former fault*: the responsibility attributed to Eve (and by extension, to all women) for the sin of eating the apple and bringing about the Fall of Man.

763–6. See Genesis 3:6, which does not specifically attribute blame to Eve for tempting Adam, but goes on to imply that he ate the apple out of love for her: 'The woman whom thou gavest to be with me, she gave me of the tree, and I did eat' (3:12).

767. *subtile*: underhand, crafty.

769. *undiscerning Ignorance*: i.e. Eve's innocence of evil before the fall.

770. *him*: Satan.

771. *bereav'd*: deprived. Without the knowledge borne of sin, Eve could not know what loss meant.

772. *condiscended*: agreed, acquiesced.

775–6. When faced with the serpent, Eve reiterates what God has told her (Genesis 3:2–3).

779. *Weaknesse*: Eve, and, by extension, femininity.

780. *Being Lord of all*: AL refers to the fact that God created Adam first and in his image (Genesis 2:7) and made him master of creation, and that Eve was created second from Adam's rib (Genesis 2:21–2).

783–4. Again, the argument relating to Adam's greater authority relies upon his prior creation.

785. *fram'd*: made, formed.

787. *strait*: strict.

788. See Genesis 2:16–17. The warning is given to Adam only; it is inferred that he has communicated it to Eve.

793. *Patience*: Eve, but also women in general.

795. *discretion*: discernment, judgement.

796. AL refers to the fact that it was Eve, not Adam, who encountered the serpent.

800. I.e., there was no one in authority over him to prevent him; *stay*: restrain, hold back.

803. *prove*: try, test.

805–6. In Genesis, Adam is not seen to instruct Eve, although she clearly knows the injunction.

807–8. AL ironically mentions the male monopoly on knowledge, while reminding her reader that it was through Eve's fall that knowledge was given to humanity.

810. *ground*: origin, i.e. if Eve was evil, then, as she was created from Adam, she must have got it from him.

811. *one of many Worlds*: Satan, who had been expelled from heaven, was able to roam over the earth.

813. *traine*: craftiness.

814. I.e., what will the same faulty sinfulness do when spread among many?

815. *Her*: Eve's.

825. *our Libertie*: the freedom of women, as Eve was free before the Fall, and the promise of freedom contained within Christ's redemptive sacrifice.

826. *challendge*: apportion, attribute; *Sov'raigntie*: supremacy, authority.

827. *our paine*: the pain of childbirth, part of God's curse after the Fall (Genesis 3:16).

838. *reprobate*: person condemned by God; *Saul*: either the OT Saul, the first king of Israel, who was rejected by God for his disobedience, and became the sworn enemy of his successor, David, or the NT Saul, who persecuted Christians until his conversion.

847. *loose*: set free. See Luke 23:6–16, where Pilate examines Jesus and finds him not guilty.

848. *the Thiefe*: Barabbas.

853. *such grace*: that of Christ.

857–60. AL attacks Pilate's actions on the grounds that they are legally indefensible, and hence his status as judge is undermined. See Matthew 27:22.

870. *yield*: i.e. give in to the crowd (Luke 23:23–4).

871. *rowt*: crowd.

873–4. AL continues subtly to discredit Pilate, hence asserting the injustice of his decision.

875–6. AL does not adhere strictly to the narrative sequence of the Gospels, where Herod is consulted before Pilate makes his final decision. This reordering constitutes a further assertion of Pilate's weakness; *reconcile thy selfe*: Pilate and Herod were enemies, see Luke 23:7–12.

881. *his great place*: Herod's status as king.

890. *robes of honour*: Christ was mocked by being dressed in the garments of kingship, a ritual humiliation derived from his claim to be the king of the Jews. See Matthew 27:28–9.

891. *Pure white*: added to the Gospel accounts by AL.

893. *penury*: poverty.

898. *Diadem*: diamond.

901. *To his*: compared with his.

905–8. I.e., to the faithful, Christ's robes, given in scorn, represent his true majesty.

913–20. AL is filling the gaps left in the Gospel accounts.

916. I.e., Pilate listens to all rumours.

919. *Caesar*: Tiberius, Pilate's superior.

921. *painted wall*: an image for hypocrisy, where 'painted' stands for falsity and deception.

922. *golden Sepulcher*: gilded tomb, i.e. Pilate's crime will bring about his death and damnation.

923. *equitie*: the application of principles of justice to correct the law; the privilege of a judge, which Pilate notably fails to exercise.

927. *latter day*: the Day of Judgement.

928. The indelible nature of Pilate's sin on the Day of Judgement is ironically contrasted with his public self-exoneration of washing his hands and disclaiming responsibility for Christ's death (Matthew 27:24).

930. *withstand*: resist.

939. *lust*: desire, will.

945. *long expected houre*: the hour of crucifixion and death.

947. *cheere*: expression, countenance.

949. *his deserts*: what he deserves, merits.

951. *satisfaction*: a requital, atonement; *generall doome*: final judgement at the end of the world.

954. *Mount Calvarie*: site of Christ's Crucifixion, called Golgotha (place of skulls), Calvary in Luke 23:33.

956. *odious sort*: i.e. Christ's treatment as a common criminal, crucified between two thieves, Matthew 27:38.

963–4. The hangman, because of his role of executioner, will be condemned to eternal damnation. The term 'hangman' is not strictly accurate, as the reference to the 'nayles' (965) used for crucifixion indicates.

966. *impiety*: lack of reverence.

969. *such grace*: in St John's Gospel Christ turns to the women as he passes on his way to the cross (19:26), but in Luke Christ predicts a series of calamities which will follow his death (23:27–9).

974. *Flora*: the goddess of spring and flowers.

977–80. AL refers to Christ's refusal to co-operate under interrogation, recounted in each of the Gospels.

985. *daughters of Jerusalem*: the term that Christ uses when he addresses the women in Luke 23:28.

991. *Eagles eyes*: eagles were renowned for their keen sight, but the point made here is to do with their spiritual insight, perceiving Christ's worth when others reject it; AL works within a tradition of seeing female weakness as rendering women more able to identify with Christ's suffering; *Sunne*: with a pun on 'Son'.

994. *innocent Dove*: a sign of peace and forgiveness, but also a frequent symbol for the Holy Spirit.

997. *presse*: crowd, throng.

1008. *faintly*: weakly.

1009–40. See John 19:25–6. AL asserts a close identification between the Virgin Mary and women.

1012. *swouned*: swooned, fainted.

1021. *Jessie floure and bud*: Christ as descendant and culmination of the ancient tree of Jesse, the father of David (see I Samuel 16; Isaiah 11:1).

1024. Cf. 'Oh death, where is thy sting?', I Corinthians 15:55.

1025. *faultlesse fruit*: offspring, i.e. Christ.

1026. *All Nations*: a reference to the visit of the three kings at Christ's birth, to offer their gifts and reverence (Matthew 2:11).

1029. *wisest persons*: the three kings.

1030. *chosen vessell*: the Virgin Mary, but the phrase is from Acts 9:15, where it refers to Saul, later St Paul.

1033. *magnified*: exalted, raised up.

1041–3. *Haile Mary*: in Luke's Gospel Gabriel actually says 'Hail, thou that art highly favoured' (1:28). The lines which follow paraphrase the angel's greeting to Mary.

1061. *cheere*: appearance, countenance.

1064. I.e., the Immaculate Conception, related in Luke 1:35.

1076. *hap*: luck, good fortune.

1083. *subject to no paine*: because Mary is free from sin, and balances out the sins of Eve.

1086. *poore degree*: low status, position.

1088. *the curse*: Original Sin.

1091. *approove*: testify to, prove.

1101. *decaies*: sins, misdemeanours.

1102. *living in his feare*: living in fear of him.

1107. *vouchsafe*: condescend to give, grant; *riches of his treasure*: Christ.

1108. I.e., It was absolute righteousness by God (and Christ) to make the ultimate sacrifice for man.

1110. *snow-white Weed*: clothing, symbolizing purity and innocence; the image is that of the incarnation of God in the shape of the pure body of Christ.

1111. *in a skarlet Die*: dyed red, i.e. with blood.

1114. AL refers to the majesty of Christ, and his humble way of life among mortals on earth.

1115. *fraile clothing*: human flesh, the body.

1117. *deerely*: at great cost.

1118–20. Those afflicted by sin are tossed about like feathers, subject to the sources of sin, the world, the flesh and the devil; *to blind*: because sin and temptation blind mortals to the truth of God's power.

1122. *blessed, yet accursed*: 'blessed' because it redeems the world, 'accursed' because it puts Christ to death.

1123. *them*: the sins of humankind.

1125. *ragged clothing*: the body, mortality; cf. line 1115.

1126. *rent*: ripped, ragged.

1128. *grace it selfe*: Christ; *disgrac'd*: the iniquities visited upon Christ.

1132. *The peoples fury*: the clamour of the crowd, calling for Christ's Crucifixion (Luke 23:21).

1137. *Simon of Cyrene*: the man made to carry the cross.

1139. *Golgatha*: Golgotha, the hill outside the city walls of Jerusalem, where Christ was crucified; see Matthew 27:33.

1142. *present*: immediate, imminent.

1144. *filth*: sin, evil, wrong-doing.

1148. *prest*: set upon, determined.

1152. *opprobrious*: scornful, abusive.

1154. *trace*: path, way.

1155. See Luke 23:33. It is Christ, not the thieves, who is 'unpitied, unbewailde'.

1157. *appailde*: beset by, dismayed, full of fear.

1167. *bowells*: internal organs.

1168. AL refers to Christ calling upon God the Father to deliver him, see Matthew 27:46 and Mark 15:34.

[. . .]

1289. *rize*: risen.

1290–92. The precious ointments brought to anoint the body of Christ become marriage gifts, as AL introduces the metaphor of Christ and the Church.

1297. [Marginal note, now footnote] *Canticles*: Song of Songs, the wedding poems of Solomon; AL draws upon their imagery in lines 1305–20.

1298. *Compunction*: remorse, conscience.

1301. *redounds*: rebounds, returns.

1322. *taske of Beauty*: the attempt to describe the glories of Christ.

1327. *holy shrine*: the Countess of Cumberland's heart is the 'shrine' which contains Christ's portrait.

1328. *Environed*: surrounded.

1330. *case*: state, situation.

1335. *almes-deeds*: charity, the giving of aid to the poor.

1336. *bring to stop*: cause to cease.

1345. *Shepheards weed*: in the guise of a shepherd, cf. the imagery of Christ as shepherd in the Gospels, particularly in John 10.

1364–5. The distinction is between the eyes of the body, and the eye of the spirit, an opposition frequently rehearsed by Paul (see Romans 8, for example).

1369. *Keyes*: the keys of heaven, traditionally associated with St Peter. See Matthew 16:19.

1370–72. While not attributing spiritual power directly to the Countess of Cumberland, AL suggests that this is exercised by virtue of the example that she sets of piety and goodness, which leads others to imitate her.

1375–6. There is an echo of Christ's power to perform miracles here; see Matthew 9:6–7; 15:30–31.

1377–80. Healing power is attributed to the Countess, through her adherence to the precepts of Christ.

1385. *rich*: spiritually powerful.

1388. *Desiring place*: ambitious for social advancement; *thou sittest them belowe*: the Countess sits beneath the proud because of her modesty and humility. The contrast is between worldly and spiritual values.

1392–3. While you can convert the wicked from their folly, you are never tempted by them.

1394–6. In other words, the Countess covers over the sins of others, in order to give them time to heal.

1397. *weake lost sheepe*: a common metaphor for sinners, see for example Matthew 9:36.

1404. *his Spouse*: the Church; *unfaind*: genuine, unfeigned.

1407. *drosse*: the residue which is left after the refinement of metals.

[. . .]

1465ff. AL moves into another stage of her argument here, citing biblical and historical precedents of virtuous and powerful women, many of whom are conventional examples. Once again she uses the topos of outdoing, to elevate the virtues and qualities of her subject over these important predecessors. See her use of these exemplary women in 'To the Vertuous Reader'.

1465. *elder times*: former times, ancient ages.

1469–70. The kingdom of Scythia was invaded by Darius, king of Persia, in revenge for the Scythians' conquest of Media. AL's notion that it was the women who put him to flight seems to come from Herodotus' account of the Scythians' inter-breeding with the Amazons: Herodotus, *The Histories*, Book IV.

1471–2. Alexander the Great was also defeated by the Scythians in 331 BC.

1473–4. *Whose worth*: the Scythian women; an odd comparison, as the Scythians were renowned for their savagery and primitive way of life.

1475. In Herodotus, the Scythian women are lax in their sexual morals, breeding with the slave class while their men are at war (*The Histories*, Book IV).

1481. *Deborah*: Deborah and Barak delivered Israel from the oppression of Sisera; her role as judger of Israel is mentioned in Judges 4:4. See 'To the Vertuous Reader', line 5.

1482. *Judeth*: the heroine who saved her people from Nebuchadnezzar's army by decapitating its leader, Holofernes (1486); see the Apocryphal Book of Judith 8–13.

1483. Deborah is also described in Judges as 'a prophetess' (4:4).

1485. *queale*: quell, cut down.

1505–12. *Hester*: Esther protected the Jewish people from the predations of their enemy, Haman, and interceded with Ahasuerus to have him hanged, see the Apocryphal Book of Esther, especially 5–7.

1508. *a spoyle*: something captured, betokening triumph; i.e. she is trying to destroy her beauty so that Haman will not want her.

1510. *the map*: epitome, outline. Cf. MS Ps. 68:11.

1516–17. *free/ From doubt of death*: alluding to the Countess of Cumberland's faith in the life to come.

1519. *Him*: Christ.

1521. *not Feare*: Esther's motivation was fear for her people, rather than faith.

1522. *No kinsmans counsell*: Esther is advised by her uncle, Mordecai, not to reveal her Jewishness in order that the overthrow of the Israelites' enemies might be accomplished (Esther 2:10).

1525. *Vanities*: dreams, fantasies.

1527. *mourning time*: mortal life, when sin must be considered and dwelt upon.

1529–35. *Joachims wife*: Susanna, accused of sexual misdemeanours by two men whose advances she had resisted, and condemned to death. She was believed by Daniel, who had the men put to death (Book of Daniel in Revised Standard Version of the Bible).

1533. *bare away the blame*: took the blame upon herself.

1535. *spirit of a Child*: the prophet Daniel, who was a child at the time of this incident.

1538. *that hand*: the hand of God.

1539. *holy Writ*: the Bible.

1546. *imbracements*: predations.

1553. *constant Lawrell*: laurel, a symbol of victory and poetic power, but also of chastity.

1557. *Queene*: of virtue and piety, presumably.

1562. *consent*: to Christ.

1565. *fame*: used to refer to the Countess's virtue; AL suggests that virtue is the only qualification for fame.

1569. *Ethyopian Queene*: the queen of Sheba, who hearing of Solomon's wealth and wisdom, came to visit him in order to test him with 'hard questions' (1581). They exchanged gifts before she returned to her homeland (I Kings 10:1–13).

1580. *faire rich presents*: these are described in I Kings 10:2.

1581. *hard questions*: difficult, knotty problems; the phrase is found in I Kings 10:1.

1593. *affect*: are affectionate, partial.

1603. *nicenesse*: fastidiousness; *respect*: norm.

1608. *imprest*: imprinted; *perfect storie*: perfect narrative, faith.

1609. *map*: representation, example; cf. line 1510 and note.

1610. *figure*: prefiguration, pale version; *Love*: the Countess's love for Christ.

1613. *faire Earthly starre*: Solomon.

1614. *glorious Sonne*: Christ, with the conventional pun on 'sun', of which Solomon is a reflection, or star.

1617. *small sparke*: Solomon's wisdom and faith, as compared to Christ's.

1622. *salvation*: the salvation offered to humankind through Christ's death and resurrection.

1625. *travels*: journeys, but also trials (as in 'travails'); *affected*: concerned, committed, involved.

[. . .]

1680. *spotlesse Lambe*: Christ, who is without stain or sin; see I Peter 1:19.

1681. *that Heathen Queene*: the queen of Sheba, whose respect for Solomon is interpreted as prefiguring the Countess of Cumberland's greater love of Christ.

1682. *the shadow*: Solomon. AL reads this as an allegory of (i) the marriage of Christ and the Church, and (ii) the relationship between the believer and Christ, exemplified in the figure of the Countess of Cumberland.

1683. *Judiciall day*: the Day of Judgement; the queen of Sheba has a place among the righteous because of the 'grace' (1681) bestowed upon her by Solomon, much as a sinner is redeemed through God's grace.

1685. *haplesse*: unfortunate, with the implication that the queen is excluded from Christ; *happie*: fortunate.

1686. *behove*: benefit, advantage.

1689. *Phoenix*: the queen of Sheba; the phoenix was the mythical bird which regenerated itself from the ashes of its funeral pyre.

1691. *earthly Prince*: Solomon.

1693–6. I.e., the queen of Sheba's devotion to Solomon was false, because she reveres a mortal king, rather than a heavenly king, Christ.

1705. *affected*: devoted in love.

1715. *seeming Trades-mans sonne*: referring to Christ's father, Joseph, generally assumed to be a carpenter; *attended*: taken notice of, waited upon.

1724. *inroules*: enrolls, in the sense of entering something in a document – here the Book of the Saved (the Book of Life).

1725. *Characters*: symbols, letters; *blood and teares*: the blood of Christ's sacrifice and tears symbolizing his suffering.

1729. *holy rivers*: cf. Revelation 22:1, 'a pure river of water of life'.

1730. *fountaine of our life*: Christ; see Revelation 21:6, 'I will give unto him that is athirst of the fountain of the water of life freely,' and previous note.

1731. *sugred*: sweetened.

1732. *christall streames*: cf. Revelation 22:1, 'water of life, clear as crystal'.

1741. *prove*: undergo, endure.

[. . .]

1829. *faine*: eagerly, happily.

1833. *sprites*: spirits.

1839. *Articke Starre*: the Pole Star, used by mariners for navigation.

The Description of Cooke-ham

1. *Cooke-ham*: a manor in Berkshire, leased to the Countess of Cumberland's brother and where she lived periodically 'until 1605 or shortly after' (Woods, p. 130n.).

2. *Grace . . . Grace . . . Grace*: favour . . . noble personage (i.e. the Countess) . . . God-given favour, virtues.

3. *Muses*: the nine deities presiding over poetry, music and the arts.

4. *powre*: ability, specifically poetic ability.

5. *princely Palace*: the house leased to the Countess; *indite*: write, give an account of.

6. *sacred Storie*: the narrative of Christ's Passion, as related in the main part of the poem.

7. *rest*: remain, reside.

10. *unfold*: reveal, disclose.

12. *desires*: cf. AL's apology for not writing 'Those praisefull lines of that delightfull place' at the beginning of 'Salve Deus' (18).

13. *Vouchsafe*: be willing, undertake.

14. *fleeting worldly Joyes*: as AL praises the Countess for rejecting worldly pleasures (see for example 'Salve Deus', 161–8), here she anticipates the transition to meditation on heavenly matters undertaken later in the poem.

15. *dimme shadowes*: poor reflections.

17. *against you*: in response to.

18. *frame*: make, prepare.

21. *Liveries*: uniforms, usually signifying the loyalty of a group of retainers to their lord.

22. *similies*: similarities. The image is of nature being close to the Countess of Cumberland herself.

26. Because AL is stressing that the Countess outdoes nature, she reverses the usual convention here, so that the sun has to be shaded from the light of virtue (presumably), shining from the Countess's eyes.

27. *cristall Streames*: cf. Revelation 22:1; *spangles*: thin pieces of metal attached to a garment – figuratively, something that glitters.

31. *Philomela*: she was changed into a nightingale, after being raped by her brother-in-law, Tereus. Her tongue was cut out, but she managed to communicate what had happened by weaving a tapestry. Her sister Procne took revenge, killing Tereus' son, and feeding the boy to him (see *Met.* VI, pp. 146–52); *leyes*: songs.

32. *delightfull Place*: Cookham is presented through the classical topos of the *locus amoenus*, or beautiful place, also used to describe the Garden of Eden. See Curtius, pp. 192–3, 195–200.

44. *Phoenix*: the mythical bird which regenerated itself from its own ashes.

45. *Arbor*: a shady alcove, enclosed by plants or trees.

49. *Burrough*: burrow.

51. *Bowe in your faire Hand*: suggesting Diana, famed for her hunting ability and her chastity.

53–5. AL's concentration on the 'Oake' as symbolizing the feminized Eden they share, indicates that it functions as an inversion and corrective of the Tree of Knowledge in the Garden of Eden, as the women here gain spiritual nourishment and understanding of virtue, not knowledge of sin and death.

57–61. Cf. Ps. 92:12, 'The righteous shall flourish like the palm tree: he shall grow like a cedar in Lebanon.'

64. *Defended Phebus*: i.e. protected you from the sun; *assaile*: attack.

70. *preferre*: advance, put forward; *sute*: request.

78. *perfit Law*: the divine plan and order, as represented in the natural world.

79. *descrie*: discern.

83. *holy Writ*: scripture, but here, by extension of the previous image of the natural world, as a metaphor for God, Christ's example in general; *faire tree*: both the Tree of Knowledge, but also the image of redemption in the shape of the cross (or tree).

85. *Moyses . . . holy Hill*: a reference to the attempt by the virtuous soul to reach God, symbolized as the hill of Sion, through meditation on God's word (see Psalm 43:3).

86–7. The Psalms of David. On their place within Protestant devotion, see Introduction, pp. xix–xxiv.

91–2. Joseph, who was sold by his brothers into Egypt. He gained such power that when famine afflicted Israel, his brothers were forced to come to him for food (see Genesis 37, 42–5); *pined*: starved.

93–5. *that sweet Lady*: Lady Anne Clifford, the Countess of Cumberland's daughter; *Bedfords*: the Russell family; *Dorset*: Anne's husband, Richard Sackville, Earl of Dorset.

98. *well framed*: well-made, well-constructed.

100. *Neere*: both in terms of physical proximity, and in terms of virtue.

102. *enforce*: elicit.

104. *frame*: position, situation.

105. *great*: noble, of high rank.

106. *degree*: social position, rank.

107. *Orbes of state*: world of politics.

108. *Parters*: dividers.

109–10. Those of high rank value honour less than their social inferiors, the true professors of honour.

111. *conceit*: thought.

112. *conster*: construe, explain, consider.

118. *turne againe*: come around again.

119. *Dorsets*: Anne Clifford's.

131. *inkeling*: slight thought, idea.

132. *frame*: turn, convert.

137. *stay you*: make you remain, prevent you from leaving.

138. *pray you*: persuade you to stay.

143. *hoarie*: greyish white.

145. *swarthy*: ark; *riveld*: wrinkled; *ryne*: rind.

147. *occasions*: obligations, responsibilities.

150. *Requiting*: rewarding.

165–6. AL's stealing of the Countess's kiss implies the possibility of equality between them, if at a remove, through their mutual love of and faith in God.

170. *it*: the kiss.

171. *deceive*: deprive.

178. *consort*: music, accompaniment.

183–96. Echoing the earlier, joyful, depiction of Cookham's natural beauty, in lines 21–46.

189–90. Cf. line 31 above; *Ditty*: song.

191–2. Echoing, with variation, lines 45–6 above.

199. *Eccho*: the wood nymph, who often represents ideal union with the landscape; *wonted*: accustomed.

207. *her noble hest*: the Countess of Cumberland's request, noted in 'Salve Deus', lines 17–19.

TEXTUAL APPARATUS

ISABELLA WHITNEY

Text: There are two extant copies of Whitney's work, one each of *A sweet Nosgay, or Pleasant Posye: contayning a hundred and ten Phylosophicall Flowers* (London, 1573) [BL C.39.b.45] and *The copy of a letter, lately written in meeter, by a yonge gentilwoman: to her unconstant Lover* (London, 1567) [Bodleian Library 8°H44(6) Art.Seld]. There are therefore no significant textual problems, but the print quality is extremely poor in places, with letters transposed and occasionally reversed or omitted. Emendations to the text are given below.

from *A SWEET NOSGAY*

To the worshipfull and right vertuous yong Gentylman, George Mainwaring Esquier . . .

7. esteemed] *emended from* exteemed

The Auctor to the Reader

79. loote] *emended from* toote

* * *

THE COPY OF A LETTER

The admonition by the Auctor, to all yong Gentilwomen: And to al other Maids being in Love

64. home] *emended from* whom

* * *

*The lamentacion of a Gentilwoman upon the death of her
late deceased frend William Gruffith Gent.*

Text: Taken from *The gorgious Gallery of gallant Inventions* (London, 1578),
the text is a verse miscellany in the tradition of Tottel's famous collection
(BL C.57.d.49 [2]). See also *A Gorgeous Gallery of Gallant Inventions*
(Menston, Yorkshire, 1972), and Martin 1997, pp. 301–10.

MARY SIDNEY (HERBERT), COUNTESS OF PEMBROKE

THE SIDNEY PSALTER (1599)

Text: The psalms reproduced here are selected from those composed by
Mary Sidney. The textual history of the Sidney Psalter is 'exceedingly
complex' (*CW* 2.337), and it is not the purpose of this edition to provide a
full apparatus, but to represent the instability of the text. Most editions to
date (Rathmell 1963, Pritchard 1992, *CW*; Martin 1997) have taken the
text designated A by Ringler as a copy-text (see *The Poems of Sir Philip
Sidney* (1962), pp. 546–52; *CW* 2.308–36). Ringler A has a strong claim to
be the most 'finished' of the fourteen extant manuscripts, but the relation-
ships between the other manuscripts indicate that Mary Sidney saw her
undertaking rather less in terms of being directed to the production of a
single authoritative text, and more as an on-going process of revision and
alteration. This is supported by Ringler's contention that the Countess
possessed two working copies, one kept at Wilton, and one at Baynard's
Castle, her London residence (p. 503). This number has been revised to
three in the light of recent work on the manuscripts (*CW* 2.338). None of
these copies is extant, but Ringler B, although incomplete, is derived from
one of them. Editors generally agree on the importance of B; Ringler asserts
that '[t]his is the most valuable of all the known manuscripts of the Psalms'
(p. 548), and the editors of *CW* opine that it 'provides the most important
evidence', 'the single most important document for tracing the complex
textual history of the poems' (2.337, 338). Waller argues that 'in a sense,
the countess had no "final" version of the work' (see 'The Countess of
Pembroke and Gendered Reading', in *The Renaissance Englishwoman in
Print: Counterbalancing the Canon*, ed. Anne M. Haselkorn and Betty S.
Travitsky (Amherst, Mass., 1991), p. 338).

Rather than assuming the absolute status of A, this edition uses instead Bodleian Ms. Rawlinson 25 (Ringler B) and Ms. Rawlinson 24 (Ringler C), on the grounds that these, but particularly B, provide useful insights into the Countess's methods of composition and revision. For many psalms B and C are close to, if not identical with, A; this version has been consulted in *CW*, but with a glance at Rathmell. B is missing a number of psalms (88–103 and 131–150), and these have been supplied from C, again in consultation with *CW*. Where the texts differ substantially, the present edition has used B or C (as relevant) as the copy-text, on the grounds that the text of A is already available in Rathmell and *CW*. Interested readers can then undertake a comparative study of the two versions. The texts presented here follow their manuscript sources in all particulars, except that B's numbering of verses according to the Geneva Bible (see *CW* 2.309) is not reproduced. Due to the differences in date between B and C, the resulting texts bear the marks of their transcriptions: B's habits of punctuation and spelling are those of the late seventeenth century, C's those of the earlier seventeenth century. Simple variants and incidentals have not been noted, and some of the other variants that remain are scribal errors. Emendations are duly noted.

'Even now that Care' taken from *The Penguin Book of Renaissance Verse*, ed. David Norbrook and H. R. Woudhuysen (Harmondsworth, 1992, 1993).

The Psalmes of Mary Sidney, Countess of Pembroke

Psalm 45

Text: B, variants from A.
2. who] that
10. mights] things
17. cleave] clive
19. faine] *emended from A. B has* feign; *possibly a transcription error. A's reading is more convincing, meaning 'keen', 'enthusiastic'*
28. Thy] thine
49. the King] a king

Psalm 47

Text: Taken from B and compared with A.
3. Triumphs] triumph
4. high of] high, and

Psalm 49

Text: One of the Pss. for which Woodforde has noted extensive revisions.
B, collated with A: readers should also consult the revisions reproduced
with the text of Ps. 49.

TITLE] audite haec omnes
10. which his] which his though great
14. in bargaining is endlesse slow] his prisoner never will forgoe
15. a longer] but longer
16. Rejected] respited;
17. At his sure summons] sure at his summons
18. leave] hoord
22. Such honourd fooles of sense] exalted men of sence
25. These though their race] Yea these, whose race
27. life] light
29. Yea . . . for soon] Nay . . . when once
34. and honours seed] though glories seede
38. To] who
39. shall] must

Psalm 50

Text: B, which differs substantially from A, can be found in Rathmell,
pp. 117–19 and *CW* 2.47–9. The revisions are discussed by Waller ('The
Text and Manuscript Variants of the Countess of Pembroke's Psalms',
Review of English Studies, NS 26, 1975), pp. 11–12.

Psalm 51

Text: B, collated with A. See Rathmell, pp. 120–21, Pritchard, pp. 48–9,
CW 2.49–51.
4. sin] sinnes
15. where] when
32. spirit] sprite
45. of] for

Psalm 52

Text: B, collated with A. Rathmell sets out this psalm in quatrains.

Psalm 53

Text: B, which differs completely from A. See Rathmell, p. 124, Pritchard, p. 50, *CW* 2.53–4.

Psalm 54

Text: B, collated with A.

Psalm 55

Text: B, collated with A.
49. find] fin'd

Psalm 56

Text: B, collated with A.
25. all are] are all

Psalm 57

Text: B, collated with A.
13. enraged] incaged
38. My] with

Psalm 58

Text: B, which differs substantially from A. See Rathmell, pp. 133–4, Pritchard, pp. 54–5, *CW* 2.61–2.

Psalm 61

Text: B, collated with A.

Psalm 63

Text: B, which differs radically from A. See Rathmell, p. 144, Pritchard, p. 60, *CW* 2.70–71.

Psalm 64

Text: B, which differs from A. See Rathmell, pp. 145–6, *CW* 2.71–2.

Psalm 65

Text: B, collated with A.
5. sin] sinns
21. damm] *emended from A. B has* Dame

Psalm 67

Text: B, collated with A.

Psalm 68

Text: B, which differs from A. See Rathmell, pp. 154–6, *CW* 2.78–81.

Psalm 69

Text: B, heavily revised in A. See Rathmell, pp. 157–60, *CW* 2.81–5.

Psalm 70

Text: B, collated with A.
2. To help me] lord now to help me
3. Shame let them have] shame lett them surely have
5. have] hold
6, 9. turned] forced
10. And for reward] and for a faire reward
11. own fall] owne foule ruine
12. Who laugh out hard] who laugh and laugh out hard
13. Ah ha when most I mone] when I most inly mone
15. trace] paths
17. Make them for ever sing] Make them with gladdnes sing
18. To God be Prayse] to god be ever praise
19. And to me bring] and faile not me to bring
22. From . . . comfort] In . . . succour

Psalm 71

Text: B, which differs from A. See Rathmell, pp. 162–4, *CW* 2.86–9.

Psalm 74

Text: B, collated with A.
31. Place] seate

46. Among] amongst
99. despights] dispight

Psalm 76

Text: B, collated with A.
TITLE] Notus in Judea
2. Israel] Jacob
9. attempts, Thy valiand] attempt, thy valiand
11, 12. were] grew
25. offring] Offrings
29. terribly] terrible

Psalm 77

Text: B, collated with A.
TITLE] Voce mea ad Dominum
10. Yet] yea
67. doth] do

Psalm 79

Text: B, collated with A.
6. sacks] sack
7. wracks] wrack
8. houses] buildings

Psalm 81

Text: B, collated with A.
28. should] shall
42. servile state] base estate
47. Hony from the rocks] honny them from Rocks

Psalm 82

Text: B, collated with A.
2. what] who
7. protect] respect

Psalm 84

Text: B, collated with A.
47. most] thrice

Psalm 86

Text: B. For A's rendering see Rathmell, pp. 205–6, *CW* 2.125–7.

Psalm 88

Text: From this point until Ps. 103, B breaks off. The text is supplied from C, and collated with A.
9. plaint] cry
12. neere my] nigh the
22. whome thou do'st] whom now thou dost
49. mercie] mercies
57. my] thy

Psalm 89

Text: C, collated with A.
TITLE] Misericordias Domini
3. endles] still void
15. mynd] minded
17. with thee among the clowds] among the cloudes with thee
20. thy] thine
31. to slide] or slide
36. to East, and West] from West to East
37. name] arme
42. triumphes] tryumph
46. thoughts] thought
71. will him my first borne roome assigne] and I my first-bornes roome will him assigne
73. times] time
83. plainelie] prophanely
96. turneles] *tearmlesse
109. tyme] prime
112. overladen] over-loden
123. servants] servant

Psalm 90

Text: C, collated with A.
19. be] thee
39. labor] laboures

Psalm 92

Text: C, collated with A.
TITLE] Bonum est confiteri
26. shall] all
35. Or] and
39. court] Courts

Psalm 93

Text: C, collated with A.
13. ties] lies

Psalm 95

Text: C, collated with A.
7. he's a] he is

Psalm 96

Text: C, collated with A.
35. feedeth] fieldeth
39. yee] you

Psalm 98

Text: C, collated with A.
11. heav'nly] earthy
13. Earthly] earthy
14. and rejoice] ô rejoice

Psalm 100

Text: C, collated with A.
6. that] this
12. all goodnes] and goodnes

Psalm 101

Text: C, collated with A.
TITLE] Misericordiam et judicium
17. myne] my
23. roote] hate

Psalm 102

Text: C, collated with A.
1. cryeng] praying
5. most miserable] my most most miserable
14. bones my flesh] flesh my bones
17. lovelie] lonely
30. yet thinck] yet think they wish
58. haste] hast
79. heavens] heaven
84. weare] beare

Psalm 104

Text: B, collated with A.
14. for] from
38. *wingy] winged
73. retires] retornes
102. in song his Worth] his worth in song

Psalm 109

Text: B, collated with A.
17. condemned go] condempn'd may goe
18. plagues] plague
20. part] port
37. may be so farr] soe farre may be
67. and] , their
73. when] where
78. Training . . . shameles] trailing . . . shamefull

Psalm 111

Text: B, collated with A.
TITLE] Confitebor tibi
12. heathen] heathens

Psalm 113

Text: B, collated with A.
6. bound] boundes

Psalm 114

Text: B, collated with A.
6. springs] spring
9. hillock] hillocks
11. why] with
15. with] by
18. O God Jehovas] Of God Jehova, Jacobs

Psalm 115

Text: B, collated with A.
12. hands] hand

Psalm 116

Text: B, collated with A.

Psalm 117

Text: B; that of A is given below (taken from *CW* 2.188).

> P raise him that ay
> R emaines the same:
> A ll tongues display
> I ehovas fame.
> S ing all that share
> T his earthly ball:
> H is mercies are
> E xpos'd to all.
> L ike as the word
> O nce he doth give,
> R old in record,
> D oth tyme outlyve.

Psalm 119

Text: B, collated with A. Those sections which differ substantially from A are noted below.

119B:14. which] that
119D:17. doth] doe
119D:22. writhed] wreathed
119D:23. make] graunt
119D:28. dayly] gladly
119D:30. judgment] judgments
119E:2. unfold] enfold
119E:13. my] mine
119E:15. treading] treadings
119E:20. Cousning] comming

A's reading of line 20 conveys the idea of futurity implicit in the biblical text, but B also makes sense, meaning 'deceitful, fraudulent'. Note that the revision rejected in B is restored to A.

119E:24. me still] my will

119G Text: A differs substantially. See Rathmell, p. 281, Pritchard, pp. 110–11, *CW* 2.198. The later version in A retracts 32 lines to 16, condensing the meaning, supporting the suggestion that MS began with paraphrases of the biblical text which she then moulded into tighter metrical and rhythmic schemes.

119H Text: B, which differs from A. See Rathmell, pp. 281–2, Pritchard, p. 111, *CW* 2.198–9.

119K:20. on] in
119N:13. reform] refraine
119N:23. sure] true
119O:4. swear] sware
119O:5. Thy] the
119O:19. my] mine
119P:2. for] from
119Q:7. so] to
119Q:22. Time] the time
119Q:24. doth] they
119Q:30. Are thy] are all thy

119S Text: B, which deviates from A. See Rathmell, pp. 288–9, Pritchard, p. 119, *CW* 2.206–7. The text of A is 16 lines, as opposed to B's 24, although there are some parallels in phrasing.

119T:14. watchings] watching
119V:8. redeem] relive
119V:27. and heare] and here

119W Text: B, which is longer than A, and differs substantially in phrasing. See Rathmell, p. 291, Pritchard, p. 122, *CW* 2.210.

Psalm 120

Text: B, collated with A.
17. I wander] wander I

Psalm 122

Text: B, which differs entirely from A. See Rathmell, p. 295, *CW* 2.214–15.

Psalm 123

Text: B, collated with A.
TITLE] Ad te levavi oculos meos
2. God] good

Psalm 125

Text: B, collated with A.
6. enforced] *enforted

Psalm 126

Text: B, collated with A.
14. lively] newly
18. bequeatheth] bequeathed
21. happily] happly

Psalm 127

Text: B, collated with A.
TITLE] Nisi Dominus
3. our] thy

Psalm 128

Text: B, collated with A
18. longest running race] running longest race

Psalm 129

Text: B, collated with A.

Psalm 130

Text: B, collated with A.
6. attending] attentive
13. On Thee] Yea makes

Psalm 132

Text: B breaks off here. The text of C is used, collated with A.
27. foote] feete
38. Kinge] kings
66. the] my
76. him himself] him self

Psalm 133

Text: C, collated with A.
TITLE] Ecce quam bonum

Psalm 135

Text: C, collated with A.
12. inviolable] inviolate
40. can] should
42. servants] servant

Psalm 137

Text: C, collated with A.
11. growe] goe
34. shall] shalt

Psalm 139

Text: C, collated with A.

Psalm 140

Text: C, collated with A.
TITLE] Eripe me Domine
6. poisoned] poisons
16. bedd] head
21. stronge] stonge

Psalm *141*

Text: C, collated with A.

Psalm *142*

Text: C, collated with A.
TITLE] Voce mea ad Dominum
6. waies] way
18. weeryeng] wearing

Psalm *143*

Text: C, collated with A.
14. nowe] at length
37. hopes] hope

Psalm *144*

Text: C, collated with A.

Psalm *147*

Text: C, collated with A.
28. maintaine] mountaine
30. foode doe] diett
37. let] letts

Psalm *148*

Text: C, collated with A.
3. amongst] among
15. banke] banck'd
37. ground] gown

Psalm *150*

Text: C, collated with A.

*   *   *

A Dialogue betweene two shepheards, Thenot, *and* Piers, *in praise of Astrea . . .*

Text: The 'Dialogue' is unique among MS's poetic output for being preserved only in print; it is found in Francis Davison, *A Poetical Rhapsody* (1602), and in no other source. There is no evidence that the visit alluded to in the title ever took place. The text is taken from the 1611 edition (BL C.122.c.27).

*   *   *

THE TRIUMPH OF DEATH TRANSLATED OUT OF ITALIAN BY THE COUNTESSE OF PEMBROOKE (?1600)

Text: Taken from the unique transcript in Petyt Ms. 538.43.1 (Inner Temple Library) sent by Sir John Harington to the Countess of Bedford, along with Pss. 51, 104 and 137.

AEMILIA LANYER

SALVE DEUS REX JUDÆORUM (1611)

There are nine known copies of *Salve Deus*, five of which include all of the dedicatory poems. The other copies omit some of the dedications probably in order to tailor them to the interests of various recipients. This edition uses the Bodleian Library copy for the dedications and 'Salve Deus' (Vet.A2.f.99). Emendations to the text are noted below. See also Woods, *The Poems of Aemilia Lanyer*, pp. xlvii–li.

The Authors Dreame to the Ladie Marie, *the Countesse* Dowager of Pembrooke

71. Ladied] *emended to* Ladies

To the Ladie Anne, *Countesse of* Dorcet

22. especially] *emended to* especiall

The Description of Cooke-ham

The text is taken from *Salve Deus Rex Judæorum* (London, 1611), BL, shelfmark BM C.71.h.15.

READ MORE IN PENGUIN

In every corner of the world, on every subject under the sun, Penguin represents quality and variety – the very best in publishing today.

For complete information about books available from Penguin – including Puffins, Penguin Classics and Arkana – and how to order them, write to us at the appropriate address below. Please note that for copyright reasons the selection of books varies from country to country.

In the United Kingdom: Please write to *Dept. EP, Penguin Books Ltd, Bath Road, Harmondsworth, West Drayton, Middlesex UB7 0DA*

In the United States: Please write to *Consumer Sales, Penguin Putnam Inc., P.O. Box 12289 Dept. B, Newark, New Jersey 07101-5289.* VISA and MasterCard holders call 1-800-788-6262 to order Penguin titles

In Canada: Please write to *Penguin Books Canada Ltd, 10 Alcorn Avenue, Suite 300, Toronto, Ontario M4V 3B2*

In Australia: Please write to *Penguin Books Australia Ltd, P.O. Box 257, Ringwood, Victoria 3134*

In New Zealand: Please write to *Penguin Books (NZ) Ltd, Private Bag 102902, North Shore Mail Centre, Auckland 10*

In India: Please write to *Penguin Books India Pvt Ltd, 11 Community Centre, Panchsheel Park, New Delhi 110017*

In the Netherlands: Please write to *Penguin Books Netherlands bv, Postbus 3507, NL-1001 AH Amsterdam*

In Germany: Please write to *Penguin Books Deutschland GmbH, Metzlerstrasse 26, 60594 Frankfurt am Main*

In Spain: Please write to *Penguin Books S. A., Bravo Murillo 19, 1° B, 28015 Madrid*

In Italy: Please write to *Penguin Italia s.r.l., Via Benedetto Croce 2, 20094 Corsico, Milano*

In France: Please write to *Penguin France, Le Carré Wilson, 62 rue Benjamin Baillaud, 31500 Toulouse*

In Japan: Please write to *Penguin Books Japan Ltd, Kaneko Building, 2-3-25 Koraku, Bunkyo-Ku, Tokyo 112*

In South Africa: Please write to *Penguin Books South Africa (Pty) Ltd, Private Bag X14, Parkview, 2122 Johannesburg*

READ MORE IN PENGUIN

A CHOICE OF CLASSICS

ANTHOLOGIES AND ANONYMOUS WORKS

The Age of Bede
Alfred the Great
Beowulf
A Celtic Miscellany
The Cloud of Unknowing and Other Works
The Death of King Arthur
The Earliest English Poems
Early Christian Lives
Early Irish Myths and Sagas
Egil's Saga
English Mystery Plays
The Exeter Book of Riddles
Eyrbyggja Saga
Hrafnkel's Saga and Other Stories
The Letters of Abelard and Heloise
Medieval English Lyrics
Medieval English Verse
Njal's Saga
The Orkneyinga Saga
Roman Poets of the Early Empire
The Saga of King Hrolf Kraki
Seven Viking Romances
Sir Gawain and the Green Knight

READ MORE IN PENGUIN

A CHOICE OF CLASSICS

Adomnan of Iona	**Life of St Columba**
St Anselm	**The Prayers and Meditations**
Thomas Aquinas	**Selected Writings**
St Augustine	**Confessions**
	The City of God
Bede	**Ecclesiastical History of the English People**
Geoffrey Chaucer	**The Canterbury Tales**
	Love Visions
	Troilus and Criseyde
Marie de France	**The Lais of Marie de France**
Jean Froissart	**The Chronicles**
Geoffrey of Monmouth	**The History of the Kings of Britain**
Gerald of Wales	**History and Topography of Ireland**
	The Journey through Wales and The Description of Wales
Gregory of Tours	**The History of the Franks**
Robert Henryson	**The Testament of Cresseid and Other Poems**
Robert Henryson/ William Dunbar	**Selected Poems**
Walter Hilton	**The Ladder of Perfection**
St Ignatius	**Personal Writings**
Julian of Norwich	**Revelations of Divine Love**
Thomas à Kempis	**The Imitation of Christ**
William Langland	**Piers the Ploughman**
Sir Thomas Malory	**Le Morte d'Arthur** (in two volumes)
Sir John Mandeville	**The Travels of Sir John Mandeville**
Marguerite de Navarre	**The Heptameron**
Christine de Pisan	**The Treasure of the City of Ladies**
Chrétien de Troyes	**Arthurian Romances**
Marco Polo	**The Travels**
Richard Rolle	**The Fire of Love**
François Villon	**Selected Poems**
Jacobus de Voragine	**The Golden Legend**

READ MORE IN PENGUIN

A CHOICE OF CLASSICS

Leopoldo Alas	**La Regenta**
Leon B. Alberti	**On Painting**
Ludovico Ariosto	**Orlando Furioso** (in two volumes)
Giovanni Boccaccio	**The Decameron**
Baldassar Castiglione	**The Book of the Courtier**
Benvenuto Cellini	**Autobiography**
Miguel de Cervantes	**Don Quixote**
	Exemplary Stories
Dante	**The Divine Comedy** (in three volumes)
	La Vita Nuova
Machado de Assis	**Dom Casmurro**
Bernal Díaz	**The Conquest of New Spain**
Niccolò Machiavelli	**The Discourses**
	The Prince
Alessandro Manzoni	**The Betrothed**
Emilia Pardo Bazán	**The House of Ulloa**
Benito Pérez Galdós	**Fortunata and Jacinta**
Eça de Quierós	**The Maias**
Sor Juana Inés de la Cruz	**Poems, Protest and a Dream**
Giorgio Vasari	**Lives of the Artists** (in two volumes)

and

Five Italian Renaissance Comedies
   (Machiavelli/**The Mandragola**; Ariosto/**Lena**; Aretino/**The
   Stablemaster**; Gl'Intronati/**The Deceived**; Guarini/**The Faithful
   Shepherd**)
The Poem of the Cid
Two Spanish Picaresque Novels
   (Anon/**Lazarillo de Tormes**; de Quevedo/**The Swindler**)

READ MORE IN PENGUIN

A CHOICE OF CLASSICS

Francis Bacon	**The Essays**
Aphra Behn	**Love-Letters between a Nobleman and His Sister**
	Oroonoko, The Rover and Other Works
George Berkeley	**Principles of Human Knowledge/Three Dialogues between Hylas and Philonous**
James Boswell	**The Life of Samuel Johnson**
Sir Thomas Browne	**The Major Works**
John Bunyan	**Grace Abounding to The Chief of Sinners**
	The Pilgrim's Progress
Edmund Burke	**A Philosophical Enquiry into the Origin of our Ideas of the Sublime and Beautiful**
	Reflections on the Revolution in France
Frances Burney	**Evelina**
Margaret Cavendish	**The Blazing World and Other Writings**
William Cobbett	**Rural Rides**
William Congreve	**Comedies**
Cowley/Waller/Oldham	**Selected Poems**
Thomas de Quincey	**Confessions of an English Opium Eater**
	Recollections of the Lakes
Daniel Defoe	**A Journal of the Plague Year**
	Moll Flanders
	Robinson Crusoe
	Roxana
	A Tour Through the Whole Island of Great Britain
	The True-Born Englishman
John Donne	**Complete English Poems**
	Selected Prose
Henry Fielding	**Amelia**
	Jonathan Wild
	Joseph Andrews
	The Journal of a Voyage to Lisbon
	Tom Jones
George Fox	**The Journal**
John Gay	**The Beggar's Opera**

READ MORE IN PENGUIN

A CHOICE OF CLASSICS

Oliver Goldsmith	**The Vicar of Wakefield**
Gray/Churchill/Cowper	**Selected Poems**
William Hazlitt	**Selected Writings**
George Herbert	**The Complete English Poems**
Thomas Hobbes	**Leviathan**
Samuel Johnson	**Gabriel's Ladder**
	History of Rasselas, Prince of Abissinia
	Selected Writings
Samuel Johnson/	**A Journey to the Western Islands of**
James Boswell	**Scotland and The Journal of a Tour of the Hebrides**
Matthew Lewis	**The Monk**
John Locke	**An Essay Concerning Human Understanding**
Andrew Marvell	**Complete Poems**
Thomas Middleton	**Five Plays**
John Milton	**Complete Poems**
	Paradise Lost
Samuel Richardson	**Clarissa**
	Pamela
Earl of Rochester	**Complete Works**
Richard Brinsley Sheridan	**The School for Scandal and Other Plays**
Sir Philip Sidney	**Arcadia**
Christopher Smart	**Selected Poems**
Adam Smith	**The Wealth of Nations (Books I–III)**
Tobias Smollett	**Humphrey Clinker**
	Roderick Random
Edmund Spenser	**The Faerie Queene**
Laurence Sterne	**The Life and Opinions of Tristram Shandy**
	A Sentimental Journey Through France and Italy
Jonathan Swift	**Complete Poems**
	Gulliver's Travels
Thomas Traherne	**Selected Poems and Prose**
Henry Vaughan	**Complete Poems**